# NAVAL SHIPBUILDERS OF THE WORLD

# Naval Shipbuilders of the World

## From the Age of Sail to the Present Day

Robert J Winklareth

Chatham Publishing

LONDON

## Dedication

This book is dedicated to my late father, August Winklareth, who, like myself, was once a worker at one of the shipyards described herein.

Copyright © Robert J Winklareth 2000

First published in Great Britain in 2000 by Chatham Publishing,
61 Frith Street, London W1V 5TA

Chatham Publishing is an imprint of Gerald Duckworth & Co Ltd

*British Library Cataloguing in Publication Data*
A catalogue record for this book is available from the
British Library

ISBN 1 86176 121 X

All maps and diagrams drawn by the author.

Typeset by Dorwyn Ltd, Rowlands Castle, Hants

Printed and bound in Great Britain by Bookcraft (Bath) Ltd

# Contents

# LIST OF PLATES

# Preface

**M**uch has been written about famous warships and the naval battles in which they participated. This book, on the other hand, is intended to provide general information on the shipyards that built those ships, both government-operated naval shipyards and private shipyards that built warships under contract. The work includes a concise history of each shipyard, a map showing its location, and for certain key shipyards, a diagram showing the general layout of the facility. In addition to shipyards, this book also covers the major naval bases and other significant naval facilities that supported the fleets of the world.

The scope of this book includes most of the shipyards throughout the world that have made a significant contribution to naval shipbuilding since the sixteenth century. The book concentrates on the major warships built by those shipyards, naming most capital ships and many smaller naval vessels produced by them. In a work of this size, it would be impossible to include every shipyard that ever produced a naval vessel, and the reader is referred to publications on shipbuilding in local regions for further information.

This book is a consolidation of data and information on naval shipbuilding derived from many sources throughout the world. In cases where shipyards are no longer in existence, the author has contacted the archives, historical societies, maritime museums, libraries, chambers of commerce, municipal officials, and other possible sources in the region of those shipyards for historical information on those facilities. As a result of this research, much detailed information on those shipyards was obtained for this work, including photocopies of pertinent book extracts, newspaper articles, and other documents which are no longer in print.

As might be expected, information on the shipyards of certain nations was especially difficult to obtain from native sources. As a result, the description of those shipyards contained in this book had to be derived from outside sources. Fortunately in the case of Japanese shipyards, excellent data and information was provided by the US Naval Forces in Japan, which still maintains two major naval bases in that country. The information contained in this book on Russian and Chinese shipyards, however, may not be as complete or current as that for other nations.

Every effort has been made to ensure the accuracy of the information contained in this work. Where inconsistencies existed in earlier publications, these were resolved by contacting reliable independent sources. The maps and diagrams presented in this work are reasonably accurate in showing the location and layout of the shipyards covered herein. The shipyard layout diagrams are not, however, to exact scale, and they therefore should not be used for precise measurement purposes.

Most long-established shipyards have undergone extensive changes over the years to keep up with new technologies and the increasing size of warships. It would be impossible for a general book of this nature to illustrate each expansion or other major change to the configuration of the shipyard during its lifetime. Since this book is intended only to provide an impression of those shipyards for comparison purposes, the reader is referred to individual publications and documents dealing with each shipyard of particular interest for more detailed information on those yards.

In certain cases, the assigned numbers for major facilities of shipyards, such as dry docks, locks, and slipways, are provided on layout diagrams where those numbers are significant to the text. The numbers are not provided in all cases since those numbers were often changed over time. At first, the facilities were numbered in chronological sequence, but then as the shipyard was expanded over the years, the numbering system may have been changed to reflect the current relative importance of those facilities. Thus, a new dry dock may have been designated as Dry Dock No. 1 to indicate its premier position as to size and capacity, thereby causing earlier dry docks to be renumbered accordingly.

In certain cases, the classification of warships has been subject to question, and even change. This was especially true at the end of the nineteenth century when armoured cruisers, turret ships, coastal defence ships, and battleships all approached the same size and configuration. For example, the American battleship uss *Maine*, which blew up in Havana Harbour in 1898 precipitating the Spanish-American War, was originally classified as an armoured cruiser. In this work, the latest accepted classification of those ships has been used, even though this may not be consistent with the information contained in certain earlier works.

Many proper names contained in this book that are not of English origin can be subject to variations in spelling depending upon the particular scholar who performed the translation. This is especially true of Japanese and Russian names that are based on non-English scripts. For example, the name of the Japanese aircraft carrier *Ryujo* has also been spelled as *Ryuzyo*. In some cases, the English spellings have changed over the years, such as the name of the Nikolaiev shipyard on the Black Sea, which is now being spelled 'Nikolayev' or 'Nikolajev'. The most accepted spelling of such names has been used in this book, with a preference for their native spelling.

The section on Great Britain addresses Royal Dockyards and British naval bases throughout the world for as long as they were operated and maintained by the Royal Navy. When certain nations achieved Commonwealth status under the British Commonwealth of Nations, or the Royal Navy otherwise departed their bases in those countries, they had to assume responsibility their own naval defence. This book treats those nations as independent countries from the time that they set up their own naval establishments. The subsequent history of the dockyards and naval bases in each of those countries is continued under the name of that country, *ie* Canada, Australia, New Zealand, and India, in the later chapters of this book.

# Acknowledgements

The author gratefully acknowledges the contributions made by the following individuals and firms in collecting and providing the information used in this work:

GREAT BRITAIN
Mr Harold Bennett, Chatham Dockyard Historical Society, Chatham, Kent, England
Tracy Shepherd, HM Naval Base Devonport, Plymouth, England
Mrs Shaline Groves, HM Naval Base Portsmouth, England
Mr Kelly Walker, Babcock International, Rosyth Royal Dockyard, Rosyth, Fife, Scotland
Dr I L Buxton, Department of Marine Technology, University of Newcastle, Newcastle-upon-Tyne, England
Mr Martin J Crowther, Cowes Maritime Museum, Cowes, Isle of Wight, England
Mr Jim Grant, Scottish Maritime Museum, Irvine, Scotland
Mr Alan Hildrew, Central Library, North Shields, Tyne & Wear, England
Ladies of Hebburn Library, South Shields, Tyne & Wear, England
Mr E A Rees, Chief Archivist, Tyne & Wear Archives, Newcastle-upon-Tyne, England
Harland & Wolff Shipbuilding and Heavy Industries Ltd, Belfast, Northern Ireland
Ms Joanne Hunter, John Brown Engineering Ltd, Clydebank, Scotland
Mr Jan Wilson, Kvaerner Govan Ltd, Govan, Glasgow, Scotland
Mr Dave Fillary, Swan Hunter (Tyneside) Ltd, Wallsend, Newcastle-upon-Tyne, England
Mr D Clark, Tyne Tees Dockyard Ltd, Hebburn-on-Tyne, England
Mr Mike Smith, Vickers Shipbuilding and Engineering Ltd, Barrow-in-Furness, England

Mr Phil Rood, Vosper Thornycroft (UK) Ltd, Woolston, Southampton, England
Yarrow Shipbuilders Ltd, Scotstoun, Glasgow, Scotland
Captain A D Balgarnie, HQ British Forces, Gibraltar
Captain Sarah M Wood, HQ British Forces, Hong Kong
Ms Joyce Pang, Hong Kong Museum of History, Kowloon

UNITED STATES
US Naval Station, Newport, Rhode Island
US Naval Submarine Base New London, Groton, Connecticut
Mr Gregory J Plunges, National Archives and Records Administration, New York, New York
US Naval Historical Center, Washington, DC
Mr Joseph M Judge, Curator, Hampton Roads Naval Museum, Norfolk, Virginia
Mr E M Baker, US Naval Base, Norfolk, Virginia
US Naval Station, Mayport, Florida
US Naval Air Station, Pensacola, Florida
Mr E A Skala, US Naval Station, Pascagoula, Mississippi
Mr H Sam Samuelson, US Naval Station, San Diego, California
Lt Lydia Leporte, US Submarine Base, San Diego, California
Mr J R Pfeiffer, US Naval Shipyard, Long Beach, California
Mr William Kooiman, National Maritime Museum, San Francisco, California
Mr C S Robert, US Naval Air Station, Alameda, California
US Naval Shipyard Puget Sound, Bremerton, Washington
US Naval Submarine Base, Bangor, Washington
Ms Jeanie Kitchens, US Naval Station, Everett, Washington
Mr D G Coulter, US Naval Base, Guantanamo Bay, Cuba
US Naval Station, Rota, Spain
US Naval Support Activity, Naples, Italy
US Naval Station, Pearl Harbor, Hawaii
Mr Jon N Nylander, US Naval Forces Japan (for information on Japanese shipyards)
Ms Julie Philips, Bath Iron Works, Bath, Maine
Mr William A Stoops, Maine Maritime Museum, Bath, Maine
Mr A Dooley, Quincy Historical Society, Quincy, Massachusetts
Ms Linda Beeler, Thomas Crane Public Library, Quincy, Massachusetts
Mr N D Ruenzel, Electric Boat Corp., Groton, Connecticut
Mr Robert B Factor, Public Library, Bridgeport, Connecticut
Ms Alice Gingold, New York Historical Society, New York, New York
New York Public Library, New York, New York
Dr Joy Holland, Brooklyn Public Library, Brooklyn, New York
Ms Dorothy J Davison, New York Public Library, Staten Island, New York
Staten Island Historical Society, Staten Island, New York
Mr Robert P Marasco, City Clerk, Newark, New Jersey

Mr James Stuart Osbourn, Public Library, Newark, New Jersey
Mr Charles J Waller, Kearny Museum, Kearny, New Jersey
Mr Roben Manker, Free Library of Philadelphia, Philadelphia, Pennsylvania
Mr James G Gear, Executive Director, J Lewis Crozer Library, Chester,
    Pennsylvania
Ms Jennifer Brown, Wilmington Library, Wilmington, Delaware
Ms Lyn B Lyon, Newport News Shipbuilding, Newport News, Virginia
Ms Anne Hansford, San Pedro Bay Historical Society, San Pedro, California
Mr Roberto Landazuri, San Francisco History Center, San Francisco,
    California
Mr Tom Lucy, Vallejo Naval and Historical Museum, Vallejo, California
Mrs E Larrimore, Seattle Public Library, Seattle, Washington
Mr Robert W Long, Naval Consultant, Seattle, Washington
Bay County Library, Bay City, Michigan
Ms Sandra J Zipperer, Wisconsin Maritime Museum, Manitowoc, Wisconsin

FRANCE
Mr Gilbert Bellec, Direction des Constructions Navales, Brest
Direction des Constructions Navales, Toulon
Mr L Lucas, Chantiers de L'Atlantique, St. Nazaire

GERMANY
Dr Hofmeister, State Archives, Bremen
Mr Hans-Joachim Erdtmann, City Library, Bremen
German Maritime Museum, Bremerhaven
Mr. Briel, City Archives, Kiel
Nadja Koch, Jochen Dietze *et al*, Blohm + Voss GmbH, Hamburg
Messrs Köhne-Lindenlaub and Müther, Fried. Krupp Historical Archives,
    Hoesch, Essen
Mr Reinhold Brenner, Thyssen Nordseewerke GmbH, Emden
Captain Hippchen, Office of Military History, Potsdam
Mr Eberhard Rössler (noted author on German U-boats), Berlin
Prof Dr Jürgen Rohwer (former Director of the Library for Contemporary
    History, Stuttgart), Weinstadt

ITALY
Admiral Giordano Cottini, Director, Military Maritime Arsenal, La Spezia
    (1997)
Rear-Admiral Dino Nascetti, Director, Military Maritime Arsenal, La Spezia
    (1998)
Mr Alfonso Camposarcone, Military Maritime Arsenal, Taranto
Mr Luigi Mor, Director, Sestri Cantieri Navale, Genoa
Ms Vera Murialdi, Stabilimento Muggiano, Cantieri Navali Italiani SpA, La
    Spezia
Cantieri Navale Fratelli Orlando, Livorno
Fincantieri Naval Shipbuilding Division, Genoa

CANADA
Ms Marilyn Gurney, Director, Maritime Command Museum, CFB, Halifax,
    NS
Lt Cmdr C E L Henderson, Hq Maritime Forces Pacific, Victoria, BC
Mr Joseph M Lenarcik, Asst. Curator, Naval and Military Museum, CFB
    Esquimalt, BC
Ms Lynn Wright, Maritime Museum of British Columbia Society, Victoria,
    BC

OTHER COUNTRIES
Mrs Heleen den Heijer, Schelde Shipbuilding, Vlissingen, The Netherlands
Wilton-Fijenoord Dock & Shipyard Co., Schiedam, The Netherlands
Mr Thomas Aronsenius, Kockums AB, Malmö, Sweden
Ms Maude Carlsson and Liselotte Lindahl, Kockums Naval Systems,
    Karlskrona, Sweden
Mr E Korchargin, Central Naval Museum, St Petersburg, Russia
Mr A P Romanov, National Library of Russia, St Petersburg, Russia
Australian Submarine Corporation Pty Ltd, Osborne (Adelaide), South
    Australia
Warrant Officer C S A Heywood MBE, Royal New Zealand Navy
    Museum, Devonport (Auckland), New Zealand
Mr Michael Cassar, Valletta, Malta
Mr Thorbjörn Jónsson, First Secretary, Ministry for Foreign Affairs,
    Reykjavik, Iceland
Mr Wee Cheng Leong, Curator, Naval Museum, Singapore

# 1 The Evolution of Naval Shipbuilding

Although there had been other primitive vessels that were adapted for warfare purposes, the first true warship of record was the 'war galley', which was used primarily in the eastern Mediterranean region from the middle of the first millennium BC. Initially, warships were merely trading vessels that were used to transport armed warriors to protect other trading vessels from the ships of hostile nations or from roving pirates. The early Phoenicians used galleys, oar-propelled ships with a single mast and square-rigged sail, for trading purposes along the Mediterranean seacoast in the seventh century BC. These galleys were later adapted as war galleys by the Assyrians, using a raised structure around the hull to provide some protection for the oarsmen as well as the soldiers carried on board.

The early galleys usually had a single bank of about two dozen sets of oars positioned on the main deck. The Greeks later fitted their galleys with additional banks of oars, staggered at different levels, to achieve greater speed, creating the bireme with two banks of oars and eventually the trireme with three banks of oars. The Romans continued the use of war galleys to support their conquests in extending the domain of their empire in the Mediterranean region. These war galleys were even more heavily protected than those of the Assyrians, and they had castle-like towers, usually on the fore deck but sometimes also on the after deck, from which soldiers could throw their spears and shoot their arrows at the enemy below. This design led to the foredeck of a ship later becoming known as the 'forecastle' or simply 'fo'c'sle'.

The use of the war galley reached its climax in the Battle of Lepanto off the western coast of Greece in 1571. At that time, over two hundred ships of the Christian alliance of Spain, Genoa, Venice, Malta and the Papal States defeated a Turkish fleet of about the same size. Most of the ships used on both sides were war galleys with single masts and lateen sails, but the Venetians also had a half dozen galleasses. The galleass was somewhat larger than a galley, had three masts with lateen sails, and was armed with several large cast-brass cannons which had just come into being at that time. The gunfire from the galleasses decided the battle before the two sides could get close enough to each another for the customary boarding and hand-to-hand combat.

Shipyards were also becoming more numerous along the Mediterranean and Adriatic coastlines to support the ever-growing need for merchant ships and warships. The Roman Empire required a large fleet of ships to transport her legions to the far corners of the empire to maintain its dominance over those distant regions. At the time of the Crusades, Venice became a centre for building ships for the Christian nations to transport their forces to the eastern Mediterranean. Meanwhile, the Turks were building a large fleet to challenge the Christian forces in the region.

While the galley dominated maritime use and naval warfare in the Mediterranean area, there were other developments in the north. During the ninth century AD, the Scandinavian Vikings displayed the ultimate in warship construction up to that time with their long, graceful and seaworthy ships. These were narrow vessels that carried one mast with a square-rigged sail and, like the galley, had about two dozen sets of oars. With these 'dragon' ships, the Norsemen went on raiding expeditions and ravaged the coastal villages of the British Isles, France, the Low Countries, and Spain. There is some evidence that they even reached the North Atlantic continent in the area around Newfoundland early in the eleventh century.

Around the twelfth century, trade was beginning to flourish among the coastal cities of northern Europe, especially along the English Channel, North Sea, and Baltic coasts. On the mainland, several key German cities united to form the Hanseatic League of merchants to further promote and control trade in the region. This led to the development of the cog, a small merchant vessels with a single mast and square sail, which later evolved into the carrack. Some cogs were also fitted as warships with fighting platforms at their bows and sterns and carrying soldiers to protect the merchant cogs from pirates and other foes. Across the English Channel, vessels similar to the cog were used by the merchants of the Cinque Ports on the south-eastern coast of England.

By the thirteenth century, ships were being built with an additional mast. These ships usually had one large square sail on the centrally-located mainmast and a triangular lateen sail attached to a smaller mizzen-mast toward the stern of the ship. By the fifteenth century, these ships evolved into the carrack, a ship with three masts, one forward and one aft of the larger centre mainmast, and raised forecastle decks and quarter-decks. The mainmast and the foremast were rigged with square sails, while the mizzen–mast was rigged with a triangular lateen sail. These ships also had a single stern rudder which was developed in the fourteenth century to replace the single or double steering oars mounted on either or both sides of earlier ships near the stern.

During this period, the caravel made its appearance. These ships usually had three masts, one large mainmast at the centre and smaller foremast and mizzen–mast, all of which were rigged with triangular lateen sails. Some

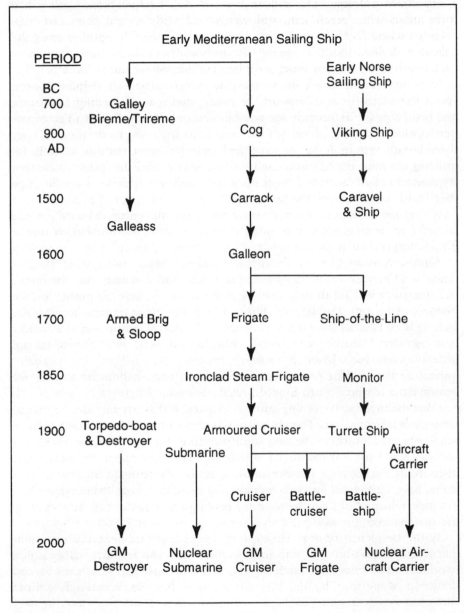

Evolution of Warships.

caravels carried an even smaller fourth mast behind the mizzen-mast, and those so-called jigger masts were also lateen-rigged. Like the carracks, these caravels also had raised foredecks and quarter-decks. Christopher Columbus' squadron consisted of three caravels, but only the smaller *Pinta* was properly rigged as a caravel with three lateen sails. The *Santa Maria* and *Niña* were rerigged as 'ships' with a large square mainsail and a square main topsail, a single square foresail, a lateen mizzen, and a bowsprit sail. Caravels were used mostly by the Portuguese as merchant vessels and had little naval significance.

In the sixteenth century, the galleon evolved from the carrack, and this type of ship was used both for trading and for warfare. The galleon was a large vessel rigged as a 'ship' with two square sails on both the mainmast and foremast, a lateen sail on the mizzen-mast, and a small square sail set on the bowsprit. The galleon was distinguished by its extremely high multi-tiered quarter-deck. With the advent of cast-brass and then cast-iron muzzle-loading cannons at the beginning of the century, the warship version of the galleon had up to two gun decks.

Although first built by England and later by other nations as well, the galleon was most noted for its use by Spain, which used the galleon to extend its rule to distant lands and bring back gold and other riches from the New World. In this latter role, the Spanish galleon was the target of privateers such as Sir Francis Drake in the latter part of the sixteenth century. The galleon was also the primary type of ship used by Spain in her ill-fated Armada sent to invade England in 1588.

Another version of the galleon was the Dutch 'fluit' (also spelled 'fluyt' or 'flute'). This vessel was designed specifically for carrying the maximum amount of cargo and thereby achieving the optimum level of profit for their owners. Although the size of fluits varied, the most common type was generally somewhat over 100ft in length and 20ft in beam, and it displaced 400–500 tons. The fluit had a bulbous bow and stern intended for the storage of extra cargo. Not designed for speed, the fluit often fell prey to marauding pirates, and during the Anglo-Dutch Wars in the latter half of the seventeenth century, many were lost to English privateers.

Shipbuilding was becoming more of a science than merely the haphazard activity that it once was. The choice of wood became very important as larger ships were kept in the water and were therefore subject to rotting. It was not unusual for ships to have lives of only five years or less due to the problem of their hulls rotting away. Earlier ships could be constructed at ground level using basic manpower for construction tasks, then merely rolled into the water on logs, which could also be used for hauling the ships out of the water for repairs and maintenance.

With the increasing size of ships, shipyards were of necessity becoming permanent establishments with improved facilities and a steady highly skilled workforce. Building and launching ways and other essential structures became fixtures at shipyards. The building of larger ships became increasingly difficult and time-consuming due to the size of their structural members and the need for exact measurements to ensure the proper fit of mating components. The

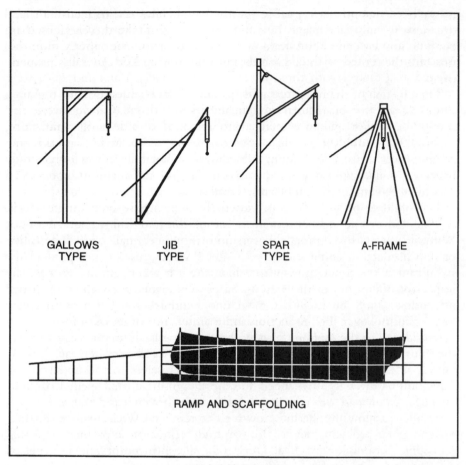

GALLOWS TYPE     JIB TYPE     SPAR TYPE     A-FRAME

RAMP AND SCAFFOLDING

Early Lift Cranes.

structural members of ships now had to be built up from smaller sections of wood and then erected on the building and launching ways. The outside planking was attached to the framework of the ship by shipwrights working on scaffolds.

Lumber and other supplies and equipment needed for construction and interior work above ground level were brought aboard the ship using long ramps extending from the ground to the working level. These ramps were set up either longitudinally along the side of the ship under construction or, where space permitted, laterally up to the side of the ship. Heavier pieces were often moved up the ramp on rollers, carts or other wheeled conveyances.

Various types of lifting devices were later developed to assist in the construction and fitting-out of ships. These lifting devices included the gallows-type, which were used for lifting very heavy objects such as rudders and positioning them on the ship. The jib-type, with the jib affixed to the base of a vertical post, and the spar-type, with the spar attached to the upper section of a vertical post, were used for general lifting tasks. The A-frame could be used alone to support heavy loads, but it was limited to moving loads for short distances in only one plane by tilting the device forward. When used in conjunction with another A-frame set up directly across the slipway from the first one, the combination had greater range in moving loads laterally between them.

The erection of the masts was perhaps one of the trickiest tasks in building a ship during that era. Masts were usually fashioned out of a single tree for strength and then placed directly onto the keel of a ship for maximum support. They could be as long as 100ft or more, up to 2ft in diameter, and weigh several tons. The A-frame was the most suitable device for erecting masts, and some shipyards erected a permanent 'mast crane' consisting basically of a tilted A-frame with lumber rear supports.

The building of large fleets of vessels for the purpose of trading and for warfare led to the further development of shipyards throughout Europe. Without any central control, however, uniformity in configuration and quality of ship production could not be guaranteed. While this was not particularly significant in the production of merchant ships, it was beginning to have an impact on the navies of the various sea powers involved. By the end of the fifteenth century, the English Crown was beginning to take steps to effect greater control over the production and maintenance of its warships.

In addition to the building of new ships, there was an urgent need to keep the ships already in service at the peak of efficiency. This required the removal of barnacles and other sea life that attached themselves to the underside of ships causing them to loose speed due the rough surface and weight of these creatures. In the past, this required the ships to be beached and turned over on their sides to allow the marine growth to be removed. With small vessels, this was no great problem, but as the size and weight of ships increased, this procedure became less practical. During the fifteenth century, the concept of the dry dock was developed and implemented.

In 1496, the first Royal dry dock was built by Henry VII at Portsmouth on the southern coast of England on the English Channel. In 1506, Henry VIII began construction of the first two Royal Dockyards at Woolwich and at Deptford, both on the Thames River near London, solely for the construction of warships for the Royal Navy. The French also recognised the importance of exercising direct control over the construction of their warships, and in 1636, its naval base at Toulon on the Mediterranean coast was established as a marine arsenal (naval shipyard). Spain eventually established a naval shipyard at Cádiz on its southern Atlantic coast, which was the chief port for the galleons sent to the New World to bring back gold for the Spanish Royal Treasury.

During the latter half of the seventeenth century, the British Admiralty established a board to define the specifications for each type of warship henceforth to be built for the Royal Navy. This was a further attempt to standardise naval shipbuilding in the interests of facilitating production, training, and subsequent support. As a result of these efforts, orders could be placed for the same type of ship at different dockyards with some reasonable assurance that they would be substantially identical. As a practical matter, there would always be some variations as technical changes were prescribed for specific ships in different stages of production.

During the eighteenth and early nineteenth century, a family of warships was developed on the basis of the various functions to be performed by each type of warship, but with a degree of standardisation within each class of warship. At the lower end of the scale were small vessels rigged as schooners, sloops, and brigs and used for coastal defence and patrolling purposes. These were generally two-masted ships of about 200-300 tons displacement, and they carried between 12 and 24 guns on a single deck. Later 'barks' were somewhat larger and had three masts, but their armament remained substantially the same.

The most versatile type of warship of the Royal Navy and other fleets during this era was the frigate. This medium-sized ship, akin to the latter-day cruiser, was used for a variety of purposes, especially long-range naval operations. Frigates were generally three-masted ships of about 1000-2000 tons displacement and carrying 28-44 guns. They were fast and highly manoeuvrable, which gave them some capability for action against larger, but more cumbersome warships. At the turn of the century, the United States built six large 44-gun frigates, including the famous USS *Constitution*, which distinguished themselves in action against British warships during the War of 1812.

The ultimate warship of the era was the 'ship-of-the-line' which carried up to 120 guns. Smaller warships, including frigates, carried most of their armament on a single gun deck, but the ship-of the line needed two and even three guns decks for the number of guns they carried. The French built the largest ships-of-the-line of the period, this trend reaching epic proportions with their 4000-ton, 120-gun *Le États de Bourgogne* in 1790. More typical of three-deckers was HMS *Victory*, flagship of Lord Nelson at the Battle of Trafalgar in 1805. This ship displaced 3500 tons, had three masts, and carried 100 guns.

Ships-of-the-line were rated by the number of guns they carried and therefore their potential effectiveness against an enemy force while in the line of battle. In the Royal Navy of Nelson's time, First Rate ships-of-the-line carried 100-120 guns on three gun decks, whereas Second Rates carried between 90 and 98 guns also on three decks. Third Rates carried between 64 and 80 guns on two decks, leaving the frigate as the next lowest category of warship.

The United States also recognised the importance of establishing naval shipyards under government control to assure the construction of warships when required to prescribed standards and specifications. In 1800, just 11 years after the establishment of a Federal government, the US Congress authorised the construction of its first six navy yards dedicated to the building of warships for the US Navy. These navy yards were scattered along the eastern seaboard of the United States, starting with Portsmouth, New Hampshire in the north, including Boston, New York, Philadelphia, and Washington, and extending southward down to Gosport (Norfolk), Virginia.

## A NEW ERA IN SHIPBUILDING

By the middle of the nineteenth century, there were several technological advances that dramatically changed naval construction. The successful application of the steam engine, invented by James Watt as early as 1765, to marine propulsion spelled the end of the age of sail. The Battle of Navarino Bay off the west coast of Greece in 1827 was the last battle ever fought between pure sailing vessels. In this battle, the combined fleet of French, English, and Russian ships defeated the Turks and secured the independence of Greece. While the steam engine had been used on commercial shipping since early in the century, it was not applied to warships, even as a secondary source of propulsion, until the middle of the century.

The first steam-powered ships used paddle wheels for propulsion, which for the most part consisted of a pair of paddle wheels located amidships on either side of the ship. There were also some sternwheelers with a single broad paddle wheel mounted at the stern. The first steam-powered warship was the *Demologos*, built by Robert Fulton for the US Navy in 1815. That ship had a single paddle wheel mounted at the centre of the ship for maximum protection, but this required the construction of a double hull like a catamaran. With its double hull and single paddle wheel, the *Demologos* did not prove successful, and Fulton returned to the more conventional side-wheeler design for his second warship, the steam frigate *Fulton II* in 1836.

Paddle steamers were really not suitable as warships since they reduced the number of guns that could be mounted on each side of the ship and their fragile paddle wheels were very susceptible to damage from enemy gunfire. The vulnerability of side paddle wheels required the extensive use of iron plating around their housings for protection. The solution to this problem soon came with the invention of the screw propeller, and by 1840, this device was being applied to new merchant ship production. The screw propeller was later adopted by the admiralties of the major naval powers, and by 1860, all new warships being built incorporated steam engines and screw propellers.

At about the same time, consideration was being given to the attachment of iron plates over the basic wood structure to protect the hull, guns, and other vitals of the ship, including the new steam engine, from enemy fire. Thus, the 'ironclad' warship came into being in the middle of the nineteenth century. In 1850, the British frigate HMS *Pegasus*, the first ironclad ship with screw propellers to be built, was placed into service with the Royal Navy. By 1860, all of the major warships being built for the British and French navies were ironclads.

In 1862, another type of warship, one that would revolutionise naval construction, made its appearance. The USS *Monitor*, the forerunner of other ships of that type, was a steam-powered, screw-propelled ship with an open flat deck and low freeboard. Its unique feature was its two 11in Dahlgren muzzle-loading guns mounted in a single revolving turret at the centre of the ship. The sides, deck and turret were armoured with heavy iron plates that could withstand the gunfire of contemporary warships. Its first encounter with the Confederate ironclad CSS *Virginia* proved that it could stand up to other ironclads, but the potential for further development of this type of warship was unlimited.

Concurrently with other advances, there were also new developments in armaments technology. Efforts by Sir William G Armstrong and Sir Joseph Whitworth of England and Friedrich Krupp of Germany led to the development of breech-loading guns. Breech-loading allowed greater flexibility in aiming the guns since they no longer had to be on carriages that were moved directly to the rear of their firing position to permit reloading. Instead of having duplicate batteries of muzzle-loading guns on both sides of a ship, a single battery of breech-loading guns could now be located along the centreline of the ship, allowing for the precise aiming of the guns at targets. Armoured gun turrets and shields for individually-mounted guns afforded protection for both the crews and the gun mechanisms.

Two other innovations that contributed to the improvement of the armament systems of warships were rifled bores and shell projectiles. The rifled bores imparted a spin to the projectile for stability and allowed the use of the new shell projectiles that were cylindrical in shape but with pointed noses for aerodynamic purposes. Projectiles filled with the new high explosives could inflict more damage on the enemy than solid shot or black powder-filled shells. Since the weight of a projectile was no longer of an indication of its destructive power, the classification of guns was changed from 'pounder' to the calibre of the gun, *ie* the diameter of the bore in inches or centimetres.

With these overlapping developments occurring at the same time, there was considerable confusion within the Admiralties and among naval architects as to which innovations should be incorporated into the design of warships and when this should be accomplished. Naval shipbuilders were also having problems in converting their yards to accommodate these new technologies. Until sails were eliminated completely, they would still have to keep their sail lofts, but now had to expand their yards to incorporate engineering works for the new steam engines being introduced. Woodworking equipment would still be required for the time being, but additional equipment for the working of iron plating and other components would now be needed. Additional storage facilities would also be needed to stock iron plating and other iron forms.

The problems resulting from the simultaneous introduction of a multitude of new technologies into the naval shipbuilding process resulted in many unsatisfactory products. It also caused the rapid obsolescence of warships that were built before all of the new technologies could be incorporated into their design and production. The transition from sail to steam was particularly vexing since it resulted in a fleet composed of a combination of pure sailing ships, vessels with both steam and sail, and pure steamers. Coupled with this was the transition from all-wood to ironclad, then to composite wood and iron, then to all-iron, and finally to all-steel vessels. On top of that, some ships of each type still had muzzle-loaders while the others had the new breech-loading guns.

It was not until the end of the nineteenth century that naval shipbuilding caught up with all of these new technologies and began incorporating them collectively into new warships. By then, steel had replaced iron plates for warship construction and protective armour plating, and the all-steel warship was born. The first major all-steel warship was the cruiser, a replacement of the ironclad steam frigate. The earliest cruisers had no armour protection and were therefore referred to as 'unprotected' or 'unarmoured' cruisers. These later evolved into the 'light cruiser' and they are therefore referred to as such in this book for the sake of simplicity. The need for some armour protection soon became apparent, and this led to the development of the 'protected' cruiser with some horizontal deck armour over its vital engine compartment and magazines for protection against plunging fire.

The ultimate in cruiser development in that period was the 'armoured' or 'belted' cruiser, which had a thick armoured belt around its mid-section, intended to protect the vital spaces within its hull against direct fire. With three different categories of cruiser at hand, a simple numerical rating system, similar to that used for ships-of-the-line, was developed to indicate the relative size, power and armour protection of cruisers. First Class cruisers were the latest armoured and protected cruisers, whilst Second Class cruisers were generally less well-armed and protected. Third Class cruisers were the least well-armed and protected.

The construction of wooden sailing ships-of-the-line came to an end in 1847 with the completion of the French 120-gun *Valmy*. While some ships-of-the-line were converted to or built with steam power, it was clearly impractical at the time to apply iron armour plates over the entire length of the ship because of the weight involved. The capital ships of the future would evolve from the smaller iron and steel vessels then being constructed. The single-turret monitor soon evolved into the double-turret monitor, and further developments in both Britain and America led to the turret ship, a precursor of the battleship.

In Great Britain, the first turret ships carried masts for sails, reflecting the Admiralty's concern that the steam engines of the time were unable to meet the demands of strategic cruising. They carried four guns ranging in calibre from 12in to 16in in two twin turrets. By 1875, sails had been removed from capital ships, and within the next five years breech-loading guns had replaced muzzle-loaders on turret ships. In the 1880s several classes of barbette ship, with 12in or 13.5in guns on open turntables were built, but the vulnerability of these unprotected mounts meant that this trend did not continue. The battleship replaced the earlier sailing ship-of-the-line as the principal capital ship. By the 1890s, battleships were the class carrying the heaviest guns with the greatest armour protection, generally displacing up to 15,000 tons and with a main armament of four 12in guns in two twin turrets, one forward and one aft, as well as substantial batteries of lighter guns.

At the same time, armoured cruisers were increasing in size and power until by the turn of the century they were approaching the size of battleships, growing from 6000 tons on average to nearly 15,000 tons, and mounting guns of up to 10in calibre. The latest armoured cruisers usually mounted their heavy guns in single or twin turrets fore and aft, with numerous lighter guns in casemates or open mounts along the ship's sides.

Design and technology associated with the battleship and armoured cruiser converged at the turn of the century and the distinction between the two types began to become blurred. For example, the USS *Maine*, a 6700-ton American warship built in 1895 and armed with four 10in guns, was originally classified as an armoured cruiser, but later reclassified as a 'Second Class battleship'. Her loss due to an explosion in Havana harbour in 1898 precipitated the Spanish-American War. Some battleships were small and suitable only for service in home waters, and these became known as 'coastal defence (battle)ships' to distinguish then from the larger ocean-going battleships. The armoured cruiser as a type ceased to be built by the major navies after 1905, and was largely obsolete by the outbreak of the First World War. The gap between battleships and light cruisers would later be bridged by the new 10,000-ton heavy cruisers armed with 8in guns built under the terms of the Washington Naval Treaty of 1922.

The transition from wood and sail to iron and steam sounded the death-knell for most of the existing private shipyards at the time. While naval shipyards were financed by their respective governments and were therefore required to keep pace with the times, this was generally not true of the private shipyards. The equipment and skills used for the construction of wooden sailing ships were not adaptable to the construction of ships made out of iron and propelled by steam engines. The last of the large sailing ships were the great clippers built for the tea trade with the Orient, such as the renown *Cutty Sark* of England and Donald McKay's famous American clippers, the *Flying Cloud* and *Lightning*.

With the demise of the private shipyards that represented the wood and sail era, a new breed of shipyard sprung up as their replacements, the corporate 'iron works'. Typical of these iron works were Thames Iron Works on the River Thames near London, Bath Iron Works in Maine, Columbian Iron Works in Baltimore, and Union Iron Works in San Francisco. As steel became the preferred material for shipbuilding purposes, many of the great steel producers of the world expanded their domain into the field of shipbuilding. These included John Brown of Sheffield, England, William Beardmore of Glasgow, Scotland, Friedrich Krupp of Essen, Germany, Mitsubishi and Kawasaki in Japan, and Bethlehem Steel in the United States.

Technological advances also improved the facilities at shipyards. The steam engine was adapted to shipyard cranes, giving them greater power to lift heavy structural members and to position them in place on ships under construction or repair. Adapted from locomotive technology, these cranes could travel on rails alongside a building berth, dock, or pier to where they were needed. Travelling cranes were later equipped with smaller and more versatile diesel engines in lieu of the massive steam engines previously used.

There were further developments at the turn of the century which had an impact on warship construction. During the American Civil War and other conflicts of that era, attempts were made to destroy enemy ships by placing and detonating explosive charges against their hulls. The spar torpedo was an explosive charge placed at the end of a pole attached to the bows of a small boat or early submersible and then rammed against the hull of the target. Other explosive devices were placed in the water and detonated when enemy ships came in contact with them. These so-called 'torpedoes' (later called mines) had obvious disadvantages and although they did cause a certain amount of damage, they were not considered as primary weapons of warfare.

The development of the 'automatic' or self-propelled torpedo in 1868 by Robert Whitehead, an English inventor from Lancashire, soon had a major impact on the nature of naval warfare. By the end of the century, the design of the torpedo had been advanced by the addition of gyroscopic controls, contra-rotating propellers, and improved propulsion systems to the point of becoming a very potent naval weapon. This led to the development of two new delivery systems for the self-propelled torpedo, one a surface vessel and the other a submersible.

Development of the torpedo-boat began as early as 1880 with steel vessels of 100 tons or less displacement being able to fire one or two earlier versions of the Whitehead torpedo. In the 1890s Great Britain developed the torpedo boat 'destroyer', ships of about 350 tons displacement that carried three torpedo tubes and had a speed of 26kts. Destroyers were also armed with a battery of quick-firing guns to defeat enemy torpedo-boats. Over the next few years, these ships continued to be improved upon by both Britain and France. By the end of the nineteenth century, construction of torpedo-boats and destroyers by the major naval powers was progressing at a fast pace. These small ships, still displacing only about 500 tons at most, could easily be turned out by the smaller shipyards that could not keep up with the increasing size of the capital ships now being built.

While the submersible had already been invented, it was not until 1900 that the first practical submarine was developed by John P Holland for the US Navy. Again there was a coming-together of several technologies that made the submarine a formidable warship before the beginning of the First World War. The diesel engine had been developed by Rudolf Diesel in Germany in 1897, and the first marine application of this engine was produced in 1910. At about the same time, the Edison storage battery became available for industrial use. The use of the highly efficient compression-ignition engine for surface travel, coupled with the use of the Edison storage battery for undersea travel, provided an ideal power plant for the submarine.

The development of the periscope also contributed to the overall effectiveness of a submarine by providing the means for the commander to track the target, estimate its range and speed, and arrive at the proper firing solution. The first production submarines were only about 100 tons in displacement and had a single bow torpedo tube, but advances over the next few years in the United States, Britain, France, and Germany significantly improved the quality of the undersea warship. By the time that war broke out in 1914, these powers were producing quality submarines that made a real contribution to their war effort.

By the end of the nineteenth century, electric power became available commercially. The original direct current (DC) electrical systems were soon replaced with alternating current (AC) systems which could be transformed to higher voltages for transmission purposes and then reduced for application. The availability of electric power, coupled with Thomas Edison's electric lamp and Nickola Tesla's induction motor, was a great boon to shipyards since they could now use electric-powered equipment and lighting to aid in their operations.

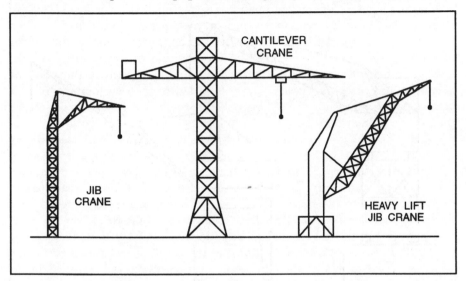

Fixed Cranes.

With the advent of commercial electric power, fixed cranes could be erected alongside a slipway to move ship components from the ground to any position on a ship under construction. These included more modern versions of the old wooden spar-type lifting devices, as well as the newer cantilever-type crane. The cantilever crane is a T-shaped device consisting of a cross member sitting atop a relatively slender fixed structure. The cross member can rotate a full 360°, and its hoist can travel the entire length of the forward boom. The cantilever crane has a capacity of about 250 tons, and the rear boom of the cross member supports the counterweights required to balance the load being moved.

The ultimate fixed crane was the hammerhead-type crane of cantilever design used mostly in American naval shipyards for the fitting out of large warships. These massive cranes had a capacity of 350 tons, and were used primarily for the installation and replacement of heavy machinery and armament systems on battleships. They generally had a large base with heavy vertical supports and strong cross-bracing to support the turntable on which the crane rotated.

Many shipyards employed an electric–powered fixed gantry crane over the slipways used for the construction of major warships as well as large commercial vessels. While the gantry structure itself is fixed, a laterally-placed travelling crane rides on rails supported along each side of the gantry for the entire length of the slipway. A hoist in turn travels along the entire width of the crane, thus allowing for the movement of ship components from the ground to any position on the ship under construction. A variation of this type

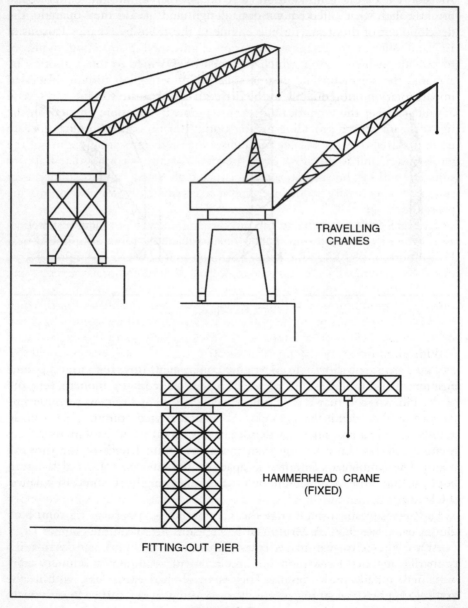

TRAVELLING
CRANES

HAMMERHEAD CRANE
(FIXED)

FITTING-OUT PIER

Heavy Lift Cranes.

of crane consists of a travelling gantry crane riding on rails above fixed supports on both sides of the slipway and running the entire length of the slipway.

## THE TWENTIETH CENTURY

At the turn of the century, there was yet another significant technological breakthrough that affected warship design and production, namely the development of the steam turbine engine in the 1880s by Charles Parsons of England. Whereas the reciprocating steam engine used steam acting on pistons to provide in-line motion, which was then transformed to rotary motion by a crank, the steam turbine engine used steam acting on turbine blades to impart rotary motion directly to the drive shaft. The steam turbine had several advantages over the reciprocating steam engine. It was more efficient in the use of steam power, providing greater output for the same amount of steam used. It was also much smaller and lighter than a reciprocating engine of the same power, and it therefore could be more readily accommodated aboard ship. The turbine, however, turned at a very high speed, and a reduction gear system was necessary to reduce the speed sufficiently for use in marine propulsion.

The effectiveness of the steam turbine engine was first demonstrated in 1894 when the steam turbine yacht *Turbinia* made its debut at Spithead near Portsmouth off the English Channel. Stealing the show at a prestigious Royal Naval Review, the *Turbinia* was able to outrun all of the other naval vessels and actually attained a speed of 34kts. Two years later, the British Admiralty ordered a steam turbine driven torpedo boat destroyer, HMS *Viper*, which became the first warship to be powered by a steam turbine engine. By 1914, over half of the major warships in the Royal Navy were driven by steam turbine engines.

The production of steam turbine engines involved very critical manufacturing processes and required the use of high-precision tooling and great skill. Most shipyards which had been able to manufacture reciprocating engines did not have the capability to produce steam turbine engines and therefore had to rely on other firms that specialised in the building of steam turbine engines. In 1889, Charles Parsons established a new company, the Parsons Marine Steam Turbine Company, at Wallsend near Newcastle-upon-Tyne in England to produce this new power plant for the various shipbuilders. Most major British warships built during the twentieth century were equipped with Parsons steam turbine engines, and even a few American warships built during and after the First World War had Parsons steam turbine engines.

At the turn of the century, Charles Curtis of the United States developed a variation in the Parsons turbine using velocity-compounded impulse stages with intermediate rows of fixed blades to redirect the steam back to the rotating blades. This steam turbine was marketed as the Curtis-Brown steam turbine engine, it and soon competed with the Parsons turbine in marine applications, especially in the United States. Several British battlecruisers built during the First World War era were also equipped with Curtis-Brown turbines. Later both General Electric and Westinghouse corporations began the manufacture of steam turbine engines for naval use, and these eventually became the standard for the US Navy.

In 1906, Great Britain revolutionised capital ship design with its new 18,000-ton battleship HMS *Dreadnought*, the first 'all-big-gun' battleship. Up until then, the typical armament arrangement on the battleships of most navies was to have two turrets on the main deck, one forward and the other aft, each carrying two 12in guns, and a number of smaller guns of different calibres mounted along both sides of the ship. In contrast, the *Dreadnought* carried ten 12in guns in five twin turrets, one forward, two aft, and two 'wing' turrets amidships on either side of the ship. The vessel's secondary armament was also standardised at twenty-four 12pdr guns. Another innovation of the *Dreadnought* was that she was the first capital ship to be equipped with steam turbine engines.

With the advent of the 13.5in gun to replace the 12in in the Royal Navy in 1911, the increased size and weight of the turret caused the abandonment of the 'wing' turret design of capital ships. All naval powers henceforth placed their main armament along the centreline of the ship. By 1913, Great Britain had introduced the 15in gun as the primary weapon for the Royal Navy, and her new battleships would carry eight of these guns in four twin turrets, two forward and two aft. The United States, however, preferred to stay with the 14in gun, and these were mounted in four triple turrets, two forward and two aft in her new battleships laid down in that period.

The availability of electric power came just in time to support the frenzy of warship construction that characterised the armaments race between the major European powers prior to 1914. Germany under Kaiser Wilhelm II was challenging the might of British Empire and had begun a massive warship construction programme that taxed the capability of her Imperial naval shipyards and contractor shipyards. Great Britain more than kept pace with the German shipbuilding programme and was able to stop the threat of German sea power at the Battle of Jutland in 1916, even with the loss of three capital ships in that engagement.

At the beginning of the First World War, the size of battleships had increased to about 30,000 tons in displacement, limiting their production to naval shipyards and a limited number of private contractor shipyards. The ultimate accomplishment in capital ship construction of this period was the mighty British battlecruiser HMS *Hood* completed by the John Brown shipyard at Clydebank near Glasgow, Scotland in 1920. The *Hood* displaced 42,000 tons, was over 850ft in length, had a speed of 32kts, and carried the same armament as contemporary battleships, eight 15in guns. She remained the most powerful capital ship in the world until the advent of a new generation of 35,000-ton battleships being build by the major naval powers in the late 1930s.

Just before the First World War, both the United States and Great Britain were beginning to experiment with naval aviation. By 1911, the US Navy had already demonstrated the feasibility of aircraft taking off and landing on temporary platforms erected on naval vessels. At the end of the War, Great Britain had converted a former Italian liner into the first flush-deck aircraft carrier, HMS *Argus*. The British soon had a second ship of this type by converting the hull of an incomplete battleship. They then converted three completed battlecruisers into aircraft carriers when disarmament treaties limited the number of capital ships that each of the world naval powers could retain after the First World War.

In 1922, the United States converted a collier for use as an experimental aircraft carrier, and when this proved successful, two battlecruisers, already laid down but not completed, were converted into aircraft carriers. The USS *Saratoga* and USS *Lexington* were both commissioned as aircraft carriers in 1927. The Japanese, similarly faced with disarmament treaty limitations on capital ships, also converted two of their battlecruisers, the *Akagi* and *Kaga*, into aircraft carriers. As the aircraft carrier established its position as a warship and as an integral part of the fleet, the major naval powers began designing and building aircraft carriers from the keel up.

At the end of the First World War, there was a concerted disarmament effort among the major world powers to limit the size of their navies. The Washington Naval Conference of 1922 and the London Naval Conference of 1930 put specific limits on the number of warships that each nation could retain or build. Those treaties also established technical limitations on their displacement and the armament that those ships could carry. This period brought hard times to the shipyards that depended on government orders for warship construction to sustain them, and many of them could not survive. The economic depression of the early 1930s also contributed to severe cutbacks if not outright closure of the shipyards affected.

The Washington Naval Treaty limited the size of cruisers to 10,000 tons and their armament to a maximum calibre of 8in. This resulted in the introduction of the 'heavy cruiser' type. In 1924, America produced two Treaty heavy cruisers of the *Pensacola* class, displacing 9100 tons and armed with ten 8in guns. Subsequent American heavy cruisers carried nine 8in guns in three triple turrets which became the standard for this type in the US Navy. The British followed suit with the 9500-ton 'County' class cruisers, armed with eight 8in guns in four twin turrets, the first of which was completed in 1928.

After the demise of the armoured and protected cruiser, the unprotected cruiser continued to evolve into the 'light cruiser', which usually displaced between 4000 and 6000 tons, and mounted guns of 6in calibre or less. A few earlier vessels in this category carried heavier guns, such as the British *Hawkins* class which were armed with seven 7.5in guns in single mounts. As the Second World War approached, light cruisers grew in size, approaching 10,000 tons, and carried up to fifteen 6in guns in triple turrets. Others were built as specialised anti-aircraft cruisers with a main armament of numerous smaller-calibre guns capable of high-angle fire.

In the 1920s and early 1930s, the only sizeable programmes for major warship construction were for heavy and light cruisers for the British and US navies. Destroyer and submarine production continued at a low rate during that period, primarily just to keep up with technological improvements and maintain a production base for future emergency needs. A few large ships were being built, such as the British battleships *Rodney* and *Nelson*, which were allowed under the naval treaty to replace an equal number of ageing battleships that were to be scrapped. The other large ships being produced at this time were conversions and new construction of a few aircraft carriers by Great Britain, Japan, and the United States.

In the early 1930s, a unique type of warship made its appearance on the world scene. By the Treaty of Versailles, Germany was limited to capital ships not exceeding 10,000 tons in displacement and main armament not exceeding 11in calibre. The result was an innovative cross between a battleship and cruiser, which the Germans called merely 'Panzerschiff' (armoured ship), but to which the rest of the world gave the more descriptive title of 'pocket battleship'. Germany built three of these ships before reverting to more conventional capital ship construction under a separate treaty with Great Britain. These pocket battleships displaced 10,000 tons (nominally) and carried six 11in guns in two triple turrets, one forward and the other aft. They were of all-welded construction for lightness, and they were powered by four diesel engines driving two screws.

With the advent of German rearmament under the Third Reich, Italian militarism proclaimed by its Fascist regime, and Japanese expansionism in Asia, there was a resurgence of naval shipbuilding activity throughout the world in the late 1930s. The expiration of the London Naval Treaty at the end of 1936 provided the legality for exceeding previously agreed upon numerical limitations on capital ships. This led to the construction of the next generation of 35,000-ton battleships by the major European powers and the United States. By 1940, the United States laid down its first 45,000-ton battleship, the USS *Iowa*, only to be outdone by the Japanese 62,000-ton battleships *Yamato* and *Musashi* laid down in the same year. The two Japanese behemoths each carried nine 18.1in guns in three triple turrets, two forward and one aft, the largest calibre guns ever mounted on a capital ship.

The era of battleship dominance in the navies of the world came to an end during the early part of the Second World War when the capabilities of the aircraft carrier were clearly demonstrated. The successful strike by British carrier aircraft against the Italian naval base at Taranto in November 1940 was the first blow. This was then followed by the devastating attack by Japanese carrier aircraft against the American naval base at Pearl Harbor in December 1941. Less than six months later, American carrier aircraft had their revenge by sinking the four Japanese carriers that attacked Pearl Harbor during the battle off Midway Island in the Pacific. Even the mighty *Yamato* and *Musashi* succumbed to the bombs and torpedoes dropped by American carrier aircraft, and from then on, the aircraft carrier reigned supreme as the ultimate warship.

After the end of the Second World War, shipbuilding activity dropped again, just as it had after 1918, but this time the circumstances were different.

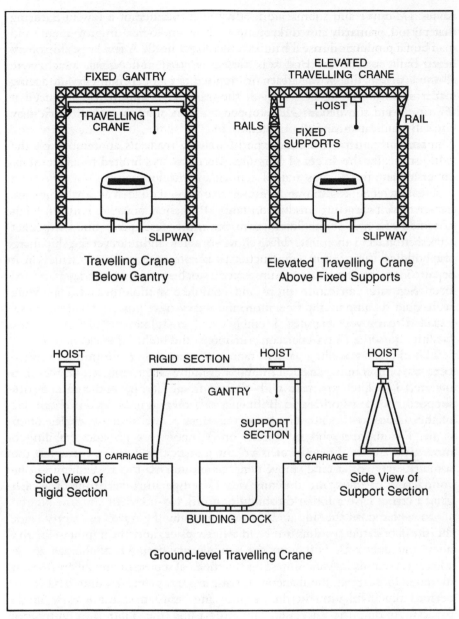

FIXED GANTRY

TRAVELLING CRANE

SLIPWAY

Travelling Crane
Below Gantry

ELEVATED
TRAVELLING CRANE

HOIST

RAILS

RAIL

FIXED
SUPPORTS

SLIPWAY

Elevated Travelling Crane
Above Fixed Supports

HOIST

CARRIAGE

Side View of
Rigid Section

RIGID SECTION

HOIST

GANTRY

SUPPORT
SECTION

CARRIAGE

BUILDING DOCK

HOIST

Side View of
Support Section

Ground-level Travelling Crane

Gantry Cranes.

Although relations with the Soviet Union had rapidly deteriorated into a 'Cold War' after hostilities had ceased, the Soviet Union did not pose a serious naval threat. There was no longer the need for a huge navy with its massive battle fleets, and therefore naval shipbuilding continued to decline throughout the latter half of the twentieth century. Many of the great shipyards were closed down during this period, and the very few that remained open now specialise in building supertankers, container ships, gas carriers, bulk cargo ships, and cruise ships. Even work at naval shipyards had to be cut back, and several of those were closed down.

The famous British naval base at Scapa Flow in the Orkney Islands off the northern coast of Scotland was closed in 1956. The great John Brown Company near Glasgow, builder of the mighty battlecruiser *Hood* and many other ships of the line, as well as the gigantic liners *Queen Mary*, *Queen Elizabeth*, and the newer *QE2*, stopped building ships in 1968. The William Cramp & Sons shipyard in Philadelphia is gone, as is the New York Shipbuilding and Dry Dock Co. yard across the river at Camden, New Jersey. The great New York Naval Shipyard (Brooklyn Navy Yard), builder of the super battleships USS *Iowa* and USS *Missouri*, is also long gone.

The few remaining shipyards realised that they would have to become more competitive by cutting production costs as much as possible. This led to the adoption of a new shipbuilding technique involving modular construction of ship sections, and then assembling those complete modules on the ship. Large shipbuilding docks were constructed to accommodate the construction or repair of the largest tanker or up to four smaller ships, two abreast and two deep. Separate fabrication shops and complete module assembly buildings were built to support the operation, and heavy travelling gantry cranes were installed to move fabricated assemblies and complete modules from those facilities onto the ship under construction in the building dock.

The ultimate travelling gantry crane came into being late in the twentieth century. This crane spans a slipway or building dock, and it consists of an inverted L-shaped structure with a rigid frame at one end and a flexible support frame at its other end. Both ends ride on rails imbedded on both sides of the slipway or dock by means of carriages placed under each leg of the crane. The support end is basically an A-frame that provides stability for movement in the direction of travel. At its top, the support end is allowed some degree of lateral movement to compensate for expansion and contraction of the crane structure due to temperature variations. Travelling gantry cranes have a lifting capability of up to 800-900 tons.

Once placed on the ship under construction by the travelling gantry crane, the pre-fabricated sections are welded into place, and the piping, electrical lines, and ductwork built into the module are then be connected to the adjacent sections of the ship. This method of construction allows several modules to be built simultaneously with a great saving in time, and it also permits the installation of the engines and other machinery early in the process. Among the successful shipyards using the modular construction technique are Harland & Wolff of Belfast, Newport News Shipbuilding and Dry Dock Co. (USA), Mitsubishi of Nagasaki (Kosho), Chantiers de l'Atlantique of St. Nazaire, and Riva Trigoso of Italy.

Currently, the most popular type of warship among the nations of the world is the small modern frigate loaded with sophisticated electronics equipment and carrying a variety of weapons including missiles, homing torpedoes, and defensive gun systems. The United States is now building a new generation of guided missile cruisers and destroyers at a relatively low rate of production, as well as an occasional aircraft carrier, to maintain a modern strike capability. These ships can be sent across the Seven Seas to help preserve the peace in troubled areas in the far corners of the world. Nuclear and conventional submarines also continue to be an important element of the navies of the world.

Another shipbuilding technique introduced late in the twentieth century is the fibre-reinforced plastic technique for smaller craft up to the size of coastal corvettes. This method is derived from the fibreglass-reinforced epoxy resin first used for small boats and then developed for use on larger pleasure boats. Under this method, the frame of the hull is constructed upside down in a covered shipbuilding bay, and it is then covered with fibre-reinforced plastic. After this step has been accomplished, the hull is turned right-side-up, and the ship is completed by normal means. Fibre-reinforced plastic for a hull material is ideal for minesweepers and new vessels designed to incorporate 'stealth' technology.

# 2 Great Britain

Great Britain consists of a group of islands separated from the mainland of Europe by the English Channel and the North Sea. Self-sufficient in ancient times, Great Britain became increasingly dependent on trade for her livelihood in the modern era. It was therefore essential that merchant ships had free access to and from the British Isles, and this meant that the entire coastline of the British Isles had to be protected by warships operating out of strategically located bases.

During the ninth century AD, Alfred the Great built a fleet of warships to defend England against the Danes, but these ships were abandoned after peace was restored, and no permanent navy was established at that time. Up until the end of the fourteenth century, English monarchs contracted with the Cinque Ports, a confederation of maritime towns along the English Channel in the south-eastern corner of England that had common interests in trade and fishing, to provide a specified number of fully-manned ships for use by the Crown for a designated period of time during the year. These Cinque ports, originally comprising Hastings, Romney, Hythe, Dover, and Sandwich were chartered by the Crown in return for the naval services that they provided.

In 1391, during the reign of King Richard II, the British Admiralty was established with a Lord High Admiral in overall charge, and this was considered to be the birth of the Royal Navy. Thirty years later, Henry V ordered the first warships to be built for the Royal Navy, the 1400-ton *Grâce Dieu* (1418), the 1000-ton *Jesus* (1420), and the smaller *Holigost* (*Holy Ghost*), *Christopher*, and *Trinity Royal*, all built around the same time. Henry VII built a number of warships at the turn of the century, including the large four-masted carrack *Regent*. In 1496, Henry VII built the first British dry dock at Portsmouth, where several warships of the Royal Navy had been built in private yards, including the *Grâce Dieu* and *Holigost*.

As soon as he ascended the throne in 1509, Henry VIII purchased plots of land at Deptford and Woolwich on the south bank of the River Thames, a short distance downstream from London, for the construction of the first

Royal Dockyards. The dockyard at Woolwich was completed in 1514, and the one at Deptford became fully operational shortly thereafter. Royal Dockyards are government-owned and operated naval shipyards involved in the construction, refit, and repair of British warships. Once established, they would have priority over private yards for the construction of warships, and also usually doubled as operational bases for elements of the Royal Navy.

Great Britain.

The large carrack *Mary Rose* was completed at Portsmouth in 1509, and in 1512, Henry VIII ordered the construction of several galleons at Royal Dockyards. In 1514, Henry VIII had the magnificent 1500-ton four-masted warship *Henry Grâce à Dieu* (*Great Harry*) built at Woolwich Royal Dockyard, and that ship became the flagship of his navy. In 1540, Henry VIII expanded the dry dock facility established by his predecessor at Portsmouth into a full dockyard, giving the Royal Navy a third dockyard. By this time, the cast-brass cannon had been developed, and warships of the Royal Navy were being equipped with this weapon. These guns were built in various sizes ranging from the 'cannon', which could fire a 50lb cast-iron ball one mile, to smaller guns firing shot under 10lb at closer ranges.

Queen Elizabeth I ascended to the throne in 1558, and in 1570, she established another Royal Dockyard at Chatham. The availability of four dockyards to turn out warships over the next several years proved to be very fortuitous for the Royal Navy in view of the threat later posed by the Spanish Armada in 1588. Spain concentrated on the construction of larger and more powerful galleons, which proved to be cumbersome in fighting the English ships during the invasion attempt. England, on the other hand, favoured smaller galleons with greater speed and manoeuvrability. As a result of her victory over the Spanish Armada, Britain became a recognised naval power.

In view of the success of these smaller and faster galleons, Britain continued with their development, and as a result, the sailing frigate evolved during the seventeenth century. The frigate, the precursor of the more modern cruiser, was a popular warship in that era because of its combination of firepower, speed, and range. Britain did not, of course, neglect the building of larger, more costly warships. In 1636, Charles I ordered the construction of the massive 1500-ton *Sovereign of the Seas.* This ship, which was built at Woolwich Royal Dockyard, had three gun decks mounting a total of 100 guns, and it became the forerunner of the British First Rate ship-of-the-line.

Two more Dockyards were established in the seventeenth century, one at Sheerness in 1665 and the other at Plymouth (later renamed Devonport) in 1689. Another Dockyard had been established at Harwich early in the century, but it closed down soon after Sheerness became fully operation, and its workload was shifted there. This expansion of dockyard capacity was primarily due to the three wars with the Netherlands, which ranged from 1652 to 1674. Subsequent to the Dutch Wars, there were various wars with France and Spain that extended throughout the eighteenth century. In 1704, Gibraltar was captured, and this led to the later establishment of a Dockyard at that stronghold.

At the beginning of the eighteenth century, the ship-of-the-line had grown to over 1700 tons displacement and carried as many as 120 cast-iron guns. During the latter part of the eighteenth century, a new weapon, the carronade, which was developed by the Carron Co. of Scotland, was introduced into the Royal Navy. The carronade was a short, large-calibre gun mounted on the upper deck that could deliver a heavy cannon ball against an enemy ship with devastating effect. Although they did not form the main armament of ships-of-the-line, carronades were mounted on the upperworks of such ships where they could engage enemy ships at close range.

The most powerful warship built during the age of sail was the First Rate ship-of-the-line that mounted 100 to 120 guns of various calibres on three gun decks. Very few of these ships, however, were produced due to their enormous cost and vast consumption of shipbuilding materials. There was a brief spurt of construction of those vessels from 1814 to 1841 when ten 120-gun monsters were built after the Napoleonic Wars and before the end of the age of sail. Second Rate ships carrying ninety to ninety-eight guns on three decks were built in greater numbers than First Rate ships during the latter half of the eighteenth century, but still not in any great numbers because of the resources required.

The most predominant ship-of-the-line during the latter half of the eighteenth and first part of the nineteenth century was the 74-gun, two-decker Third Rate. Nearly one hundred of those ships were produced between 1750-99, and another forty between 1800-25. Those ships were the workhorse of the battle fleet, and their numbers far exceeded those of the First and Second Rate ships combined in every major naval battle fought during that period. Although private shipyards were usually assigned warship construction at the lower end of the naval spectrum, several of the larger yards were awarded contracts for 74-gun ships due to the great demand for them. Many of these ships were the first to bear the names that are now famous in the annals of naval history.

During the Napoleonic Wars, private shipyards at Milford (Milford Haven), Falmouth, and North Yarmouth were contracted by the Admiralty to build warships for the Royal Navy to supplement the capacity of the Royal Dockyards. After those wars, further contracting ceased, and the Admiralty decided to expand a naval support facility established at Pembroke across from Milford into a Royal Dockyard in 1814. Another Royal Dockyard was also established early in the nineteenth century at Haulbowline (Cobh) in County Cork, Ireland, but that dockyard was ultimately used only for the repair and maintenance of warships, and it was later turned over to the Republic of Ireland.

The Royal Dockyards had a difficult time keeping up with the rapid advances in technology that occurred during the middle of the nineteenth century. First came the steam engine, and in 1843, a factory was established at the Woolwich Royal Dockyard for the manufacture and repair of steam engines for warships of the Royal Navy. Five years later in 1848, a steam engine manufacturing and repair facility was established at Portsmouth Royal Dockyard. The Devonport Royal Dockyard was expanded northward into Keyham to provide a steam facility for that dockyard in 1853.

At first, the Admiralty did not have full confidence in the reliability of the steam engine, and it was used only as an auxiliary source of power with greater reliance still being given to sail. As a result, the Royal Dockyards had to maintain dual facilities, a sail loft as well as an engine works, to satisfy both needs. It was not until the 1870s that the Admiralty began to build capital ships with only steam power. With continued advances in steam engine design from the single-expansion engine to the compound engine and then the triple-expansion engine, the Admiralty decided to discontinue the manufacture and repair of steam engines at Royal Dockyards and to rely exclusively on private engineering firms to provide the machinery for warships. The later introduction of the complex steam turbine engine to replace the reciprocating steam engine confirmed the wisdom of that decision.

Next came the introduction of iron and steel into the construction of warships. By the middle of the nineteenth century, the use of iron plates over critical sections of a wooden warship to protect its steam engine and main armament gained acceptance by the Royal Navy as well as by other navies throughout the world. At about the same time, the composite hull, in which the keel, frames, and stems were made out of wrought iron, but the sides were still made out of wooden planking, gradually evolved. Then hulls were constructed with sides of iron plating riveted together instead of wood planking, and finally the all-steel ship appeared. Metallurgical advances in steel armour plating led to improved protection for warships and greatly reduced weight compared with the equivalent protection afforded by iron plates.

In 1863, the first British armoured battleship, HMS *Achilles*, was built at Chatham Royal Dockyard. She displaced nearly 10,000 tons and was about 380ft long, but was still a hybrid sail-steam vessel. Other dockyards, as well as Chatham, continued building improved warships that gradually evolved into the all-steel, solely steam-powered, armoured cruisers that made their appearance at the turn of the century. Due to the many technological advances that were taking place, greater reliance had to be placed on private shipyards for the construction of warships for the Royal Navy. The Royal Dockyards at Deptford and Woolwich could not keep up with these new requirements, and as a result, they were both closed down in 1869.

The availability of commercial electric power at the turn of the century was a great boon to the shipbuilding industry. The electrification of the shipyards lead to the development of shipyard cranes and gantries that facilitated the movement of heavy structural members, steel plates, and machinery throughout the yard and their eventual installation aboard the ships under construction. The introduction of the incandescent light bulb at the same time allowed for the extension of working hours in winter months and even round-the-clock operations at critical periods.

As a result of the arms race with Germany at the beginning of the twentieth century, the ability of Royal Dockyards to keep up with warship construction orders became severely taxed. The Admiralty had, therefore, to turn even more to private shipyards to supplement the shipbuilding capacity of Royal Dockyards prior to and during the First World War. The last Royal Dockyard to be established in the British Isles was at Rosyth near Edinburgh, Scotland during the First World War, but it was intended primarily for repair and maintenance. At the end of the war, work at the other Royal Dockyards gradually began to shift to repair and maintenance activities.

After the First World War, shipbuilding requirements for the Royal Navy dropped significantly, and this not only affected the Royal Dockyards, but also the private shipyards that were heavily engaged in producing warships. In 1926, the Admiralty decided that all work at Royal Dockyards would henceforth be limited to refit, repair, and maintenance operations. This was to allow some of the private shipyards to survive the drought of shipbuilding orders and to maintain a capacity for building warships in the event of future needs. While Royal Dockyards were kept busy during the Second World War, they continued to decline after the end of the war, and several had to be closed down.

The first casualty was Pembroke Royal Dockyard, which had already been closed down in 1926. It was reactivated in 1939 to assist in the war effort, but soon after the end of the war, it was shut down again in 1947. The next to go was Sheerness Royal Dockyard, which closed down in 1960. Chatham ceased operations in 1984 to become a Historic Dockyard, and it is now being preserved as a museum. Rosyth Royal Dockyard continues to repair and maintain warships for the Royal Navy, but it is now being operated by the Facilities Management Division of Babcock International Group under contract with the Admiralty.

Devonport Royal Dockyard built several modern frigates after the end of the Second World War, but it now specialises in fleet maintenance, including the modernisation of aircraft carriers, frigates, and submarines. Portsmouth lost its standing as a Royal Dockyard in 1984, but it continues to serve as a naval base.


## ROYAL DOCKYARDS

### Portsmouth

The most important British dockyard, which currently still operates as a naval base for the Royal Navy, is at Portsmouth on the central south coast of England on the English Channel near the port of Southampton. Although Portsmouth had been used for over 250 years before as a harbour and supply depot for British warships, the PORTSMOUTH ROYAL DOCKYARD actually began as a dry dock facility built by Henry VII in 1496. The famous 600-ton, 78-gun warship *Mary Rose*, pride of King Henry VIII's fleet, was built in the dry dock in 1509. Over the years, additional facilities were added to the yard, and in 1540, the site was established as a Royal Dockyard intended for use primarily for the repair and maintenance of warships.

Located only a short distance across the English Channel from the northern coast of France, Portsmouth was vulnerable to attacks from the Continent, and in 1545, a French fleet attacked the base causing considerable damage. Not wishing to expose its vessels to the French threat, England transferred much of the naval workload intended for Portsmouth to Chatham, and in 1550, all of the ships at Portsmouth were sent to Chatham in the relative safety of the River Medway. After a decline of nearly one hundred years, naval activity resumed at Portsmouth in 1650, and for the first time, a shipbuilding programme was undertaken at the yard. New facilities added at the yard included a slipway in 1651, a ropery in 1654, and a double dry dock in 1656-8.

From 1650 to 1700, Portsmouth built over thirty warships, including the 100-gun ships-of-the-line *Charles Royal* (1673), *James Royal* (1675), and *Coronation* (1685), the 90-gun *Vanguard* in 1678, the 80-gun *Russell* in 1692, and the 70-gun ships *Expedition* and *Eagle*, both in 1679. In 1698, the Great Ship Basin was built at the yard, and two more dry docks were added in 1698 and 1700 respectively. During the first half of the eighteenth century, the yard built fifteen warships, including the 90-gun Second Rate ship-of-the-line *Victory* in 1737, the 74-gun *St. George* in 1740 and *Ramillies* in 1749, two 64-gun ships, two 60-gun ships, and one 54-gun ship.

Portsmouth Royal Dockyard produced twenty-eight warships in 1750-9, including the 100-gun *Britannia* in 1762, the 98-gun *St. George* in 1786, the 80-gun *Neptune* in 1756, the 74-gun ships, *Newcastle* (1750), *Ajax* (1767), *Elizabeth* (1769), *Warrior* (1781), and *Bulwark* (1787), three 64-gun ships, one 60-gun and one 50-gun ship. The workforce at Portsmouth averaged about 1000 men throughout most of the eighteenth century, but it reached a peak of 1750 men early in the century. The Great Ship Basin was enlarged in 1795-1801, and three more dry docks were added to the shipyard in 1801-03.

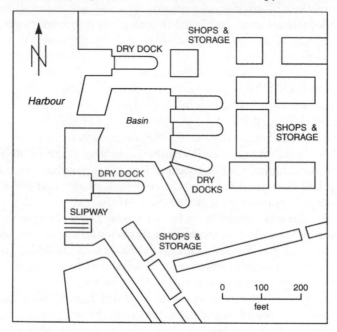

Portsmouth in 1800.

Portsmouth continued to build wooden sailing warships until the middle of the nineteenth century, completing ten such ships from 1800-48. Those ships included the 74-gun ships-of-the-line *Scipio* in 1800 and *Bellerophon* in 1818 and one Fourth Rate ship in 1823. Portsmouth completed its last sailing vessel, the 74-gun *Leander*, in 1848. In 1837, the Admiralty had approved the use of steam as auxiliary power for its warships, and action was taken to equip Royal Dockyards with the facilities to manufacture and repair steam engines. In 1848, the Great Steam Basin was opened at Portsmouth for the fitting out of steam engine-powered warships, and Portsmouth soon began the production of ironclad steam-powered vessels. Two additional dry docks were constructed at the yard in 1850 and 1865, respectively.

In 1867, Portsmouth Royal Dockyard was extended to accommodate the construction of larger steam-powered iron warships. An additional 180 acres of land, just to the north of the dockyard, was acquired to supplement the existing 120-acre tract of land then occupied by the shipyard. New facilities were subsequently added to the site, including three separate basins and four new dry docks. With this expansion and a workforce of 1100 men, Portsmouth soon became the lead dockyard for the production of capital ships for the Royal Navy. The shipyard built the turret ships *Devastation* (1871), *Inflexible* (1876), *Imperieuse* (1884), *Colossus* (1886), *Camperdown* (1889), and *Trafalgar* (1890). The *Inflexible*, with its four 16in guns in two armoured turrets, can be seen as one of the precursors of the 'all-big-gun' battleship.

In view of this full-scale production of capital ships, the workforce at the shipyard rose to over 7500 employees by 1890. In 1896, the fourteenth and largest dry dock at the yard, was constructed. Portsmouth began building battleships with the *Royal Sovereign* (1892), *Centurion* (1894), *Majestic* (1895), *Prince George* (1896), *Caesar* (1898), *Hannibal* (1898), and *Canopus* (1899). During that period, the yard also built the protected cruisers *Royal Arthur* in 1891 and *Crescent* in 1892, and six light cruisers between 1890 to 1897. After the turn of the century, Portsmouth built the battleships *Formidable* in 1901, *London* in 1902, *Zealandia* in 1905, and *Britannia* in 1906.

In 1906, Portsmouth also produced HMS *Dreadnought*, the first 'all-big-gun' battleship which revolutionised naval construction throughout the world. That ship was followed by the Dreadnought-type battleships *Bellerophon* (1909), *St Vincent* (1909), *Neptune* (1911), *Orion* (1912), *King George V* (1912), and *Iron Duke* (1914). Also built at Portsmouth during the early part of the twentieth century were the armoured cruisers *Kent* in 1903 and *Suffolk* in 1904 and the light cruiser *Pandora* in 1901. Wartime production of ships included the battleships *Queen Elizabeth* in 1915 and *Royal Sovereign* in 1916, the first ships of two new classes of battleships to mount 15in guns. During the First World War, Portsmouth also built five submarines, the first two ships of the 'J' class and the first three ships of the 'K' class.

In 1912, Portsmouth was further improved by the enlargement of its third basin, and this led to the construction of two locks to allow additional entry into the basin. During the First World War, a 250-ton capacity crane and two 10-ton capacity travelling cranes were installed at the yard. By the end of the war, Portsmouth had fourteen dry docks in operation, including three 560ft in length and one 770ft in length, as well as two 850ft locks and two 460ft locks. The dockyard also had one 750ft slipway for battleships and four basins, three of which were of large size. The workforce at Portsmouth averaged about 8000 during the first part of the century, but during the First World War, it reached a peak of over 15,000 men.

During the inter-war years, Portsmouth built three of the new 'County' class 10,000-ton heavy cruisers mounting eight 8in guns. These were the *Suffolk* (1928), *London* (1929), and *Dorsetshire* (1930). Both the *Suffolk* and *Dorsetshire* contributed to the discovery and sinking of the German battleship *Bismarck* in May 1941. The *Suffolk* first sighted the *Bismarck* in the Denmark Strait off the coast of Iceland, and the *Dorsetshire* fired the fatal torpedoes that ultimately sank the German battleship. Portsmouth also produced the light cruisers *Effingham* (1925), *Neptune* (1934), *Amphion* (later renamed *Perth* and transferred to the Royal Australian Navy) (1935), and *Aurora* (1937), as well as one 'D' class destroyer in 1932.

During the Second World War, most of the shipbuilding for the Royal Navy was performed under contract with private shipyards. Although within range of Luftwaffe airfields in German-occupied France and therefore subject to periodic air raids, Portsmouth was able to produce the light cruiser *Sirius* in 1942 and two 'T' class submarines in 1945. After the war, Portsmouth built four modern frigates for the Royal Navy. The frigate HMS *Andromeda*, completed in 1968, was the last ship built at Portsmouth Royal Dockyard. With the workload declining, the Dockyard was reclassified as a naval base in 1984, and as such, it continues to provide logistic support to the fleet.

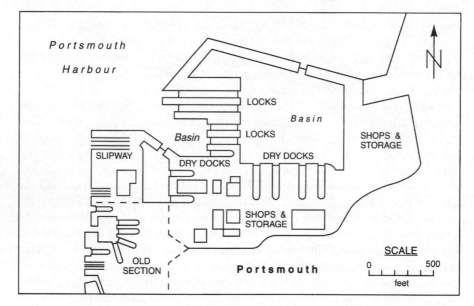

Portsmouth in 1945.

In addition to its continuing role as a naval base, Portsmouth is also a Historic Dockyard, and it now houses the Royal Naval Museum. On permanent display at Portsmouth is HMS *Victory*, Nelson's famous flagship at the Battle of Trafalgar in 1805. Also on display is the *Mary Rose*, a warship built for Henry VIII in 1509. The ship sank off Portsmouth in 1545, but she was raised in 1982 and subsequently restored. A third feature of the yard is HMS *Warrior*, the powerful hybrid sail-steam warship that was the pride of Queen Victoria's navy in 1860.

### Deptford
Deptford was one of two Royal Dockyards established by Henry VIII in 1509, the other being Woolwich. DEPTFORD ROYAL DOCKYARD was conveniently located on the south bank of the River Thames only 3 miles east of the heart of London. During the sixteenth century, Deptford built numerous warships

for the Royal Navy, including the galleon *Ark Royal*, Lord Howard of Effingham's flagship when he fought against the Spanish Armada in 1588. England's victory against Spain established her status as a naval power, and in 1588, Deptford was expanded to increase its capacity for building and repairing warships. During the seventeenth century, Deptford continued building ships for the Royal Navy, including several ships-of-the-line and frigates.

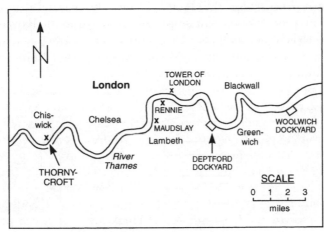

The River Thames.

With three dry docks, but only one set of building ways, Deptford was more suited to ship repair rather than to shipbuilding, but the yard did continue to build quite a number of ships for the Royal Navy. From 1700-49, Deptford produced thirty warships, including twenty-two ships-of-the-line and three frigates, as well as rebuilding twenty-eight additional warships. Among the ships-of-the-line built at Deptford were the 80-gun *Cumberland* in 1710, the 74-gun *Culloden* in 1747, and the 70-gun ships *Northumberland* (1705), *Restoration* (1706), *Resolution* (1708), *Burford* (1722), *Berwick* (1723), *Berwick* (II) (1743), and *Kent* (1746).

During the latter half of the eighteenth century, Deptford produced forty-three warships, including thirty-two ships-of-the-line and four frigates. Among the ships-of-the-line built were the 98-gun ships *Impregnable* (1786), *Windsor Castle* (1790), and *Neptune* (1797) and the 74-gun ships *Dublin* (1757), *Norfolk* (1757), *Hercules* (1759), *Dragon* (1760), *Superb* (1760), *Kent* (1762), *Albion* (1763), *Monarch* (1765), *Magnificent* (1766), *Marlborough* (1767), *Egmont* (1768), *Resolution* (1770), *Grafton* (1771), *Cumberland* (1774), *Culloden* (1776), *Alexander* (1778), *Alcide* (1779), *Goliath* (1781), *Vanguard* (1787), *Brunswick* (1790), and *Mars* (1794).

Several Deptford ships built during the latter half of the eighteenth century made significant contributions to the glory of the Royal Navy in naval battles. The *Hercules, Marlborough,* and *Resolution* all participated in the Battle of the Saintes in 1782. The *Impregnable* fought in the Battle of the Glorious First of

June in 1794, and the *Alexander* contributed her firepower against the French in the Battle of the Nile. The *Monarch* was among the several British ships-of-the-line that engaged the Danes in the Battle of Copenhagen in 1801.

From 1800-23, Deptford produced thirty-four sailing warships, including seventeen ships-of-the-line and eleven frigates. Among the ships-of-the-line built were the 104-gun *Queen Charlotte* in 1810, the 80-gun *Cambridge* (1815), and the 74-gun ships *Courageous* (1800), *Colossus* (1803), *Fame* (1805), *Bombay* (1808), *Blake* (1808), *Hogue* (1811), *Blenheim* (1813), *Hero* (1816), and *Russell* (1822). The Deptford Royal Dockyard was temporarily closed from 1828 to 1842 due to declining workload, but shipbuilding resumed in 1843 with the construction of the 52-gun *Worcester*. The last sailing vessel built by the yard was the 50-gun *Phaeton* in 1848

Deptford produced the first steam-powered vessel specifically constructed for naval use, the *Comet*, which was built in 1822. From 1822-50, Deptford produced eleven paddle warships, but then shifted to screw-propelled warships. From 1847-69, Deptford built nearly forty screw-driven warships, including three frigates, three corvettes, and eight sloops. The most renowned vessel produced by Deptford was the 1900-ton paddle frigate *Terrible*, which was built in 1845 and saw service in the Crimean War. The 3100-ton screw frigate *Hannibal* (1854) was the largest ship built at Deptford. Due to declining workload, the Deptford Royal Dockyard was closed permanently in 1869.

## Woolwich

Woolwich was the second Royal Dockyard established by Henry VIII in 1509. Like Deptford, WOOLWICH ROYAL DOCKYARD was also located on the south bank of the River Thames, but further downstream, about eight miles east of London. In 1546, Woolwich built the magnificent galleon *Henry Grâce à Dieu* (*Great Harry*), which became the flagship of Henry VIII's navy. Like Deptford, Woolwich built numerous warships for the Royal Navy during the sixteenth and seventeenth centuries. In 1637, Woolwich built the 1500-ton, three-decked 104-gun *Sovereign of the Seas*, which was the first true British First Rate ship-of-the-line.

During the first half of the eighteenth century, Woolwich produced twenty-one warships, including fourteen ships-of-the-line and three frigates, as well as rebuilding thirty-one additional ships. Among the ships-of-the-line built by Woolwich in that period were the 100-gun ships *Royal Sovereign* in 1701 and *Britannia* in 1719, the 74-gun *Devonshire* in 1745, and the two 80-gun ships *Somerset* in 1731 and *Devonshire* (II) in 1810. By the middle of the eighteenth century, Woolwich had 20 acres of land with a 1500ft river frontage, and was equipped with five slipways, one double dry dock, one single dry dock, a mast pond with a mast house, and a rigging house.

From 1750-99, Woolwich built thiry-five additional warships, including twenty-three ships-of-the-line and five frigates. The ships-of-the-line were the 100-gun *Royal George* built in 1756, the 98-gun ships *Queen* in 1769 and *Boyne* in 1790, the 90-gun ships *Blenheim* in 1761 and *Prince* in 1788, the 80-

gun ship *Princess Amelia* in 1757, and the 74-gun ships *Mars* (1759), *Thunderer* (1760), *Triumph* (1764), *Bedford* (1775), *Edgar* (1779), *Minotaur* (1793), and *Centaur* (1797). The *Bedford* fought in the Battle of the Saintes in 1782, the *Queen* was involved in the Battle of the Glorious First of June in 1794, and the *Edgar* was at the Battle of Copenhagen in 1801. The *Minotaur* participated in both the Battles of the Nile and Trafalgar in 1798 and 1805, respectively.

Continuing into the nineteenth century, Woolwich produced thirty-six sailing warships, including seventeen ships-of-the-line and eleven frigates between 1800-50. Among the ships-of-the-line were the 120-gun *Nelson* in 1814, the 110-gun *Trafalgar* in 1841, the 98-gun *Ocean* in 1806, the 84-gun *Thunderer* in 1831, and the 74-gun ships *Plantagenet* (1801), *Invincible* (1808), *San Domingo* (1809), *Redoubtable* (1815), *Black Prince* (1816), *Talavera* (1818), and *Hawke* (1820). Woolwich built its first paddle warship in 1827, and from then until 1848, the dockyard produced twelve additional paddle-wheelers. In 1843, the Woolwich Steam Factory was opened for the manufacture and repair of steam engines and boilers for ships of the Royal Navy.

Woolwich shifted to the production of screw-propelled vessels in 1846, and from that year until 1869, the dockyard produced twenty screw-propelled warships, including three wooden ships-of-the-line, the 121-gun *Royal Albert* in 1854 and the 91-gun ships *Edgar* in 1858 and *Anson* in 1860, three ironclad frigates and three ironclad corvettes. The Woolwich Royal Dockyard was closed in 1869, at the same time as its sister dockyard, Deptford. Both Deptford and Woolwich had physical limitations that precluded them from building larger iron and steel warships and keeping up with other technological advances, especially in the field of steam engines.

*Chatham*

Chatham is located on the River Medway, about 30 miles south-east of London. The Royal Navy rented ship storehouses at Chatham since 1547, when Jillingham Water (later called the River Medway) was used as a secure anchorage for the British fleet. In 1559, Queen Elizabeth I acquired the facilities at Chatham as a Royal Dockyard. In view of the strategic location of the dockyard, Upnor Castle was built in 1561-7 to provide security for the base. Originally known as Jillingham Dockyard, the facility was renamed CHATHAM ROYAL DOCKYARD in 1567. In 1571, a mast pond was constructed at the facility, and in the following year, the shipyard was expanded by the acquisition of more land and the construction of additional storehouses and a forge.

The first dry dock was built Chatham Dockyard in 1581, mostly for the repair of fleet warships, and in 1584, a graving dock was added. In 1586, the first Chatham-built warship, the 5-gun pinnace *Sunne*, was completed. At the turn of the century, the workload at the yard exceeded its capability, and another 70-acre tract of land upriver from the original dockyard was purchased for a new dockyard. In 1619, a 330ft-long double dry dock was constructed at the new site. This was soon followed by additional facilities, including new storehouses, wharves, mast ponds, a ropery, and a sail loft. In

1623, the second dry dock was constructed at the new shipyard, and one year later a second graving dock was built.

By 1628, the dockyard had a workforce of 225 men. The second dry dock built in 1619 was lengthened and converted into a double dock to accommodate two ships in 1645. By 1660, nearly 325 workers were employed at the yard. In 1667, during the Second Anglo-Dutch War, disaster struck the area when a Dutch squadron raided the Medway fleet anchorage and sank sixteen British warships. By the end of the seventeenth century, the dockyard had produced over seventy warships, including the 1400-ton, 100-gun *Prince* in 1670, the first major warship that it produced for the Royal Navy, the 1700-ton, 100-gun *Britannia* in 1682, and four 80-gun ships between 1692-7.

In 1685, two additional dry docks were built just to the east of the first two dry docks, and this was followed by a new 660ft warehouse, new mast houses, and additional wharf space in 1686. From 1700 to 1714, the dockyard was completely modernised, including the addition of two new slipways in 1700, and Chatham had nearly 500 workers in 1700. In 1737, a new slipway was built to replace one of the older slipways that was demolished. During the first half of the eighteenth century, Chatham had built fourteen warships and had rebuilt an additional twenty-three naval vessels. Production in that time frame included the 70-gun ship-of-the-line *Stirling Castle* in 1705 and another 70-gun ship of the same name in 1742, as well as two 64-gun, three 60-gun, one 54-gun, and three 50-gun ships.

From 1750-99, Chatham produced thirty-eight warships, including twenty-six ships-of-the-line and five frigates. Among the ships-of-the-line were the 110-gun *Ville de Paris* in 1795 and the 100-gun ships *Victory* in 1765, *Royal George* in 1788, and *Queen Charlotte* in 1790. *Victory* was Nelson's flagship at the Battle of Trafalgar in 1805, and it was aboard her that he succumbed to his mortal wound received during the battle. Other ships-of-the-line produced during that period were the 98-gun ships *Sandwich* (1759), *Barfleur* (1768), and *Temeraire* (1798). The *Barfleur* saw action in the Battle of the Saintes in 1782, and the *Temeraire* was also a participant in the Battle of Trafalgar.

Additional ships-of-the-line built by Chatham during the latter half of the eighteenth century included the 90-gun ships *Union* (1756), *Namur* (1756), *Ocean* (1761), *Prince George* (1772), and *Formidable* (1777), the 74-gun *Lenox* (1758), *Valiant* (1759), *Bellona* (1760), *Ramillies* (1763), *Alfred* (1778), *Montague* (1779), and *Leviathan* (1790), as well as five Fourth Rate ships with armaments ranging from seventy guns down to fifty guns. The *Leviathan* was the third Chatham-built ship-of-the-line which fought at Trafalgar. The third and fourth slipways were constructed at Chatham Dockyard in 1762, and in 1771, the fifth and sixth slipways were added to the yard. By 1772, the workforce at Chatham Dockyard had increased to 1250 men.

The yard continued to produce wooden sailing warships well into the nineteenth century, completing fifty-nine such vessels between 1800 and 1850. Those ships included the 120-gun ships *Howe* (1815), *Prince Regent* (1823), *Royal George* (1827), and *Waterloo* (1833) and the 106-gun *Trafalgar* in 1820. Also built during that period were the 98-gun *Impregnable* in 1810, the 92-gun

*London*, and the 84-gun ships *Formidable* (1825), *Powerful* (1826), and *Monarch* (1832). In addition, Chatham produced several Third Rates, including the 76-gun *Warspite* in 1807, the 74-gun ships *Revenge* (1805), *Defence* (1815), *Hercules* (1815), and *Minotaur* (1816), and the 70-gun *Cumberland* in 1842, as well as two 50-gun ships.

A fifth dry dock was added to Chatham dockyard in 1820. Early in the nineteenth century, the age of steam and iron was gradually overtaking sail and wood. In 1832, Chatham built its first steam-powered warship, the paddle sloop *Phoenix*. From 1833-49, the dockyard produced twenty paddle wheel vessels for the Royal Navy, but screw-propulsion was quickly replacing the paddle wheel. Chatham built its first screw-propelled warship, the gunboat *Teazer*, in 1846, and from 1853-63, the dockyard produced eighteen wooden screw-propelled warships. Among those ships were the 91-gun ships-of-the-line *Orion* (1854), *Renown* (1857), *Hero* (1858), and *Hood* (1859) and the 80-gun ships *Cressy* in 1853 and *Irresistible* in 1859.

From 1836-54, Chatham Royal Dockyard was modernised with the replacement of certain old slipways with new covered ones and the construction of a new covered seventh slipway in 1853. The last major wooden warship produced at the dockyard was the screw-propelled ship-of-the-line *Royal Oak*, which was built in 1863. Chatham completed its first ironclad vessel, the armoured frigate *Achilles*, in 1863, and from 1864-85, the shipyard was extended to accommodate the increasing size of steam-powered iron ships contemplated by the Admiralty. A 180-acre plot of land on St Mary's Island to the north of the dockyard had been acquired, and work was begun on the construction of three large basins and four new dry docks.

Chatham Royal Dockyard produced the central-battery ironclads *Bellerophon* (1866), *Lord Warden* (1867), *Hercules* (1868), *Sultan* (1871), *Alexandra* (1877), and *Temeraire* (1877), the turret ships *Monarch* in 1869 and *Agamemnon* in 1883, and the barbette ship *Rodney* in 1888. After the Royal Dockyards at Deptford and Woolwich had been closed in 1869, some of the equipment at those yards was transferred to Chatham, which then undertook a major naval construction programme of producing battleships for the Royal Navy. Those battleships included the *Hood* (1891), *Barfleur* (1894), *Magnificent* (1895), *Victorious* (1896), and *Illustrious* (1898).

Also produced by Chatham at the end of the nineteenth century were the armoured cruisers *Warspite* in 1888 and *Immortalité* in 1889, the protected cruisers *Blake* in 1889 and *Hawke* in 1894, and eight light cruisers from 1887-97. In 1897, the ninth dry dock was begun, and in 1900, the eighth slipway had been completed at the dockyard. Continuing with warship construction into the twentieth century, Chatham produced the battleship *Goliath* in 1900, and that ship was followed by the battleships *Irresistible* (1902), *Venerable* (1902), *Prince of Wales* (1904), *Albemarle* (1903), and *Africa* (1906). In addition, Chatham built the armoured cruisers *Devonshire* in 1904 and *Shannon* in 1908, as well as three light cruisers from 1900-04.

Surface ship production during the First World War consisted of the light cruisers *Lowestoft* and *Arethusa*, both in 1914, and the *Conquest* and *Calliope*, both in 1915. In 1908, Chatham began building submarines, completing twenty-four such craft by the end of the war. By that time, the workforce at Chatham had grown from 6000 in 1906 to 11,000 men in 1908, just two years later, and it would eventually reach a peak of 12,000 workers by the end of the First World War. During the war, the dockyard had three building slips, three large closed basins, nine dry docks, and a variety of floating dry docks in operation. Of the dry docks, one was of 650ft length, four of 460ft , and the remaining four were suitable only for small craft.

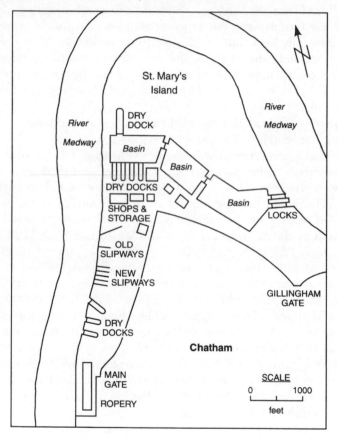

Chatham Dockyard in 1945.

The 9600-ton light cruiser *Hawkins*, mounting seven 7.5in guns, was begun during the war and completed in 1919. In 1926, Chatham Dockyard completed the light cruiser *Emerald*, which had been started by Armstrong-Whitworth. The dockyard then built the 10,000-ton 'County' class heavy cruiser *Kent* in 1928, but after that, the workload steadily declined until 1933, when its workforce reached a low of 7000 men. Chatham built the light cruiser *Arethusa* in 1934 and the light anti-aircraft cruiser *Euryalus* in 1939. The shipyard resumed submarine production in 1925 with the gigantic 2500-ton experimental submarine *X-1*, which carried four 5.2in guns in two twin turrets. Chatham built a total of fifteen submarines before the outbreak of the Second World War, and during the war, it produced an additional eleven submarines.

After the end of the war, Chatham completed one submarine that had been begun during the war, and it then produced six *Oberon* class submarines from 1961-8 (two of which were for the Royal Canadian Navy). In 1968, a nuclear submarine refit complex was completed at Chatham, but soon thereafter, reduced workload began to affect all of the Royal Dockyards. In 1984, the Chatham Royal Dockyard was officially closed, but action was promptly taken to preserve the yard as a Historic Dockyard. Chatham Historic Dockyard now has on display the refurbished Chatham-built submarine *Ocelot*, and it also houses the Royal National Lifeboat Collection and other galleries on the building of wooden ships and the making of rope.

### Sheerness

In 1665, Sheerness, a port at the mouth of the River Medway, was chosen by King Charles II for a dockyard. The SHEERNESS ROYAL DOCKYARD was attacked by the Dutch fleet in 1667 while still under construction, and it did not became fully operational until 1677. At first, it was used for ship repair and maintenance, but it later began to build warships for the Royal Navy, including the 32-gun *Sheerness* in 1691 and the 60-gun *Medway* in 1693. During the first half of the eighteenth century, Sheerness produced eight warships, including one 54-gun and one 50-gun ship, and rebuilt an additional two warships.

From 1750-99, Sheerness produced ten warships, including the 64-gun *Polyphemus*, the largest sailing vessel built at the dockyard, one 60-gun ship, and three 50-gun ships. The *Polyphemus* saw action in both the Battle of Copenhagen in 1801 and the Battle of Trafalgar in 1805. By the turn of the century, the dockyard covered over 25 acres of land, and had two slipways, two dry docks, and one tidal dock. From 1800-48, the dockyard built six sailing warships, including one 50-gun, 4th rate ship and one 46-gun frigate. In 1815, the Sheerness Royal Dockyard acquired another 50 acres of land, increasing the size of the facility to nearly 80 acres.

Gradually shifting to the production of steam-powered vessels, Sheerness built its first paddle warship, the *Salamander*, in 1832. The dockyard produced an additional seven paddle warships from 1833-43, after which it built eleven wooden screw-propelled vessels from 1843-69, beginning with the sloop *Rattler*. Sheerness then produced eleven more wooden screw-propelled warships in 1851-69 before turning to the construction of iron ships. The first iron warships built by Sheerness were the 2000-ton corvettes *Encounter*, built in 1873, and *Diamond*, built in 1874. From 1887-1903, the dockyard produced six light cruisers, eight corvettes, and nineteen sloops for the Royal Navy.

At the beginning of the twentieth century, naval shipbuilding was discontinued at Sheerness, and the shipyard was then used primarily for the repair and maintenance of warships. Before the First World War, the yard had five small dry docks that could accommodate only small craft, but during the war, Sheerness was equipped with a 680ft floating dry dock to accommodate larger vessels. Sheerness also served as a destroyer base prior to and during the war. After the war, the workload declined, but the dockyard was retained for ship maintenance service before and during the Second World War, after which the workload again dropped off, and Sheerness Royal Dockyard was finally closed down in 1957 and sold off in 1960.

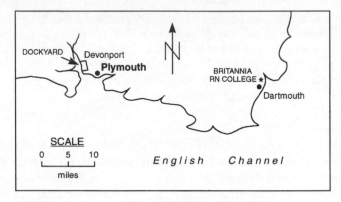

Plymouth.

## Plymouth (Devonport)

The second most important Royal Dockyard was at Plymouth on the south-western coast of England along the English Channel. PLYMOUTH ROYAL DOCKYARD was established in 1689 on 40 acres of land by the joint-reigning monarchs of England, William III and Mary II. Work began in 1691 with the construction of a new stone dry dock, which was unique at the time since earlier dry docks were built out of wood. In 1692, the dry dock and a wet basin were completed, and this was soon followed by the construction of two building slipways, workshops, and storehouses, including the Great Square Storehouse which could accommodate the supplies and equipment for as many as forty ships-of-the-line. The initial workforce at the yard was only seventy-five men.

By 1700, the workforce at Plymouth had exceeded 500 men, and the yard had already produced several warships, including two 48-gun and two 32-gun ships. In 1724, a third building slip was installed at the yard, and this was followed in 1727 by the construction of a double dry dock that could accommodate two ships lengthwise. The dockyard was expanded in 1730 by the acquisition of 15 acres of land to the south of the yard, and a mast pond was built at the new site. By 1740, the Plymouth Dockyard had received its third slipway, and its workforce had increased to 700 employees. Further improvements were made to the yard from 1760-1800 with the acquisition of 15 more acres of land and the addition of three new slipways, three new storehouses, a fourth dry dock, and a new ropery.

During the first half of the eighteenth century, Plymouth Dockyard had completed thirty-six warships, including the 80-gun ship-of-the-line *Norfolk* in

1729, seventeen Fourth Rates and three frigates. From 1750-99, Plymouth produced forty-five warships, including twenty-four ships-of-the-line and two frigates. Among the ships-of-the-line were the 100-gun *Royal Sovereign* in 1786 and the 98-gun ships *Duke* in 1777 and *Glory* in 1788. There were also nine Third Rates produced, including the 80-gun ships *Foudroyant* in 1774, *Caesar* in 1793, and the second *Foudroyant* in 1798 and the 74-gun ships *Hero* (1759), *Defence* (1763), *Royal Oak* (1769), *Conqueror* (1773), and *Caesar* (1783).

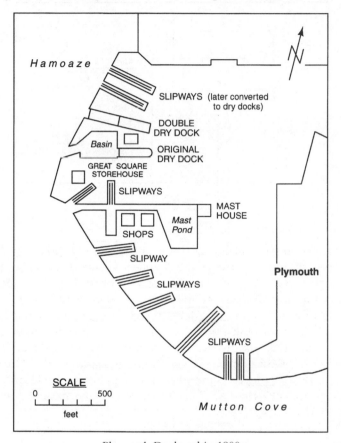

Plymouth Dockyard in 1800.

Several Plymouth-built ships distinguished themselves in various naval actions during Britain's wars in the late eighteenth and early nineteenth century. The *Duke* participated in the Battle of the Saintes in 1782, and the *Glory* fought during the Battle of the Glorious First of June in 1794. The *Defence* was engaged in both the Battle of the Glorious First of June and the Battle of Trafalgar, and the *Conqueror* was also at in the Battle of Trafalgar in 1805.

By 1800, there were 1100 workers employed at the shipyard. Plymouth continued building wooden sailing ships during the first half of the nineteenth century, completing a total of sixty-one such vessels from 1800-48, including eighteen ships-of-the-line and seven frigates. Among the ships-of-the-line produced were the 120-gun ships *Caledonia* (1808), *St Vincent* (1815), *Britannia* (1820), and *St George* (1840), the 110-gun *Hibernia* (1804), and the 104-gun *Royal Adelaide* (1828). Also included were the 92-gun *Nile* (1839), the 90-gun ships *Algiers* (1815), *Albion* (1842), and *Aboukir* (1848), the 78-gun *Hindustan* (1841), and the 76-gun ships *Union* (1811) and *Vigo* (1817).

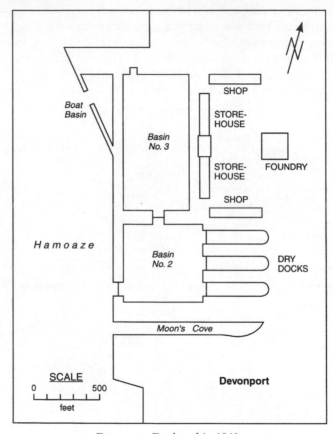

Devonport Dockyard in 1860.

In 1843, the name of the Plymouth Royal Dockyard was changed to DEVONPORT ROYAL DOCKYARD, following the change in the name of the local town from Plymouth Port to Devonport in 1824. The Devonport Dockyard kept pace with technological advances when iron and steam began taking over from wood and sail in the mid-nineteenth century. Steam was introduced into the Royal Navy in 1820, and in 1832, Devonport built its first steam warship, the paddle-wheeled sloop *Rhadamanthus*. By 1850, the workforce at the yard was up to 3000 employees. In 1852, the yard produced the 70-gun ship-of-the-line *Sans Pariel*, the first large ship modified during construction to accept an auxiliary steam engine with a screw propeller. In subsequent years, a number of existing sailing ships were returned to

Devonport and other dockyards for retrofit with steam engines and screw propellers.

In 1845, 75 acres of land north of the existing dockyard was purchased for the construction of the KEYHAM STEAM YARD complex to facilitate the construction of steam-powered warships and the manufacture and repair of steam engines. Work was begun on the new yard one year later, and the facility was opened in 1853 although it had not been fully completed by that time. The Keyham Steam Yard was equipped with three dry docks and two basins, and it featured a complex of covered workshops, storehouses, foundries, and offices that encompassed 10 acres of land. The Keyham Steam Yard was separated from the original shipyard, now referred to as the South Yard, by the town of Devonport, so a tunnel was built in 1854-6 to connect the two yards.

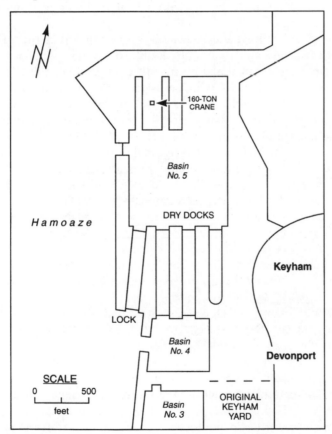

The Keyham Extension 1910.

In 1863, Devonport produced its first ironclad warship, HMS *Ocean*, and from 1888 to 1901, it built twelve light cruisers for the Royal Navy, as well as the protected cruiser *Edgar* in 1894. While initially the Admiralty intended to have its Royal Dockyards produce the engines for the warships that they built, it soon became apparent that it was not feasible for the yards to keep pace with the technological advances of the nineteenth century. From the simple expansion engine, the steam engine progressed to the compound engine (double-expansion), triple-expansion, and even quadruple-expansion engine before the reciprocating engine itself was finally overtaken by the steam turbine.

The Admiralty decided that Royal Dockyards would no longer manufacture and repair engines, but would simply take advantage of the latest advances in steam engine development being made by private shipyards and engineering firms. Devonport received much of the machinery for the ships that it produced from Hawthorn Leslie, but it also received some engines from John Brown and Vickers Barrow. As the number and size of warships required by the Royal Navy increased toward the end of the nineteenth century, it again became necessary to extend the Devonport Dockyard. In 1896, another 115 acres of land north of the Keyham Steam Yard was acquired for a new fitting out facility.

The new so-called 'Keyham Extension' was completed in 1907. The facility had one 460ft single and two 740ft double dry docks. The new yard also featured a large 35-acre enclosed fitting-out basin with a 730ft entrance lock. Upon completion, the basin, which was subsequently called the 'Prince of Wales' Basin', it was equipped with two 30-ton and one 20-ton steam travelling cranes and two 75-ton electric cranes. In 1909, a huge 160-ton capacity electric cantilever-type crane was installed there.

After the turn of the century, Devonport Royal Dockyard built a number of capital ships, including the pre-Dreadnought battleships *Ocean* (1900), *Implacable* (1901), *Bulwark* (1902), *Queen* (1904), *King Edward VII* (1905), and *Hibernia* (1907). The total workforce had been gradually increasing, and by 1907, it had reached 7500 employees. The yard then produced the Dreadnought-type battleships *Temeraire* (1909), *Collingwood* (1910), *Centurion* (1913), and *Marlborough* (1914). The *Marlborough* was the last British capital ship that was built to use coal as fuel, all subsequent ships being equipped with oil-burning power plants. Devonport also produced the armoured cruiser *Minotaur* in 1908, as well as the battlecruisers *Indefatigable* in 1911 and *Lion* in 1912.

Wartime production at Devonport included the 15in gun battleships *Warspite* in 1915 and *Royal Oak* in 1916. The *Royal Oak* was the first capital ship lost in the Second World War when she was torpedoed by a German submarine in October 1939 while anchored at her base of Scapa Flow in the Orkney Islands off the northern coast of Scotland. The *Warspite* became one of the most famous battleships of the Second World War, participating in many naval actions beginning with the Norwegian campaign. During the First World War, Devonport also produced the light cruisers *Aurora* in 1914 and *Cleopatra* in 1915, as well as five 'J' and 'K' class submarines. At the beginning of the First World War, the workforce at Devonport was about 12,300 workmen, but by 1919 it had grow to 16,000.

After the war, Devonport became the centre for the conversion of certain previously built warships and hulls into aircraft carriers. The shipyard first converted the hulls of two battleships partially completed by Armstrong-Whitworth into the carriers *Eagle* and *Hermes*, both in 1923, and then converted the existing battlecruisers *Courageous* and *Glorious* in 1925, and finally rebuilt the battlecruiser *Furious* into an aircraft carrier in 1925. The *Courageous* became the first major naval casualty of the Second World War when she was sunk by a German U-boat on 17 September 1939, just two weeks after the war had begun. The *Glorious* was later sunk by German battleships off the coast of Norway on 8 May 1940 during the Norwegian operation.

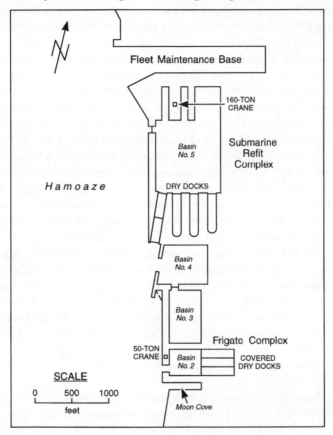

Devonport in 1980.

In 1924, Devonport completed the *Cavendish* class light cruiser *Frobisher*, which was begun during the war. After 1925, work became scarce at the yard, and by 1927 the workforce had been reduced to about 11,000 men before picking up again in the late 1920s. Devonport built the heavy cruisers *Cornwall* (1928), *Devonshire* (1929), and *Exeter* (1931) and these were followed by the light cruisers *Leander* (1933), *Orion* (1934), *Apollo* (1936), and *Birmingham* (1937). The *Apollo* was subsequently turned over to the Royal Australian Navy in 1938, becoming the *Hobart*. The *Exeter* was one of three cruisers that intercepted the German pocket battleship *Admiral Graf Spee* off the coast of South America in December 1939 and caused that ship to be scuttled by her crew in Montevideo harbour a few days later.

Due to its proximity to German airfields in occupied France, production at Devonport during the Second World War was limited to the light cruiser *Trinidad* in 1941 and four 'T' class submarines in 1943-6. Despite considerable damage from bombs early in the war, the Devonport Dockyard also performed numerous refits and repairs on a variety of warships during the war. Devonport continued to build warships for the Royal Navy after the Second World War, but only on a very limited basis. In 1953, the yard built the modern frigate *Salisbury*, and this was followed by five more frigates from 1959-68.

Shipbuilding at Devonport was discontinued in 1971, after which the shipyard became a ship repair and maintenance facility. In 1977, a Frigate Rebuild Complex was constructed at the yard by converting the three dry docks leading into Basin No. 2 into covered docks and permanently separating Basin No. 2 from Basin No. 3. The complex was equipped with four tower cranes, one of 50-ton capacity on the seawall and three 12-ton capacity cranes on the north and south sides of the basin. A new Fleet Maintenance Base, consisting of workshops, storehouses, and berths for nine ships, was built at the northern end of the yard in 1978. This was followed in 1980 with a Submarine Refitting Complex encompassing the area around Basin No. 5.

In 1980, Devonport was the largest Royal Dockyard with 330 acres of land, 2½ miles of waterfront, and over 15,000 employees, including 1100 apprentices. In 1987, a contract was awarded to Devonport Management Ltd, which included Brown & Root Ltd, for the commercial management of the dockyard. That arrangement continued until 1994, when all naval activities in the Devonport area were integrated into HM Naval Base Devonport. The entire naval complex now encompasses nearly 625 acres of land with all of the facilities of the former dockyard, including five basins, twelve dry docks, and twenty-five tidal berths.

### Pembroke

During the Napoleonic Wars, the Admiralty contracted with a private shipyard at Milford Haven, located at the south-western tip of Wales, for the construction of warships for the Royal Navy from 1810-13. That area seemed to be a good site for shipbuilding, and the Admiralty, in keeping with its policy of having warships built primarily at Royal Dockyards, purchased an 80-acre tract of land at nearby Pater in 1810 for the construction of such a dockyard. Originally called the Pater Yard, the PEMBROKE ROYAL DOCKYARD was established in 1815 during the reign of King George III, and at that time, the yard had only two open slipways.

By 1816, Pembroke had already begun building warships with the launching of two 28-gun frigates. The shipyard constructed a covered slipway in 1820, and during the 1830s, it received additional slipways and a dry dock. Pembroke continued building small wooden-hulled, sailing vessels until the middle of the nineteenth century, when it began converting to the construction of steam and iron ships. During the last half of the nineteenth century, Pembroke evolved into a major shipbuilding facility with over a dozen building ways, and a score of shops with widespread shipbuilding equipment and skills. By 1900, the shipyard had thirteen building slipways and one dry dock, 400ft long and 75ft wide, and it was employing over 2000 workers of various skilled trades.

The first steam warship produced at Pembroke Royal Dockyard was the broadside-battery ironclad frigate *Prince Consort*, which was built in 1864. That ship was followed by the central-battery ironclads *Zealous* and *Lord Clyde*, both in 1866, and the *Iron Duke* in 1871. The dockyard then began to build all-steel vessels, including the turret ships *Thunderer* (1877), *Dreadnought* (1879), *Ajax* (1893), *Edinburgh* (1887), and *Nile* (1891) and the barbette ships *Collingwood* (1887), *Anson* (1889) and *Howe* (1889). Pembroke also built the armoured cruisers *Shannon* in 1877 and *Aurora* in 1889, as well as ten light cruisers from 1879 to 1895.

Graduating to the construction of capital ships, Pembroke then built the battleships *Empress of India* (1893), *Repulse* (1894), and *Renown* (1897). After the turn of the century, the shipyard could no longer compete with the other dockyards in the production of capital ships even though the yard was later equipped with two large slipways. Pembroke produced the armoured cruisers *Drake* (1902), *Cornwall* (1904), *Essex* (1904), *Duke of Edinburgh* (1906), *Warrior* (1906) and *Defence* (1909) and the protected cruisers *Andromeda* (1900) and *Spartiate* (1902).

During the First World War, Pembroke built four 'C' class light cruisers, the *Caryfort* and *Cordelia*, both in 1915, the *Cambrian* in 1916, and the *Curaçoa* in 1918. The *Curaçoa* suffered a tragic fate during the Second World War when the ship was accidentally sliced in two by the liner *Queen Mary* in September 1942 with the loss of 340 lives. The *Curaçoa* was escorting the *Queen Mary*, which was carrying nearly 10,000 American troops en route from New York to Scotland at the time, when she sailed across the path of the liner while zigzagging in limited visibility.

During the War, Pembroke was used primarily for the repair and maintenance of ships for the Royal Navy, and at that time, the yard had a workforce of 2500 people. After the war, the workload at all Royal Dockyards declined, and in 1926, Pembroke was closed in favour of keeping Portsmouth, Devonport, and Chatham gainfully employed. The facility was used as a naval air station after 1931, but in 1939, Pembroke was re-established as a dockyard to assist in the war effort. The yard continued to serve as a ship repair and maintenance facility throughout the Second World War, but after the war, the workload again declined. Pembroke Royal Dockyard was closed permanently in 1947.

*Rosyth*

At the beginning of the twentieth century, it became apparent to the Admiralty that the existing Royal Dockyards could not possibly handle the repair and maintenance of the large number of steel, steam-powered warships being produced and contemplated for the Royal Navy. The Admiralty therefore began planning in 1903 for another Royal Dockyard at Rosyth on the north bank of the Firth of Forth, about 12 miles north-west of Edinburgh, which would be used strictly for warship repair and maintenance. In 1905, the new dockyard was authorised by Parliament, and after plans were finalised in 1908, construction began in 1909. The original plans called for only one dry dock, but in 1911, a second dry dock was built, and in 1913, a third dry dock was authorised. All of these dry-docks were 850ft long and could accommodate the largest battleships then on the drawing boards.

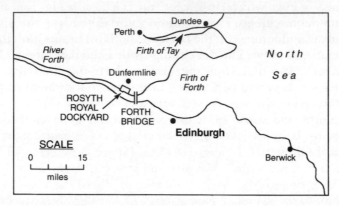

The River Forth.

At the beginning of the First World War, Rosyth Royal Dockyard was still not fully operational as a dockyard, but due to its favourable location, it soon became a major naval base for the Royal Navy. A destroyer and submarine basin were ready for use early in the war, and it had a limited

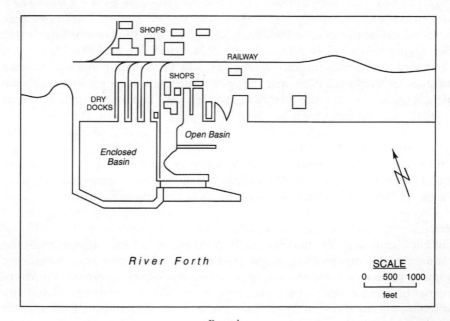

Rosyth.

capability for ship repair and maintenance functions by the end of the war. Rosyth was the base for Vice-Admiral Sir David Beatty's Battle Cruiser Fleet from which he sailed to engage Admiral von Hipper's battlecruisers at the Battle of Jutland (31 May-1 June 1916). In 1917, Rosyth became the base for the British Home Fleet for the remainder of the war.

After the war, Rosyth ceased operations and was put in a care and maintenance status, which just kept the facility ready for any future contingency requirements. That occasion came in the late 1930s when war clouds were again looming on the horizon and Rosyth was brought back up to full operational status. The dockyard provided yeoman service during the Second World War in retrofitting and modernising warships, repairing battle-damaged ships, and performing maintenance for vessels of the Royal Navy. At the end of the war, Rosyth was kept open as a ship and submarine refitting centre, and since 1987, this function has been continued under contract with Babcock Rosyth Defence Ltd., a subsidiary of Babcock International Group.

### Harwich
A Royal Dockyard was established at Harwich on the east coast of England, about 60 miles north-east of London, early in the seventeenth century. Considered to be a backup dockyard to Sheerness, HARWICH ROYAL DOCKYARD was used primarily for the refit and repair of ships for the Royal Navy. Harwich was temporarily closed in 1660, but during the Second Dutch War, it was reopened again in 1664. Over the next twenty years, Harwich produced a number of ships-of-the-line and smaller warships for the Royal Navy. In 1681, the yard received its second building slipway, but it still had no dry dock.

In view of its limited capabilities, Harwich was not used extensively during the eighteenth and nineteenth centuries. During the First World War, the dockyard was revived for ship repair work, and it was equipped with a floating dry dock for that purpose. Harwich also served as a naval base primarily for destroyers and submarines. Harwich Dockyard was closed after the end of the war, and the yard was subsequently privatised.

### Haulbowline
In the late nineteenth century, work began on another Royal Dockyard at Haulbowline (Cobh) on the Great Island in Cork Harbour on the southern coast of Ireland, which was still under British control at the time. HAULBOWLINE ROYAL DOCKYARD became operational in 1894 with the completion of its first dry dock, which was nearly 420ft long. The yard was intended only as a fleet maintenance facility, and it had no building ways. The yard was later equipped with a second dry dock that was over 600ft long. Haulbowline employed an average of about 1000 workers, but its workforce increased significantly during the First World War. After the war, shipyard activities ceased at the facility, and the dockyard was subsequently turned over to the Irish Free State.

## NAVAL BASES AND NAVAL STATIONS

Naval bases differ from Royal Dockyards in that they have no shipbuilding capability, and at the most, they have only a limited ship repair capability. Naval bases usually serve in a support role for the Royal Navy, providing logistics support for units of the fleet to include refuelling and the provisioning of supplies, equipment, and repair parts. They may also serve as the headquarters for certain units of the fleet, and as such, they would provide administrative support for naval personnel, such as medical and dental services, recreational facilities, and other essential functions. Naval stations have an even more limited role, serving primarily as refuelling stations, their other support functions being limited.

*Scapa Flow*
The principal British naval base in both World Wars was at Scapa Flow off the northern coast of Scotland. Scapa Flow is a body of water about 8 miles in length from east to west and 6 miles in width from north to south located among the Orkney Islands. The anchorage is protected from the Atlantic

Scapa Flow.

Ocean and North Sea by the surrounding islands, but it has easy access to those bodies of water through the Pentland Firth. Although Scapa Flow was used as a base by the Vikings as early as the eleventh century, it was not considered as a suitable base for the Royal Navy until the nineteenth century.

During the First World War, Scapa Flow served as the main base for Admiral Sir John Jellicoe's Grand Fleet, and it was from here that he sailed to engage the German High Seas Fleet at the Battle of Jutland (31 May-1 June 1916). At the end of the war, most of the units of the German High Seas Fleet surrendered at Scapa Flow and were interned with their crews remaining on board. When the German crews believed that the British would take over their ships before the peace treaty was officially signed, they scuttled many of them to avoid their possibly being used against Germany.

During the Second World War, Scapa Flow was the anchorage of the Home Fleet and served as a refuelling and resupply station as well as the fleet headquarters. As the international situation deteriorated prior to the war, the fuel oil storage capacity at the Lyness Naval Base on the eastern coast of the island of Hoy was increased by 100,000 tons with the construction of large underground storage tanks. Action was also undertaken at that time to improve the defences of Scapa Flow by the laying of anti-submarine booms and the sinking of blockships in some of the more vulnerable channels between the various islands surrounding the anchorage.

On 14 October 1939, just six weeks after the outbreak of war, a German submarine (*U-47*, commanded by Lt. Comdr. Günther Prien) penetrated the eastern defences of Scapa Flow through one of the still open passages between the islands of Burray and Mainland. There off the coast of East Mainland, the *U-47* torpedoed the battleship *Royal Oak* (*Royal Sovereign* class) while it was at anchor, and the ship sank with the loss of over 800 lives. The channel was later sealed with a blockship, and causeways were eventually constructed between the islands, but the damage had already been done. Since Scapa Flow did not have any major shipbuilding or repair facilities to sustain naval activity after the war, the base was closed in 1957.

### Other Naval Bases in the British Isles

During the Second World War, the Royal Navy used other ports and anchorages in the British Isles for refuelling and resupply purposes, especially those that were out of range of the Luftwaffe. These included the Firth of Forth near Edinburgh, Firth of Clyde near Glasgow, and Londonderry in Northern Ireland. In earlier times, the British had built a string of naval bases along the southern coast of England on the English Channel for protection against the French, Dutch, and Spanish fleets, but their vulnerability to air attack limited their usefulness in the Second World War.

### Royal Naval College

The original Naval Academy, where all officers of the Royal Navy receive their formal training, was established at Portsmouth in 1733, and in 1806, its name was changed to Royal Naval College. In 1869, the ROYAL NAVAL

COLLEGE moved to Greenwich at the site of the former Naval Hospital, which had been established in 1694 but was no longer needed as a veteran's hospital. The Royal Naval College, now known as the BRITANNIA ROYAL NAVAL COLLEGE, moved from Greenwich in 1933 to Dartmouth, a small town on the south-western coast of England on the English Channel about 30 miles east of Plymouth. The Royal Naval College facility at Greenwich was then converted into the National Maritime Museum.

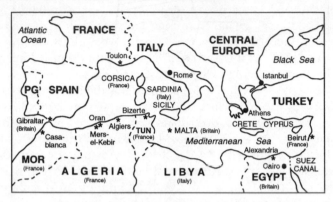

The Mediterranean 1940.

## British Overseas Bases

With a far-flung colonial empire, Great Britain had to become a great naval power to protect its global interests. This necessitated the building of a huge fleet of warships and the establishment of naval bases and naval stations throughout the world to keep the vital sea lanes open to her widespread possessions. The Mediterranean was the second most important area of naval interest to Great Britain, especially since the opening of the Suez Canal in 1869. It was essential that this important waterway be kept open since it represented Britain's lifeline with her colonies in eastern Africa and southern Asia. In the Mediterranean Sea, the Royal Navy had three major bases, Gibraltar, Malta, and Alexandria.

### Gibraltar

The famous GIBRALTAR NAVAL BASE at the southern tip of the Iberian Peninsular guarded the western entrance to the Mediterranean Sea, and it was therefore a key link in the British defence network. Gibraltar was taken by Great Britain from Spain in 1704 during the War of the Spanish Succession, and it remained in British hands as a result of the Treaty of Utrecht (1713). Beginning early in the eighteenth century, Britain strengthened the fortifications of that peninsular until it achieved the reputation of being impregnable.

Early in the twentieth century, the defences of Gibraltar were modernised to include the construction of a naval dockyard with three graving docks measuring 850 × 90ft, 550 × 90ft, and 450 × 90ft. A fourth dry dock, located a short distance up the coast from the dockyard, was suitable only for

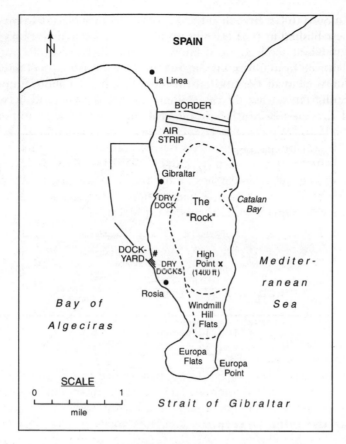

Gibraltar in 1945.

torpedo craft due to its small size. No slipways were ever considered for the dockyard since its primary mission was to provide a base for the fleet and to perform limited repairs and maintenance on its vessels. During the Second World War, Gibraltar was the home base of 'Force H' which was to have a crucial role in the sinking of the German battleship *Bismarck* in May 1941. Gibraltar continues to serve as a base for the Royal Navy at the present time.

*Malta*

The British occupied the island of Malta in 1800 at the invitation of the native population to thwart the efforts of Napoleon Bonaparte to take over the island. Recognising the strategic value of the island, the British soon established the MALTA NAVAL BASE at the Grand Harbour of Valletta to include a dockyard, arsenal, and supply depot for the Royal Navy. In 1848, the first dry dock, measuring 525 × 85ft, was built at the dockyard, and this was followed by an additional 525 × 85ft dry dock in 1871. Two more dry docks, measuring 470 × 80ft and 520 × 94ft feet, were added by the end of the century. In 1908, three new dry docks were built to replace the two original dry docks, including a 700 × 95ft double, a 536 × 73ft single, and a 550 × 95ft single dry dock.

The Malta dockyard proved to be of great value to Allied forces during the First World War, but after the war, its workload declined. The location of Malta in the Mediterranean Sea off the southern coast of Sicily and between that island and the coast of North Africa gave it particular strategic importance in the Second World War. After Italy entered the war on the side of Germany in 1940, Malta was intensively bombed by Axis aircraft, especially since it was along the route for the shipment of supplies to Rommel's Afrika Korps. These air attacks did considerable damage to the base and resulted in the sinking of several ships in Valletta harbour. When the tables were turned, Malta became an important base for the Allied invasion of Sicily.

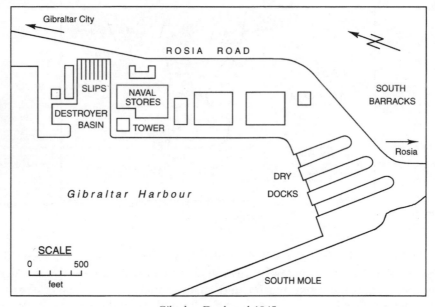

Gibraltar Dockyard 1945.

After the war, the workload again dropped, and the Malta Dockyard was finally closed in 1958. The facilities are now being operated by the private firms of Malta Drydocks and Malta Shipbuilding Co. Ltd. for the building and repair of merchant ships.

## Alexandria

The Egyptian port city of Alexandria was acquired by Great Britain in 1882 after an Egyptian uprising against Europeans was put down by an Anglo-French fleet and Egypt was occupied as a British protectorate. The ALEXANDRIA NAVAL BASE was soon established to protect the eastern end of the Mediterranean Sea and the northern terminus of the Suez Canal. The Suez Canal was opened in 1869, and it was an important waterway for trade

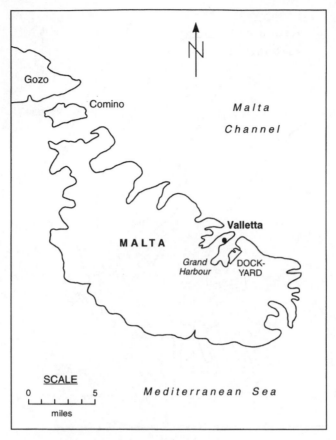

Malta.

between Europe and the Far East, cutting weeks off earlier voyages around the Cape of Good Hope. In time of war, the canal became the lifeline of the British Empire which extended around the world. Although not classified as a dockyard, Alexandria did possess a 550ft dry dock that could accommodate cruiser-size vessels.

*Africa*
Great Britain had two other major naval bases in Africa, one at Freetown in Sierra Leone on the west coast of Africa, and the other at Simonstown (Simon's Town) near Cape Town in South Africa on the Cape of Good Hope at the southern tip of the continent. Both of these bases provided primarily logistics support to elements of the Royal Navy operating in those respective areas. FREETOWN NAVAL BASE was once the Headquarters of the Royal Navy's South Atlantic Region when the British were hunting down the German pocket battleship *Admiral Graf Spee* which was raiding Allied shipping in that area during the fall of 1939. The raider was finally brought to bay in December of that year by a British task force off the coast of Uruguay in South America.

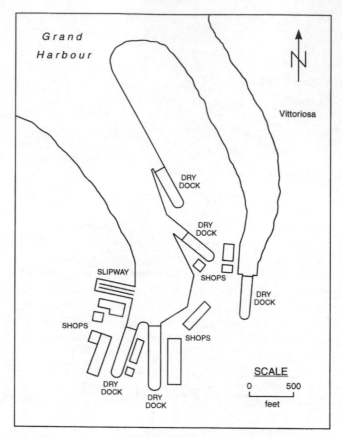

Malta Naval Base 1945.

The SIMONSTOWN NAVAL BASE was located on Simon's Bay (now called False Bay) on the eastern side of the small peninsula that constitutes the Cape of Good Hope, about 20 miles south of the town of Capetown. The Cape of Good Hope is actually not the southernmost point of Africa, that distinction being held by Cape Agulhas, about 110 miles south-east of the Cape of Good Hope. The Simonstown Dockyard was equipped with a 750ft dry dock and a 25-acre tidal basin, which could accommodate Dreadnought-type battleships.

*India*

The first Europeans to arrive in India were the Portuguese at the end of the fifteenth century. One hundred years later, around 1600, the Dutch came to India with their East India Company, and they were soon followed by the English in 1619. The French then began to establish settlements in 1666, but after a succession of wars between England and France, the French as well as the Dutch had to relinquish their interests in India. By the eighteenth century, England had established dominance over India and ruled the country with a succession of viceroys named by the Crown.

British occupation of India was marked by numerous uprisings, and in the

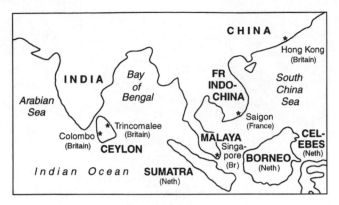

Southeast Asia 1945.

nineteenth century, nationalist movements sprung up with demands for Indian independence. India finally achieved self-determination in 1947 with the establishment of the Dominion of India as a part of the British Commonwealth of Nations. The land, however, was partitioned along religious boundaries, and the new Dominion of Pakistan was also established concurrently. The island of Ceylon (now Sri Lanka) off the southern tip of India, which was first colonised in 1795, won its independence in 1948.

Great Britain had naval bases at Bombay on the western coast of India, at Calcutta in the eastern part of the country, and two major bases on the island of Ceylon. One base was at Colombo, the capital city of Ceylon on the west coast of the island, which had a deep harbour protected by a breakwater. The COLOMBO NAVAL BASE was established at the turn of the century as a fortified coaling station after the Royal Navy switched from sail to steam power. The base at Colombo was subsequently equipped with a dry-dock over 700ft long that could accommodate a Dreadnought-size battleship, and it was used extensively as a warship repair and maintenance facility during the Second World War.

Trincomalee on the north-eastern coast of Ceylon features one of the finest natural harbours in the world. Trincomalee Bay is protected on three sides, and it is of sufficient size to accommodate the anchorage of a large fleet of ships. First held by the Dutch in 1639, the harbour was taken by the French in 1673 and again in 1782, but it was recovered by the Dutch both times. The Dutch surrendered the port to a British fleet in 1795. During the Second World War, TRINCOMALEE NAVAL BASE became an important facility for the Allies in their efforts to recapture the territories taken by Japan in south-east Asia. After the Second World War, the base was abandoned, and like the one at Colombo, it was taken over by the government of Sri Lanka. (Continued under Other Countries: India.)

## Singapore

The primary British naval base in south-east Asia had been at Singapore at the southern tip of the Malay Peninsula. Great Britain acquired the island of

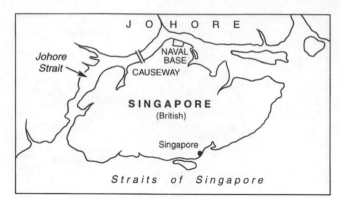

Singapore.

Singapore in 1824 by purchase from the local ruler of that region of Malaya. In 1921, the SINGAPORE NAVAL BASE was established at the northern end of the island on the Jahore Strait, and it became one of the most important British naval facility in the Far East. In 1938, the base was expanded to include a dockyard with a dry dock of sufficient size to accommodate the largest warship afloat.

Protected by coastal artillery aimed against an attack from the sea, Singapore quickly fell to invading Japanese forces, which attacked the stronghold from the rear after coming down the Malay Peninsula in February 1942. The Japanese used the facilities of Singapore as a forward base while they continued their expansion into the Dutch East Indies (later Indonesia). After the Japanese surrender in August 1945, the British returned to Singapore, and in 1959, the island became a self-governing state. The dockyard facilities were later taken over by a private firm, Sembawang Shipyard, and it now provides ship repair and maintenance services for the entire Far East region.

*China*
Great Britain acquired the island of Hong Kong on the coast of the South China Sea near the Chinese city of Canton in 1841, and it immediately established Hong Kong as a free port for international trade. In 1856, the HONG KONG NAVAL BASE was established on the north shore of Hong Kong Island. Great Britain occupied Kowloon across the strait from Hong Kong Island in 1860, and in 1898, a 99-year lease was obtained for the New Territories on the mainland to the north-west of Hong Kong Island. Hong Kong became an important coaling station for the Royal Navy after it had converted to steam power, and in 1902, a 550ft dry dock was added at the base to allow for the repair of British warships in that region.

As oil replaced coal as the preferred fuel for warships of the Royal Navy, fuel storage tanks were constructed at the Hong Kong naval base. Upon Japan's entry into the Second World War in December 1941, Hong Kong was soon occupied by Japanese forces. After the end of the war, Hong Kong continued to serve the needs of the Royal Navy until 1958 when overseas

China (1914).

naval activities were severely curtailed due to budget cuts. In 1993, the naval base activities were transferred to nearby Stonecutters Island, although the headquarters remained on Hong Kong Island. When the 99-year lease on Hong Kong territories terminated in June 1997, the entire area of the Crown Colony was turned over to the Republic of China.

Great Britain also acquired another naval base on the coast of China for a period of time. In 1898, the Chinese naval base at Wei-Hai-Wei (Weihai) on the Korea Bay at the north-eastern corner of Shantung Province was leased to the Royal Navy for use as a naval base and coaling station. The WEI-HAI-WEI NAVAL BASE was strategically located directly across the bay from the famous fortified harbour of Port Arthur, which was captured by Japan in 1894, but later acquired by Russia in 1898. Wei-Hai-Wei was never fortified or developed into anything but a coaling station, and in 1921, it was returned to the China in accordance with agreements reached at the Washington Conference of that year.

*Australia*
Australia was discovered by the English explorer, James Cook, in 1770, and

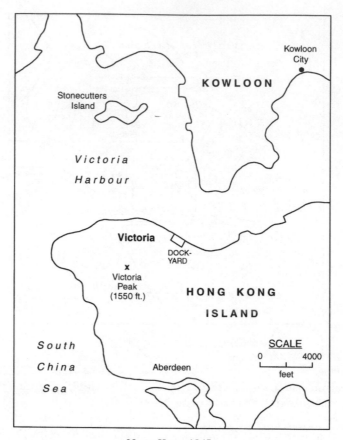

Hong Kong 1945.

further explorations of the island continent continued over the next one hundred years. From 1820 to 1850, there was considerable agitation for self-government in the country, and in 1850, the Australian Colonies Government Act was passed, allowing a certain degree of self-determination. The Federal Commonwealth of Australia was established in 1901 from the federation of the provinces of Victoria, New South Wales, Queensland, South Australia, and Western Australia. In 1911, the Royal Australian Navy was officially established.

The Royal Navy had several naval bases and naval stations in Australia, the most important of which was at Sydney, the capital of New South Wales on the eastern coast of Australia. Other British naval bases in Australia were at Brisbane in Queensland, Melbourne in Victoria, Adelaide in South Australia, King George Sound in Western Australia, and Hobart on the island of Tasmania. Under the Australian Nation Defence Act of 1887, the colonies of Australia and New Zealand were required to make an annual contribution for the maintenance of modern warships provided by Great Britain for the defence of those colonies. The Royal Australian Navy initially consisted of warships acquire from Great Britain, either by purchase or by loan from the Royal Navy. (Continued under Other Countries: Australia.)

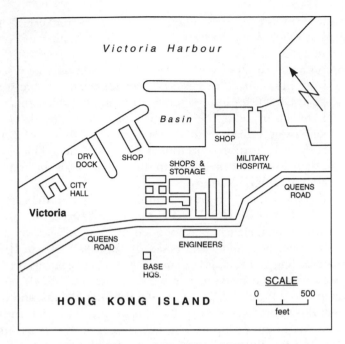

Hong Kong Naval Base 1945.

## New Zealand

New Zealand had a similar history to that of its larger neighbour, Australia. The two major islands that comprise New Zealand, North Island and South Island, were mapped by James Cook in 1769, and they were subsequently visited by explorers from France, Spain, Russia, and America. New Zealand was first settled by English missionaries early in the nineteenth century, and as the settlements grew, the people began to seek self-rule over their affairs. In 1852, self-government was allowed by the Crown, and in 1856, a parliament was established. This was followed by a constitution in 1870, but New Zealand still remained a colony.

In 1907, New Zealand finally became a Dominion within the British Commonwealth of Nations, following Australia by six years. Britain had one major naval base in New Zealand, and that was at Auckland on the North Island. Initially, the New Zealand Navy was composed of warships acquired from Great Britain, either by purchase or on loan from the Royal Navy. (Continued under Other Countries: New Zealand.)

## Canada

French explorers reached Canada early in the sixteenth century, and in 1534, the colony of New France was established. In the seventeenth century, English settlers from New England and New York began to expand northward and encroach on territory claimed by France. Frequent fighting occurred between English and French colonists during the middle of the seventeenth century to the middle of the eighteenth century, especially when England and France were formally at war with each other. During the Seven Years War, English forces captured Quebec and Montreal, forcing the surrender of New France to England in 1760.

Canada continued to grow with the influx of additional new settlers and expansion westwards. During the mid-nineteenth century, there were strong forces at work in Canada for internal unification and self-determination of the Canadian provinces. In 1840, the provinces of Upper Canada were united with those of Lower Canada, and in 1867, the Dominion of Canada was established from the federation of its four primary provinces. This gave Canada self-rule, but with continued allegiance to the crown under the concept of the British Commonwealth of Nations.

The Royal Navy had two major bases in Canada, one on the east coast, and the other on the west coast. The Royal Navy's main base on the east coast was at Halifax, Nova Scotia. Halifax was founded in 1749, and it soon became an important maritime port and naval base. The HALIFAX NAVAL BASE served mainly as a refuelling and resupply point for its warships, but its dockyard also provided ship repair and maintenance services for naval vessels operating in that region. In 1759, the King's Yard was established at Halifax, and during the remainder of the eighteenth century and throughout the nineteenth century, the dockyard was improved upon. The HALIFAX DOCKYARD has never built any ships and remained primarily a ship repair facility.

On the west coast, Canada's primary base was the naval dockyard at Esquimalt located near Victoria, the capital of in British Columbia, on the southern tip of Vancouver Island. During the first half of the nineteenth century, there were constant disputes between American and British interests over the north-west territory. Britain established Fort Vancouver in 1825 and Fort Victoria in 1843 to promote its rights in that region. The issue was finally resolved by the Washington Treaty of 1846, which established the 49th Parallel (49° north latitude) as the dividing line between American and British territory. Great Britain was recognised as having rights to all land above that parallel as well as all of Vancouver Island which laid mostly above that line.

The harbour at Esquimalt on Cape Breton was surveyed in 1846, and a naval base was established there two years later in 1848. In 1861, the ESQUIMALT NAVAL BASE became the headquarters of the British Pacific Station, and within the next twenty-five years, a 450ft dry dock was constructed at the site to allow for the repair and maintenance of British warships up to the size of light cruisers. The ESQUIMALT DOCKYARD, like the Halifax Dockyard, did not have a shipbuilding capability.

In 1902, the British decided to give up its two dockyards in Canada, and in 1905, the Royal Navy departed from Halifax and Esquimalt. The Royal Navy's headquarters for North American naval operations was thereupon transferred from Halifax to Bermuda. Both Halifax and Esquimalt Dockyards were formally transferred to the Dominion of Canada in 1910, the year in which the Royal Canadian Navy was created. The Royal Canadian Navy initially consisted of warships acquire from Great Britain, either by purchase or by loan from the Royal Navy. (Continued under Other Countries: Canada.)

*Bermuda*

England colonised Bermuda, a small group of islands in the Atlantic Ocean about 1000 miles due east of Savannah, Georgia, in 1612. Early in the nineteenth century, Great Britain established a naval base at Bermuda, and in 1869, the BERMUDA NAVAL BASE was equipped with a large 545ft floating dock to allow for the repair and maintenance of Royal Navy vessels operating in that region. At the turn of the century, the base was extended, and it was then equipped with a second floating dry dock in 1906. The base served as a coaling station for warships of the Royal Navy after the conversion to steam-power, but it was later equipped with oil storage tanks when that fuel replaced coal early in the twentieth century. Bermuda became the headquarters of the Royal Navy's North Atlantic naval operations upon its transfer from Halifax in 1905.

*The Caribbean*

The island of Jamaica was discovered by Columbus in 1494, and the island was held by Spain until 1655 when it was captured by the English. British title to Jamaica was recognised by the Treaty of Madrid in 1670, and the British established the JAMAICA NAVAL BASE on the island late in the eighteenth century. Jamaica became a Crown Colony with Kingston as its capital in 1866. Finding Bermuda to be more suitable for a naval base and coaling station in the western Atlantic region, Britain transferred its naval operations from Jamaica to Bermuda in the nineteenth century. Great Britain also had a naval base on the island of Antigua in the Leeward Islands of the Lesser Antilles Group, which it colonised in 1632. The ANTIGUA NAVAL BASE was not used to any great extent, and it was finally abandoned at the end of the nineteenth century.

*Iceland*

After the fall of Denmark in May 1940, Great Britain occupied Iceland to keep it from falling into German hands. The British also took advantage of the opportunity to establish refuelling and resupply bases for British warships on

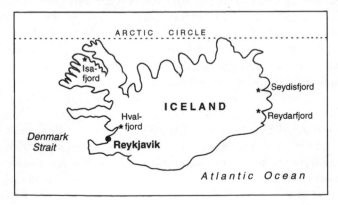

Iceland.

convoy or patrol duty in the North Atlantic. Britain's most important naval base in Iceland was at HVALFJORD, which is located just to the north of the capital at Reykjavik. Other bases included ISAFJORD in the north-west corner of the island and SEYDISFJORD on the east coast of the island. The British also used REYDARFJORD, a small fjord just south of Seydisfjord, as a refuelling station. After the end of the Second World War, the British abandoned those bases and turned them back to Iceland.

## PRIVATE SHIPYARDS IN ENGLAND

Privately-owned shipyards were contracted to construct many of the warships of the Royal Navy, particularly when the authorisation for new ship construction exceeded the capacity of Royal Dockyards. This was especially true during periods of national emergency, such as the French and Dutch wars and the two more recent World Wars. During the age of sailing vessels, private shipyards were generally limited to building smaller warships up to 74-gun ships-of-the-line, leaving the construction of larger First and Second Rate ships to Royal Dockyards. Initially, naval shipbuilding took place primarily along the River Thames and the English Channel, but those shipyards were subsequently overshadowed by those on the River Tyne and then the River Clyde.

Many of the private shipyards contracted to build the 74-gun ships-of-the-line also produced ships for the Honourable East India Co. Those so-called 'East Indiamen' were among the largest merchant sailing vessels built during the late eighteenth–early nineteenth century. Many of these ships were armed to protect them from marauding pirates, and they could readily be converted into auxiliary frigates. In fact, the *Bonhomme Richard*, used by the American naval hero, John Paul Jones, to defeat the 44-gun frigate HMS *Serapis* off Flamborough Head in 1779, was a converted East Indiaman.

### Thames Yards

The greatest concentration of British shipbuilding, including naval construction, during the age of sailing vessels was just to the east of London. Most of the shipyards were located along the loop formed by the River Thames around the Isle of Dogs, two to three miles east of the Tower of London. This area was also the site of the great harbour complexes known as the East India Docks and the West India Docks.

### Blackwall

The most prolific shipyard on the River Thames was at Blackwall. The yard, located just to the west of the East India Docks, was originally established in the late sixteenth century, and it operated under a series of leases until 1639, when it was taken over by Henry Johnson. HENRY JOHNSON began building warships some fourteen years later with two 62-gun ships-of-the-line, the *Dreadnought* in 1653 and the *Torrington* in 1654. Those ships were followed by the 70-gun ships

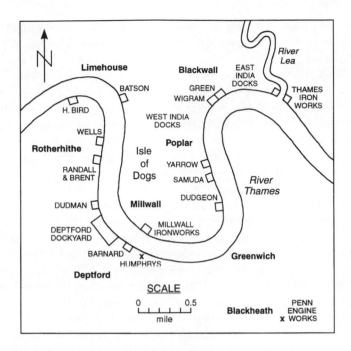

The Isle of Dogs.

*Warspite* (1666), *Essex* (1679), *Kent* (1679), *Exeter* (1680), and *Suffolk* (1680). Henry Johnson died in 1683, and the shipyard was taken over by his son, Henry, who built two 48-gun ships in 1695-6 before giving up the enterprise.

After many years of idleness, the Blackwall shipyard was finally leased by Philip Perry in 1732. As P. PERRY & CO., Philip Perry and his son, John, built the 60-gun ship *Weymouth* in 1736 and two 50-gun ships in 1741-5. By the middle of the eighteenth century, the yard had one double dry dock, two single dry docks, several building ways, and a wet fitting-out basin. In the twelve-year period, 1756-67, Perry produced thirty-one large ships, including twenty-seven East Indiamen and several warships. The firm's naval construction included one 60-gun ship in 1759 and two 64-gun ships in 1761-5. Philip Perry died in 1776, and the yard was taken over by his son, John.

John Perry built another two 64-gun ships in 1778-9, and in 1781, he built four 74-gun ships-of-the-line, the *Venerable*, *Victorious*, *Hannibal*, and *Theseus*. The *Theseus* was a participant in the Battle of the Nile in 1798. Perry then built two 44-gun frigates in 1784, the 74-gun *Bombay Castle* in 1789, and one 38-gun frigate in 1794. In 1796, Perry's son-in-law, George Green, become a partner in the firm, and two years later in 1798, John and William Wells gave up their shipyard in Rotherhithe to join Perry and Green. PERRY, WELLS & GREEN built three 74-gun ships, the *Kent*, *Ajax*, and *Dragon*, in 1798. The yard then built a succession of East Indiamen and a few small warships over the next few years.

In 1805, Perry, Wells & Green built the three 74-gun ships-of-the-line *Magnificent*, *Elizabeth*, and *Valiant*. Those ships were later followed by the 74s

*Ajax* and *Berwick* in 1809 and the *America* in 1810. John Perry died in 1810, and his share of the company was bought by Robert Wigram. WIGRAM & GREEN went on to build two more 74s, the *Barham* in 1811 and the *Pembroke* in 1813. In 1813, the yard also produced one 60-gun, one 58-gun, and five 50-gun ships, as well as three 38-gun frigates.

Wigram & Green then turned to the exclusive production of East Indiamen and other merchant vessels. Sir Robert Wigram died in 1819, and he left his share of the shipyard to his two sons, Money and Henry, but it was Money Wigram who took the most active part in looking after the Wigram interests in the shipyard. Wigram & Green produced their first steamer, the *City of Edinburgh*, in 1821, and they gradually shifted to the production of steamships only. In 1843, the Blackwall shipyard was divided between the Greens and the Wigrams, with Richard and Harry Green taking over the eastern half of the yard and Money Wigram and his sons taking over the western half of the yard.

R. & H. GREEN, after taking over the eastern half of the Blackwall shipyard, continued to concentrate on the production of merchant vessels until the Crimean War (1854-6). Green produced fourteen screw-propelled gunboats and eleven other small warships in 1855-6. In 1864, the yard built the 5700-ton armoured wooden frigate *Arapiles* for Spain, the largest ship built at the yard. Two years later, Green built its first iron ship, the 1450-ton sailing vessel *Superb*. The yard produced two small warships in 1875 and 1882, before building its last warship, an experimental torpedo-boat, in 1886. After that, R. & H. Green built mostly coastal paddle steamers and a variety of other merchant ships before ending shipbuilding in 1902.

Soon after taking over the western half of the Blackwall shipyard, MONEY WIGRAM & SONS built their first ship, the *Terpsichore*, a wooden sailing warship. Like R. & H. Green, the Wigrams also built a number of small warships in support of the Crimean War, including seven screw-propelled paddle gunboats and nine other types of vessels in 1855-6. Over the next twenty years, the shipyard produced nineteen vessels, including five small warships, until 1856, when it built its last ship. The Wigram yard finally closed completely seven years later in 1863.

Another Blackwall shipyard was that of DITCHBURN & MARE. Thomas Ditchburn and C. J. Mare had already established a partnership at Deptford in 1837, and in the following year, they took over a shipyard at the mouth of the River Lea where it emptied into the River Thames in the Blackwall District. At first, the yard built mostly merchant steamers, but in 1843-5, it produced seven paddle wheel warships. In 1846, Thomas Ditchburn retired, leaving the yard in the sole possession of C. J. Mare. C. J. MARE & CO. built four additional paddle wheel warships in 1846-7 as the yard moved over to the production of screw-propelled warships. From 1846-56, the yard produced twenty-seven small screw-propelled warships up to 2600 tons displacement.

Around the middle of the nineteenth century, C. J. Mare purchased additional land nearby to provide greater facilities for the production of warships. The five slips in the upper yard then ranged from 240 to 400ft in length, and the three slips in the lower yard included two slips of 400ft in length and one slip of 370ft in length. Beset by financial difficulties, C. J. Mare built its last ship in 1856, and in the following year, the company was reconstituted as Thames Iron Works and Shipbuilding Co.

THAMES IRON WORKS & SHIPBUILDING CO. soon received Admiralty orders for warships, and in 1860, it produced the broadside battery ironclad *Warrior*, which had both sail and auxiliary steam power. The 380ft *Warrior* was the largest warship in the world at that time, displacing over 9200 tons, and that ship was soon followed by the 10,690-ton broadside-battery ironclad *Minotaur* in 1863. The production of warships for the Royal Navy continued with three 3500-ton turret ships in 1869-74. During that period, Thames also produced ironclads for foreign navies, including one for Spain in 1865, one for Greece in 1867, one for Prussia in 1869, and four for Turkey in 1869-75.

In 1872, the company was incorporated as the THAMES IRON WORKS & SHIPBUILDING CO. LTD., and after 1875, the yard switched over to the production of all-steel vessels. By 1880, the shipyard had 30 acres of land in West Ham on the east side of the River Lea and 5 acres in Blackwall. The all-steel warships produced for the Royal Navy after that time included the battleships *Superb* in 1880, *Benbow* in 1888, and *Sans Pareil* in 1890, as well as the protected cruisers *Blenheim* in 1890 and *Theseus* and *Grafton*, both in 1892.

Before the turn of the century, Thames Ironworks also built a number of warships for foreign governments, including one 6400-ton broadside battery ironclad for Turkey in 1864, one 7000-ton ironclad for Spain in 1865, the 9800-ton central-battery ironclad *König Wilhelm* for the North German Confederation in 1868, two 9000-ton central-battery ironclads for Turkey in 1876, and the battleships *Fuji* (1896) and *Shikishima* (1899) for Japan. Smaller foreign warships produced by the yard included two additional vessels for Spain, two additional vessels for Turkey, five ships for Greece, two ships for Portugal, and one ship for Russia.

In 1899, the firm acquired the engine works of John Penn & Sons in Greenwich, and the company became THAMES IRON WORKS, SHIPBUILDING & ENGINEERING CO. LTD. with the addition of that engineering function. Thames Iron Works continued warship production for the Royal Navy into the twentieth century with the battleships *Albion* (1901), *Duncan* (1903), *Cornwallis* (1904) and *Thunderer* (1912) and the 13,550-ton armoured cruiser *Black Prince* in 1904. The company went bankrupt in 1911, and it closed its doors after completing the battleship *Thunderer* in 1912.

*Rotherhithe*

The greatest rival to the Blackwall yard in shipbuilding was the Randall & Brent yard in Rotherhithe, located on the south bank of the River Thames, about 2 miles east of the Tower of London. J Randall established a shipyard at the site around the middle of the eighteenth century, and he was soon joined by Daniel Brent as a partner. From 1756-1813, RANDALL & BRENT produced fifty-three warships, including fifteen Third and Fourth Rate ships and eight frigates. The 74s produced during the latter half of the eighteenth century included the *Suffolk* (1765), *Vengeance* (1774), *Fortitude* (1780), *Ganges* (1782),

*Defiance* (1783), *Culloden* (1783), *Ramillies* (1785), and *Audacious* (1785).

The last four of those ships achieved fame for their participation in naval battles with the Royal Navy. The *Defiance* fought against the Danes in the Battle of Copenhagen in 1801, and it was also engaged against the Franco-Spanish fleet at the Battle of Trafalgar in 1805. The *Culloden* and the *Ramillies* were both involved in the Battle of the Glorious First of June in 1794, and the *Audacious* was involved in the Battle of the Nile in 1798.

After the turn of the century, Randall & Brent continued to build Third Rates, including the 74-gun *Illustrious* (1803), *York* (1807), and *Edinburgh* (1811) and the 72-gun ship *Benbow* in 1813. Between 1801-12, the yard also produced six East Indiamen. Soon thereafter, J Randall left the firm, and management of the yard was taken over by the Brent family. S. & D. BRENT become one of the earliest steamship builders in the world, producing the *Diane*, one of the first successful steamships built in Great Britain, in 1817. The firm, however, soon came upon hard times, and it completed only four more steamers before going out of business in 1821.

Around 1745, John and William Wells took over the Wells family shipyard at Rotherhithe, which was established at the beginning of the century, and they built the 42-gun frigate *Larke* in 1703. The reactivated WELLS SHIPYARD produced its first warship, the 60-gun *Tiger*, in 1747, and 10 years later, the Wells family began to build warships in earnest. From 1757 to 1798, the yard produced twenty-nine warships, including ten ships-of-the-line and two frigates. Among the ships-of-the-line built by Wells were the 74-gun ships *Shrewsbury* (1758), *Cornwall* (1761), *Invincible* (1765), *Thunderer* (1783), *Terrible* (1785), *Swiftsure* (1787), and *Dragon* (1798). The *Thunderer* was engaged in the Battle of the Glorious First of June in 1794, and the *Swiftsure* fought the French at the Battle of the Nile in 1798.

Other Rotherhithe shipbuilders involved in naval construction included RICHARD BURCHETT, who produced four warships from 1703-10, including one 60-gun ship-of-the-line and two frigates, one a 44-gun and the other a 42-gun ship. ELIAS BIRD built eight warships from 1740-9, including one 60-gun and one 50-gun ship and two 44-gun frigates. HENRY BIRD produced twelve warships from 1740-60, including two 44-gun frigates. Henry Bird was also involved in naval shipbuilding at Northam on the English Channel coast for a short period of time from 1755-9. ROBERT INWOOD built six warships, including two 32-gun ships, in 1756-63.

*Millwall*

William Fairbairn, with his partner, Andrew Murray, established a shipyard in Millwall, at the south-western section of the Isle of Dogs, in 1835. FAIRBAIRN built one of the earliest iron steamers, the *Sirius*, in 1837, and in 1842-5, he produced two paddle warships for the Royal Navy. At its peak of production, the yard employed 2000 people, but the firm went bankrupt in 1846. Despite financial difficulties, the yard remained open until 1849, after it had completed the 1400-ton iron steam frigate *Megaera*. When the yard closed in 1849, the land was purchased by ROBINSON & CO.

Henry and Alfred Robinson were joined by John Scott Russell, a noted hull designer, to form the partnership of ROBINSON & RUSSELL. Russell soon took over complete control of the firm, and it then became JOHN SCOTT RUSSELL CO. The shipyard built three iron paddle steamers for Prussia in 1851, but two were acquired and placed in service by the Royal Navy. The shipyard then produced eight small warships for the Royal Navy in 1854-60. The firm's greatest achievement during that period was the construction of the famous *Great Eastern* in 1858 at a new shipbuilding facility adjacent to the original shipyard. The 18,900-ton, 680ft long *Great Eastern* was the largest merchant ship ever produced up to that time.

John Scott Russell Co. built its last ship in 1861, and the yard was then taken over by C J Mare of Blackwall fame. C J Mare operated the yard as the MILLWALL IRONWORKS & SHIPBUILDING CO., and it had an area of 22 acres and a river frontage of 1500ft. With a workforce that peaked at 4000, the company built several sailing and screw-propelled merchant ship, but only one warship, from 1862-6. The *Northumberland*, a 10,800-ton broadside-battery ironclad, was built in 1866. Beset by financial problems, the shipyard closed in 1866 after completing the *Northumberland*.

In 1856, Joseph Westwood and Robert Baillie took over the Millwall shipyard once owned by the Napier family of Clyde fame and then by Robinson & Russell, adjacent to the new John Scott Russell Co. shipyard. In 1859, WESTWOOD & BAILLIE built their first ship, a steam yacht, and in 1861, the firm built the 3700-ton armoured frigate *Resistance*. The company went bankrupt in 1862, and the 4100-ton broadside-battery ironclad *Valiant*, then under construction at the yard, had to be completed by Thames Iron Works & Shipbuilding Co.

### Deptford

In addition to the Deptford Royal Dockyard, there were several private shipyards in Deptford that produced warships for the Royal Navy. WILLIAM BARNARD established a shipyard near the Deptford Royal Dockyard around 1780, and from that time until 1819, he with various partners produced twenty-six warships and twelve East Indiamen. The warships produced by Barnard included the 74-gun ships *Tremendous* (1784), *Zealous* (1785), *Orion* (1787), *Repulse* (1797), *Northumberland* (1798), *Marlborough* (1807), *Rodney* (1809), and *Devonshire* (1812), three 64-gun ships, two 38-gun and two 36-gun frigates. The *Tremendous* and *Orion* both participated in the Battle of the Glorious First of June in 1794, and the *Orion* was also involved in the Battle of Trafalgar, as was the Barnard-built 64-gun ship *Africa*. Barnard ceased building ships in 1820.

DUDMAN & CO. established a shipyard at Deptford in 1780, and it included five building slips and two double dry docks. From 1783-1812, the firm produced twenty-two warships and three East Indiamen. The warships included the 74-gun *Carnatic* (1783), *Renown* (1798), *Sceptre* (1802), and *Sultan* (1807), as well as three 36-gun frigates. Another Deptford yard, ADAMS & CO., produced five warships from 1773-85, including the 74-gun ships *Hector* in

1774 and *Majestic* in 1785 and one 50-gun ship in 1774. The *Majestic* was a participant in both the Battle of the Glorious First of June in 1794 and the Battle of the Nile in 1798.

THOMAS WEST produced thirteen warships from 1740-66, including the 74-gun ships *Warspite* in 1758 and *Russell* in 1764 and two 60-gun ships. The *Russell* was involved in both the Battle of the Saintes in 1782 and the Battle of Copenhagen in 1801. ROBERT CASTLE built nine warships, including two 70-gun and one 66-gun ship at Deptford in 1666-95. BRONSDEN & CO. produced four warships in 1740-4, including one 60-gun and two 50-gun ships and one 44-gun frigate. JOHN BUXTON, JR. produced ten warships in 1740-57, including one 44-gun frigate. Another Deptford yard, the DURRELL SHIPYARD, built one 44-gun frigate in 1687.

*Poplar*
Joseph and Jacob Samuda established a shipyard at Poplar on the north-eastern side of the Isle of Dogs, in 1843. From 1855-91, SAMUDA BROS. built thirteen warships for the Royal Navy and six warships for foreign governments. The Royal Navy ships included the 4900-ton central-battery ironclads *Belleisle* in 1876 and *Orion* in 1879 and two light cruisers in 1891. Samuda's foreign orders included two ironclads for Brazil in 1867, the 5600-ton central-battery ironclad *Kronprinz* for the Kingdom of Prussia in 1867, the 7700-ton armoured frigates *Kaiser* and *Deutschland* for the German government in 1875, and the 3700-ton armoured frigate *Fuso* for Japan in 1877. In 1893, the yard, which by then encompassed over 6 acres of land with a river frontage of 370ft, was closed.

Another Poplar shipbuilder, ALFRED YARROW, got started in 1868, and he first specialised in the construction of steam launches, completing 350 of those craft by 1875. Yarrow then produced several steamers before building his first torpedo-boat for the Royal Navy in 1877. In 1893, Yarrow received a contract to build the first destroyers for the Royal Navy, the *Havock* and the *Hornet*. From then until 1907, Yarrow built fifty-seven more destroyers for the Royal Navy and five for foreign customers. Beset by labour problems, Yarrow moved his shipbuilding operations to Scotstoun on the River Clyde after completing his last destroyer in 1907.

Just to the south of Poplar on the south-eastern side of the Isle of Dogs was the shipyard of John and William Dudgeon, which was established in 1860. From 1862-74, J. & W. DUDGEON produced thirty-two ships, including the 9300-ton turret ship *Neptune* in 1874 and three other naval vessels for the Royal Navy. Dudgeon is perhaps best noted for its production of ten screw-propelled blockade runners for the Confederate Navy from 1862-5 during the American Civil War.

*Limehouse*
The Limehouse District of London is located on the north bank of the River Thames, about 2 miles east of the Tower Of London. John and Robert Batson established a shipyard there around 1737, and in 1739, J. & R. BATSON built

their first warship, a 20-gun vessel. From 1756-87, the yard produced eleven warships, including the 74-gun *Captain* in 1787, a 64-gun ship in 1783, and three 44-gun frigates. The SNELGROVE SHIPYARD built six warships from 1691-1745, including one 60-gun and one 50-gun ship and two 44-gun frigates. JOHN GREAVES produced nine warships at Limehouse, including two 44-gun frigates, in 1743-83.

Other Limehouse shipbuilders included ROBERT CARTER, who built six warships at that site from 1740-7, including one 60-gun ship in 1744 and three 44-gun frigates. HILL & MELLISH produced seven warships, including a 38-gun frigate, and several East Indiamen from 1794-8. GRAVES AND PURNELL built one 38-gun frigate in 1781 and a 36-gun frigate in 1785, and JOHN BARTON produced two 36-gun frigates there in 1813.

## Chiswick

In 1862, JOHN I. THORNYCROFT established a shipyard at Chiswick, a western suburb of London on the north bank of the River Thames, and there he started building launches and steam yachts. In 1876, the yard built the first torpedo-boat for the Royal Navy, HMS *Lightning* (TB-1), after which it began to specialise in the production of torpedo-boats for the Royal Navy and for foreign nations. From 1878-1902, Thornycroft produced ninety-five torpedo-boats for the Royal Navy and eighty-three for foreign customers, including twenty-four for Italy, seventeen for Denmark, twenty-one for six other European nations, five for Australia, four for New Zealand, three for India, and one for Egypt.

In 1893, Thornycroft built its first torpedo boat destroyer, HMS *Daring*, for the Royal Navy, and from 1894-1906, the yard produced twenty-five additional destroyers for the Royal Navy, eight for Japan, and one for Sweden. At that time, the yard covered 6 acres of land and employed 1700 people. In 1904, Thornycroft purchased a shipyard at Woolston, a suburb of Southampton, and began transferring work to that facility. Production continued at both yards until 1909, when the Chiswick yard was closed down completely. The last warships produced at Chiswick were five coastal destroyers built in 1906.

## Gravesend

WILLIAM CLEVELEY, one of the smaller builders of naval vessels, had a shipyard at Gravesend on the south bank of the River Thames, about 30 miles east of London. From 1780-98, Cleveley produced eleven warships, including the 74-gun ships *Colossus* in 1787 and *Achilles* in 1798, one 64-gun and one 50-gun ship, and one 38-gun and one 36-gun frigate. The *Achilles* fought at the Battle of Trafalgar in 1805.

Across the way on the north bank of the River Thames, THOMAS PITCHER & SONS had their shipyard at Northfleet. Pitcher produced twenty-five warships from 1794-1813 intermingled with twenty-three East Indiamen and three West Indiamen built from 1789-1825. The yard's warships included the

74-gun ships *Superb* (1798), *Eagle* (1804), *Cumberland* (1807), *Venerable* (1808), *Egmont* (1812), *Gloucester* (1812), and *Medway* (1812), as well as one 64-gun ship and three 36- to 38-gun frigates.

*Engineering Works on the River Thames*
In addition to shipbuilders, there were a number of engineering works on the Thames that specialised in the production of steam engines and related machinery for warships built for the Royal Navy and other customers. Royal Dockyards and many private shipbuilders did not build their own engines, and they had to rely on these engineering works to design and build the machinery for their ships. Several of the engineering firms also built ships, but they were noted primarily for their engineering activities.

The greatest producer of marine steam engines for early steam-powered British warships was MAUDSLAY SONS & FIELDS, which at one time had a virtual monopoly in this field. The firm began as a partnership between Henry Maudslay, who had a machine shop in Westminster, and Joshua Field in 1805. In 1814, they moved their operations to Lambeth on the south bank of the River Thames across from the heart of London. Maudslay built its first marine steam engine for a River Thames steamer in 1814, and from 1814-99, the firm produced numerous marine engines for steamships and warships. In 1845, Maudslay provided the engine for the paddle warship *Terrible*, its first naval contract.

Maudslay produced the engines for two wooden screw-propelled frigates in 1855-6, and thereafter, the firm supported the construction of iron and then steel ships. Maudslay provided the engines for seven broadside-battery ironclads in 1861-3, eight central-battery ironclads in 1866-82, two turret ships in 1886-90, and two barbette ships in 1888-9. The firm also produced the machinery for two light cruisers in 1877-8, six battleships in 1889-1900, one armoured cruiser in 1886, and one protected cruiser in 1900. In addition, Maudslay built the engines for a number of major Italian, Prussian, and Russian warships. The firms customers included Royal Dockyards and the local shipbuilders of Thames Iron Works and Samuda Bros. Maudslay went bankrupt in 1900, and the firm ceased the production of marine steam engines after that.

JOHN PENN & SONS began producing marine steam engines at Greenwich in 1825. John Penn died in 1843, and the business was taken over by his son, John Penn, Jr. The main engine works was subsequently established at Blackheath, about a mile south-east of Greenwich, where it covered 7 acres of land and had a workforce of 1200. Its engine assembly shop was housed in a building 180ft long by 50ft wide, and it was supported by cranes up to 50-ton capacity. The firm initially provided steam engines for four wooden, screw-propelled warships from 1853-7, and it then produced the engines for seven broadside-battery ironclads in 1861-4 and four central-battery ironclads in 1866-71.

John Penn, Jr. retired in 1874, but the Penn family continued to operate the shipyard under the same name for another thirty-eight years. The firm provided the engines for four turret ships in 1873-83, four battleships from

1892-8, three armoured cruisers from 1876-88 and five light cruisers from 1885-97. In 1899, John Penn & Sons was acquired by Thames Iron Works, and from then on, its output was primarily in support of ships produced by Thames Iron Works, including four battleships from 1901-11 and one light cruiser in 1911. Penn's customers included Royal Dockyards and the local shipbuilders of Millwall Ironworks and Dudgeon. The Penn engine works was closed down in 1912 when its parent company, Thames Iron Works Shipbuilding & Engineering Co., went out of business.

HUMPHRYS, TENNANT & DYKES LTD began building marine steam engines in the mid-nineteenth century, and the firm soon developed a reputation for producing single piston engines for small boats. Edward Humphrys had been the manager of the John Penn & Sons engine works until 1852, when he was released and went on to form his own business. The Humphrys firm built numerous compound engines for commercial liners before providing engines for warships. Naval orders included the machinery for two central-battery ironclads in 1877, seven turret ships in 1869-90, four barbette ships in 1887-9, seven battleships in 1892-1904, and three armoured cruisers in 1901-06.

Thames Iron Works used Humphrys engines for many of their warships until they acquired John Penn & Sons in 1899, and after that they used their own Penn engines. Humphrys greatest achievement was providing the 44,000-horsepower steam turbine engines for the battlecruiser HMS *Invincible* being built by Armstrong on the Tyne in 1907. The yard closed a year later in 1908 due to financial difficulties.

John Barnes began building marine steam engines at Ratcliff on the north bank of the River Thames, about one and a half miles east of the Tower of London, in 1822. Under a variety of partnership arrangements, BARNES & RAVENHILL provided the engines for seventeen warships from 1826-41, including three Royal Navy central-battery ironclads in 1866 and two German screw-propelled frigates in 1871. In 1839, Barnes and Ravenhill

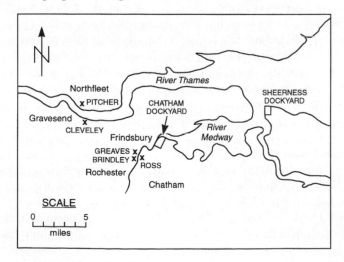

The Thames and the Medway.

began a shipbuilding venture in Blackwall, and from then until 1847, the company built five Rhine paddle steamers, two British paddle steamers, and two small warships for the Royal Navy.

In 1821, John Rennie, Jr. and George Rennie took over the Albion Ironworks begun by John Rennie, Sr. on the south bank of the River Thames at Blackfriars, directly across from the City of London. From 1838-1909, J. & G. RENNIE provided the engines for thirteen warships, including the ironclad frigate HMS *Boadicea* in 1871. In 1858, the firm started a shipyard at Greenwich, and from 1859-1909, it produced some twenty-five vessels, including six gunboats, two for the Royal Navy, two for Brazil, and two for Mexico. In 1915, J. & G. Rennie left London, closing down both facilities. JOHN SEAWARD began building marine steam engines for commercial steamers in 1829, and from then until his death in 1858, he built the engines for thirteen small warships of the Royal Navy.

*River Medway*
Private shipyards on the River Medway were concentrated around the town of Rochester and its northern suburb of Frinsbury across from Chatham. Here they were in close proximity to Chatham Royal Dockyard, where their ships could be properly outfitted and armed.

JOSHUA & THOMAS BRINDLEY established a shipyard at Rochester on the west bank of the River Medway late in the eighteenth century. From 1794-1814, the yard produced nineteen warships, including the 74-gun ships *Aboukir* (1807), *Cressy* (1810), and *Asia* (1811), as well as two 38-gun and two 36-gun frigates. At about the same time, JOHN AND MARY ROSS established a shipyard on the east bank of the River Medway across from Rochester. The Ross shipyard produced twelve warships from 1795-1814, including the 74-gun ships *Vigo* in 1810 and *Stirling Castle* in 1811. The yard also built three 38-gun and one 36-gun frigates in that period.

The GREAVES SHIPYARD, located on the west bank of the River Medway at Rochester, built one 32-gun ship in 1785 and the 74-gun *Bellerophon* in 1786, which participated in both the Battle of the Glorious First of June in 1794 and the Battle of Trafalgar in 1805. Another Rochester shipbuilder, J. HENIKER, produced five warships, including one 64-gun, one 60-gun, and one 50-gun ship, from 1758-74. The remaining Rochester shipyard of note was that of JOHN PELHAM, who from 1807-15 produced eight warships for the Royal Navy, including one 58-gun ship and one 36-gun frigate.

**The English Channel**
During the age of sail, the southern coast of Hampshire, near the important port city of Southampton, and the Isle of Wight was the second most important area of naval construction in Great Britain. Being located near the large Royal Dockyard and naval base at Portsmouth, shipyards in that region were awarded many contracts by the Admiralty when their own Royal Dockyards could not keep up with the demand for new warships. Proximity to a Royal Dockyard was advantageous since the ships built at such sites could

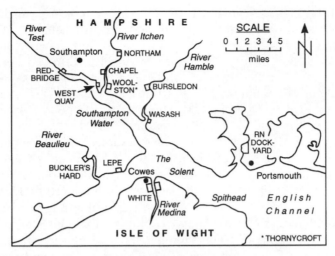

The Solent.

be readily towed to the dockyard for final fitting-out. In the age of steam, however, the importance of naval shipbuilding in that area declined in favour of increased activity on the Clyde, the Tyne, and other locations.

*Buckler's Hard*

The greatest naval shipbuilding centre along the Channel coast was at Buckler's Hard on the west bank of the River Beaulieu about 50 miles south of Southampton. The construction of naval vessels at Buckler's Hard began in the late seventeenth century after Bailey's Hard, an earlier site 7 miles further upriver, became inadequate for the building of larger vessels. In 1698, RICHARD HERRING built the 48-gun ship *Salisbury*. The 680-ton *Salisbury*, which measured 134ft in length and 34ft in beam, was one of four ships contracted out to Hampshire shipyards by the Admiralty at the time. The three sister-ships of the *Salisbury* were built at Southampton, Northam, and Cowes. To build the *Salisbury*, Richard Herring had a workforce of about 100 men, including 40 shipwrights and 16 sawyers.

In 1743, JAMES WYATT took over the yard at Buckler's Hard, but his efforts lasted only three years after producing a single 24-gun ship in 1745 and one 18-gun ship in 1746. The yard was then acquired by JOHN DARLEY, who began building the 44-gun *Woolwich*. John Darley went bankrupt in 1748, and the *Woolwich* had to be completed by Moody Janverin at nearby Lepe in 1749. Buckler's Hard was then taken over by HENRY ADAMS in 1749, and he promptly produced a 24-gun sloop in the first year. That ship was later followed by two 24-gun ships in 1756 and two 32-gun ships in 1757-8.

Henry Adams continued to build warships intermingled with merchant vessels at Buckler's Hard for the next 35 years. Those warships included two 28-gun ships and one 32-gun ship in 1793. In 1774, he launched the 64-gun *Vigilant* from a new slipway installed at the yard. This was followed by a 44-gun frigate in 1777, a 50-gun ship in 1779, and another 28-gun ship, also in

1779. In 1781, Henry Adams built the 64-gun *Agamemnon*, which displaced 1380 tons and measured 160ft in length and 44ft in beam. The *Agamemnon*, Nelson's first capital-ship command and reputedly his favourite, fought in the Battle of the Saintes in 1782, the Battle of Copenhagen in 1801, the Battle of Trafalgar in 1805 and the Battle of San Domingo in 1806.

Henry Adams then built a 44-gun frigate in 1782, a 32-gun ship in 1783, and the 64-gun *Indefatigable* in 1783. Those ships were followed by a 44-gun frigate in 1787 and the 74-gun, *Illustrious* in 1789. The 1640-ton, 140ft long *Illustrious* was one of three sister-ships awarded to Hampshire private shipbuilders at the time, the others being the *Elephant* built by George Parsons at Bursledon and the *Saturn* produced by Thomas Raymond at Northam. A 36-gun frigate built in 1791 was the last warship produced by Henry Adams before he turned the yard over to his sons, Balthazar and Edward, in 1793.

BALTHAZAR AND EDWARD ADAMS continued to build warships for the Royal Navy, including a 32-gun ship in 1794, a 38-gun frigate in 1797, and two 16-gun ships. They built the 74-gun *Spencer* in 1800, and that ship was followed by a 36-gun frigate in 1801, three 18-gun ships in 1802, and one 36-gun frigate in 1803. In 1804, the Adams Brothers built another 74, the *Swiftsure*. By that time, the workforce at the shipyard consisted of some 90 people, including 35 shipwrights. Next came four 16-gun brigs in 1804-6, a 38-gun frigate in 1807, and the 74-gun *Victorious* in 1808.

The Adams Brothers had not been receiving an adequate return from their naval construction projects, and after completing the 74-gun *Hannibal* (III) at a loss in 1810, they went bankrupt in the following year. Although the firm was dissolved, the brothers attempted to continue to build ships at Buckler's Hard independently. EDWARD ADAMS held on for another year, and he completed two 18-gun ships in that period. BALTHAZAR ADAMS lasted until 1813, and he completed two 20-gun ships before giving up naval construction completely in favour of building strictly merchant vessels. This ended naval shipbuilding at Buckler's Hard.

### Lepe

Lepe is located on the northern bank of The Solent near the mouth of the River Beaulieu, about 4 miles east of Buckler's Hard and 9 miles south of Southampton. MOODY JANVERIN began building naval vessels at Lepe with the 50-gun ship *Greenwich* in 1747. After producing a 28-gun ship in 1749, Janverin completed the 44-gun frigate *Woolwich*, which had been under construction by John Darley at Buckler's Hard before he went bankrupt in 1748. Janverin left Lepe after completing the *Woolwich*, but one additional naval vessel was later built at the yard. In 1765, Henry Adam's of Buckler's Hard used the Lepe yard to build the 64-gun *Europe*, which displaced 1370 tons and was 160ft long.

### Bursledon

The second most important Hampshire shipyard involved in naval construction was at Bursledon on the River Hamble, about 3 miles upriver from Southampton Water and 4 miles south-east of Southampton. WILLIAM WYATT established a shipyard at Bursledon before 1690, and he immediately began to build Third Rate and Fourth Rate ships for the Royal Navy. In 1692, he built the 80-gun, 1160-ton *Devonshire*, and this was followed by the Fourth Rate *Winchester* one year later. William Wyatt died in 1693, and the shipyard was taken over by his widow, Anne Wyatt. ANNE WYATT completed two 80-gun ships, the *Lancaster* in 1694 and the *Cumberland* in 1695, before turning the shipyard over to Richard Herring.

RICHARD HERRING built a 24-gun ship in 1696, within a year after acquiring the Bursledon yard, but naval shipbuilding then ceased at Bursledon until the 1740s. PHILEMON EWER took over the Wyatt shipyard in 1724, but it was not until nearly 20 years later that he began to build warships for the Royal Navy. Naval production resumed with a 14-gun sloop in 1744, a 50-gun ship in 1745, a 24-gun ship in 1746, and the 60-gun, 1200-ton *Anson* in 1747. During this same period, RICHARD HEATHER built a 24-gun ship in 1745 and a 44-gun frigate in 1747 at another nearby site in Bursledon before he moved on to Gosport. In 1749, JOHN SMITH built a 44-gun frigate at Bursledon, and later in 1758, MOODY JANVERIN produced a 28-gun ship at the site.

In 1780, Thomas Calhoun entered into a partnership with John Nowlan, and they acquired one of the three shipbuilding sites at Bursledon. CALHOUN & NOWLAN subsequently produced four 36-gun frigates in 1781-4, and those ships were followed by two 32-gun ships in 1786-7. The firm went bankrupt upon completion of the last ship, and John Nowlan subsequently moved to Northam where he took over that yard from Thomas Raymond in 1790.

In 1780, GEORGE PARSONS acquired another of the three shipbuilding sites at Bursledon, and he soon produced one 32-gun frigate in that same year and a 36-gun frigate in 1783. In 1786, George Parsons built the 74-gun *Elephant*, one of three sister-ships produced at the time. The 1640-ton *Elephant*, which was nearly 140ft long, was a participant in both the Battle of the Glorious First of June in 1794 and the Battle of Copenhagen in 1801. Other ships of that class included the *Illustrious*, built by Henry Adams at Buckler's Hard, and the *Saturn*, built by Thomas Raymond at Northam. After completing a 44-gun frigate in 1786, George Parsons had no naval work for seven years.

George Parsons resumed naval shipbuilding at Bursledon with a 16-gun ship in 1793, a 32-gun ship in 1794, and a 40-gun frigate in 1797. Those ships were followed by four 36-gun frigates in 1799-1804. By that time, the shipyard had a workforce of forty, including fifteen shipwrights. George Parsons then built a 16-gun ship in 1804, a 36-gun frigate in 1805, and a 38-gun frigate in 1807. After completing that last ship, George Parsons gave up the shipyard which he had held for over 25 years.

In 1807, the Bursledon shipyard was acquired by the partnership of Richard Blake and John Scott, and in 1808, BLAKE & SCOTT produced its first warship, a 18-gun brig. A second slipway was added to the yard during the next two years, and in 1812, it was used to launch the 74-gun *Rippon*. The *Rippon* displaced 1740 tons and measured 175ft in length and nearly 50ft in beam. At about the same time, Richard Blake entered into a second partnership, this time with John Tyson. BLAKE & TYSON built warships at one of the alternative sites in Bursledon, including three brigs in 1809-12 and a 38-gun frigate in 1813. Those were the last sailing naval vessels produced at Bursledon.

## West Quay

In 1681, JOHN WINTER purchased a tract of land at West Quay on the western side of a small peninsular between the River Test and the River Itchen, just to the south of Southampton. This area has since been extended to form the harbour complex now known as Southampton Docks. John Winter began building Third and Fourth Rate ships at that site in 1690. He produced the 80-gun ships *Cornwall* in 1692 and *Norfolk* in 1693, as well as the 48-gun *Southampton*, also in 1693. John Winter then left West Quay and moved to Northam on the River Itchen, where he continued his shipbuilding activities.

In 1694, JAMES PARKER began building warships in the area, and in 1696, he launched a 32-gun ship at Southampton. Two years later in 1698, James Parker built the 48-gun *Dartmouth*, one of four ships in that class. Sister-ships of the *Dartmouth* included the *Worcester* built by Robert Winter at Northam, the *Salisbury* built by Richard Herring at Buckler's Hard, and the *Jersey* built by Joseph Nye at Cowes. This ended naval shipbuilding at West Quay in favour of better facilities available an Northam and Chapel on the nearby River Itchen.

## Redbridge

The shipyard at Redbridge near the narrow mouth of the River Test, about four miles west of Southampton, was used by WILLIAM WYATT of Bursledon fame in 1794 to build a 32-gun ship. The Redbridge yard was taken over by John Stigant in 1694, but it was then leased to John Knowler one year later. JOHN KNOWLER build a 32-gun ship in 1696, but no large warships were produced at Redbridge after that time. In 1796-8, Redbridge was used for the construction of small experimental warships, including two 18-gun ships and four even smaller schooners.

## Northam

In 1693, JOHN WINTER, a shipbuilder at West Quay on the River Test, acquired a tract of land for a shipyard at Northam on the west bank of the River Itchen at the north-east sector of Southampton. With his brother, Robert, John Winter built the 80-gun ship *Dorsetshire* and the 60-gun *Sunderland* for the Royal Navy in 1694. Upon completion of the 48-gun *Worcester* in 1698, naval shipbuilding ceased at the yard and throughout all of Hampshire until the 1740s.

GEORGE ROWCLIFFE took over the Winter shipyard at Northam in 1739, and in 1741, he produced his first naval vessel, a 28-gun ship, followed by two 44-gun frigates in 1743, a 24-gun ship in 1744, and the 50-gun, 980-ton *Advice* in 1746. George Rowcliffe died in 1746, and the shipyard was taken over by Henry Bird ten years later in 1756. HENRY BIRD, with his son, Henry Bird, Jr., built a 24-gun naval vessel in 1757, and one year later, they produced the

74-gun *Resolution*. After completing another 24-gun warship in 1759, the shipyard was idle for three years. In 1762, Henry Bird went into a partnership with Humphrey Davis, and BIRD & DAVIS produced only one 14-gun ship in 1763 before discontinuing naval construction.

In 1778, THOMAS RAYMOND leased the Northam shipyard, and he soon began producing warships for the Royal Navy, including a 32-gun ship in 1780 and two 44-gun frigates in 1782. Thomas Raymond went bankrupt in 1783, but he continued to supervise the construction of the 64-gun ship-of-the-line *Stately* in 1784, a 44-gun frigate in 1785, and the 74-gun *Saturn* in 1786 for the Royal Navy. In 1790, Thomas Raymond vacated the Northam shipyard, and the site was taken over by John Nowlan, the former partner of Thomas Calhoun at Bursledon. JOHN NOWLAN produced only one naval vessel, a 32-gun ship, in 1794 before his death one year later. There was no naval construction at the yard for the next ten years.

In 1805, the Northam shipyard was acquired by ROBERT GUILLAUME, and he immediately began producing warships for the Royal Navy. He produced two 12-gun brigs in 1805-6, a 22-gun sloop in 1806, and two 18-gun brigantines in 1807 before building a 38-gun frigate, also in 1807. Over the next two years, the yard produced four small naval vessels with less than twenty guns each, and it then built a 36-gun frigate in 1809 and a 38-gun frigate in 1810. Also in 1810, Robert Guillaume built the 74-gun *Conquestadore*, the last major warship built in Hampshire. The *Conquestadore* was one of a mass order for sixteen such vessels to be built in private yards and one of the four built in Hampshire. The last naval vessel built by Robert Guillaume was a 36-gun frigate completed in 1811.

In 1812, the Northam shipyard was taken over by the partnership of WILLIAM AND JAMES DURKIN. The Durkins built only one naval vessel, an 18-gun ship, in 1813, and their work after that consisted mainly of building and repairing small packet boats. In 1824, the yard was acquired by JOHN KING, a shipbuilder on the Thames, who used the yard to produce several sailing vessels.

In 1837, as the age of sail was slowly ebbing, the Northam shipyard was acquired by Day, Summers & Co., owners of an iron works in Millbrook. Under DAY, SUMMERS & CO., Ltd., the shipyard enjoyed a long history of producing paddle steamers, coastal vessels, and other merchant vessels well into the twentieth century. The yard, however, was not involved in naval construction to any significant degree during that period, and it played only a minor role in such activity during the First World War. The shipyard was sold to John I. Thornycroft Co. Ltd. in 1929, and it was used thereafter primarily as a ship repair facility.

### Chapel

As West Quay diminished as a shipbuilding centre, shipyards were developed at Northam and then Chapel, which is also located on the west bank of the River Itchen, about five miles south of Northam in the eastern part of Southampton. Robert Carter built two naval vessels for the Royal Navy at

Chapel in 1746, a 24-gun ship and the 50-gun *Colchester*, after which production was limited to merchant vessels. In 1772-7, the yard was leased by ROBERT FABIAN, who produced the 50-gun *Renown* in 1774. In 1777, THOMAS RAYMOND acquired the Chapel shipyard, and he built two 28-gun ships in 1778-80 before going bankrupt in 1783.

There was little activity at Chapel until after the turn of the century, when ROBERT ADAMS took over the yard. He also went bankrupt in 1807, but only after producing five small naval vessels carrying 10-16 guns each. RALPH THOMPSON then acquired the yard, and he built one 18-gun ship in 1807 before giving up the yard to William Burridge, who converted the facility into a wharf.

### Woolston

In 1910, JOHN I. THORNYCROFT CO. LTD. acquired an existing shipyard at Woolston, on the east bank of the River Itchen across from and two miles south of Chapel. Thornycroft had been building ships at its Chiswick yard on the River Thames, but the firm needed larger facilities for its increasing ship construction programme. The Woolston facility had a river frontage of 2000ft and other advantages over the restrictive confines of the upper Thames. The Thornycroft Woolston Works soon began building paddle steamers, and in 1907, it built its first destroyer, HMS *Tartar*, for the Royal Navy. The Chiswick yard was eventually closed down in 1909, leaving all production to the Woolston Works.

By 1914, the Woolston Works had built an additional sixteen destroyers, as well as a number of other small craft, for the Royal Navy. Production during the First World War included twenty-four destroyers, three submarines, and a variety of other small warships for the Admiralty. By the end of the war, the facilities at Thornycroft Woolston included thirteen slipways, three of which were covered, and those slipways could accommodate ships up to 400ft in length. Thornycroft had a workforce of 5000 at that time. After the First World War, Thornycroft switched over to the production of small merchant vessels, and it was not until 1926 that it resumed building warships.

Over the next thirteen years, Thornycroft produced ten destroyers for the Royal Navy, five destroyers for Chile, and two destroyers and several other small naval vessels for Canada. During the Second World War, the shipyard built sixteen destroyers, several sloops, and a number of other warships. Many naval orders were cancelled at the end of the war, but Thornycroft was allowed to continue work on two destroyers, which it completed in 1948. In 1952, Thornycroft built one destroyer and several minesweepers, and during the period 1957-67, it produced five frigates and a variety of other warships for the Royal Navy.

In 1966, John I. Thornycroft Co. Ltd. was taken over by Vosper Ltd. of Portsmouth, which had also been building small naval craft, to become VOSPER THORNYCROFT LTD. In 1977, the Woolston Works was nationalised, and in 1985, it came under the state-controlled British Shipbuilders, but a year later in 1986, the shipyard was returned to private ownership. From 1978 to

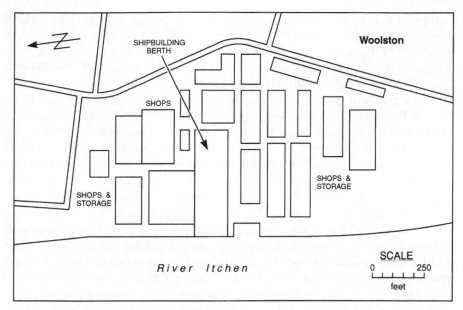

SHIPBUILDING
BERTH

Woolston

SHOPS

SHOPS &
STORAGE

SHOPS &
STORAGE

*River Itchen*

SCALE

0            250

feet

Vosper–Thornycroft.

1989, Vosper Thornycroft built ten minesweepers for the Royal Navy and a number of patrol craft and other small warships for foreign nations. Since 1966, Vosper Thornycroft had built nearly 300 ships for over thirty different users, and it continues to design and build small warships for a variety of customers. The current facilities of Vosper Thornycroft feature a covered main shipbuilding berth, and the company now employs over 3000 personnel in all departments.

*Isle of Wight*
In 1694, JOSEPH NYE began naval shipbuilding at Cowes near the mouth of the River Medina on the northern tip of the Isle of Wight, and one year later, he went into a partnership with George Moore. The firm built a 32-gun ship in 1696, and in 1698, it produced the 48-gun, 680-ton *Jersey*, one of four ships of the same type built at Hampshire yards at that time. The completion of that ship heralded an end of naval construction by private yards in the area until the 1740s.

PHILEMON EWER acquired Joseph Nye's former yard in 1745, and he immediately began the construction of warships for the Royal Navy. In 1746, he built the 44-gun frigate *Salisbury*, and that ship was followed by the 70-gun *Vanguard* in 1748. Philemon Ewer died in 1750, and the yard was taken over by his son-in-law, PLEASANT FENN. Pleasant Fenn built a 28-gun ship in 1758, but did no further naval construction. Robert Fabian, who began shipbuilding at Chapel in 1772, also leased the shipyard at Cowes two years later in 1774. ROBERT FABIAN built a 28-gun ship in 1777 before producing the 64-gun *Repulse* in 1780. He then produced a 32-gun ship in 1781 and a 44-gun frigate in 1784.

Robert Fabian died in 1786, and the yard was taken over by his son, Robert Fabian, Jr. ROBERT FABIAN, JR. continued the work begun by his father, and he launched the 74-gun *Veteran* in 1787. The shipyard was acquired by Robert Adams in 1803, but five years later, it was taken over by Daniel List. DANIEL LIST built two small warships at East Cowes in 1808-10 and one at Fishbourne, about 4 miles south-east of Cowes. In 1812-14, he produced three 36-gun frigates at Binstead, about 5 miles south-east of Cowes.

THOMAS WHITE moved to West Cowes in 1815, and there he established the Thetis shipyard. His first ship was a 350-ton West Indiaman, and he continued to produce primarily merchant sailing vessels for the next 40 years. In 1859, his grandson, J. SAMUEL WHITE, took over the shipyard, as well as other shipbuilding activities on both sides of the River Medina. In 1860, White acquired the Falcon shipyard in East Cowes, and in 1889, he established an engine works in West Cowes, thus allowing him to use the East Cowes yard to build hulls and the West Cowes yard to outfit his ships. In 1885, White built its first torpedo-boat for the Royal Navy, and in the next 10 years, the yard produced thirty additional torpedo-boats and two A class destroyers.

In 1898, the White company was incorporated as J. SAMUEL WHITE CO. LTD. In 1911, White's West Cowes outfitting yard was equipped with an 80-ton hammerhead crane. By 1914, the Falcon (East) Yard had eight shipbuilding berths, the largest of which could accommodate ships up to 340ft long. During the war, improvements were made to the yard, including the extension of two slipways and the reconstruction of two older slipways with concrete slabs, steel sheds, and electric overhead travelling cranes. Up until the outbreak of the First World War, White had produced twenty-five destroyers for the Royal Navy and two destroyers for Chile. Four additional destroyers intended for Chile were taken over by the Admiralty in 1914 as a wartime measure.

White built an additional sixteen destroyers, two submarines, and a number of other warships for the Royal Navy during the First World War. At the end of the war, many orders for naval vessels were cancelled, but White was allowed to complete six of those warships. By the end of the war, the workforce at White's had reached 4500 employees, but as the workload began to decline after the war, that number gradually decreased. In 1920, White reverted back to merchant ship production, but from 1928 to 1939, the yard built seven destroyers and four sloops for the Royal Navy, three destroyers for Argentina, and two destroyers for Poland.

Production during the Second World War at White included fourteen destroyers and a number of other vessels for the Royal Navy. One additional destroyer was completed in 1947, but orders for an additional six destroyers had been cancelled. After the war, White again reverted to the production of small merchant vessels, but eventually a few orders from the Admiralty did come in. In 1950, White built one destroyer, and during the period 1954-9, it produced five frigates for the Royal Navy, two frigates for the Indian Navy, and several other naval vessels. From 1960 to 1965, the firm produced two frigates for the Royal Navy and two more for the New Zealand Navy. With the delivery of its last ship, the frigate HMS *Arethusa*, in 1965, the White shipyard was closed and the facilities were subsequently sold to British Hovercraft.

## East Coast

### Harwich and Ipswich

Naval construction at Harwich, off the North Sea coast, about 40 miles north of the mouth of the River Thames, began in the late eighteenth century. BARRETT & MUNDY produced two warships for the Royal Navy, the *Ipswich* and the *Yarmouth*, which were launched in 1694 and 1695, respectively. The TURNER shipyard built a 24-gun ship in 1755, and BARNARD & CO. produced two ships-of-the-line, the 74-gun *Arrogant* in 1764 and the 50-gun *Centurion* in 1774. Better shipbuilding facilities elsewhere finally led to the demise of shipbuilding in the Harwich area.

At Ipswich on the River Orwell, about 10 miles north-west of Harwich, J. BARNARD, the predecessor of Barnard & Co. of Harwich, built the 50-gun *Hampshire* in 1741. In the early part of the nineteenth century, the BAYLEYS shipyard at Ipswich built a 74-gun ship for the Royal Navy. As with Harwich, shipbuilding at Ipswich soon declined in favour of other locations having greater advantages.

### Hull

John Frame, a shipbuilder from Wapping on the River Thames near London, opened a new shipyard at Hull (Kingston-upon-Hull) on the River Humber, about 175 miles north of London late in the seventeenth century. Since this was done with the encouragement of the Admiralty, Frame was rewarded with a contract to build the 80-gun ship *Humber* at the new facility. She was launched in 1698, and this was the last warship built in the area until the 1740s. Naval shipbuilding resumed with a 50-gun ship built by the REED shipyard in 1744 and a 24-gun ship by BLAYDES in 1755. At the beginning of the nineteenth century, the GIBSON shipyard produced a 74-gun ship-of-the-line.

In 1853, as steam and iron were gradually replacing sail and wood, CHARLES AND WILLIAM EARLE began a shipbuilding business at Hull. In 1871, the company was incorporated as EARLE'S SHIPBUILDING & ENGINEERING CO. LTD., and soon thereafter, the company began to receive orders from the Admiralty. Earle's built two armoured corvettes for the Royal Navy in 1874. Turning to foreign orders, Earle's built two central-battery ships for Chile in 1874-5, and in 1878, it built an armoured corvette for Japan.

Earle's later built the armoured cruiser *Narcissus* in 1889, the protected cruisers *Endymion* and *St. George*, both in 1894, and two light cruisers in 1901, for the Royal Navy. Up until 1881, Earle's also built iron merchant ships, but in the following year, it switched over to building ships strictly out of steel. In addition to its warship production, the yard specialised in the construction of passenger/cargo ships, commercial steamers, and ferry boats. In 1900, the company went into liquidation and was idle for a year.

In 1901, a new company was formed under the same name, and the new owners poured substantial sums of money into the expansion and modernisation of the yard. By 1914, Earle's had produced some thirty-five ships, and the yard built three sloops and several tankers for the Royal Navy during the First World War. After the end of the war, Earle's resumed commercial production, and the yard built a number of cargo liners, lake steamers, and other vessels until 1931. Its workload continued to decline, and in 1932, the shipyard was taken over by National Shipbuilders Security Ltd. and dismantled.

### Tyne & Wear

Once the most important shipbuilding region on the British Isles, Tyneside was later overtaken by the River Clyde at the end of the nineteenth century. Shipbuilding naturally evolved around the great port city of Newcastle-upon-Tyne, which prospered as a result of its coal exports since the eighteenth century. The River Tyne had long been navigable to the port of Newcastle, and that prompted the establishment of shipbuilding activities on both sides of the river from Elswick to Jarrow. Of far lesser importance was shipbuilding on the River Wear, which empties into the North Sea about eight miles south of the River Tyne.

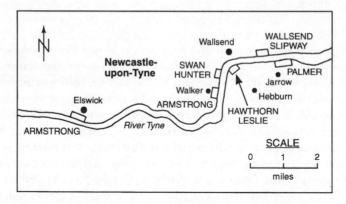

Tyneside.

During the age of sail, warship orders were rare in view of the area's remoteness from Royal Dockyards, which were usually used for outfitting ships built at private shipyards. At the beginning of the nineteenth century, GEORGE ROW did receive an order for a 74-gun ship-of-the-line, which he built at Newcastle. Another 74 was also built by SIMON TEMPLE of Shields in that period. It was not, however, until the age of steam and iron that Tyne and Wear yards came into prominence.

### ARMSTRONG

The name most associated with naval shipbuilding and naval ordnance at Tyneside is that of 'Armstrong'. In 1847, William G Armstrong established the ARMSTRONG ENGINEERING WORKS at Elswick, a western suburb of

Newcastle on the north bank of the River Tyne. The facility began on a 5-acre tract of land that featured four small workshops, and it was initially involved in the development and production of hydraulic machinery. The Elswick plant gradually expanded, and by 1852, it had a workforce of 325. In 1854, at the beginning of the Crimean War, Armstrong began studies on the improvement of field guns, and this led to the founding of the ELSWICK ORDNANCE WORKS in 1859.

The Elswick Ordnance Works was established as a separate facility for the express purpose of building breech-loading guns for the British Army, and it produced 3000 field pieces through 1863. In 1868, Armstrong got involved in shipbuilding by leasing the shipyard of Mitchell & Swan at Walker, another suburb of Newcastle on the west bank of the River Tyne, but further downstream. In the 1870s, Armstrong began to design and build a number of cruiser-type vessels at the Walker yard, and this led to the construction of the first modern protected cruiser, the *Esmeralda*, which was produced for Chile in 1882. The *Esmeralda* would be the first of a long line of 'Elswick' cruisers designed and built by Armstrong for foreign customers.

In 1882, Armstrong merged with Mitchell & Swan to form SIR W. G. ARMSTRONG, MITCHELL & CO. LTD. By that time, Armstrong had been knighted for his accomplishments in the development and production of superior ordnance for the military, especially for the development of a breech-loading gun. In 1883, Armstrong built another shipyard at Elswick, and thereafter, ships were built at both the Elswick and Walker yards. Armstrong continued to build protected cruisers for foreign governments, including two for China in 1886, one for Romania in 1888, and one for Argentina in 1890. Armstrong built the turret ship *Victoria* in 1890 and then produced two Second Class cruisers and three Third Class cruisers in 1891-2, all for the Royal Navy.

Armstrong built two A-class destroyers in 1894, and the firm was subsequently selected to build one of the first three experimental turbine-powered destroyers for the Royal Navy in 1899. From 1892-6, Armstrong produced seven more protected cruisers for South American nations, including three for Chile, two for Argentina, and two for Brazil. In 1897, Armstrong merged with the Sir Joseph Whitworth Co. Ltd. of Manchester, which had been a strong competitor of Armstrong in the development and production of heavy ordnance for the military forces, forming SIR W. G. ARMSTRONG, WHITWORTH & CO. LTD.

Joseph Whitworth had established an ordnance engineering firm at Openshaw near Manchester around the middle of the century. He began with the design and development of small arms, and ultimately, he invented the Whitworth rifle. Whitworth's attention then turned to larger-calibre weapons, and he produced field guns for the British Army in the late 1860s. Like Armstrong, Whitworth was subsequently knighted for his military and technical contributions to the nation. The Whitworth Works was incorporated as Sir Joseph Whitworth Co, Ltd in 1874, and ten years after the death of Whitworth in 1887, his heirs agreed to the merger with Armstrong in 1897.

After the merger with Whitworth, Armstrong continued to build warships for the Royal Navy and for foreign navies. During the remainder of the nineteenth century, Armstrong produced two coastal defence battleships, the *Harald Haarfagre* and the *Tordenskjold*, for Norway in 1897, the battleship *Yashima* for Japan in 1897, two more protected cruisers for Chile and two for China in 1897-8, one protected cruiser for Spain in 1898, and two light cruisers for the United States, the *New Orleans* in 1898 and the *Albany* in 1900. The yard also built one Third Class cruiser for the Royal Navy in 1898. In 1900, the year in which Sir William Armstrong died, his industrial empire covered 230 acres of land, and it employed over 25,000 workers.

The Elswick shipyard had a frontage of 2500ft, and its facilities included three large slipways and six smaller ones, but it had no dry dock. The Elswick yard also was equipped with a 150-ton hydraulic crane, and it had a machine shop 1000ft long. The original Walker yard, later referred to as the High Walker shipyard or the 'Navy Yard', had 70 acres of land with a river frontage of over 5000ft. The High Walker yard, which had become the primary producer of warships, had eight slipways ranging in length from 800 to 1000ft. The nearby Low Walker shipyard had only 30 acres of land, a waterfront length of 1000ft, six slipways ranging in length from 450 to 650 feet, and it was used primarily for the construction of commercial vessels.

After the turn of the century, Armstrong produced the pre-Dreadnought battleships *Swiftsure* in 1904 and *Superb* in 1909 and the battlecruiser *Invincible* in 1908. The yard also built the armoured cruisers *Lancaster* (1901), *Hampshire* (1905), and *Achilles* (1907), the light cruiser *Newcastle* in 1910, five Third Class cruisers in 1904-14, and one F-class destroyer in 1908. The firm also built two additional battleships, the *Norge* and the *Eidsvold*, for Norway in 1900, two additional battleships, the *Hatsuse* and *Kashima* for Japan in 1901 and 1906, respectively, and a protected cruiser for Turkey in 1903. Up until 1910, the Elswick Ordnance Works had been producing complete 12in gun turrets for capital ships of the Royal Navy.

In 1912, Armstrong completed the Dreadnought battleship *Monarch* for the Royal Navy. The *Monarch* was one of the first capital ships to mount the new 13.5in guns, causing those ships to be referred to as 'Superdreadnoughts'. Armstrong had built a unique 27,500-ton battleship for Brazil, with fourteen 12in guns in seven twin turrets, but when Brazil could not pay for the vessel, the incomplete ship was sold to Turkey early in 1914. As the war clouds loomed in Europe, Britain confiscated the ship, and it entered service with the Royal Navy as HMS *Agincourt* in August 1914. When the war broke out, Armstrong was building a battleship with ten 14in guns for Chile, but that ship was also requisitioned and completed as HMS *Canada* in 1915.

During the war, Armstrong built the battleship *Malaya*, one of the 15in gun *Queen Elizabeth* class, in 1916 and the battlecruisers *Courageous* and *Furious*, both in 1917. The *Courageous* and *Furious* were later converted to aircraft carriers by Devonport Royal Dockyard under the terms of the Washington Naval Treaty. Armstrong produced the hulls of two battleships, the *Eagle*, a sister-ship of the *Canada*, and the *Hermes*, both of which were also completed as aircraft carriers at Devonport. Wartime production also included the light cruisers *Birmingham* in 1914, *Centaur* and *Concord*, both in 1916, *Danae* in 1918, and the *Delhi* and *Dunedin*, both in 1919, as well as eight submarines.

Armstrong had begun work on the light cruiser *Emerald* in 1918 and launched the ship in 1920, but the vessel was finally completed by Chatham Dockyard in 1926. From 1900 to 1910, the total workforce at Armstrong remained relatively constant at about 25,000 employees, but as the First World War approached, the number of workers gradually increased until reaching a peak of 31,000 by the end of the war. After the war, Armstrong won an order to build one of two new battleships authorised as replacements for older battleships, and HMS *Nelson* was completed in 1927. During the post-war period, Armstrong also completed three submarines for the Royal Navy.

After the war, Armstrong produced a number of merchant ships, including the liners *Ausonia* (1921) and *Ascania* (1925) for Cunard, the *Berlin* (1925) for Germany, and the *Gripsholm* (1925) for Sweden. In 1928, Armstrong, Whitworth & Co. Ltd. merged with its arch rival, Vickers Ltd. of Barrow-in-Furness, and formed VICKERS-ARMSTRONG, LTD. Vickers-Armstrong (Tyne) then built the passenger liner *Arkadia* for Greece in 1931.

Armstrong was selected to build the lead ship of the five new 35,000-ton battleships of the *King George V* class authorised for the Royal Navy after the expiration of the disarmament treaties. The yard completed HMS *King George V* in 1940. In that period, Vickers-Armstrong (Tyne) also produced the two *Southampton* class light cruisers *Newcastle* and *Sheffield*, both in 1937, as well as three destroyers and three submarines prior to the Second World War. Armstrong then became the lead shipyard for the famous 'Tribal' class destroyers, and it built eight of the twenty vessels of that class that were eventually produced.

Production during the Second World War included the aircraft carrier *Victorious* (1941), the aircraft maintenance carrier *Perseus* (1945), the light cruiser *Swiftsure* (1944), eighteen additional destroyers, and three submarines. After the war, Vickers-Armstrong production at its Tyne facility was gradually phased down in favour of keeping production going at its Barrow facility, and by the 1950s, shipbuilding at the Tyne facility had virtually ceased.

Despite its start as an engineering works at Elswick, Armstrong generally did not produce the machinery for the vessels that it built, especially in the later years. The firm often obtained its turbine engines directly from Parsons, but the nearby Wallsend Slipway and Engineering Co. Ltd. provided most of its machinery requirements. Armstrong occasionally used machinery produced by its sister Vickers Barrow facility, and at other times, it obtained engines from other shipbuilders, such as Hawthorn Leslie and John Brown. Boilers were usually obtained from firms that specialised in their manufacture, such as Babcock & Wilcox and Yarrow.

## SWAN HUNTER

In 1860, Wigham Richardson established the Neptune Shipyard at Walker, an eastern suburb of Newcastle-upon-Tyne on the north bank of the River Tyne, to build iron ships. The Neptune yard was located a short distance to the north-east (downstream) from the Mitchell & Swan shipyard, also in Walker, later taken over by Armstrong in 1868. In 1899, Wigham Richardson was incorporated as WIGHAM RICHARDSON LTD., and four years later in 1903, the firm merged with C. S. Swan & Hunter, Ltd. In the meanwhile, C. S. Swan and John Hunter established a partnership in 1872, and in 1895, the partnership was incorporated as C. S. SWAN & HUNTER LTD. Two years later in 1897, Swan Hunter acquired a shipyard at Wallsend, a town on the north bank of the River Tyne four miles to the north-east of Newcastle-upon-Tyne.

Over the next four years, Swan Hunter built a number of commercial vessels, including the passenger liners *Ultonia* (1898) and *Ivernia* (1900). In 1903, C. S. Swan & Hunter Ltd merged with Wigham Richardson Ltd. to form SWAN, HUNTER & WIGHAM RICHARDSON LTD. In that same year, the new company acquired additional facilities as well as a controlling interest in the Wallsend Slipway & Engineering Co., which would provide the machinery for most of the ships that it produced. By 1907, the Swan Hunter Shipyard covered 78 acres of land and had a river frontage of 4000ft. The yard had seventeen building berths, eleven of which had overhead cranes and four of which were covered, two graving docks, and two floating dry docks. Its workforce then numbered 7000.

Swan Hunter continued the production of passenger liners, including the *Mauritania* (1907), *Franconia* (1911), and *Laconia* (1912) for the Cunard Line as well as the *Argentina* for Spain in 1913. The firm also began taking orders for warships from the Admiralty, and it built four destroyers for the Royal Navy before the outbreak of the First World War. Wartime production included the light cruisers *Comus* (1915) and *Coventry* (1918), over twenty-five destroyers, and three submarines. By the end of the war, Swan Hunter had four additional slipways, all of which had overhead cranes, bringing the total to twenty-one with fifteen having overhead cranes. By then the workforce had reached a peak of 8000.

After the war, Swan Hunter resumed the production of merchant ships, building the passenger liners *Laconia* (II) (1922) and *Aurania* (1924) for the Cunard Line, *Giulio Cesare* (1921) for Italy, *Cuba* (1923) for France, and *Sobieski* (1939) for Poland. In the 1930s, Swan Hunter also produced the light cruisers *Sydney* (1936) and *Edinburgh* (1938), as well as ten destroyers. During the Second World War, HMAS *Sydney* disappeared without a trace after an encounter with the German auxiliary cruiser *Kormoran*, which also sank as a result of damage inflicted by the *Sydney* during the battle.

During the Second World War, Swan Hunter produced the battleship *Anson* (1942), the light cruisers *Mauritius* (1941), *Newfoundland* (1943), and *Superb* (1945), and over fifteen destroyers. The shipyard began work on the aircraft carrier HMS *Albion* in 1944, but that ship was not launched until 1947, and it was finally completed in 1954. Swan Hunter also began work on another aircraft carrier in 1942, the *Vengeance*, but with the war winding down in 1945, work was suspended and it was towed to Portsmouth Dockyard. In 1956, the incomplete carrier was purchased by Brazil, and after extensive modernisation at Portsmouth, the ship joined the Brazilian Navy as the *Minas Gerais* in 1960. Swan Hunter also completed the light cruiser HMS *Lion*, which was begun by Scott's of Greenock on the River Clyde but was cancelled after its launch in 1945.

After the Second World War, Swan Hunter produced five destroyers for the Royal Navy in 1948-54. The firm later built the passenger liners *Bergensfjord* for Norway and *De Grasse* for France, both in 1956. In 1966, Swan Hunter merged with Smith's Dock Co. Ltd. of Middlesborough on the River Tees, about 35 miles south-east of Newcastle-upon-Tyne, under ASSOCIATED SHIPBUILDERS LTD. The name was soon changed, however, to SWAN HUNTER GROUP LTD. to take advantage of the reputation and recognition of the Swan Hunter name. In 1969, the company changed its name again to SWAN HUNTER SHIPBUILDERS LTD. Nationalised in 1977, the company was later privatised again, and it is now called SWAN HUNTER (TYNESIDE) LTD.

WALLSEND SLIPWAY

The WALLSEND SLIPWAY CO. LTD. was established in 1871 at Wallsend, a town on the north (left) bank of the River Tyne about four miles north-east of Newcastle-upon-Tyne. The firm was formed by several steamship companies that banded together to provide a joint facility for the repair of their vessels. In 1874, the company began to build engines and boilers, and four years later in 1878, it changed its name to WALLSEND SLIPWAY & ENGINEERING CO. LTD. In 1891, the firm began the construction of a large graving dock, which it completed in 1895. In 1903, Swan, Hunter and Wigham Richardson Ltd. acquired a controlling interest in the company. The company continued to specialise in the manufacture of marine engines and the repair of ships, leaving shipbuilding to others.

Wallsend Slipway provided the machinery for most of the warships built by Swan Hunter, ranging in size from light cruisers to battleships and aircraft carriers. The firm also supported Armstrong and the Royal Dockyards at Portsmouth and Devonport by providing the machinery for some of the warships built by those yards. After building marine engines for some one hundred years, including two world wars, Wallsend Slipway ceased engine production in the 1970s. The shipyard continued in the business of repairing ships with its then four dry docks, and in 1977, Wallsend Slipway became a member of British Shipbuilders Ltd. as part of the Tyne Shiprepair Group Ltd. One year later in 1978, the name of the company was changed to WALLSEND SLIPWAY ENGINEERS LTD., and it went out of business a short time later.

HAWTHORN LESLIE

In 1853, Andrew Leslie established a shipyard at Hebburn near Jarrow on the south bank of the River Tyne across from Newcastle. Before his retirement in 1886, Leslie built over 250 merchant ships, including forty cargo liners and twenty-five other cargo ships, and he also built several vessels for Russia. Upon Leslie's retirement, his company merged with the engineering firm of Robert and William Hawthorn to form R. & W. HAWTHORN, LESLIE & CO. LTD. It was only natural for these two companies to come together since Leslie used the engines produced by the Hawthorn Brothers in many of his ships. Robert Hawthorn had been building steam engines for locomotive, stationary and marine applications since 1820, and had developed a considerable expertise in that field.

After the merger, Hawthorn Leslie continued to build merchant ships for the commercial trade, including cargo liners, other cargo ships, tankers, and ore carriers. Hawthorn Leslie built the light cruiser *Bellona* in 1891 and three A-class destroyers in 1895 for the Royal Navy. The company then received an order to build the first experimental turbine destroyer with the new Parsons steam turbine engine for the Royal Navy, HMS *Vixen*, which it completed in 1900. Hawthorn Leslie then received a further order to build the second of three experimental steam turbine destroyers for the Royal Navy, HMS *Velox*, which it completed in 1904. By 1906, the yard had seven slipways of up to 680ft in length, a 450 × 68ft dry dock, and 3000 employees.

With the design of steam turbine destroyers firmed up by the Admiralty, Hawthorn Leslie went on to build twenty more destroyers through 1913. During the First World War, warship production by Hawthorn Leslie included

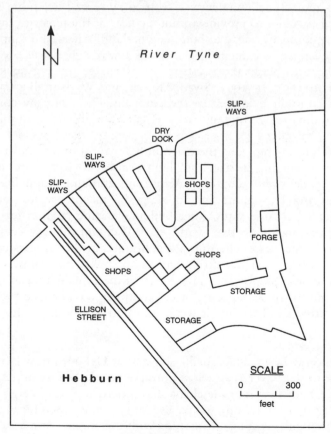

Hawthorn Leslie.

the light cruisers *Champion* (1915) and *Calypso* (1917) and fifteen additional destroyers. The firm also provided the machinery for a number of battleships and smaller warships built by Royal Dockyards and other private shipbuilders, including the battleships *Collingwood* (1910), *Monarch* (1913), *Centurion* (1913), *Marlborough* (1914), *Warspite* (1915), and *Royal Oak* (1916). During the war, Hawthorn Leslie also completed ten cargo liners. By the end of the war, the yard had added four more slipways for a total of eleven, and its workforce had reached a total of over 6000.

After the war, Hawthorn Leslie built several small passenger liners and a number of passenger-cargo ships, tankers, and tramp steamers. During the post-war period, the shipyard also produced the heavy cruiser *Sussex* (1929), the light cruiser *Manchester* (1938), twelve destroyers, two sloops, and the machinery for the heavy cruiser *Kent*, which was built by Chatham Dockyard in 1928. One of the destroyers built by Hawthorn Leslie was the famous HMS *Kelly* which distinguished herself in action during the early part of the Second World War. Hawthorn Leslie also built several sloops for Portugal in the early 1930s.

Production during the Second World War included the aircraft carrier *Triumph* (completed in 1946), the light cruisers *Naiad* (1940), *Cleopatra* (1941), and *Diadem* (1944), and ten destroyers. Hawthorn Leslie also provided the machinery for several additional warships produced by other builders. After the war, Hawthorn Leslie built five destroyers of the 'Battle' class up to 1948. The shipyard later completed two modern frigates, four naval oilers, and several other ships for the Royal Navy. In the post-war era, Hawthorn Leslie also produced some fifty tankers and fifteen dry cargo or bulk carriers. In 1977, the shipyard was nationalised, and with shipbuilding orders continuing to decline, the shipyard finally closed down in 1982.

## PALMERS

In 1851, Charles M Palmer and his brother, George, entered into a partnership as PALMER BROS. & CO., and in the following year, they established a shipyard at Jarrow on the south bank of the River Tyne about six miles east of Newcastle-upon-Tyne. The shipyard was subsequently expanded into a fully operational facility with the addition of engine works, boiler works, blast furnaces, and iron and steel works. After building a number of colliers and other commercial steam-powered vessels, Palmer produced the armoured floating battery *Terror* in 1856 and the ironclad frigate *Defence* in 1861 for the Royal Navy. These were followed by the armoured turret ships *Cerebus* in 1868 and *Gorgon* in 1871. In 1865, after the retirement of George Palmer, Charles Palmer incorporated the company as PALMERS SHIPBUILDING AND IRON CO. LTD.

In 1872, the company completed the ironclad frigates *Swiftsure* and *Triumph* for the Royal Navy. At the turn of the century, Palmers received numerous orders for warships from the Admiralty, including the battleships *Resolution* (1893), *Revenge* (1895), *Russell* (1903), *Lord Nelson* (1908) and *Hercules* (1911), the armoured cruisers *Orlando* (1888) and *Undaunted* (1889), eight light cruisers from 1886 to 1905, and twenty-five destroyers. During the period before the First World War, Palmers also built nearly 600 merchant ships, including fifty cargo liners, twenty tankers, and ten steamers.

By 1906, the Palmer Jarrow shipyard had six slipways, one dock 440 × 70ft in size, and a workforce of 7000. At that time, Palmer began leasing the idle shipyard of Robert Stephenson & Co. in nearby Hebburn to supplement its shipbuilding capacity. The Richardson yard had seven slipways, but of even greater importance was its much larger 700 × 90ft dry dock. During its prior existence, Richardson had built one light cruiser for the Royal Navy in 1891. In 1912, Palmers eventually purchased the Richardson shipyard for the primary purpose of merchant ship construction.

During the First World War, production included the battleship *Resolution* (1916), the battlecruiser *Queen Mary* (1915), the light cruiser *Dauntless*, twenty

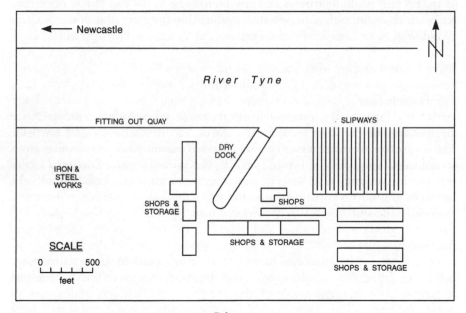

Palmers.

destroyers, and two submarines. The *Queen Mary* was one of the three battlecruisers sunk at the Battle of Jutland a year after her completion. During the war, Palmers also built the passenger liner *Colombo* for Italy in 1917. By the end of the war, Palmers had added another slipway, bring the total up to fourteen for both the Jarrow and Hebburn yards together, and the combined workforce had reached 9000 employees.

After the war, Palmers produced fifty tankers and ten cargo liners from 1920-30. In 1930 the firm completed the heavy cruiser *York*, and within the following two years, it built four destroyers. With shipbuilding workload continuing to diminish, Palmers went out of business after completing its last merchant vessel in 1927, and the shipyard was subsequently acquired by National Shipbuilders Security Ltd. In 1934, the dry dock of Palmers

Hebburn Dock was taken over by Vickers-Armstrong, and it continued to operate throughout the Second World War as PALMERS HEBBURN CO. LTD., a subsidiary of Vickers-Armstrong Ltd. In 1935, the rest of the shipyard was demolished,

## DOXFORD

The shipyard of WILLIAM DOXFORD & SONS LTD. was established in 1891 at Sunderland on the River Wear about ten miles south-east of Newcastle-upon-Tyne. From 1894 to 1901, the yard built six destroyers for the Royal Navy, and during the First World War, it produced an additional fifteen destroyers. During its existence, Doxford built merchant ships of up to 20,000-ton displacement and marine engines of all sizes and types, including reciprocating steam engines, turbine steam engines, and diesel engines. After the First World War, the yard no longer produced any major vessels for the Royal Navy, and its production of merchant vessels was very limited over the years. William Doxford & Sons Ltd. went out of business in 1966.

## West Coast

### Barrow-in-Furness

In 1871, a shipyard was established by BARROW IRON SHIPBUILDING CO. at Barrow-in-Furness on the Irish Sea about 100 miles north of Liverpool, England. Barrow initially built a few wooden steamship liners, and in 1877, it built its first warship for the Royal Navy, the frigate *Foxhound*. After converting to steel in 1881, Barrow built several steel steamship liners, averaging about 6000 tons displacement, in the next seven years. In 1886, Barrow built one of the first torpedo warships for the Royal Navy, the torpedo cruiser HMS *Fearless*, and several gunboats. In 1888, the shipyard became NAVAL CONSTRUCTION & ARMAMENTS CO. LTD., and during the next 10 years, it built several cruisers for the Royal Navy, including three light cruisers in 1889-90. In 1897, the shipyard was acquired by Vickers, Son & Co.

Edward Vickers had set up a steelworks in Sheffield before 1830, and with the expansion of that facility into an important armaments factory, he began to seek another outlet for his steel and ordnance products. In 1897, Vickers acquired the Naval Construction & Armaments Co. Ltd., as well as one of his arch rivals in the armaments industry, the Maxim Nordenfeldt Co., and the new firm became known as VICKERS, SON & MAXIM LTD. Vickers built two submarines for Sweden in 1887, and then it built the Royal Navy's first submarine, HMS *Holland*, in 1901. Vickers became the primary submarine producer for Great Britain Vickers, going on to produce over forty submarines before the end of the First World War. Many of Vickers' design innovations were incorporated into submarines produced by other shipbuilders.

The new Vickers company continued to receive Admiralty orders for surface vessels, and before the outbreak of the First World War, it had produced the battleships *Vengeance* (1901), *Triumph* (1904), *Dominion* (1905) and *Vanguard*

(1910) and the battlecruiser *Princess Royal* (1912). By 1906, the Vickers yard had six large slipways and six smaller slipways, but no dry dock. Its workforce was at 10,500 with nearly 4000 persons involved in shipbuilding and the remainder in gun-mounting and machinery. Vickers had also produced the protected cruisers *Powerful* (1897), *Niobe* (1899), and *Amphitrite* (1900), the armoured cruisers *Hogue* (1902), *King Alfred* (1903), *Euryalus* (1904), and *Natal* (1907), and two light cruisers in 1905, all for the Royal Navy.

For foreign navies, Vickers built the battleships *Mikasa* (1902), *Katori* (1905) and *Kongo* (1913) for Japan, the battleships *Minas Gerais* (1908) and *São Paulo* (1909) for Brazil, and the armoured cruiser *Rurik* for Russia in 1906. The battleship *Mikasa* was Admiral Togo's flagship at the Battle of Tsushima when the Japanese fleet destroyed the Russian fleet in 1904 during the Russo-Japanese War. The *Kongo* was a Dreadnought-type battlecruiser that was acquired by the Japanese as a prototype for building three more ships of this class in their own shipyards. Vickers also had many orders for large merchant ships during the period.

In 1911, Vickers, Son & Maxim Ltd. became just VICKERS LTD. In that year, Vickers completed the light cruiser *Liverpool*. Production during the First World War included the battleships *Emperor of India* (1914), *Erin* (1914), and *Revenge* (1916), as well as the light cruisers *Penelope* (1914), *Phaeton* (1915), *Cassandra* (1917), *Curlew* (1917), and *Calcutta* (1919). Vickers had begun work on the light cruiser *Diomede* before the end of the war, and it was allowed to complete that ship in 1922.

At the end of the war, the Vickers shipbuilding yard covered 50 acres of land, not including its engineering and other functions. The yard had a total of thirteen building berths, ranging in length from 330 to 520ft and including seven covered berths. All berths were served by electric or steam travelling cranes, and the fitting out basin had two 150-ton capacity hammerhead cranes and an assortment of other cranes. By then, Vickers had constructed a 500 × 60ft graving dock as well as two floating dry docks, one 420ft long with a lift capacity of over 5000 tons and the other with a 2000-ton lift capacity. The total workforce, including all departments, had grown to 30,000 employees.

After the war, Vickers concentrated on the production of merchant ships, including over a dozen passenger liners ranging from about 15,000 tons to over 20,000 tons. Most notable of these were the Cunard liners *Scythia* (1920), *Antonia* (1921), and *Carinthia* (1925). Vickers also received an order from the Admiralty for one of the 'County' class heavy cruisers, and it completed HMS *Cumberland* in 1928. In 1928, Armstrong, Whitworth & Co. Ltd. of Newcastle-upon-Tyne, a rival of Vickers in the armaments industry, experienced financial difficulties and merged with Vickers, forming a new company, VICKERS-ARMSTRONG LTD. To avoid confusion with the Tyne facility of Vickers-Armstrong, the Barrow facility will be refereed to as Vickers-Armstrong (Barrow) or just as 'Vickers'.

During the 1930s, Vickers built the light cruiser *Ajax* (1935), six destroyers, and some thirty submarines for the Royal Navy. The light cruiser *Ajax* would later gain fame as one of the three British cruisers that intercepted the

German pocket battleship *Admiral Graf Spee* off the coast of Uruguay and caused that ship to be scuttled by its own crew in Montevideo harbour in December 1939. Vickers also built several submarines for other countries during this period, as well as a training cruiser and three destroyers for Argentina. Vickers continued to build merchant ships, including several large passenger liners ranging up to over 20,000 tons. As the Second World War approached, Vickers switched over completely to the production of warships for the Royal Navy.

Production at Vickers continued to concentrate on submarine construction, and it built over eighty submarines in the period. During the war, Vickers also built the aircraft carriers *Illustrious* (1940) and *Indomitable* (1941), the aircraft maintenance carrier *Pioneer* (1944), the light cruisers *Nigeria* (1940), *Jamaica* (1942), *Spartan* (1943) and *Uganda* (1943) and four destroyers. Vickers had begun work on two additional aircraft carriers, the *Majestic* and the *Hermes*, but these ships could not be completed prior to the end of the war. The *Majestic* was later completed in 1955 and acquired by Australia where it was renamed the *Melbourne*. The *Hermes* was finally launched in 1953 and completed in 1958 for the Royal Navy.

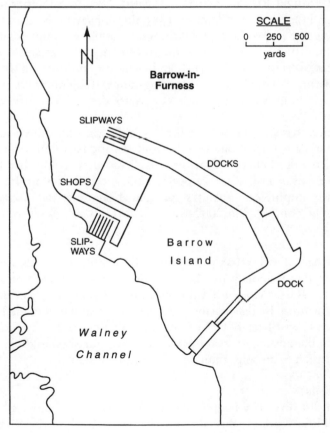

Vickers Barrow in 1941.

After the end of the war, Vickers resumed production of merchant ships, and from 1947 to 1960, it built some ten liners, including the 42,000-ton *Oriana* in 1960. In 1951, the shipyard began the construction of large tankers, building nearly twenty of these vessels by 1965, including the 62,000-ton supertanker *British Admiral* (1965). During the 1950s, Vickers built several warships for foreign navies, including two destroyers for Venezuela in 1953. Submarine production resumed in 1955, and six diesel-powered submarines were built for the Royal Navy in the next ten years. In 1960, Vickers produced Britain's first nuclear-powered submarine, HMS *Dreadnought*.

Vickers built the frigate *Mohawk* for the Royal Navy in 1963, four nuclear-powered ballistic missile submarines of the *Resolution* class in 1968, and six nuclear-powered attack submarines of the *Swiftsure* class in 1974-81. The yard also built two Type 42 guided missile destroyers in 1975 and 1979 respectively and the aircraft carrier HMS *Invincible* in 1977. For its foreign customers, Vickers produced two destroyers for Chile in 1959, two destroyers for Iran in 1969, three diesel-powered submarines for Brazil from 1971-5, and a Type 42 guided missile destroyer for Argentina in 1976.

Vickers was nationalised in 1976, and in 1981, the company began trading as VICKERS SHIPBUILDING & ENGINEERING LTD., a member of British Shipbuilders Ltd. Four years later, in 1985, the shipyard was again privatised, and it continued to produce submarines and other warships for the Royal Navy. From 1983-91, Vickers built seven nuclear attack submarines of the *Trafalgar* class, and in 1993, it began the production of *Vanguard* class submarines armed with the long-range Trident strategic missile. The yard has built three of those vessels to date, the fourth is nearing completion.

In addition to submarines, Vickers is also currently involved in the production of new amphibious assault vessels for the Royal Navy. In 1998, the yard completed the helicopter carrier HMS *Ocean* after its hull had been built by Kvaerner Govan Ltd. of Glasgow, Scotland, and it is now in the process of building two amphibious assault ships, the *Albion* and *Bulwark*, which are expected to be competed in 2002-3.

## River Mersey

During the age of sail, warships produced by private shipyards were usually fitted out at Royal Dockyards. In view of its remoteness from any Royal Dockyard, the River Mersey did not become a significant naval shipbuilding centre at that time. In that period, rare Admiralty orders included a 50-gun ship produced by O'KILL & CO. of Liverpool in 1744 and a few smaller naval vessels. With the advent of steam power and iron for shipbuilding, the River Mersey emerged as an important area for naval construction.

## CAMMELL LAIRD

The Cammell Laird story begins in 1824 when William Laird established the Birkenhead Iron Works at Birkenhead on the west bank of the Mersey River directly across the river from the port area of Liverpool. A few years later, he went into shipbuilding with his son, John, and began building steamers for the commercial trade as well as gunboats for foreign navies. In 1861, the company began trading as LAIRD BROS. LTD., but the shipyard was actually managed by William Laird's sons. Laird Bros. then produced the ironclads *Scorpion* and *Wivern* (both in 1861), the *Agincourt* (1865), and the *Vanguard* and *Captain* (both in 1870) for the Royal Navy. The firm also built two ironclads for Brazil in 1865, and two ironclads for The Netherlands in 1866-8. During the 40 years of existence of Laird Bros. from 1861-1903, the company produced some 300 merchant vessels.

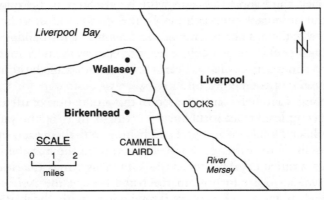

Merseyside.

Near the turn of the century, Laird Bros. began building battleships for the Royal Navy, including the *Royal Oak* (1894), *Mars* (1897), *Glory* (1900) and *Exmouth* (1903). In addition, the shipyard produced the battleships *Libertad* (1890) and *Independencia* (1891) for Argentina. Laird Bros. also got involved in producing smaller warships for the Admiralty, building two fast torpedo-boats in 1893 and completing the construction of over fifteen destroyers in 1894-1901. In 1903, Laird Bros. merged with Charles Cammell & Co., which produced armour plating for warships at its Sheffield steel works, to form CAMMELL, LAIRD & CO. LTD.

In 1905, Cammell Laird had two medium-size and five small slipways, three medium-size and two small dry docks, and a workforce of 3500. The company then acquired additional land to the south of the existing facility to expand its capability. With this new land, the size of the total shipyard was increased to nearly 100 acres. Six new slipways, ranging in size from 650 to 1000ft in length, were constructed in the new southern section of the yard. The centre section of the yard, between the old northern yard and new southern yard, was expanded to include a 15-acre outer basin with a 150-ton hammerhead crane, a 3-acre inner basin, and two new large dry docks, one 850ft and the other 700ft in length.

By 1907, the workforce at Cammell Laird had increased to 8000 employees. The company continued to build warships for the Royal Navy, including two light cruisers in 1904-1905 and fifteen destroyers of various classes from 1904-14. In 1912, Cammell Laird built the light cruiser *Melbourne* for the Australian Navy, and in the following year, it produced the Dreadnought *Audacious* for the Royal Navy. The firm also produced a number of passenger/cargo liners during that period, including the passenger liner *Argentina* in 1913 and the liners *Bergensfjord* and *Stavangerfjord*, both in 1913, for Norway. Production during the First World War included the 'C' class light cruisers *Caroline* (1914), *Castor* (1915), *Constance* (1916), *Caledon* (1917), and *Cairo* (1919), as well as some twenty destroyers.

Two light cruisers begun by Cammell Laird for Greece during the war were taken over by the Admiralty as a wartime measure. One was completed as the *Birkenhead* in 1915, and the other joined the Royal Navy as the *Chester* in 1916. Cammell Laird also had begun work on the new battlecruiser *Howe* in 1916, but the order was cancelled before the ship could even be launched. During the war, the old north yard was used primarily for building destroyers and other small craft less than 400ft in length, whereas the new south yard was used for the construction of larger vessels. By the end of the war, Cammell Laird had nearly 15,000 people on its rolls.

After the war, Cammell Laird reverted to the production of merchant ships, and it soon completed three small liners in 1920-2. In 1924, the yard built the 20,000-ton liner *De Grasse* for the French Line, and altogether, the shipyard completed some forty passenger/cargo liners during the 1920s. In the inter-war period, Cammell Laird produced the light cruiser HMS *Capetown* in 1922, and it received an order for one of the battleships of the *Nelson* class, HMS *Rodney*, which it produced in 1927. The *Rodney*, with the battleship *King George V*, was in on the kill of the German battleship *Bismarck* in May 1941.

Cammell Laird built the light cruiser HMNZS *Achilles* for New Zealand in 1933, as well as four destroyers in the 1930s. The *Achilles* was one of the three cruisers that tracked down the German pocket battleship *Admiral Graf Spee* at the beginning of the Second World War and caused that ship to be scuttled by her crew in the harbour of Montevideo, Uruguay. Reverting to the construction of merchant ships, Cammell Laird built several tankers and other merchant vessels in the early 1930s. One of Cammell Laird's crowning achievements was the completion of the 36,000-ton Cunard passenger liner *Mauretania* in June 1939, just three months before the outbreak of war. The *Mauretania*, like her larger cousins, the *Queen Mary* and *Queen Elizabeth*, served as a troopship during the war.

In 1938, Cammell Laird built the aircraft carrier *Ark Royal*, which had a distinguished carrier in the Second World War. The first British warship designed from the keel up as an aircraft carrier, she participated in several naval engagements early in the war. In 1941, her planes crippled the German battleship *Bismarck*, leaving her to be sunk by the British battleships *King George V* and *Rodney*. The *Ark Royal* was sunk by a U-boat in the Mediterranean later that year.

As the Second World War approached, Cammell Laird was awarded a contract to build one of the new 35,000-ton battleships of the *King George V* class, HMS *Prince of Wales*, which it completed in 1941. Although not yet fully ready for combat, the *Prince of Wales* immediately participated in the action against the German battleship *Bismarck*. The ship was later sunk by Japanese bombers off the coast of Malaya on 10 December 1941, just a few days after the Japanese attack on Pearl Harbor.

During the war, Cammell Laird built the aircraft carrier *Venerable* (1945), the light anti-aircraft cruisers *Dido* (1940) and *Charybdis* (1941), twenty destroyers, and some forty submarines. After the war, Cammell Laird again reverted to the construction of merchant ships, and from 1946 to 1985, it built sixty tankers and forty cargo liners. The company was restructured and renamed CAMMELL LAIRD (SHIPBUILDERS & ENGINEERS) LTD. in 1953. In 1955, Cammell Laird completed the 43,000-ton aircraft carrier *Ark Royal*, the largest warship ever built in Great Britain, and in 1960, the yard completed the 36,000-ton liner *Windsor Castle*. Admiralty orders during the post-war period also included the one guided missile destroyer, ten submarines, and three frigates.

In 1970, the company was again reorganised, becoming just CAMMELL LAIRD SHIPBUILDERS LTD., and production was concentrated on cargo liners, oil tankers, gas tankers, container ships, and bulk carriers. In 1977, Cammell Laird became part of British Shipbuilders Ltd. and continued construction of the same product line. Between 1982 and 1985, the yard built two Type 42 destroyers, and in 1985, the firm merged with Vickers Barrow. In 1989, the

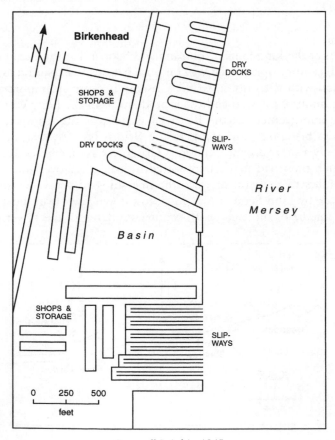

Cammell Laird in 1945.

shipyard completed a Type 22 frigate for the Royal Navy, but with its workload continuing to decline, Cammell Laird ceased production and closed its shipyard in 1993.

### Bristol

Although Bristol, which is located at the mouth of the River Severn, about 120 miles west of London, was an important port city as early as the twelfth century, it never developed into a major shipbuilding centre despite a few notable achievements. The *Great Western*, one of the first steamships to cross the Atlantic, and the *Great Britain*, the first iron ship and the first screw-propelled iron ship to cross the Atlantic, were both built in Bristol. Its remoteness from Royal Dockyards for fitting-out purposes precluded Bristol from receiving orders from the Admiralty for naval construction. As an exception to the rule, FRANCIS BAYLEY was given the contract to build the Fourth Rate *Oxford* at Bristol in 1677.

## PRIVATE SHIPYARDS IN SCOTLAND, WALES, AND NORTHERN IRELAND

### Clyde Yards

The union of the kingdoms of England and Scotland at the beginning of the eighteenth century opened the way for both nations to expand trade with one another and with the outside world. Glasgow became an important port for the importation of tobacco and other products from the New World, and this led to the improvement of the River Clyde to accommodate the increasing size of ships bringing those items to the British Isles. At first, the river was dredged only a short distance, and Port Glasgow was established to handle the cargo which then had to be transported by barges or overland to Glasgow some 20 miles to the east. In 1711, the first shipyard was established on the River Clyde by John Scott at Greenock just down river from Port Glasgow.

By the middle of the eighteenth century, dredging of the River Clyde was

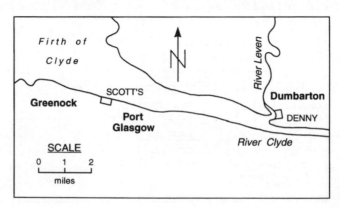

Clyde West.

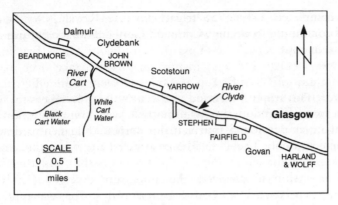

Clyde East.

accomplished all the way up to Glasgow, making that city a port in its own right. In 1790, the 20-mile long Forth and Clyde Canal was opened, linking the River Clyde just east of Glasgow with the River Forth at Grangemouth, 20 miles west of Edinburgh. The deepening of the River Clyde channel to Glasgow soon attracted additional shipbuilding activities to the area. Shipbuilding and related works expanded along both sides of the River Clyde during the last half of the nineteenth century, drawn to the area by a good large-city workforce, academic engineering support from the universities, and excellent shipbuilding features.

Although numerous sailing ships had been produced by Clyde shipbuilders during the age of sail, the area had been virtually ignored by the Admiralty in providing contracts for naval construction. Too far removed from any Royal Dockyard where ships built by private firms could be fitted-out and armed, the Clyde was not a significant factor in naval shipbuilding until the advent of steam power. Then the new Clyde shipyards, specialising in steam power and iron construction, came into their glory and eventually overtook the Tyne and Wear yards in the production of warships and large commercial vessels. By 1880, there were nearly seventy shipbuilding activities stretching from Glasgow down to the Firth of Clyde, which incidentally provided a good protected testing-ground for newly-built ships.

Late in the nineteenth century, the railway was extended to Glasgow, connecting the Clyde region with the rest of Britain. This reduced the value of the Forth and Clyde Canal to insignificance, and there was little traffic on the canal after that time. In addition to several large warships and liners built on the River Clyde over the years, the area also became noted for its submarine production. Since 1912, when the first submarine produced on the Clyde was built by Scott's, Clyde shipyards have produced eighty submarines for the Royal Navy and other world powers. Scott's built more than half that number and the remainder were built primarily by Beardmore, Fairfield, and Denny. While nowhere near as prolific as Vickers-Armstrong at Barrow-in-Furness, Scott's ranked second in British submarine production.

The First World War brought an increase in shipbuilding activities on the

Clyde, primarily as a result of increased orders for warships by the Admiralty. After the war, the shipbuilding workload dropped dramatically, and this caused a severe economic strain on shipyards throughout Great Britain. National Shipbuilders Security Ltd. was formed in 1930 to take over many of the smaller shipyards of Great Britain and operate them more efficiently without competition. This stopgap measure was not completely successful in avoiding shipyard closures, and several Clyde shipyards went out of business. Although most of the major shipyards survived this period, William Beardmore & Co. Ltd. became a casualty of the decline in workload, and it ceased operations in that same year.

The shipyards that survived the inter-war drought in shipbuilding production experienced a resurgence of orders for warships from the Admiralty as the Second World War approached. After the war, however, shipbuilding production again took a plunge, but this time the impact would be even more severe. After years of struggling to remain afloat, John Brown, Fairfield, Yarrow, Stephen, and Connell merged their shipbuilding activities under the Upper Clyde Shipbuilders Ltd. in 1968. This desperate measure, like that of the earlier National Shipbuilders Security Ltd., was not successful, and NSS Ltd. was dissolved three years later in 1971. Yarrow was the only survivor of that enterprise, and it continues to build ships today.

## SCOTT'S

In 1711, John Scott founded the SCOTT'S SHIPBUILDING & ENGINEERING CO. LTD., the oldest shipbuilding company in the world. The Scott's shipyard was located at Greenock on the south bank of the River Clyde about 25 miles west of Glasgow. Initially, Scott's built only fishing boats and other small craft, but in 1760, it began building larger vessels. In 1767, Scott's built its first graving dock, and in 1825, it acquired the William Brownlie iron and brass foundry, which later became known as the Greenock Foundry. Scott's built the steam-propelled frigate HMS *Greenock* in 1849.

Greenock Foundry provided the machinery for the battleships *Canopus* built by Portsmouth Dockyard in 1900 and *Prince of Wales* built by Chatham Dockyard in 1904. In 1905, Scott's built the armoured cruiser *Argyll* for the Royal Navy. In 1906, Scott's had six large and four small slipways, a graving dock 370ft long and 45ft wide, a 540 × 170ft fitting-out basin with a 120-ton capacity electric jib crane and an 80-ton electric travelling crane. Its workforce averaged 2500 shipyard workers and another 1800 employees in its engine works. Between 1910 and 1922, Scott's produced the battleships *Colossus* (1911) and *Ajax* (1913), the light cruisers *Caradoc* (1917), *Dragon* (1918) and *Durban* (1921), and ten destroyers.

Scott's also built the liners *Alaunia* (1913), *Andania* (1913), and *Albania* (1920). The yard is perhaps best known for its submarine production for the Royal Navy, which began in 1912 and has been continuous ever since. Scott's produced six submarines, including four of the 'S' class which were designed by Scott's and therefore so-designated, between 1914 and 1918. By the end of the war, Scott's workforce had reached a total of 6000 employees for both its shipbuilding facility and engine works. In the inter-war period, Scott's built the light cruisers *Galatea* (1935) and *Glasgow* (1937), the latter being of the new *Southampton* class, six destroyers, and several submarines.

During the Second World War, Scott's entire production capability was devoted to building ships for the Royal Navy, including the light cruisers *Bonaventure* (1940), *Scylla* (1942) and *Royalist* (1943), some twenty destroyers, and about ten submarines. Scott's had begun work on the light cruiser *Lion*, but after the end of the war, the ship was completed by Swan Hunter on the River Tyne. In recent years, Vickers-Armstrong of Barrow-in-Furness was given exclusive production of nuclear submarines while Scott's continued to build the conventional diesel-powered submarines.

BEARDMORE

In 1821, David Napier, a noted engineer and shipowner, built an engineering works at Lancefield on the right bank of the River Clyde near the centre of Glasgow and became famous for providing innovative engines for new steam vessels. In 1836, David Napier left for London and turned over his engineering works to his younger cousin, Robert Napier, who became the pioneer of shipbuilding on the River Clyde. Robert Napier formed the ROBERT NAPIER AND SONS company that same year, and in 1841, he moved across the river and established a shipyard at Govan. During its nearly sixty years of existence (1841-1900), Robert Napier built nearly 500 vessels ranging from wooden sailing ships to steam-driven steel vessels.

While the ships produced by Robert Napier were mostly merchant vessels, the yard also built warships, including four ironclad steam frigates for the Royal Navy in 1862-70. Napier went on to build the armoured cruisers *Northampton* (1878) and *Galatea* (1889) and three light cruisers in 1885-6. In addition to the ships built for the Royal Navy, Robert Napier also built an ironclad steam frigate for Denmark in 1863 as well as an ironclad ram and a monitor for The Netherlands in 1868. Robert Napier went out of business in 1900, and his shipyard was taken over by William Beardmore. Napier's Govan yard had three large and two small slipways and a workforce of 3000 employees at that time.

In the mid-nineteenth century, the Beardmore family established a forge at Parkland on northern bank of the River Clyde just east of Glasgow. By the end of the century, William Beardmore had developed the family-owned Parkland Forge into one of the largest steel-producing works in Great Britain. Looking for a steady outlet for the steel produced at the forge, William Beardmore procured land at Dalmuir just west of Clydebank in 1899 with the intention of building a shipyard at that site. When the Robert Napier shipyard at Govan became available in 1900, William Beardmore acquired the yard and retained the labour pool available at that site to get a jump-start on his plans for building ships.

In 1900, Beardmore was incorporated as the WILLIAM BEARDMORE & COMPANY LIMITED. Beardmore completed the armoured cruisers *Berwick* (1903) and *Carnarvon* (1904) at the Govan yard before moving the shipbuilding activities of the company to his earlier-acquired Dalmuir site. Once established at the Dalmuir site, Beardmore received numerous orders for warship construction from the Admiralty. In 1906, the Dalmuir shipyard had six large and four small slipways, a 200-ton capacity crane, and could accommodate ships up to 900ft long. Beardmore's workforce by that time was up to 10,000 employees, and the yard soon produced the battleships *Agamemnon* (1908), *Conqueror* (1912), and *Benbow* (1914). Beardmore also built two light cruisers in 1911-13. The battleship *Ramillies* was laid down by Beardmore in November 1913, but damage sustained during launching in September 1916 caused the ship to be towed to Liverpool for repairs. The Cammell Laird shipyard at Birkenhead performed the necessary repairs and completed the ship at that site one year later. During the First World War, Beardmore built the light cruisers *Galatea* in 1914, the *Inconstant* and *Royalist*, both in 1915, and the *Hawkins* class cruiser *Raleigh* in 1920. Also produced by Beardmore in this period were some fifteen destroyers and six submarines.

Having concentrated on the production of warships, the Beardmore shipyard declined rapidly at the end of the war, especially after an important order for a new battlecruiser had just been cancelled by the Admiralty. Beardmore was able to get orders for two liners, the *Lancastria* (1922) for the Cunard Line and the *Conte Biancamano* (1925) for the Italian Line. Beardmore later received an order from the Admiralty for one of the new 'County' class heavy cruisers being acquired for the Royal Navy in the late 1920s, and it completed the *Shropshire* in 1929. A year later, the William Beardmore company went out of business, and the shipyard was closed. The equipment at the shipyard was disposed of, and the facility itself was subsequently used for shipbreaking.

JOHN BROWN
Two brothers and former employees of Robert Napier, James and George Thompson, founded the CLYDEBANK FOUNDRY, an engineering works at Finnieston on the north bank of the Clyde River near the centre of Glasgow, in 1847. Three years later, they moved across the river and established a shipyard at Govan called the CLYDEBANK IRON SHIPYARD. From 1850-70, James and George Thompson built over 120 ships, and in 1866, Clydebank had 1500 employees. In 1872, the company went into receivership and the land was eventually taken over by Govan Dry Docks. The sons of George Thompson, James Roger Thompson and George Paul Thompson, then took over the company and purchased land further downstream on the north bank of the River Clyde, just opposite the mouth of the River Cart.

Over the next twenty-five years (1872-97), JAMES AND GEORGE THOMPSON LTD. built 140 ships, including the pre-Dreadnought battleship *Ramillies* (1893) and twelve light cruisers from 1885-92. Thompson also laid down the protected cruiser *Terrible* before the shipyard was taken over by the CLYDEBANK ENGINEERING AND SHIPBUILDING CO. LTD. in 1897. During the next two years, the Clydebank Engineering and Shipbuilding Co. Ltd. produced some thirty or more ships, including the pre-Dreadnought battleship *Jupiter* (1898) and several destroyers. The yard completed the protected cruiser *Terrible* in 1898.

John Brown started a steelmaking business in Sheffield, England in 1837. While this venture prospered over the next several decades, orders for steel plate and other steel products fluctuated considerably. John Brown then began to seek a more permanent outlet for the products of his steelworks, which were especially suited to shipbuilding. In 1899, John Brown acquired the Clydebank Engineering and Shipbuilding Co. Ltd. and established the JOHN BROWN CO. LTD. as the shipbuilding division of his steel works. In 1906, the John Brown shipyard had nine large slipways, and the company employed about 7500 people.

Prior to the First World War, John Brown built the armoured cruisers *Europa* (1899), *Sutlej* (1902), *Bacchante* (1902), *Leviathan* (1903) and *Antrim* (1905), the pre-Dreadnought battleship *Hindustan* in 1905, the battlecruisers *Inflexible* in 1908 and *Australia* in 1913, and two light cruisers in 1911-13. During that period, John Brown Co. also produced over fifty merchant vessels, including several large liners such as the *Saxonia* (1900), *Carmania* (1905), *Caronia* (1905), *Lusitania* (1907) and the *Aquitania* (1914). The *Lusitania* was torpedoed and sunk by a German submarine off the coast of Ireland on 7 May 1915 with the loss of 1200 lives, including 125 Americans, which contributed to the entry of the United States into the war two years later.

Wartime production included the Dreadnought battleship *Barham* in 1915 and the battlecruisers *Tiger* (1914), *Repulse* (1916) and *Hood* (1920). The *Barham* was sunk in November 1942 by a German submarine while operating in the Mediterranean. The *Hood* was considered to be the 'Pride of the Royal

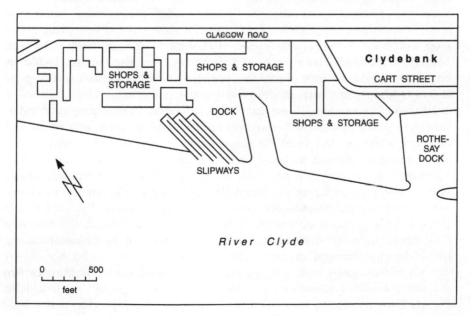

John Brown in 1945.

Navy' while she served as the flagship of the fleet from 1920 until the outbreak of the Second World War. She was lost in the epic battle against the German battleship *Bismarck* near Iceland in May 1941. John Brown also built the light cruisers *Canterbury* in 1916 and *Ceres* in 1917, as well as some fifty destroyers during the First World War.

By the end of the war the John Brown shipyard covered 80 acres of land and had a frontage of over 3000ft along the River Clyde. The yard had five large building berths ranging from 600 to 950ft in length, and five smaller building berths 450 to 600ft in length. The facility had a 5-acre tidal basin that was supported by a variety of cranes, including two of 150-ton capacity. The shipyard and the engine works had a combined workforce of some 9000 employees. At the end of the war, further naval construction ceased, and John Brown was barely able to survive on the limited orders for warships and merchant ships placed during the inter-war period.

When the Admiralty placed orders for several 'County' class heavy cruisers in the late 1920s, John Brown was awarded contracts for two of them, the *Australia* (1927) and *Canberra* (1928), both of which were purchased by the Royal Australian Navy. During that period, John Brown also built several destroyers as well as the hull for the light cruiser *Enterprise* (1926), which was later completed at Devonport Dockyard. In 1937, John Brown produced the light cruiser *Southampton,* which was the lead ship of a new class of modern light cruisers to be built for the Royal Navy.

In the inter-war years, John Brown turned again to the construction of merchant vessels. The shipyard built several Cunard liners during that period, including the *Franconia* (1923) and *Alaunia* (1925). John Brown received a big boost in prestige and financially by being selected to build the huge Cunard liners *Queen Mary* (81,000 tons) and *Queen Elizabeth* (84,000 tons), completed in 1936 and 1940, respectively. The *Queen Elizabeth*, painted overall in a dark grey, sailed on her maiden voyage in complete secrecy under wartime conditions and safely arrived in New York harbour without fanfare. Both ships would later serve as troop transports, primarily to bring American troops to Britain and then to return them home again after the war.

With war approaching in the late 1930s, shipbuilding was again diverted to warship construction. John Brown received an order to build one of the five new 35,000-ton battleships of the *King George V* class, the *Duke of York*, which the shipyard completed in 1941. The firm later received an order for HMS *Vanguard,* the last battleship ever built for the Royal Navy, which John Brown completed in 1944. During the Second World War, John Brown also produced the aircraft carrier *Indefatigable* (1944), the light cruisers *Fiji* (1940) and *Bermuda* (1942), and some twenty-five destroyers. The *Fiji* was the first of a new class of light cruisers designed in the late 1930s, and the *Bermuda* was the last of the eight ships produced of that class.

After the war, shipbuilding again took a downward turn, and John Brown was able to obtain a few orders to keep its shipyard going. In 1953, John Brown built the Royal Yacht *Britannia*, and in 1959, it produced the light cruiser *Tiger*. In 1969, the shipyard had just completed the Cunard liner *Queen*

*Elizabeth II (QE2)* of 66,000 tons, the last of the large ships built by John Brown before closing down the shipyard. In 1968, John Brown had became part of the Upper Clyde Shipbuilders Ltd., but without any further orders for ships, it began phasing out shipbuilding operations in that year. John Brown then became involved strictly in marine power engineering as JOHN BROWN ENGINEERING LTD. In 1997 the company was taken over by the Kvaerner Group and the facility was renamed the JOHN BROWN ENGINEERING WORKS of the Thermal Power Division, Kvaerner Energy Ltd.

FAIRFIELD

In 1852, John Elder became a partner in a marine engineering company in Govan which subsequently changed its name to RANDOLPH, ELDER & CO. in 1860. In 1863, the company acquired a 60-acre tract of land at Fairfield, just to the west of Govan on the south (left) bank of the River Clyde, and one year later, it established a shipyard there. With the retirement of the other partners, John Elder became the sole owner of the company, and in 1870, its name was changed to JOHN ELDER & CO. The company soon received Admiralty orders, and it built six steel corvettes for the Royal Navy in 1879 as well as the armoured cruiser *Nelson* in 1881. Elder also produced three passenger liners in 1883-5. In 1888, the company was reconstituted as the FAIRFIELD SHIPBUILDING & ENGINEERING CO. LTD.

The company soon became one of the major shipbuilders of the British Isles. Before the turn of the century, Fairfield had already produced the armoured cruiser *Australia* (1888), the protected cruisers *Diadem* (1899) and *Argonaut* (1900), and six light cruisers in 1889-99. During that period, the yard also built three passenger liners in 1890-3. From 1900 to the beginning of the First World War, Fairfield built the battleship *Commonwealth* in 1905, and the battlecruisers *Indomitable* in 1908 and *New Zealand* in 1912. Fairfield also produced the armoured cruisers *Cressy* (1901), *Donegal* (1901), *Aboukir* (1902), *Good Hope* (1902), *Bedford* (1903) and *Cochrane* (1907), three light cruisers in 1905-11, twelve destroyers; and eight submarines. The *Cressy, Aboukir*, and the Vickers-produced *Hogue* were the first major warships sunk by a German submarine during the First World War, demonstrating the true value of this new weapon for the first time. All three ships were sunk in rapid succession by *U-9* in the North Sea in September 1914, just one month after the outbreak of war. In the same period, the company also produced the passenger liners *Empress of Britain* (1906), *Royal George* (1907), *Royal Edward* (1907), *Empress of Asia* (1913), and *Empress of Russia* (also 1913). During the First World War, Fairfield continued its warship production with the battleship *Valiant* and the battlecruiser *Renown*, both in 1916 and the light cruisers *Undaunted* (1914), *Cardiff* (1917), *Carlisle* (1919) and *Colombo* (1919). The yard also built seventeen destroyers and two submarines before war production ceased. Fairfield had already begun work on the *Hood* class battlecruiser *Rodney* in 1916, but that order was cancelled before the ship could even be launched.

At the end of the war, the Fairfield shipyard encompassed 70 acres of land and had a frontage of 2600ft on the River Clyde. The yard had eleven slips up to 900ft in length, ten dry docks up to 900ft in length, a 6-acre basin with a 270ft entrance, and a 250-ton crane. At that time, Fairfield had 8500 employees. Shipbuilding work slackened after the end of the war, and Fairfield was hard-pressed to stay afloat. During the period between wars, Fairfield was able to get orders for the heavy cruisers *Berwick* (1928) and *Norfolk* (1930), the light cruisers *Despatch* (1922) and *Liverpool* (1938), and a couple of destroyers.

Fairfield also built the passenger liner *New York* for Greece in 1922 as well as a number of other merchant vessels. As the Second World War approached, Fairfield was given an order for the battleship *Howe*, one of five battleships of the new *King George V* class, which was completed in 1942. During the war, Fairfield produced the aircraft carriers *Implacable* (1944) and *Theseus* (completed in 1946), the light cruisers *Phoebe* (1940) and *Bellona* (1943), and twelve destroyers. In the post-war period, the yard built five destroyers as well as the passenger liners *Empress of Britain* (1955) and *Queen Anna Maria* (1956), the latter for Greece.

As work continued to decline, Fairfield went into receivership in 1965, and in the following year, the company FAIRFIELD (GLASGOW) LTD. was established. In 1968, Fairfield was absorbed into Upper Clyde Shipbuilders Ltd. and production ceased. The Fairfield facility has since been taken over by KVAERNER GOVAN LTD., and it is now being used to produce liquid petroleum gas (LPG) carriers, chemical tankers, and a variety of speciality ships.

DENNY

William Denny founded the company WILLIAM DENNY & SON in 1818, at Dumbarton on the west bank of the River Leven near its effluence into the River Clyde, about 15 miles north-west of Glasgow. In 1844, the company was renamed WILLIAM DENNY & BROTHERS, and in 1867, it expanded across the River Leven to the east bank where the Leven shipyard was established. In 1905, Denny was placed on the Admiralty list of qualified warship builders for the Royal Navy, and prior to 1914, Denny had already built ten destroyers. During the First World War, Denny produced an additional twenty-five destroyers as well as two submarines. The company also built the liner *Uruguay* for Spain in 1913.

At the end of the war, the Denny shipyard covered 60 acres of land, and it had ten building berths up to 550ft in length. The yard had two wet basins, one over 900ft in length and the other 475ft in length, supported by a variety of cranes up to 110-ton capacity. The Denny payroll included nearly 4000 employees. In the inter-war years, Denny built six destroyers for the Royal Navy. As the war clouds loomed on the horizon in the late 1930s, Denny again geared up for warship production.

During the Second World War, Denny built twelve destroyers, eight sloops, and a number of other vessels for the Royal Navy. The yard also built two sloops for the Indian Navy during that period. As with other shipbuilders, Denny felt the pinch of the post-war decline in shipbuilding requirements, and it closed its doors in 1963. From 1844 until it ceased to exist in 1963,

William Denny & Brothers built nearly 1500 ships, including over one hundred warships for the Royal Navy.

STEPHEN

Although its origins date back to the middle of the eighteenth century, ALEXANDER STEPHEN & SONS was established in 1851 at Kelvinhaugh on the north bank of the River Clyde near Glasgow. There Stephen built some 150 vessels before moving across the river to Linthouse near Govan on the south bank of the River Clyde in 1870. At its new location, Stephen concentrated on the construction of merchant vessels during the remainder of the nineteenth century and early part of the twentieth century. During the First World War, however, the yard built ten destroyers for the Royal Navy.

At the end of the war, the Stephen shipyard encompassed 52 acres of land with a water frontage of 1500ft on the River Clyde. The yard had seven building berths up to 700ft in length, and at that time, its workforce totalled 3500 employees. Stephen resumed with the production of merchant vessels after the war, but with the international situation deteriorating in the late 1930s, Stephen reverted back to warship production. During the Second World War, the yard built the aircraft carrier *Ocean* (1945) and the light cruisers *Kenya* (1940), *Hermione* (1941), and *Ceylon* (1943). Also built during the war were sixteen destroyers, including two 'Tribal' class ships in 1939 and seven 'Hunt' class vessels in 1941-3, as well as two sloops.

After the war, the shipyard produced two 'Battle' class destroyers in 1948 and one *Daring* class destroyer in 1950. The yard also built the liner *Olympia* (1953) for Greece and several other merchant ships, but with continuously dropping workloads, it became more and more difficult to keep the shipyard in operation. In 1968, Stephen became part of Upper Clyde Shipbuilders Ltd., but without any further orders, it ceased production in that year after completing its 700th vessel, including nearly 550 vessels at its Linthouse site.

YARROW

In 1906, Alfred Yarrow moved his shipbuilding operations from Poplar on the River Thames near London to Scotland. He established YARROW CO. LTD. at Scotstoun, a western suburb of Glasgow on the north (right) bank of the River Clyde. The Yarrow shipyard covered twelve acres of land and had a frontage of 750ft along the River Clyde, and its original workforce consisted of 1500 employees. Yarrow became a leading producer of destroyers, building thirty-five destroyers for the Royal Navy and fifteen additional destroyers for foreign navies by the end of the First World War. Yarrow was also noted for its marine boilers, providing many boilers for ships produced by other shipyards as well as for its own ships.

By the end of the war, Yarrow's workforce had risen to 2000 employees. The yard had nine building berths up to 400ft in length and a wet fitting-out basin 350 × 85ft in size and with a 50-ton capacity crane. Yarrow remained solvent in the inter-war period by continuing to build vessels for the commercial market and completing eight more destroyers. During the

Second World War, Yarrow produced sixteen destroyers and six sloops for the Royal Navy.

Although associated with Upper Clyde Shipbuilders Ltd. from 1968 to 1971, Yarrow received sufficient orders for merchant ships to remain solvent. In 1977, the company became YARROW SHIPBUILDERS LTD., part of British Shipbuilders Ltd, a national corporation of British shipbuilders. In its 70-year existence on the River Clyde (1906-77), Yarrow built almost 1000 ships. Yarrow is now part of GEC Marine, an international group of marine concerns, and it specialises in the production of modern frigates for the Royal Navy and other NATO countries.

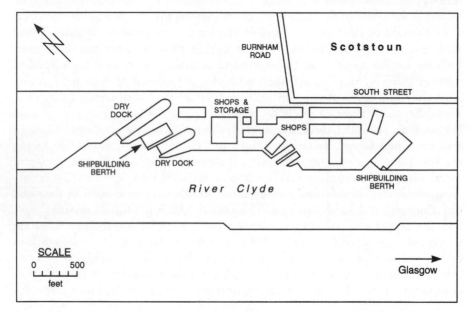

Yarrow in 1945.

INGLIS

The brothers Anthony and John Inglis formed a business partnership as A. & J. INGLIS LTD. at the Whitehall Foundry in Anderston on the River Clyde in 1847. In 1862, the Inglis brothers acquired a plot of land at Pointhouse at the mouth of the River Kelvin where it empties into the Clyde just west of Glasgow. Inglis became part of Harland & Wolff in 1919, but it continued to build ships under its own name. Inglis built some 500 ships during its one hundred years of existence (1862-1962), including two destroyers in 1905-11.

Inglis was on the waiting list to be closed down by the National Shipbuilders Security Ltd. when in 1936, the deteriorating international situation indicated the need for increased warship production. During the Second World War, Inglis built several frigates and corvettes for the Royal Navy. The shipyard finally closed down in 1962 when Harland & Wolff ceased its operations on the River Clyde.

## London & Glasgow

In 1864, a group of London and Glasgow entrepreneurs formed the LONDON & GLASGOW IRON SHIPBUILDING CO. LTD. and acquired Smith and Rodger's Middleton shipyard at Govan. London & Glasgow built a number of merchant ships during the latter half of the nineteenth century, including the liner *Princess Royal* in 1876. The yard also built six light cruisers in 1892-9 and three destroyers for the Royal Navy in that period. At the turn of the century, London & Glasgow had three large and three small slipways as well as a workforce of 3000 employees.

After the turn of the century, London & Glasgow produced the armoured cruisers *Monmouth* (1903), *Cumberland* (1904) and *Roxburgh* (1905). The shipyard then built the protected cruiser *Sydney* for the Australian Navy in 1911. London & Glasgow went out of business in 1912, and its Middleton yard was then acquired by Harland & Wolff Ltd. In its 48 years of existence from 1864 until 1912, London & Glasgow produced over 250 ships, all made out of iron or steel.

## Harland & Wolff

Early in the twentieth century, the HARLAND & WOLFF LTD. company of Belfast, Northern Ireland shipbuilding fame, decided to expand its operations to Scotland. In 1912, the firm acquired the former London & Glasgow Middleton shipyard and two adjacent yards in Govan on the River Clyde near Glasgow. At the beginning of the First World War, the Govan shipyard of Harland & Wolff had six large slipways. During the war, the yard produced six 'R' class destroyers, as well as several monitors and other smaller vessels for the Royal Navy, but their power plants were provided by the company's Belfast engine works.

Harland & Wolff continued to expand along the River Clyde by acquiring other shipyards in the area, including Caird & Co. of Greenock in 1916, A. & J. Inglis Ltd. of Pointhouse, Glasgow in 1919, A. McMillan & Sons Ltd. of Dumbarton in 1920, and finally D. & W. Henderson of Meadowside, Glasgow in 1935.

Harland & Wolff production on the River Clyde consisted mostly of passenger and cargo ships, tankers, ore carriers, whalers, tugs, and barges. Except for the construction of several frigates and corvettes by its Inglis subsidiary during the Second World War, no further Admiralty orders were received by Harland & Wolff shipyards on the River Clyde. In 1962, Harland & Wolff terminated its operations on the River Clyde, but it continues its shipbuilding activities at its Belfast facilities to the present time.

## Hanna & Donald

The HANNA & DONALD company began building ships in 1851 at the Abercorn shipyard near Paisley. The shipyard was located on the east bank of the White Cart Water branch of the River Cart about four miles south of Clydebank. In 1870, the company took on another partner, and it became HANNA, DONALD & WILSON. During its twenty-five years of existence until 1895, the company built only some thirty ships, including two 'A' class destroyers for the Royal Navy in 1894. Beset with problems in getting those destroyers accepted by the Admiralty, the company went out of business the next year.

## Wales

Wales does not have a major shipbuilding industry, being noted primarily for its steel production, and therefore it was not involved in naval shipbuilding to any great degree. The most significant Welsh shipyard was the Pembroke Naval Dockyard, which is described above. The MILFORD HAVEN SHIPBUILDING CO. did produce a few ships for the Royal Navy, including one sloop in 1884, but that was the extent of naval construction by private shipyards in Wales. The port of Milford Haven was an important eastern terminal for transatlantic convoys during the Second World War.

## Northern Ireland

HARLAND & WOLFF
In 1858, Edward James Harland acquired control of a shipyard at Queen's Island near Belfast, Ireland, and in 1861, he asked his assistant, Gustav Wilhelm Wolff, to become his partner, thereby establishing the HARLAND & WOLFF company. In 1881, the company began building its first steel ships, and prior to the First World War, it built several liners, including the passenger liners *Olympic* (1911) and *Titanic* (1912) for Cunard, the *Statendam* (1898), *Rijndam* (1901), and *Rotterdam* (1908) for The Netherlands, and the *America* (1905) for

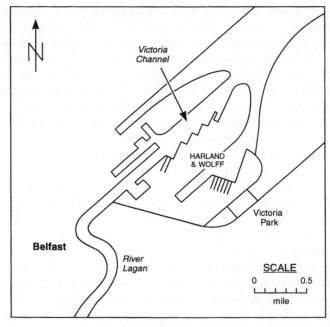

Harland & Wolff in 1945.

the United States. The *Titanic* sank in the North Atlantic after striking an iceberg on her maiden voyage with the loss of nearly 1600 lives.

In 1905, Harland & Wolff had six large and three small slipways, as well as one large 825 × 80ft dry dock and three smaller dry docks. Harland & Wolff's workforce amounted to 12,000 employees at the time. The company continued to expand, and two years later in 1907, the yard had an additional large dry dock measuring 850 × 100ft. By then, the workforce at the yard had climbed to 15,000 workers. At that time, the yard concentrated on the construction of passenger liners, and the only government work was for marine machinery. That condition would soon change, and with the outbreak of the First World War, Harland & Wolff turned to warship production.

Harland & Wolff built the battlecruiser *Glorious* in 1917, the light cruiser *Vindictive* in 1918, and several smaller vessels for the Royal Navy. The *Glorious* was later converted to an aircraft carrier at Devonport Naval Dockyard to avoid her dismantlement under the terms of the Washington naval disarmament treaty that limited the number of capital ships for each major power. By the end of the war, the Harland & Wolff shipyard had been expanded to include two additional large slipways, 860 × 100ft in size, in its main yard and six large slipways in its new yard. Total employment had reached 20,000 workers at that time.

After the war, Harland & Wolff reverted to the production of merchant ships, and from 1920 to 1932, it built twenty-nine passenger liners, including the *Doric* (1923), *Laurentic* (1927), *Britannic* (1930), and *Georgic* (1932) for Cunard and the *Veendam* (1923) and *Statendam* (1929) for The Netherlands. Between wars, Harland & Wolff built the light cruisers *Penelope* in 1936 and *Belfast* in 1939 for the Royal Navy. The firm also produced twenty passenger and cargo liners ranging up to 26,000-ton displacement from 1936 to 1939. Production during the Second World War included the aircraft carriers *Formidable* (1940), *Glory* (1945), and *Warrior* (1946), the light cruisers *Black Prince* (1943) and *Ontario* (ex-*Minotaur*) (1945), and thirty-four 'Flower' class corvettes.

During the war, Harland & Wolff also produced twenty-eight cargo liners and nineteen tankers to support the war effort. After the war, Harland & Wolff built the aircraft carriers *Magnificent* (1948), *Eagle* (1951), *Centaur* (1953), and *Bulwark* (1954) for the Royal Navy and the aircraft carrier *Bonaventure* (1957) for the Canadian Navy. From 1947 to 1961, the shipyard produced twenty passenger liners, including the 45,300-ton *Canberra* built for the Pacific & Orient Line. Within the twelve years following the end of the war, Harland & Wolff also produced fifty cargo liners and seventy tankers ranging up to 50,000 tons. With the increasing size of ships, especially oil tankers, it became necessary to upgrade the facilities at Harland & Wolff.

The first step was to replace six narrow slipways with five wider ones and to equip them with new 80-ton capacity cranes in the early 1960s. The new shipbuilding concept of prefabricating ship modules in separate shops and then assembling the modules at a central location led to further improvements later in that decade. In 1969, a huge 1825 × 305ft building dock was put into

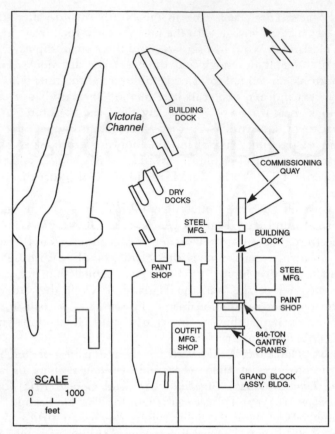

Harland & Wolff in 1980.

service, and that dock was serviced by two 840-ton capacity travelling gantry cranes. A module pre-fabrication shop and related support workshops occupy 900,000ft$^2$ of covered space on the 185-acre facility.

In 1975, the British government bought out Harland & Wolff, making the shipyard a government-owned facility. The yard, however, did not become part of the national British Shipbuilders Ltd., to which most of the other shipyards belonged. The shipyard was again privatised in 1989 under a management and employee buyout from the government. As one of the three major British shipbuilding companies still in production, Harland & Wolff now specialises in the construction of oil tankers, LPG carriers, and bulk carriers.

# 3 United States
## of America

Shipbuilding began as a commercial enterprise in the American colonies early in the seventeenth century with shipyards gradually springing up at the mouths of several rivers that flowed into the Atlantic Ocean along the Eastern seaboard from Maine down to Georgia. The first vessels were small boats used mostly for fishing or local trade, and these gradually increased in size to include coastal vessels used in trade among the colonies. The influx of skilled shipwrights among new immigrants, including some former Royal Dockyard workers, helped to improve the quality of the newer ships being built. This also led to the development of bigger and better shipyards in the colonies.

By 1680, colonial shipyards had reached the stage of proficiency that allowed them to receive a contract from the Crown to construct a Fourth Rate ship for the Royal Navy. HMS *Falkland* was built by a private shipyard in Newcastle (Portsmouth), New Hampshire in 1694, heralding the birth of naval shipbuilding in America. The *Falkland* was followed by another warship, the *Bedford*, around 1700, but the building of those warships in the colonies caused such concern among British shipbuilders that no new warships were built in America for nearly half a century. In 1747, the 24-gun frigate *Boston* was built by Benjamin Hallowell of Boston, after which the 44-gun ship *America* was produced at Portsmouth, New Hampshire in 1749.

At the beginning of the Revolutionary War, the colonies had no navy of their own, and had to rely on the arming of merchant ships under their control to face the enormous power and resources of the Royal Navy. In October 1775, just three months after the Declaration of Independence was signed, Congress authorised the purchase and fitting out of two warships for the Colonial Navy. Later that month, a committee was formed to administer colonial naval operations and establish rules of conduct for its personnel. These acts were construed as constituting the birth of the Continental Navy, and therefore also the birth of the US Navy.

In December 1775, Congress authorised the construction of thirteen frigates for the Continental Navy in accordance with naval plans and specifications. These ships were to be built by various private shipbuilders distributed among the colonies: four in Pennsylvania, two each in Massachusetts, Rhode Island, and New York; and one each in New Hampshire, Connecticut, and Maryland. This programme did not have much success since several of these ships had to be destroyed before entering service to avoid their falling into British hands. The remainder that did put to sea were eventually either sunk or captured without making any significant impact on the war effort.

The Continental Navy did achieve a number of notable successes in engagements with British forces, but these were rare and far between. In one of these exploits, John Paul Jones in his former East Indiaman *Duc de Duras*, renamed *Bonhomme Richard*, defeated the new British frigate *Serapis* in September 1779. Although the *Bonhomme Richard* was ultimately lost as a result of this engagement, John Paul Jones' feat was especially outstanding since he was greatly outgunned by his superior opponent. After the Revolutionary War, the new Federal government did not have the resources to support a navy, and it sold its few remaining warships.

The American shipping industry was enjoying considerable success in competing with European powers in trade throughout the world. At the end of the eighteenth century, however, pirates along the Barbary Coast of northern Africa began to prey on American merchant ships plying their trade in the Mediterranean Sea. This caused Congress to reconsider the need for having a standing navy to protect American shipping from any hostile forces, and in 1794, it authorised the construction of six frigates to provide protection for American merchantmen. The frigates were built in private shipyards spread along the east coast of the United States, and they were completed three years later in 1797.

By the late eighteenth century, the United States was rapidly becoming recognised as a significant trading power. In 1797, the Naval Committee of Congress recommended the establishment of a Federal navy yard to continue the construction of warships for the United States Navy. Two years later, the Navy Department was established as a branch of the Federal government. In 1800, Congress authorised the establishment of six Federal navy yards along the Atlantic Coast, and within the next year or so, the necessary land was purchased and construction began. These navy yards were located at Portsmouth, New Hampshire, Boston, New York, Philadelphia, Norfolk and Washington.

Shortly after the turn of the century, Congress authorised the construction of a total of over 175 gunboats for coast defence purposes and against the Barbary pirates. The vast majority of these orders went to over thirty private shipyards along the eastern seacoast and on some inland waterways, and only about thirty were produced by the new navy yards. These contracts were let in relatively small increments over the period 1805 to 1811, and the ships that were produced became known as the Federal 'gunboat navy'.

Prior to the Civil War, two additional navy yards were established, one at Pensacola, Florida in 1826 and the other at Mare Island near Vallejo, California in 1854. The former was never fitted out to build major warships, but the Mare Island Navy Yard went on to become one of the major builders of warships for the US Navy. In 1845, the US Naval Academy was established at Annapolis, Maryland. The Civil War, which erupted in 1861, kept the Northern navy yards occupied in building Federal warships to blockade Southern ports and to support military campaigns along the Gulf Coast and up the Mississippi River. A ninth navy yard, the Puget Sound Navy Yard, was established in 1891 at Bremerton, Washington across Puget Sound from the town of Seattle.

During the latter half of the nineteenth century, there were several technological developments that revolutionised naval architecture. The steam engine had been developed to the point where marine applications became feasible, and after a period of dual sail and steam propulsion systems, sail was dropped completely in favour of steam. The initial paddle wheel method of propulsion was quickly replaced by the more efficient screw propeller. The use of iron plating over wood for protection against enemy gunfire first gained favour in Europe, but the successful application of this technique on the Confederate frigate *Virginia* convinced the Federal Navy to follow suit and begin using iron and then steel plates for armour protection.

Another naval development was the breech–loading gun, which allowed more flexibility in the arrangement of the main armament of a warship. No longer were rows of rigidly placed guns on each side of a warship required. Guns could now be placed on rotating mounts conveniently placed anywhere on the decks. This led to the development of the rotating turret with multiple guns that could be located along the centreline of the ship where the guns could fire to either side of the ship. By the last decade of the nineteenth century, the so-called 'New Navy' would begin to have all-steel ships with steam engines and screw propellers. These ships would also have centreline-mounted main armament gun turrets supplemented by smaller guns located on either side of the ship.

The first of the all-steel ships that appeared about 1890 had little if any armour protection, and they were classified as protected cruisers or unprotected cruisers depending upon the amount of armour they carried. A few years later, the armoured cruiser, with a full belt of side armour, made its appearance. The first American armoured cruiser, the famous USS *Maine* (ACR-1), displaced 6700 tons, and it was later reclassified as a small battleship. The first true battleship, the USS *Indiana* (BB-1) of 1896, displaced 10,300 tons and carried four 13in guns. By the time of the First World War, battleships increased in displacement to 32,000 tons and they carried twelve 14in guns in four triple turrets.

The invention by Robert Whitehead, a British engineer, of the self-propelled torpedo late in the nineteenth century prompted the development of suitable delivery systems for this new instrument of war. The first successful delivery system was the surface torpedo-boat which could approach an enemy vessel at high speed, launch its torpedoes at some distance from the target, and then beat a hasty retreat before it was hit by enemy fire. These torpedo-boats were produced in large quantities by the major naval powers, and the United States was no exception. The relatively small and flimsy torpedo-boat was soon supplanted by the larger and more powerful torpedo boat destroyer, which in turn was replaced by the even larger and better armed destroyer.

Another torpedo delivery system, which would become the most effective vehicle for torpedo warfare, was the submarine. An American inventor, John Holland had been trying to get the US Navy interested in his new invention, the submersible torpedo-boat, late in the nineteenth century, but to no avail. Finally in 1900, after further development of this weapon, the navy gave Holland an order for one boat, the USS *Holland*, which proved to be reasonably successful. By the time that the First World War broke out in 1914, the submarine had advanced to the point of being a very formidable weapon of destruction.

Before the end of the nineteenth century, the United States found itself at war with Spain, precipitated by the sinking of the US battleship *Maine* in Havana harbour in evening of 15 February 1898. The US Navy defeated the Spanish fleet in two major engagements in far-distant corners of the world. The US Asiatic Fleet under Admiral George Dewey destroyed the Spanish Far East squadron in the Battle of Manila Bay in the Philippines on 1 May 1898. Two months later, two separate US squadrons, one under Admiral William T Samson and the other under Admiral Winfield S Schley, converged on Santiago, Cuba, where they trapped a Spanish squadron under Admiral Cevera. On 3 July 1898, the American force destroyed the Spanish ships one-by-one as they attempted to escape from the harbour.

The American victory over Spain established the United States as a naval power. As a result of the Spanish-American War, the United States annexed the Philippines and Hawaiian Islands in 1898. In the following year, the United States also annexed Wake Island and American Samoa. In 1901, two additional navy yards were established, one at Charleston, South Carolina and the other at Pearl Harbor in the Hawaiian Islands. These yards were not intended for the construction of major warships, but rather to provide additional bases for the refit and repair of warships for the fleet. American naval bases were also established early in the twentieth century at Cuba, Puerto Rico, and the Philippine Islands for use mostly as refuelling stations.

At the turn of the century, the US Navy reclassified several warship types and established a new numbering system for all ships in the navy. The armoured cruiser *Maine* (ACR-1) was reclassified as a battleship, but since the *Maine* and the 6100-ton battleship *Texas* were relatively small and suitable only for coastal defence duties, they were not included under the new battleship numbering system. The USS *Indiana* was the first battleship to come under the new numbering system as BB-1. The remaining twelve armoured cruisers (ARC-2 through ARC-13) were not included in the new cruiser numbering system, and were gradually phased out of service.

The new cruiser numbering system began by redesignating the scout cruisers *Chester* (CS-1), *Birmingham* (CS-2), and *Salem* (CS-3) as light cruisers CL-1, CL-2, and CL-3, respectively. The next cruisers to fall within this numbering system were the ten light cruisers of the *Omaha* class (CL-4 through CL-13) built from 1923 to 1925. The older protected cruisers *Chicago* (no previous number), *Olympia* (C-6), *Columbia* (C-12), *Minneapolis* (C-13), *St Louis* (C-20), and *Charleston* (C-22) were then retroactively brought under the new numbering system as heavy cruisers CA-14 through CA-19, respectively. The reclassification of four additional cruisers as light cruisers bought the number up to CL-23.

From then on, all cruisers shared the same numbering system, whether they carried the prefix CA as heavy cruisers or CL as light cruisers. Destroyers were numbered in the DD series beginning with the USS *Bainbridge* (DD-1), built in 1902, and similarly, submarines were numbered in the SS series beginning with the USS *Holland* (SS-1) built in 1900. Later of course came aircraft carriers (CV), destroyer escorts (DE), destroyer leaders (DL), guided missile cruisers (CG), guided missile destroyers (DDG), guided missile frigates (FFG), and a host of naval auxiliary vessels, each with their own separate numbering systems.

Anxious to show America's new naval strength, President Theodore Roosevelt sent a force of sixteen battleships with their hulls painted white on a trip around the world. Led by the flagship, the 16,000-ton battleship *Connecticut* (BB-18), the 'Great White Fleet' sailed out of Hampton Roads in December 1907. The flagship was followed by four sister ships, the *Louisiana* (BB-19), *Vermont* (BB-20), *Kansas* (BB-21), and *Minnesota* (BB-22). Then came the five 15,000-ton battleships *Virginia* (BB-13), *Nebraska* (BB-14), *Georgia* (BB-15), *New Jersey* (BB-16), and *Rhode Island* (BB-17), and finally, the battleships *Illinois* (BB-7), *Alabama* (BB-8), *Wisconsin* (BB-9), *Maine* (BB-10), *Missouri* (BB-11), and *Ohio* (BB-12) brought up the rear. The fleet returned to the United States fourteen months later, sailing into San Francisco Bay.

In 1904, the Unites States negotiated with the newly-formed Republic of Panama to build a canal through the Isthmus of Panama and the establish of a Canal Zone under US jurisdiction. The Panama Canal was completed in 1914, allowing for the more expeditious movement of warships between the East and West Coasts. Navy involvement in the First World War consisted primarily of providing escorts for convoys of merchant ships to the British Isles. As such, there was little urgency to increase warship production which was then proceeding at the rate of one battleship a year with the corresponding construction of cruisers and destroyers to make up balanced fleets for both the Atlantic and Pacific Oceans.

During the First World War, America and Great Britain began to experiment with the use of aircraft on naval vessels to serve primarily as the eyes of the fleet over the horizons. In 1919, Congress authorised the conversion of the 19,000-ton collier USS *Jupiter* as a developmental 'aeroplane carrier'. Renamed the USS *Langley* (CV-1) after an aviation pioneer, America's first aircraft carrier was commissioned in 1922, and it then began to undertake a series of tests that would prove the feasibility of naval aviation.

After the First World War, warship production throughout the world was drastically reduced, and the number of capital ships that could be retained by each nation was restricted by the terms of disarmament treaties. America was in the process of constructing six 35,000-ton battlecruisers authorised by Congress in 1916, but under the terms of the new international treaties, these ships could not be completed. In 1922, Congress authorised the conversion of two of those incomplete battlecruisers into aircraft carriers. In 1927, America's first real aircraft carriers, the USS *Lexington* (CV-2) and the USS *Saratoga* (CV-3) joined the fleet. These would be the forerunners of some seventy-five aircraft carriers that would be completed during the twentieth century.

It was not until the late 1930s that the major powers renewed their shipbuilding activities, especially in the area of capital ships. This activity was intensified as the Second World War approached when it became clear that the ambitions of the Axis nations could not be appeased. In 1939, the United States began the construction of six new generation 35,000-ton battleships followed by four 45,000-ton super-battleships, all carrying nine 16in guns. During the war, the United States produced over thirty fleet aircraft carriers, including twenty of the 27,000-ton *Essex* class, three super carriers of the 45,000-ton *Midway* class, and nine light carriers built on cruiser hulls.

In addition to battleships and fleet aircraft carriers, the US Navy also built two battlecruisers, fifteen heavy cruisers, thirty large light cruisers, ten anti-aircraft cruisers, nearly 125 escort carriers, and hundreds of destroyers, destroyer escorts, and other small craft during the war years. Escort carriers, intended to provide air cover for Atlantic convoys, were converted from merchant ship hulls, and destroyer escorts, somewhat smaller than fleet destroyers, were designed specifically for anti-submarine warfare against the U-boat threat. The United States came out of the Second World War with the strongest navy in the world, overtaking the British navy, which had held that distinction for the previous 150 years.

The final two US navy yards were established at San Francisco and Long Beach, California in 1940, just in time to lend their weight to the construction and repair of warships for the US Navy during the Second World War. In September 1945, the term 'navy yard' was officially dropped in favour of the more formal term 'naval shipyard', and the names of all of the navy yards were changed accordingly. After the war, naval construction again dropped off, and even with the Cold War with the Soviet Union, there was never a serious threat requiring a large naval force for protection. One by one, most of the famous 'naval shipyards' gradually ceased operations and closed down.

The US Navy recognised that nuclear energy would be ideal for use on submarines, since nuclear power plants would greatly extend their endurance and allow them to remain submerged for extended periods of time. One of the early proponents of nuclear energy for naval applications was Admiral

Hyman G Rickover, who became known as the 'father of the American nuclear navy'. In 1954, the first nuclear-powered submarine, USS *Nautilus* (SSN-571) was commissioned, and it was followed by over 200 more nuclear-powered submarines that would be built in the United States during the twentieth century.

In 1953, the US Navy introduced a new type of warship into the fleet, the destroyer-leader or 'frigate'. The first ship of this type, the 5600-ton USS *Norfolk*, was originally intended to be a large, cruiser-size, anti-submarine warfare ship, but it actually was more suited as the flagship of a destroyer flotilla. Designated as DL-1, the *Norfolk* was soon followed by four additional frigates (DL-2 to DL-5) in 1953 and 1954. Two of these frigates, the *Mitchner* (DL-2) and *McCain* (DL-3), were later equipped with anti-aircraft missiles and reclassified as guided missile destroyers (DDG) due to their smaller size.

The US Navy began introducing anti-aircraft missiles on naval vessels in 1956 when the heavy cruisers *Boston* (CA-69) and *Canberra* (CA-70) were converted to accommodate the 'Terrier' surface-to-air missile. The after triple 8in gun turret and the 5in dual gun mount on each ship were replaced with two twin missile-launchers during the conversion conducted by the New York Shipbuilding Company at their facilities in Camden, New Jersey. At first, these ships were designated as heavy guided missile cruisers (CAG-1 and CAG-2, respectively), but they were later redesignated as just guided missile cruisers (CG-1 and CG-2).

The two heavy cruiser conversions were soon followed by the similar conversion of six *Cleveland* class light cruisers. These conversions were completed in 1956 and 1957 at the New York Naval Shipyard, Boston Naval Shipyard, and at three private shipyards. These converted light cruisers were first designated CLG-3 to CLG-8, respectively, but then they were later renumbered as CG-3 to CG-8 when all guided missile cruisers were considered the same and included under the same numbering system. Three additional heavy cruisers of the *Baltimore* class were converted to guided missile cruisers in the early 1960s, and these were renumbered as CG-10, CG-11, and CG-12.

From 1959 to 1961, the navy built ten guided missile frigates of the *Farragut* class (DLG-6 to DLG-15), and these were followed by nine *Leahy* class ships (DLG-16 to DLG-24) in 1962 to 1964. Nine more guided missile frigates of the *Belnap* class (DLG-26 to DLG-34) were built from 1965 to 1967. The Navy later decided to reclassify its latest guided missile frigates (DLG-13 to DLG-37) as guided missile cruisers, so they were renumbered as CG-13 to CG-37, using the same numbers as before.

In 1956, the navy converted the *Gearing* class destroyer, USS *Gyatt* (DD-712) to accommodate the 'Terrier' missile. After the successful conversion, the *Gyatt* was redesignated as DDG-712, but the navy later decided to introduce a new numbering system for guided missile destroyers, so it was subsequently redesignated as DDG-1 in 1957. Eight new destroyers under construction (DD-952 to DD-959) were also equipped with the 'Terrier' missile system. These destroyers were redesignated as DDG-952 to DDG-959, but they were later renumbered as DDG-2 to DDG-9 under a new numbering system.

In 1966, the US Navy began building destroyer escorts armed with anti-aircraft guided missiles, the first being six ships of the *Brooke* class (DEG-1 to DEG-6). In 1975, the navy reclassified many of its ships in the destroyer leader (DL), destroyer (DD) and destroyer escort (DE) range. Most destroyer leaders, formerly called frigates, were upgraded to cruisers, and all destroyer escorts now became known as frigates (FF). Those first destroyer escorts that were armed with guided missiles were reclassified as guided missile frigates, but kept their same numbers (FFG-1 to FFG-6). In 1977, the navy began building some fifty-five guided missile frigates of the *Oliver Hazard Perry* class (FFG-7 to FFG-61).

While nuclear power was ideal for submarines, its application to surface ships required further evaluation. The first nuclear-powered guided missile cruiser, the USS *Long Beach* (CGN-1), was completed in 1961 by the Bethlehem Steel Co. shipyard at Quincy, Massachusetts. The *Long Beach* was subsequently renumbered as CGN-9 to conform with the new numbering system for guided missile cruisers. In the same year, the first nuclear-powered aircraft carrier, USS *Enterprise* (CVAN-65) joined the fleet. This gigantic ship was the largest warship ever built to that time, displacing nearly 90,000 tons and over 1000ft in length.

US Navy Yards and Naval Bases on the East Coast.

The *Enterprise* would be followed by seven more nuclear-powered aircraft carriers of the slightly larger *Nimitz* class through the remainder of the twentieth century.

Nuclear power for smaller surface ships was hard to justify in view of the high cost involved and the relative ease of refuelling ships by conventional means. The nuclear-powered frigate USS *Bainbridge* (DLGN-25) was built in 1963, and that ship was subsequently reclassified as a nuclear guided missile cruiser (CGN-25). In 1975, the navy built two more nuclear guided missile frigates (DLGN-36 and DLGN-37), which were later reclassified as nuclear guided missile cruisers (CGN-36 and CGN-37). From 1976 to 1980, the navy acquired four nuclear guided missile cruisers of the *Virginia* class (CGN-38 to CGN-41). These would be the last nuclear-powered cruisers built by the navy in the twentieth century, leaving nuclear power strictly to the domain of submarines and aircraft carriers.

During the 12-year period 1982 to 1994, the US Navy received twenty-seven guided missile cruisers of the *Ticonderoga* class (CG-47 to CG-73). These 9600-ton vessels are armed with a variety of the latest offensive and defensive weapon systems and are equipped with four gas turbine engines that can drive each ship at a speed of over 30kts.


## AMERICAN NAVAL SHIPYARDS

### PORTSMOUTH NAVAL SHIPYARD

Portsmouth, New Hampshire is located on the Picataqua River, which separates Maine and New Hampshire, about 60 miles north of Boston. The region was first settled in 1624, and the town of Portsmouth soon developed as a port and shipbuilding centre. In 1690, Portsmouth was contracted to build the first warship to be produced in the colonies for the Royal Navy, the 54-gun HMS *Falkland*. In 1692, Portsmouth became the first seat of the provisional government of the New Hampshire colony. Portsmouth continued constructing warships for the crown, but in 1749, it built its last ship for the Royal Navy, the 44-gun, two-decker *Boston*, later renamed *America*. After that, Portsmouth began building ships for the colonies and then the Continental Navy.

In 1800, the PORTSMOUTH NAVY YARD was established as one of the six original navy yards authorised by the Federal Congress that year. The navy yard was originally situated on Fernald's Island, a 45-acre tract of land in the Piscataque River, which was actually part of Maine and closer to Kittery, Maine than to Portsmouth, New Hampshire. In 1814, the Portsmouth Navy Yard produced its first warship, the 74-gun ship-of-the-line USS *Washington*. This was followed three years later by the 74-gun *Alabama*, which was subsequently converted into a store ship and renamed *New Hampshire*. The yard went on to produce the 44-gun frigate *Santee* (1820) and the 50-gun *Congress* (1841), as well as five sloops-of-war and one armed schooner, before steam power replaced sail.

Portsmouth Navy Yard had 150 workers in 1848 when it began building steam-powered warships, beginning with the 11-gun steam frigate *Saranac*. In 1852, Portsmouth received a 350 × 105ft wooden floating dry dock that could accommodate ships up to 5000 tons displacement. The dock was placed in the small channel between Fernald's Island and the adjacent Seavey's Island. From 1857 to 1863, the yard produced nine steam sloops. In 1862, the workforce at Portsmouth had increased to over 2000 workers. In 1866, the government acquired Seavey's Island for the enlargement of the navy yard, bringing the size of the yard up to 200 acres. Portsmouth built the 60-gun steam frigate *Franklin* in 1863, the largest steam-driven warship produced by an American navy yard up to that time.

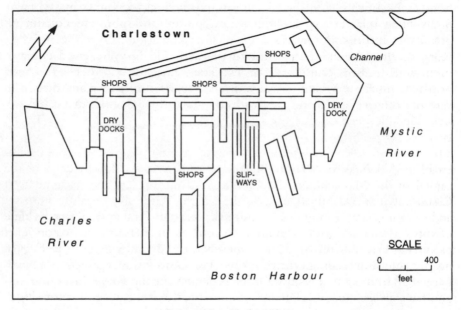

Boston Navy Yard in 1945.

During the Civil War, the Portsmouth Navy Yard produced a total of twenty-six ships, including six side-wheelers, three sloops-of-war, two ironclads, and a screw steamer. After the Civil War, the production of surface vessels for the US Navy dropped off at the Portsmouth Navy Yard, and the yard took advantage of this lull to gradually improve its facilities. In 1906, a granite dry dock, 750 × 100ft in size, was completed, and this was followed by a 725 × 195ft granite and concrete dry dock in 1914. When the United States entered the First World War in 1917, the workforce was 2000 employees, but with war production, that figure jumped to 5700 workers by the time that the war ended late in the following year. Most of the wartime activity involved ship repair and maintenance, and during that period, the yard repaired over 120 naval vessels.

The Portsmouth Navy Yard began to concentrate on the production of submarines during the First World War, and in 1917, it completed its first submarine, the *L-8* (ss-48). That ship was followed by the *O-1* (ss-62) in the following year. From 1920-3, the yard produced eleven submarines of the 'S' class, and four more of various classes during the remainder of the 1920s. During the 1930s, the Portsmouth yard built fourteen submarines mostly of the 'P' class and subsequent 'S' class. One of the latter was the ill-fated uss *Squalus* (s-1; ss-192), which sank nearby during sea trials in 1939 due to a malfunction of the main induction valve. Although twenty-six officers and men were lost in the accident, thirty-three men were rescued from the sunken craft by a bell-shaped diving chamber, which had been developed a short time earlier.

The *Squalus* was subsequently raised, refurbished, and recommissioned as the uss *Sailfish* in 1940. An additional eighty-seven submarines were produced from 1939-48 at the shipyard, which was renamed as the PORTSMOUTH NAVAL SHIPYARD in 1945. From 1951-9, ten more conventional submarines were built before production was switched to nuclear submarines. Over the next ten years, the yard built nine nuclear submarines, and in 1969, production of submarines ceased. The Portsmouth Naval Shipyard was thereupon used primarily for the overhaul, conversion, and repair of nuclear submarines. The yard now covers nearly 300 acres of land.

BOSTON NAVAL SHIPYARD

The town of Boston was founded in 1630, just ten years after the Pilgrims established the nearby Plymouth colony, and in 1632, Boston became the capital of the Massachusetts Bay colony. As Boston grew, the settlements at Charlestown and Cambridge across the Charles River also began to flourish, and soon a small shipbuilding industry developed in the region. By the time of the American Revolution, private shipyards in the area were capable of producing warships for the Continental Navy, and two frigates were built at nearby Newburyport in 1776. After the Revolution, private shipyards continued to produce warships for the Federal Navy, including the famous 44-gun frigate *Constitution*, built at Boston in 1797, and the 32-gun frigate *Essex* built at Salem in 1799.

In 1800, Boston was chosen as one of the six sites authorised by the Federal Congress for the establishment of navy yards to produce warships for the US Navy. That year, a 25-acre tract of land was purchased for the navy yard at Charlestown across the Charles River from Boston, and in the following year, the BOSTON NAVY YARD was established. In 1805, the yard made a minor contribution to the US gunboat navy intended for operations against the Barbary Coast pirates of northern Africa by building one gunboat. The facilities of the yard were improved in 1812, to include the first covered shipbuilding ways in the nation. In 1813, the Boston Navy Yard completed the 18-gun sloop-of-war *Frolic*, built by Josiah Barker at the yard under government supervision.

In 1814, Josiah Barker and his partner, Ed Hartt, completed the 74-gun ship-of-the-line *Independence* at the Boston Navy Yard. In 1818, the Boston Navy Yard completed the 74-gun *Vermont*, but construction was halted on a sister-ship, the *Virginia*, which was broken up on the stocks before she was ever launched. The yard then built the 44-gun sailing frigate *Cumberland* in 1825, and from 1821 to 1844, it produced six sloops-of-war, two brigs, and two armed schooners In 1822, the yard employed ninety workers, but that figure gradually grew over the years, reaching 450 employees in 1835 and 870 people in 1854. In 1833, Boston constructed its first dry dock, which made of granite and measured 390 × 45ft.

In 1837, the Boston Navy Yard completed the first and only rope walk (ropery) in the US Navy. The 1300ft long structure was powered by a steam engine, and it eventually also made wire rope. As sails gave way to steam power, the yard began to convert to the production of steam-powered warships. Among the early steam-powered warships produced by Boston was the screw-propelled frigate *Merrimack* (1855), which later received notoriety as the Confederate ironclad CSS *Virginia* after being converted at the Norfolk Navy Yard. Another famous ship produced by the Boston Navy Yard was the screw-propelled sloop *Hartford* (1858), which served as Admiral David G Farragut's flagship during his attack up the Mississippi River to Vicksburg in 1862.

During the American Civil War, the Boston Navy Yard built two monitors and a number of other steam warships. The workforce at the Boston Navy Yard numbered 2550 men at the beginning of the war in 1861, but during the war, the figure rose gradually to a peak of 3200 workers in 1864. After the war ended in 1865, the workforce dropped again to 2000 men in 1866 and to 1000 in the following year. In the post-Civil War era, the Boston yard produced the screw-propelled frigates *Guerriere* (1867) and *Ammonoosuc* (1868), but did not complete two other vessels of this type which it had begun. The yard also produced seven screw-propelled sloops in the same period.

The workload at the Boston Navy Yard declined during the 1880s, and employment was down to 200 workers in 1888, but in 1890, there was an upswing in activity at the yard. Although used primarily for repair work and manufacturing in the 1890s, the workforce at the yard rose from 400 workers at the beginning of the decade to 1400 in 1898, during the Spanish-American War. Boston's second dry dock, a granite and concrete structure measuring 730 × 100ft, was completed in 1905. By that time, there were over 2000 workers employed at the yard. During the First World War, the Boston Navy Yard continued to serve primarily as a ship repair centre, as well as an embarkation point for American troops being sent to Europe, and its workforce reached 10,000 workers.

The Boston Navy Yard resumed shipbuilding in 1915, and it completed three naval oilers from 1917 to 1921. In 1920, the US Navy purchased a 50-acre tract of land with a large dry dock, measuring 1170 × 150ft, from the State of Massachusetts in South Boston, about two miles down river from the main navy yard. This addition, which became known as the South Boston Annex, greatly enhanced the Boston Navy Yard's capability to repair even the larger warships anticipated in the future. With the reduced workload after the war, employment at the yard dropped to 3000 people in 1922 and to a low of 1500 workers in 1932.

In 1926, two employees at the Boston Navy Yard, A M Leahy and C G Lutts, invented the 'die-lock' method of producing anchor chain. This method, which used two C-shaped sections with mating ends that were forged together to make a single link, was stronger and more economical to manufacture than the forged iron and forged steel chain previously used. Using this method, the yard produced most of the anchor chain for naval vessels built during the Second World War. Up until 1933, the Boston Navy Yard had been used primarily for the repair and outfitting of ships, but after that, it began to receive orders for the construction of destroyers, and ten of those ships were completed by 1939.

In 1938, the yard underwent a major improvement programme, which affected mostly the shop area at the main yard. The facilities at the South Boston Annex were also greatly enhanced in 1938 by the addition of another dry dock and two additional piers, as well as improvements to its shop areas. In 1938, the total workforce of the Boston Navy Yard was only 2800, but that figure soon climbed as the world plunged into its second world war. During 1939 alone, the number of employees at the yard rose from 4000 to 6000 workers, and by 1943, it had reached a peak of 50,000 employees, including an increasing number of women and minority workers. By this time, the size of the yard had increased to a total of 230 acres.

Production during the Second World War included twenty-six destroyers, sixty-four destroyer escorts, and thirty-four tank landing ships, but the Boston Navy Yard continued to be used primarily as a repair facility. One new slipway was constructed in 1941 to increase its shipbuilding capacity. In addition to serving American warships, the yard occasionally performed repairs and maintenance on Allied warships. In 1941, the yard repaired the British battleship *Rodney*, which had suffered structural damage as a result of firing its main armament during the recent battle with the German battleship *Bismarck*. As the war drew to a close, the workforce at the yard had dropped to 22,000 workers in May of 1945. Post-war naval construction at the Boston Naval Shipyard was limited to a total of nine submarines.

After the war, there remained a need to keep the US Navy in a state of readiness, and improvements were made at the renamed BOSTON NAVAL SHIPYARD to ensure its capability to provide that service. In 1946, a 100-ton capacity crane was added to the yard to assist in its fitting out of warships. In 1957, Boston converted the destroyer USS *Gyatt* into the US Navy's first guided missile destroyer. After that, the workload at the yard continued to decline to point where the Boston Naval Shipyard was no longer required by the navy, and the yard was disestablished in 1974. Now known again by its popular name, the CHARLESTOWN NAVY YARD serves primarily as the custodian for the famous frigate USS *Constitution*, as well as the operation of the museum associated with the history of that ship.

NEW YORK NAVAL SHIPYARD
New York harbour, one of the greatest harbours in the world, was first explored in depth in 1609 by Henry Hudson of the Dutch East India

Company, which was involved primarily in trading of furs. The Dutch began to settle in the region, and in 1625, the colony of New Netherland was founded. In that same year, the Dutch purchased Manhattan Island from the natives, renamed it New Amsterdam, and established it as the seat of government for the colony. After the Dutch allied themselves with the French in 1662, the English attacked Dutch settlements in the New World, and in 1664, they conquered New Amsterdam and renamed the colony New York for the Duke of York.

The features of New York harbour were not only favourable for maritime trade, but also for shipbuilding. Over the years, several small shipyards were established in the region, and by the time of the American Revolution, New York had a limited capability to construct warships for the Continental Navy. In 1776, work began on two frigates at Poughkeepsie, just up the Hudson River from New York harbour, but subsequently they had to be destroyed on their stocks to keep them from falling into British hands. In 1781, John Jackson and his brothers, Samuel and Treadwell, acquired the site for a shipyard on the East River in Brooklyn. In 1798, the Jackson brothers built the 28-gun frigate *Adams* for the Federal Navy.

In 1800, Congress approved the establishment of six Federal navy yards, and New York was selected as one of the locales for such a yard. The NEW YORK NAVY YARD was officially established in February 1801, and in the following year, the Jackson Brothers shipyard in Brooklyn was purchased as the site for the new navy yard. The New York Navy Yard encompassed a total of 200 acres and was located on the south bank of the East River, directly across from the lower east end of Manhattan Island. Although the yard built two gunboats in 1805, it was at first used primarily as a supply depot, fitting out some 100 naval vessels during the War of 1812. In 1817, the New York Navy Yard began building warships for the US Navy, starting with the 74-gun ship-of-the-line *Ohio* in 1820.

The New York Navy Yard built the US steamer *Fulton 2* in 1835, and this was followed by the 44-gun frigates *Savannah* and *Sabine* in 1842 and 1855 respectively. In 1851, the yard constructed its first dry dock, which was made of granite and measured 330 × 65ft. At the beginning of the Civil War in 1861, the New York Navy Yard had a workforce of over 1600 men, and this was increased to 5400 men by the end of the war in 1865. In 1862, the New York Navy Yard completed the fitting out of USS *Monitor*, the namesake of a new type of warship that would revolutionise naval shipbuilding. The *Monitor* was designed by the Swedish engineer, John Ericsson, and the ship itself was produced by the Continental Iron Works at Greenpoint, Long Island.

During the Civil War, the New York Navy Yard built four screw-propelled steam sloops, two monitors, and one ironclad vessel. Although the workload dropped after the Civil War, the New York Navy Yard built two screw-propelled steam frigates and three screw-propelled steam sloops in 1867-8. In 1868, the yard underwent a massive modernisation programme. The 3900-ton, 19-gun steam frigate *Trenton*, completed at the yard in 1876, was the last wooden-hulled steam frigate build by the US Navy. From then on, the New York Navy Yard would produce only all-steel warships for the 'New Navy'.

In 1890, the second dry dock, measuring 440 × 90ft, was constructed at the yard. In 1894, the New York Navy Yard built the protected cruiser *Cincinnati* (C-7), and this was followed a year later by the armoured cruiser *Maine* (ACR-1), which was subsequently reclassified as a small battleship. The *Maine* achieved immortality when she blew up in Havana harbour in 1898, killing over 250 men and precipitating the Spanish-American War. The New York Navy Yard built its third dry dock, a 610 × 105ft structure, in 1897. Both the second and third dry docks had initially been made of wood, and then eventually had to be replaced with docks made of more durable concrete some time later.

After the turn of the century, the New York Navy Yard began a long career of turning out capital ships for the US Navy. For this purpose, both slipways at the yard were extended in 1903 to accommodate these larger vessels. This naval construction activity began with the pre-dreadnought battleships *Connecticut* (BB-18) in 1906 and *New Hampshire* (BB-25) in 1907. With the advent of the all-big-gun battleship design developed in Great Britain with its HMS *Dreadnought*, the New York Navy Yard then built several Dreadnought-type battleships. Those ships included the *Florida* (BB-30) in 1911, the *Arkansas* (BB-33) in 1912, and the *New York* (BB-34) in 1914.

The New York Navy Yard built its fourth dry dock, 700 × 120ft in size, out of granite and concrete in 1913. Although the yard already had two improved slipways, two new slipways were added in 1917. Production included the battleships *Arizona* (BB-39) in 1916, the *New Mexico* (BB-40) in 1918, the *Idaho* (BB-42) in 1919, and the *Tennessee* (BB-43) in 1920. These ships were all of about 33,000 tons displacement and carried twelve 14in guns in four triple turrets, two forward and two aft. The ill-fated USS *Arizona* was sunk at Pearl Harbor when a bomb dropped by an attacking Japanese aircraft blew up her forward magazine, killing nearly 1200 officers and men on board. The sunken *Arizona* remains as a permanent memorial at Pearl Harbor with most of her casualties entombed in the ship.

Two other battleships under construction, the *South Dakota* (BB-49) and *Indiana* (BB-50) were incomplete at the end of the war and further work was cancelled. By the end of the First World War, the workforce at the New York Navy Yard had climbed to 18,000, but that figure soon began to drop as the workload declined during the post-war period. In the 1930s, the New York Navy Yard was kept busy building cruisers and destroyers for the US Navy. These included the heavy cruiser *New Orleans* (CA-32) in 1934, the light cruisers *Brooklyn* (CL-40) in 1937 and *Helena* (CL-50) in 1939, and two destroyers of the *Farragut* class in 1935.

Returning to battleship construction, the New York Navy Yard laid down the USS *North Carolina* (BB-55), the first of a series of new generation 35,000-ton battleships carrying nine 16in guns in three triple turrets, two forward and one aft, in 1937. As the international situation deteriorated in the late 1930s, a tract of land to the east of the New York Navy Yard was acquired for expansion purposes, increasing the size of the yard to nearly 300 acres. Also in 1939, Slipway No. 1 at the yard was extended to 1000ft to accommodate the new super-battleships on the drawing boards. In 1941, a large 350-ton capacity hammerhead crane was installed at the fitting-out basin.

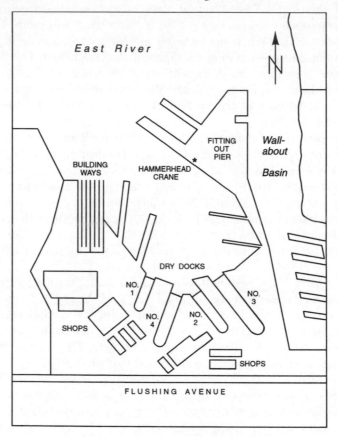

New York Navy Yard in 1941.

Two large 1100 × 150ft dry docks, the yard's fifth and sixth, were constructed at the eastern end of the yard in 1942, and a seventh dry dock was built at the navy yard Annex across the Hudson River in Bayonne, New Jersey in the following year. The New York Navy Yard completed the 45,000-ton super-battleships *Iowa* (BB-61) in 1943 and *Missouri* (BB-63) in 1944. The *Missouri* became famous as the site for the signing of the Japanese surrender at the end of the Second World War while anchored in Tokyo Bay. Another battleship, the USS *Maine* (BB-69) of the even larger *Montana* class, was laid down in 1943, but the ship was cancelled in 1944.

With the age of the battleship at an end, the New York Navy Yard turned its attention to the building of aircraft carriers. During the war, the yard produced four aircraft carriers of the 26,000-ton *Essex* class, including the

*Bennington* (CV-20) and *Bon Homme Richard* (CV-31), both in 1944, the *Kearsarge* (CV-33) in 1946, and the *Oriskany* (CV-34), launched in 1945 but not completed until 1950. In 1945, the renamed New York Naval Shipyard also completed the large fleet aircraft carrier USS *Franklin D. Roosevelt* (CVB-42, later CVA-42), one of three new 45,000-ton aircraft carriers of the *Midway* class.

Continuing with the construction of aircraft carriers, the New York Naval Shipyard produced the *Saratoga* (CVA-60) in 1956, the *Independence* (CVA-62) in 1959, and the *Kitty Hawk* (CVA-63) and *Constellation* (CVA-64), both in 1961. In 1964-5, the yard produced three amphibious transport docks for the navy. With limited demands for naval construction and the desire to maintain an industrial base for the production of defence systems, the New York Naval Shipyard was closed in 1966. The property was eventually sold to the city of New York which established the site as an industrial park.

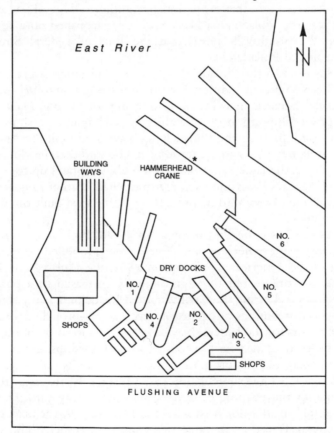

New York Naval Shipyard in 1945.

PHILADELPHIA NAVAL SHIPYARD
The Delaware Valley was first settled in the 1640s by Swedes who called their colony New Sweden. In 1655, the colony surrendered to a Dutch expedition from New Amsterdam, and the settlement came under Dutch control. Nine

years later in 1664, when England conquered New Netherland, the settlement became an English colony. In 1681, William Penn received a charter for the colony of Pennsylvania, and a new site, called Philadelphia, was selected by Penn for development as the capital of the colony. During the early part of the eighteenth century, the Delaware Valley had developed into a major shipbuilding centre, and by 1750, over 300 ships had been built in the region.

In 1774, Philadelphia became the meeting place for the First Continental Congress which contributed to the early seeds being sown for American independence from Britain. During the Revolutionary War, Philadelphia shipbuilders produced several warships for the Continental Navy, including four frigates. One of the early acts of the United States Congress after the end of the war was to authorise the establishment of navy yards to build standard warships for the new Federal Navy. Philadelphia was chosen as one of the sites for the six navy yards that were initially authorised in 1800, and in the following year, the Philadelphia Navy Yard was established on a 12-acre tract of land in the Southwalk District at the foot of Federal Street in the downtown area of Philadelphia.

From 1805 to 1810, the Philadelphia Navy Yard produced thirteen gunboats for the US Navy with an additional seven gunboats going to private shipyards in the Philadelphia area. In 1813, the 74-gun ship-of-the line *Franklin* was still built in a private shipyard in Philadelphia, but subsequent warships were built by the navy yard. In 1820, the Philadelphia Navy Yard built the 74-gun *North Carolina* as well as the 44-gun frigate *Raritan*. The yard then produced the 120-gun *Pennsylvania*, the largest ship built in the United States up to that time, in 1822. John Ericsson's experimental screw-propelled steamer *Princeton* was built at the Philadelphia Navy Yard in 1844. In 1851, the yard built the world's first floating dry dock.

From 1850 to 1859, the Philadelphia Navy Yard built seven war steamers, including two side-wheelers and five screw-propelled vessels. At the beginning of the American Civil War in 1861, the Philadelphia Navy Yard employed 345 workers, but this figure rapidly increased to a peak of 2000 employees in 1865. During the Civil War, the Philadelphia Navy Yard built the screw-propelled steam frigate *Antietam*, seven screw-propelled steam sloops, and two monitors for the Federal Navy. The existing location of the navy yard proved to be less than ideal for the construction of warships, and after the Civil War, a survey was made of other more suitable locations for the yard.

In 1868, the US Government purchased League Island from the City of Philadelphia for the purpose of developing a new navy yard. The 800-acre island is located on the north bank of the Delaware River near the mouth of the Schuykill River about three miles south of the city. The size of the yard was subsequently expanded to 1300 acres by filling in the waterway around the northeast side of the island. After the new yard had been equipped to build and repair ships, both the old and new shipyards were used until 1876, when the old yard was closed. In 1889, work was begun on the first dry dock for the Philadelphia Navy Yard, a 420 × 90ft wooden structure that was completed in 1891. This was followed in 1910 by a second and larger dry dock, which was made of granite and concrete and measured 700 × 100ft.

During the First World War, the workload at the Philadelphia Navy Yard consisted primarily of ship repair and maintenance, and its workforce rose to 12,000 employees during that period. An even larger third dry dock, measuring 1020 × 140ft, was built at the Philadelphia Navy Yard in 1916-18. Another improvement at the yard during the war was the construction of a large foundry capable of casting propellers for naval vessels. That facility was the navy's first and only propeller manufacturing plant, and it achieved international fame as such. Toward the end of the war, a 350-ton capacity hammerhead crane had been installed on Pier No. 4, which was 1000ft long and was used primarily for ship outfitting purposes.

No major naval construction took place at the Philadelphia Navy Yard until after the end of the First World War. Two of the six 45,000-ton battlecruisers of the *Lexington* class authorised by Congress in 1916, the USS *Constitution* (CC-5) and the USS *United States* (CC-6), were laid down at the yard in 1920. Work was suspended, however, in 1922 due to the naval armaments restrictions imposed by the Washington Treaty, and their incomplete hulls were scrapped. Of the six battlecruisers, only the *Lexington* (CC-1) and *Saratoga* (CC-3) were saved by their subsequent conversion into aircraft carriers at other shipyards.

In the 1930s, the Philadelphia Navy Yard built the heavy cruisers *Minneapolis* (CA-36) in 1934 and *Wichita* (CA-45) in 1939, the light cruiser *Philadelphia* (CL-41) in 1937, and five destroyers from 1935 to 1939. In 1939, the yard had a workforce of 4500 employees, and that figure would be increased ten-fold during the Second World War. Wartime production included the 35,000-ton battleship *Washington* (BB-56) in 1941 and the 45,000-ton super-battleships *New Jersey* (BB-62) in 1943 and *Wisconsin* (BB-64) in 1944. Work was in progress on another such battleship, the *Illinois* (BB-65), when the war ended and further construction was terminated. The Philadelphia Navy Yard also built two destroyers and twenty-two destroyer escorts in 1943-5.

The shipyard, renamed the PHILADELPHIA NAVAL SHIPYARD in 1945, produced the 27,000-ton *Essex* class aircraft carriers *Antietam* (CV-36), *Princeton* (CV-37), and *Valley Forge* (CV-45) and the 13,600-ton heavy cruisers *Los Angeles* (CA-135) and *Chicago* (CA-136), all between 1945-6. Coincidentally, the *Antietam*, *Los Angeles*, and *Chicago* were all christened on the same date, 20 August 1944, in a joint ceremony. By 1945, the workforce at the yard had reached 47,000 employees. Total production at the yard during the war included the construction of fifty-three warships and the overhaul and conversion of some 1200 additional ships.

By 1950, the number of employees at the Philadelphia Naval Shipyard had dropped to 6,800 workers, but it then rose again to 14,000 employees at the height of the Korean War in 1953. After that, the workforce levelled out to an average of 9000 workers during the 1960s. In the post-war period, the Philadelphia Naval Shipyard built the guided missile frigates *Dahlgren* (DLG-12) and *Pratt* (DLG-13) in 1961. From 1961 to 1968, the yard produced five helicopter-carrying amphibious assault ships, and in 1970, it built the amphibious command ship *Blue Ridge*. In 1971, the Philadelphia Naval Shipyard built its last ship, and for a while, the yard was used for ship refitting and ship repairs.

In 1990, the Philadelphia Naval Shipyard covered 1400 acres of land with a waterfront space of over 4 miles, and it contained over 1300 buildings. In that year, the US Defense Department announced that the shipyard would be among several installations that would be closed. By 1994, much of the yard had been turned back to the city of Philadelphia, and in 1995, the yard completed its last task of modernising the aircraft carrier *John F Kennedy* (CVA-67). The Philadelphia Naval Shipyard was disestablished in 1995.

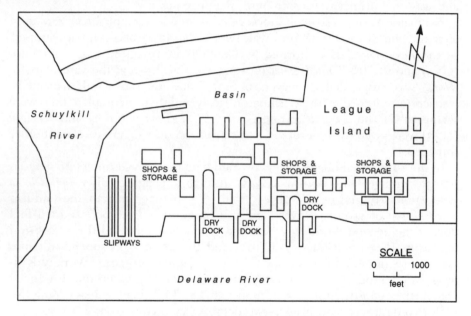

Philadelphia Naval Shipyard in 1945.

WASHINGTON NAVY YARD

In 1790, Congress authorised the acquisition and development of a ten-mile square area of land somewhere near the Potomac river for the establishment of a national capital for the United States. Major Pierre L'Enfant, a French engineer who served with the Continental Army, was chosen to select the specific site and plan the layout for the capital city. After this was accomplished, work began on the Capitol Building, and Congress transferred the seat of government to the new city of Washington in the Federal District of Columbia in 1800. One of the first acts by Congress in that year was the authorisation for the acquisition of six navy yards to build standard warships for the Federal Navy under the direct supervision of the Navy Department.

Washington was selected as one of the sites, probably to allow members of Congress to see at first hand what their naval appropriations were being spent

on. A 570-acre tract of government land on the north bank of the Anacostia
River near its confluence with the Potomac River, about one mile southeast
of the Capitol Building, was chosen as the site for the navy yard. There was no
other shipbuilding activity in that region, and the site was not considered to
be ideal for building ships, but work proceeded on the construction of the
necessary facilities for a navy yard. The navy yard was soon designated as the
home port for the Federal Navy.

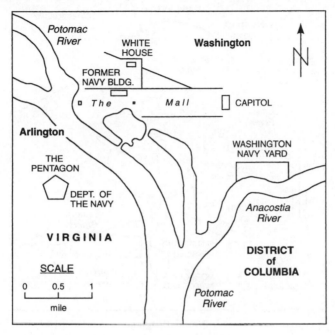

Washington DC.

The Washington Navy Yard produced fourteen gunboats for the Federal
Navy from 1805 to 1810. In 1814 during the War of 1812, the yard was
destroyed by fire, first by the Americans to prevent military equipment from
falling into British hands and then by the invading British forces that sacked
the city. After the war, the Washington Navy Yard was restored, and in 1819, it
built the 2500-ton, 74-gun ship-of-the-line *Columbus*. The yard then went on
to build the 44-gun frigates *Potomac* and *Brandywine* in 1822 and 1825,
respectively, and the 54-gun frigate *Columbia* in 1836. Thereafter naval work
was gradually transferred to other yards with better facilities, and during the
Civil War, only two monitors for the Federal navy were produced by the
Washington Navy Yard.

The last major ship built by the Washington Navy Yard was the screw-
propelled sloop *Nipsic*, which was completed in 1879. By that time, the yard
was beginning to concentrate on the manufacture of heavy shipboard
equipment, such as anchors and chain, and at the turn of the century, it
became a naval armaments centre. As the Naval Gun Factory, the yard

produced heavy guns for US naval vessels built at other navy yards, especially during the two World Wars. In 1962, production of naval ordnance ceased, and the western half of the Washington Navy Yard was subsequently taken over by the Southeast Washington Federal Centre. The eastern half of the navy yard, however, remains open to host the US Naval Historical Centre, the US Navy Library, the Navy and Marine Corps museums, and other naval activities.

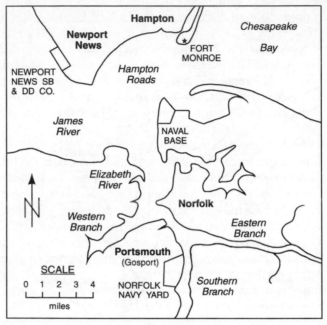

Norfolk, Virginia.

NORFOLK NAVAL SHIPYARD

The first successful settlement in Virginia was accomplished at Jamestown by the Virginia Company of London in 1607, and in 1624, Virginia became a royal colony. Groups of settlers began expanding out from Jamestown to other areas, and one party heading south along the James River established a settlement on the southern shore of Hampton Roads, one of the greatest natural harbours in the world. In 1682, the settlers laid out the town of Norfolk to serve as the county seat, and Norfolk was incorporated as a borough in 1736. During the early part of the eighteenth century, Norfolk became the port of entry into the colony.

In 1767, a ship repair service was begun by Andrew Sprowle across the Elizabeth River in Gosport (now Portsmouth), but the colonial government of Virginia requisitioned the yard as a dockyard before the Revolution. When the Revolutionary War started, the dockyard was in rebel hands, but it was abandoned in 1779 after the colonials destroyed everything that could be of use to the British. The American Revolutionary War ended in 1781, and in 1788, the United States became a constitutional republic. In 1794, the new

Federal government leased the Gosport shipyard from the state of Virginia, and in 1801, the US Navy purchased the yard after Congress authorised the establishment of six Federal navy yards, including one at Norfolk. The GOSPORT NAVY YARD soon began building ships for the Federal Navy, and it completed the 2600-ton, 74-gun ships-of-the-line *New York* and *Delaware* in 1818 and 1820 respectively.

The Gosport Navy Yard, soon renamed the NORFOLK NAVY YARD continued its production of warships for the Federal Navy, completing the 36-gun frigate *Macedonian* in 1822. In 1827-33, a granite dry dock, 320 × 80ft in size, was constructed at the Norfolk Navy Yard, and it represented the US Navy's first dry dock. The Norfolk Navy Yard built the 44-gun frigate *St Lawrence* in 1848, and during the 1850s it completed five sloops-of-war and several other warships. In 1861, the Federal forces at the Norfolk Navy Yard set fire to all facilities and ships to preclude their falling into Confederate hands.

The Confederates, upon taking over the Norfolk Navy Yard, were able to salvage the hull of the frigate USS *Merrimack* and convert it into the ironclad CSS *Virginia*. The *Virginia* sailed north and wrought havoc on Federal ships at Hampton Roads until the ship was stopped by the *Monitor*, which had just arrived on the scene from New York, in 1862. Between 1877 and 1880, the Norfolk Navy Yard built two screw-propelled sloops. In 1889, the yard completed its second dry dock, a wooden structure 490 × 85ft in size. Norfolk completed the protected cruiser *Raleigh* (C-8) in 1892, and it then built the pre-Dreadnought battleship *Texas* in 1895.

The Norfolk Navy Yard completed its third dry dock in 1908, but it was later extended to 725ft in 1911. During the First World War, the Norfolk Navy Yard was used primarily for ship repair and maintenance functions. The yard then had one slipway that could be used for the construction of Dreadnought-size battleships, as well as a new 1000 × 110ft graving dock (its fourth) with a 50-ton electrical crane. The Norfolk Navy Yard was improved by the construction of three additional granite dry docks, two of which were 550 × 110ft and the other 1000 × 110ft, during the war. Other improvements included a new foundry and an enlarged workshop area that were completed in 1917. In 1914, the yard had 2700 employees, but that figure increased to a maximum of over 11,000 by the end of the war.

In 1920, construction began on the 43,200-ton battleship *North Carolina* (BB-52), but work was suspended after the ship was only one-third complete as a result of Washington Treaty limitations on capital ships. In 1920, the Norfolk Navy Yard also undertook the conversion of the collier *Jupiter* into America's first aircraft carrier, the *Langley* (CV-1), which became the test bed for the development of US naval aviation upon its completion in 1922. The Norfolk Navy Yard built four destroyers in 1920 and seven more in the 1930s. In 1933, the old wooden dry dock of 1889 was replaced with one made of concrete. Post-war employment at the yard dropped to a low of 2500 workers in 1924, but then it gradually rose to 4000 in 1934 and 6500 in 1938.

The Norfolk Navy Yard was upgraded from 1938–40 with the construction of a 350-ton capacity hammerhead crane in 1939, a number of shop improvements, and expansion to the south. As the Second World War approached, the workforce at the yard began to take a dramatic upswing. From 7600 workers at the beginning of the war in 1939, employment reached 28,600 by the time Pearl Harbor was attacked in December 1941. The workforce at the Norfolk Navy Yard reached a peak of 43,000 in February 1943, but that figure gradually declined to 32,000 by the end of the war in 1945. Production during the Second World War included the 35,000-ton battleship *Alabama* (BB-60) in 1942 and the 27,000-ton *Essex* class aircraft carriers *Shangri-La* (CVA-38), *Lake Champlain* (CVA-39), and *Tarawa* (CVA-40) in 1944–5. The yard also produced four destroyers from 1940–2, and ten destroyer escorts in 1943.

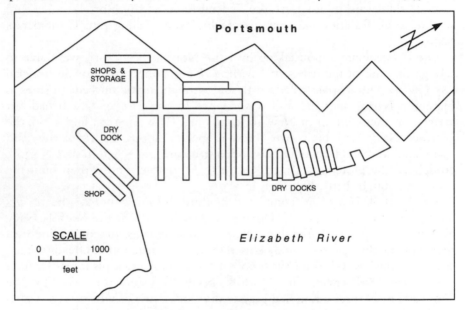

Norfolk Naval Shipyard in 1945.

Slipway No. 1 at the Norfolk Navy Yard had been lengthened from 700ft to 900ft in 1939 to accommodate the construction of the new 45,000-ton super-battleships then on the drawing boards. One of those ships, the *Kentucky* (BB-66), was laid down in 1944, but work was suspended at the end of the war. The Norfolk Navy Yard was one of the largest shipyards in the world, and during the war, it produced some one hundred ships of various types for the US Navy. The NORFOLK NAVAL SHIPYARD, as the yard was renamed in 1945, had 31,800 employees at the end of the war. The yard currently continues to repair, overhaul, and modernise naval vessels.

## CHARLESTON NAVAL SHIPYARD

The colonisation of South Carolina began in 1670 with the English settlement at Charleston. By the beginning of the eighteenth century, Charleston had become an important port, first for the export of rice and then for cotton. Charleston Harbour afforded excellent port facilities, and it could be easily defended by artillery on land masses at its mouth. Shipbuilding was not a major industry at Charleston, and only a few warships were built by private shipyards after the Revolutionary War. Charleston became the site where the American Civil War began when Confederate forces fired on the Federal garrison at Fort Sumter in the mouth of Charleston Harbour in 1861.

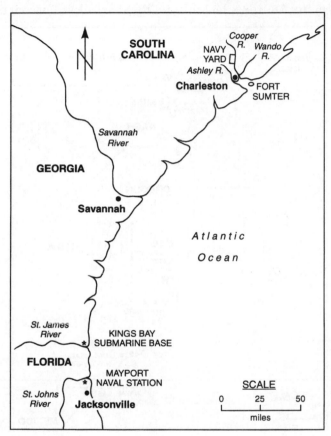

US Southeast Coast.

In 1901, Congress authorised the establishment of a navy yard at Charleston, and in that year, the government purchased land on the west bank of the Cooper River, about five miles north of the city, for that purpose. The land included the 170-acre Chicora Park bought from the city of Charleston and the 260-acre Lawton Place, a private plantation just to the south of the park. In addition, the city donated to the navy another 760 acres of mostly marshland further south of the selected area. The yard was initially equipped with two small slipways and a 550 × 100ft dry dock. During the First World War, the CHARLESTON NAVY YARD, which had been rated as a second class navy yard, built just one destroyer and several gunboats.

The Charleston Navy Yard actually specialised as a ship repair facility, and it continued to serve in this role until the late 1930s. Just prior to and during the Second World War, the yard built twenty destroyers, twenty-six destroyer escorts, 113 landing ships, and a number of auxiliary vessels and smaller warships for the US Navy. After the war, the Charleston Naval Shipyard reverted to ship repair and maintenance, including ship conversions. As the workload declined over the years, the Charleston Naval Shipyard was selected for closure in the late 1980s, and in 1991, the shipyard was decommissioned.

US Navy Yards and Naval Bases on the West Coast.

## PENSACOLA NAVY YARD

Florida was acquired from Spain in 1819, and the Pensacola Navy Yard was established in 1826 to serve primarily as a warship repair facility on the Gulf Coast. The facility was never intended to construct warships, and when it was no longer required even for ship repair services, the Pensacola Navy Yard was decommissioned as a shipyard in 1914. With naval interest in aircraft on the rise, its facilities were immediately taken over for naval aviation development, and Pensacola was established as the first US naval air station. Known as the 'Cradle of Naval Aviation', Pensacola continues to be used as the primary training centre for naval and Marine aviators, and it is the home of the famous aerial exhibition team, the 'Blue Angels'.

## MARE ISLAND NAVAL SHIPYARD

The California Territory was ceded to the United States by Mexico under the Treaty of Guadalupe Hidalgo in 1848, and in 1850, California entered the Union as a free state. In 1852, land was acquired on Mare Island across from Vallejo, California for a Federal navy yard, and Commodore David G Farragut, later of Civil War fame, was designated to became its first commandant. With Farragut supervising its construction, the MARE ISLAND NAVY YARD was established in 1854, becoming the first docking and ship repair facility on the west coast. The yard built the screw-propelled sloop-of-war *Mohican* in 1876, but it concentrated on ship repairs until the end of the First World War. Mare Island's first graving dock was completed in the early 1890s.

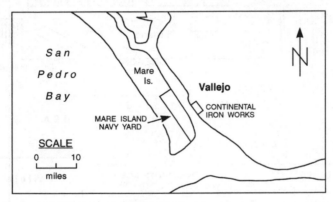

Vallejo in 1940.

In 1914, the Mare Island Navy Yard had two granite dry docks, one of 730 × 120ft and the other 460 × 95ft in size. During the First World War, an additional 880 × 100ft concrete dry dock was constructed at the yard, as was a 600ft-long slipway capable of accommodating a Dreadnought-type battleship. The Mare Island Navy Yard completed the battleship *California* (BB-44) in 1921, but work on the 43,000-ton super-battleship *Montana* (BB-51) was cancelled in 1922 due to the limitation on capital ships imposed by the Washington Naval Treaty. The yard had a workforce of 2500 people in 1920, and it gradually increased over the next few years to 2800 employees in 1925.

In the inter-war period, the Mare Island Navy Yard produced the heavy cruisers *Chicago* (CA-29) in 1931 and *San Francisco* (CA-38) in 1934, three destroyers, and three submarines. In 1936, the yard had 5000 workers, and this figure grew rapidly to 12,000 in 1939 and to over 14,000 in 1941. During the Second World War, the facilities at Mare Island Navy Yard had been increased by two floating dry docks to supplement its existing four concrete dry docks, and it had a total of eight shipbuilding ways. By that time, additional land had been acquired, and the shipyard had expanded to 1500 acres.

Production during the Second World War included the construction of thirty-nine destroyer escorts and twenty-four submarines, as well as the repair of numerous US and Allied warships. The workforce of the yard reached a peak of over 20,000 in 1943, but that figure had come down again to 12,000 in 1946. After the war, the renamed MARE ISLAND NAVAL SHIPYARD continued to build submarines, completing two conventional submarines through 1959 and then building seventeen nuclear-powered submarines from 1959 to 1972. With little additional work forthcoming, the Mare Island Naval Shipyard ceased to operate in 1994.

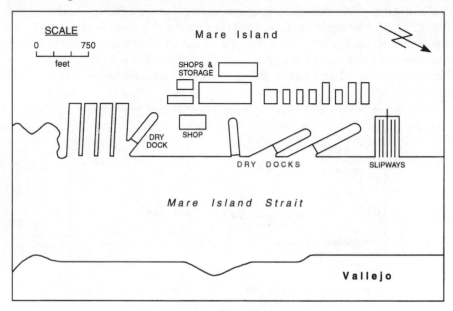

Mare Island Naval Shipyard in 1945

## PUGET SOUND NAVAL SHIPYARD

During the eighteenth century, the Pacific northwest region was open country exploited by rival British and American fur traders. As a result of American immigration into the area at the beginning of the nineteenth century, the Pacific northwest territory was claimed by the United States. In 1846, Great Britain recognised American sovereignty over the territory south of the 49th parallel, and two years later, that region was officially established by the Congress as the Oregon Territory of the United States. The first white settlement in the territory became the town of Seattle in 1851. Two years later in 1853, the area north of the Columbia River was separated from Oregon and became the Washington Territory.

The town of Tacoma at the southern end of Puget Sound was founded in 1875, and the Washington Territory became a state in 1889. The suitability of Puget Sound for maritime activity became readily apparent at the outset of its development. Seattle soon became an important port for trade between the territory and the outside world, and this was later followed by Tacoma also becoming a notable trading centre. The Puget Sound area was also recognised for it shipbuilding potential, and before the end of the nineteenth century, shipbuilding began to be undertaken along its shores. In 1891, the US Navy established the PUGET SOUND NAVY YARD on a 190-acre tract of land at Bremerton, Washington on the Sinclair Inlet, just across the Puget Sound and about fifteen miles west of Seattle.

The Puget Sound Navy Yard, also popularly referred to as the Bremerton Navy Yard, specialised in ship repair and overhaul rather than shipbuilding. In 1917, work began on the construction of slipways for the construction of scout cruisers, but the workload for such vessels never materialised during the First World War. The yard did, however, build six submarines, twenty-five minesweepers, and a host of smaller naval vessels during the war. By that time, Puget Sound Navy Yard had expanded to 315 acres, and it had two dry docks, including one wooden structure, 620 × 75ft in size and one granite and concrete dock 800 × 115ft in size. It was not until the post–First World War era, however, that the Puget Sound Navy Yard began to build major warships for the navy.

In the 1930s, the Puget Sound Navy Yard produced the heavy cruisers *Louisville* (CA-28) in 1931 and *Astoria* (CA-34) in 1934, as well as six destroyers

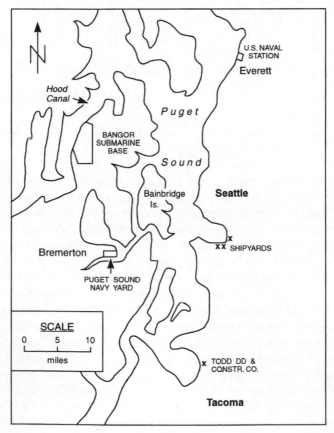

Puget Sound.

in 1935-9. The uss *Astoria* was one of the three American heavy cruisers sunk by Japanese cruisers during the Battle of Savo Island while protecting the American landings at Guadalcanal in August 1942. Five of the surviving battleships damaged during the Japanese air raid on Pearl Harbor were repaired and modernised here before returning to the fleet. During the Second World War, the Puget Sound Navy Yard built eleven destroyers and eight destroyer escorts, and in the post-war period, it produced one more destroyer and two more destroyer escorts.

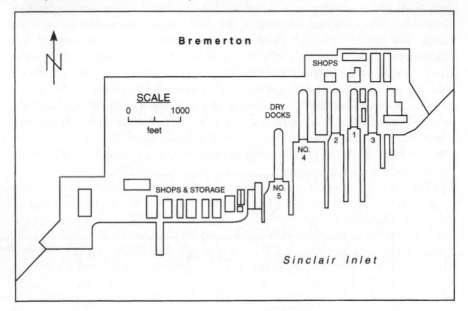

Puget Sound Naval Shipyard.

By 1945, employment at the yard reached a high of 32,000 workers, and in that year, the yard was renamed the PUGET SOUND NAVAL SHIPYARD. After the end of the war, the workload dropped, but the yard was kept busy in the 1950s by modifying several *Essex* class aircraft carriers with new angled decks that greatly increased their efficiency. In the 1960s, the Puget Sound Naval Shipyard produced six guided-missile frigates, including the *Coontz* (DLG-9) and *King* (DLG-10), both in 1960, *Gridley* (DLG-21) in 1963, *Reeves* (DLG-24) in 1964, *Jouett* (DLG-29) in 1966, and *Sterett* (DLG-31) in 1967. The latter four vessels were later reclassified as guided missile cruisers and were redesignated as CG-21, CG-24, CG-29, and CG-31, respectively, keeping their original numbers.

In 1962, the Puget Sound Naval Shipyard built its sixth dry dock, which measured 1180 × 180ft and was one of the largest in the world at that time. The shipyard is now charged with the repair and overhaul of naval surface ships and submarines on the West Coast and to provide logistics support for the ships based at that facility. The shipyard currently serves as the home port for two nuclear aircraft carriers, one guided missile cruiser, and several naval auxiliary vessels. Puget Sound Naval Shipyard presently covers 690 acres of land, and its facilities include six dry docks, nine piers, and over 380 buildings. The workforce of the yard currently stands at about 10,000 civilian employees.

### SAN FRANCISCO NAVAL SHIPYARD

The SAN FRANCISCO NAVY YARD, one of the last two shipyards authorised by Congress, was established in 1940. The yard was located at the site of a former private shipyard situated on the south side of Hunters Point on the west bank of San Francisco Bay, about 25 miles south of San Francisco. The original shipyard was expanded to accommodate the needs for major ship repairs, and by the end of the Second World War, the yard had six dry docks and it could handle the largest warships of that time. After the war, the renamed SAN FRANCISCO NAVAL SHIPYARD began to build ships, producing the guided missile frigates *Mahan* (DLG-11) in 1960, *Halsey* (DLG-23) in 1963, and *Horne* (DLG-30) in 1967. The *Halsey* and *Horne* were later reclassified as guided missile cruisers and renumbered CG-23 and CG-30, respectively. The yard also produced two nuclear submarines in 1968. The San Francisco Naval Shipyard is no longer an active shipyard.

### LONG BEACH NAVAL SHIPYARD

The LONG BEACH NAVY YARD, like the San Francisco Navy Yard, was one of the last two navy yards authorised by Congress, and it was also established in 1940 before America's entry into the Second World War. The shipyard is located on Terminal Island in San Pedro Bay near Long Beach, California, about 25 miles south of Los Angeles. Originally known as US Naval Dry Docks, Terminal Island, the shipyard became operational in 1943, and it served primarily as a ship repair facility during the Second World War and in the post-war era. At the end of the war, the shipyard had a workforce of 16,000 civilian employees. The facility was named TERMINAL ISLAND NAVAL SHIPYARD in 1945, and in 1948, it was renamed as the LONG BEACH NAVAL SHIPYARD. No longer required by the navy, the Long Beach Naval Shipyard was disestablished in 1997.

### PEARL HARBOR NAVAL SHIPYARD

The Hawaiian Islands were discovered in 1778 by the English navigator, Captain James Cook, and early in the nineteenth century, there was an influx of American missionaries seeking to convert the natives to Christianity. England and France had designs on the islands, but the local inhabitants maintained their independence from any foreign domination for many decades. In 1887, the then pro-American ruler of Hawaii gave the United States exclusive rights to maintain a ship coaling and repair station at Pearl Harbor on Oahu Island. With the encouragement of Americans on the islands, the native leaders sought annexation of Hawaii by the United States. In 1900, Congress approved the annexation of the Hawaiian Islands, and they became a territory of the United States.

Within a year of the annexation of Hawaii, the ship repair and coaling station being used by the US Navy was officially established as a Federal navy yard. The PEARL HARBOR NAVY YARD was never intended as a shipbuilding facility, but rather a shipyard for the repair and maintenance of US warships operating in the Pacific region. Pearl Harbor was a good harbour that could accommodate a large number of ships, and it was located about ten miles northwest of Honolulu. A large 800 × 115ft graving dock was built at the yard during the First World War, and at the time of the Japanese attack on Pearl Harbor in December 1941, two additional dry docks were nearing completion just to the northwest of the existing dry dock (see Pearl Harbor Naval Station).

## AMERICAN NAVAL BASES AND NAVAL STATIONS

The US Navy had two primary naval bases for its surface fleet, one on the east coast at Norfolk, Virginia and the other on the west coast at San Diego, California. In view of the independent nature of submarine operations, submarine bases are usually maintained separately from surface warship bases. Submarines armed with ballistic missiles are further segregated at two new bases established for that purpose, one at Kings Bay, Georgia on the East Coast and the other at Bangor, Washington on the West Coast. In addition to its several large 'naval bases', which have broad multi-purpose support functions for elements of the fleet, the United States also maintains a number of smaller 'naval stations' with more limited functions in the United States and in certain overseas locations.

### East Coast
The NEWPORT NAVAL STATION was established on Narragansett Bay near Newport, Rhode Island in 1884, and in that same year, the Naval War College was established at that site. During the American Civil War, the US Naval Academy was temporarily transferred to Newport, but it returned to Annapolis after the end of the war. In the early part of the twentieth century, the main anchorage of the US Atlantic Fleet was in Narragansett Bay, the entrance to which was protected by a number of forts, including Fort Adams which was built at the end of the eighteenth century, located just two miles southwest of the town of Newport.

The Newport Naval Station became a first class naval station, and it supported the Atlantic Fleet while anchored in Narragansett Bay. Prior to the First World War, the station began to specialise in the production of torpedoes, and it soon became the primary torpedo manufactory for the US Navy. Today, there are two sections of the Newport Naval Station, one of which is located on Coaster's Harbor Island off the northern end of Newport. It is there that the Naval War College and the Naval War College Museum are located. About two miles north of Newport is the other section of the Newport Naval Station, which hosts the Naval Undersea Warfare Center and Destroyer Squadron Six.

In 1868, the state of Connecticut donated over 100 acres of land on the east (left) bank of the Thames River to the US government for the development of a naval base. The site was situated about five miles north of the town of

Groton, Connecticut and across the river from New London. Construction at the site began in 1872, but lack of funds handicapped further development, and the facility was downgraded to a coaling station in 1881. In 1916, the naval station was converted into a submarine base, the so-called NEW LONDON SUBMARINE BASE became the 'Birthplace of the US Submarine Force'.

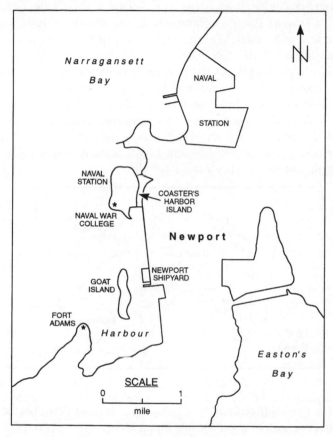

Newport.

Upon America's entry into the First World War, the New London Submarine Base became very active in the training of submariners for the fledgling US submarine force. The base was greatly expanded over the years, and it now occupies over 1300 acres of land, more than ten times its original size. The base continued to develop as a submarine training facility for the US Navy, and it is now the home of the Submarine School as well as the home port for twenty-one nuclear submarines. The US COAST GUARD ACADEMY, which was established in 1876, moved to its present site at New London on the west bank of the Thames River in 1932.

The US NAVAL ACADEMY was established in 1845 on the south bank of the Severn River near its effluence into the Chesapeake Bay at Annapolis, Maryland, the capital of the state of Maryland. During the Civil War, the US

Naval Academy was temporarily located at Newport, Rhode Island, but it returned to Annapolis after the end of the war. The tomb of the American naval hero, John Paul Jones, rests in the Naval Academy Chapel. The grounds of the Naval Academy are also the site of a naval museum and the headquarters of the US Naval Institute.

The NORFOLK NAVAL BASE is the world's largest naval base, covering some 3300 acres at Sewell's Point on Hampton Roads, about five miles north of the downtown area of Norfolk, Virginia. The base serves as the host installation for the Headquarters of the US Atlantic Fleet and numerous naval support activities. Norfolk is also the home port for five nuclear aircraft carriers, twelve nuclear submarines, one nuclear guided missile cruiser, nine conventional guided missile cruisers, eleven guided missile destroyers, eleven destroyers, eleven guided missile frigates, twelve amphibious support ships of various types, and a host of auxiliary naval vessels. In the case of Norfolk, the submarine base is part of the Norfolk Naval Station, and it does not have a separate facility as some other naval bases do.

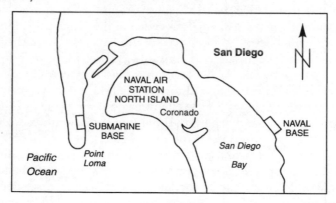

San Diego.

Located at the southern end of Chesapeake Bay near Virginia Beach, about ten miles to the east of the Norfolk Naval Base, is the LITTLE CREEK NAVAL AMPHIBIOUS BASE. The base was established in 1945 as the main operating base for the amphibious forces of the US Atlantic Fleet. Little Creek also serves as the home port for eight dock landing ships and a number of coastal patrol craft.

The CHARLESTON NAVAL BASE, one of the largest naval bases in the country, is co-located with the Charleston Naval Shipyard at Charleston, South Carolina. The base serves primarily as a logistics support activity and an operational base for destroyers, frigates, and auxiliary naval vessels. At one time, the base also supported submarine operations, but in 1979, its submarine operations were transferred to the newly opened submarine base at Kings Bay, Georgia.

In 1976, construction began on the KINGS BAY SUBMARINE BASE at Kings Bay, Georgia on the north (left) bank of the St. Mary's River at the mouth of the river across the state border from Florida. The primary purpose of Kings

Bay is to serve as the East Coast home base of the *Ohio* class 'Trident' ballistic missile submarine force, and it is the home port of ten such vessels. The Kings Bay Submarine Base also is the host installation for the Trident Refit Facility.

The MAYPORT NAVAL STATION is located at St Johns Point at the mouth of the St. Johns River where it flows into the Atlantic Ocean just to the north of Jacksonville, Florida. Mayport is the home base for one conventional aircraft carrier, four guided missile cruisers, three guided missile destroyers, five destroyers, and eight guided missile frigates.

### Gulf Coast

The PASCAGOULA NAVAL STATION is located at Spanish Point, an island in Pascagoula Bay, about two miles southwest of the city of Pascagoula, Mississippi. The naval station was opened in 1992, and it now serves as the home port for two guided missile cruisers and two guided missile frigates.

### West Coast

San Diego was first settled by the Spanish around 1700, and it came under American control when California was ceded to the United States by Mexico in 1848. California became a state in 1850, and two years later, the lower half of the Point Loma Peninsula was set aside for military use. The land was initially taken over by the Army, becoming Fort Rosecrans in 1898, but in 1959, the fort was designated as a historic landmark, and it was turned over to the navy. In 1919, the city of San Diego donated some 75 acres of land along the northern shore of San Diego Bay, about four miles southeast of the centre of the city, to the US government for a naval base.

The SAN DIEGO DESTROYER BASE was established in 1922 with its primary mission of storing many of destroyers that had been deactivated after the end of the First World War, mostly of the famous four-stacker, flush-deck type. At the onset of the Second World War, the base took on the additional function of ship repairs, and in 1943 was renamed as the SAN DIEGO NAVAL REPAIR BASE. In 1946, the base became the SAN DIEGO NAVAL STATION, and since that time, its primary mission has been to provide logistic support for the US Pacific Fleet. The San Diego Naval Station is now the home port of eight guided missile cruisers, five guided missile destroyers, seven destroyers, twelve guided missile frigates, sixteen amphibious support ships of various types, and a number of naval auxiliary vessels.

In 1963, the SAN DIEGO SUBMARINE SUPPORT FACILITY was established at Ballast Point on the western shore of San Diego Bay along the Point Loma Peninsula about six miles southwest of the city of San Diego. After the construction of a number of piers along the shore of San Diego Bay, the San Diego Submarine Support Facility was redesignated as the SAN DIEGO SUBMARINE BASE in 1981. The San Diego Submarine Base is now the home port for six nuclear-powered attack submarines. All submarine operations and related naval activities off the coast of California are controlled from the San Diego Submarine Base, and the base serves as the host installation for a submarine development activity and a submarine training facility.

The NORTH ISLAND NAVAL AIR STATION was established in 1917, and in 1963, it was officially recognised as being the 'Birthplace of Naval Aviation'. The station is located on North Island near the town of Coronado and across the San Diego Bay from the city of San Diego. The primary mission of North Island, also known as the CORONADO NAVAL AIR STATION, is to provide aviation support services to the Pacific Fleet and to perform maintenance on naval aircraft. The base is now also the home port for one conventional aircraft carrier.

The ALAMEDA NAVAL AIR STATION, located directly across San Francisco Bay from the city of San Francisco, was established as a naval air station in 1940. In addition to supporting naval aviation activities in the San Francisco area, Alameda also provided support for naval surface vessels. Over the years, the station served as the home port for several aircraft carriers as well as other naval vessels. It was disestablished in April 1997.

Naval Bases in the Caribbean.

In 1974, construction began on the BANGOR SUBMARINE BASE on the Hood Canal near Bangor, Washington, about twenty-five miles northwest of Seattle. The submarine base became operational in 1977, and it now serves as the home port for eight nuclear-powered 'Trident' ballistic missile submarines and one nuclear attack submarine of the US Pacific Fleet.

The EVERETT NAVAL STATION is located on Possession Sound at the north end of Everett, Washington, about thirty miles north of Seattle. In 1984, Everett was selected as the site for a new naval base in the Puget Sound area to serve as the home port for naval vessels under the Strategic Homeport Concept. The Everett Naval Station was established in 1994, replacing the old

Puget Sound Naval Station at Sand Point, which was subsequently closed in 1995. Everett now serves as the home port for two guided missile destroyers, two destroyers, and two guided missile frigates. Everett also serves as the headquarters of the Commander, Naval Surface Group Pacific Northwest.

## Caribbean

The GUANTANAMO BAY NAVAL STATION is located at Guantanamo Bay on the southern coastline of Cuba near the city of Santiago. It was established in 1898 as an advance base to support the Santiago campaign by the American Naval Squadron. After Cuba became independent from Spain as a result of the Spanish-American War, it leased the Guantanamo Bay facility to the United States in 1903 for use as a coaling station. This lease was formalised by a treaty signed in 1934, making the Guantanamo Bay Naval Station the oldest overseas base of the United States. Over the years, the station served mostly as a fleet anchorage for training exercises in the Caribbean, and it now serves primarily as a naval air station.

The ROOSEVELT ROADS NAVAL STATION was established at the eastern tip of Puerto Rico, about thirty miles southeast of San Juan, during the Second World War. Puerto Rico is the smallest and most easterly of the large islands in the Greater Antilles chain in the West Indies. In 1493, Columbus took possession of the island in the names of King Ferdinand and Queen Isabella of Spain. The island was attacked by Sir Francis Drake in 1595, and over the years, the French, Danes, and Dutch also tried to exert some influence over the island. Although the inhabitants were agitating for independence from Spain, Puerto Rico was ceded to the United States in 1898 after the Spanish-American War before its independence was achieved.

The main base of the Roosevelt Roads Naval Station occupies 8000 acres of land on the mainland of Puerto Rico. The US Navy also uses the nearby offshore island of Vieques for naval gunfire and bombing practice, as well as for a naval ammunition storage facility. The large range areas at both ends of the island leave only the centre portion free for commercial and private use. Another nearby island, Culebra, had been used for gunfire and bombing practice, but that use was discontinued in 1975.

The Isthmus of Panama was first explored by Spain in 1501, and it soon became a Spanish colony. It was attacked by Sir Francis Drake in 1572, but the English did not attempt to settle in the area. In 1822, the local inhabitants proclaimed their independence from Spain, and the colony immediately united with Colombia. The desirability of a canal through Panama linking the Atlantic and Pacific Oceans for trade purposes had long been recognised. In 1879, a French company under Ferdinand De Lesseps, builder of the Suez Canal, undertook the project of building the Panama Canal, but it could not be completed.

In 1903, Panama, at the instigation of the United States, declared its independence from Colombia, and in the following year, it leased a strip of land through the isthmus to the United States for the construction of a canal. The United States then occupied the Canal Zone and began its effort to build the Panama Canal. While the canal was being constructed, the United States began to fortify both ends of the canal, establishing naval stations at Cristobal near Colon on the northern (Atlantic) entrance and at Balboa near the city of Panama at the southern (Pacific) entrance to the canal.

The Panama Canal was finally completed in 1914. Each naval station at either end of the canal had a single dry dock, 1100ft long and 110ft wide, and they initially had storage facilities for a large stockpile of coal. In 1979, the United States agreed to turn over the operation of the canal to Panama and the Canal Zone was abolished. Although most of its military bases in Panama have been closed down, the United States still maintains the PANAMA NAVAL STATION at Balboa.

### Europe

The US Navy currently maintains two naval bases in Europe, and as a member of the North Atlantic Treaty Organisation (NATO), it also has access to additional naval bases and ports of treaty nations. The NAPLES NAVAL SUPPORT ACTIVITY at Naples, Italy supports US naval operations in the Mediterranean Sea and in the Middle East region. The ROTA NAVAL STATION at Rota, Spain, just to the west of the southern tip of Spain, provides logistics support for US Navy vessels operating in the eastern half of the Atlantic.

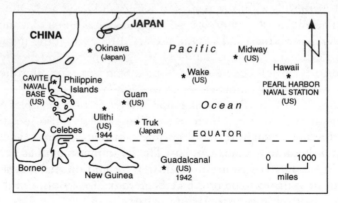

Naval Bases in the Pacific.

### Pacific Ocean

In 1908, seven years after the establishment of the Pearl Harbor Navy Yard, the US Navy established the PEARL HARBOR NAVAL STATION to support elements of the fleet. The naval station was co-located with the navy yard, but it was separately administered with respect to the conduct of naval operations. The naval station gradually expanded into a fully-fledged naval base with a variety of functions and activities, including the Headquarters of the Pacific Fleet. The Pearl Harbor Naval Station is now the most important American naval base in the Pacific region, and it is also the home port for three guided missile cruisers, two guided missile destroyers, four destroyers, and two guided missile frigates.

With dock space limited, the base had to rely on many warships being anchored in the waters surrounding Ford Island at the centre of the harbour. A unique mooring system for major warships was used at the Pearl Harbor Naval Station, consisting of large concrete mooring stanchions placed in a row just off both the north shore and the southeast shore of Ford Island. Each ship was tied up to a pair of these stanchions, and external electric power could be provided to the ship through them. At the time of the Japanese attack on Pearl Harbor in December 1941, the row of stanchions along the southeast shore was used to moor the battleships of the fleet, and the area became known as 'Battleship Row'.

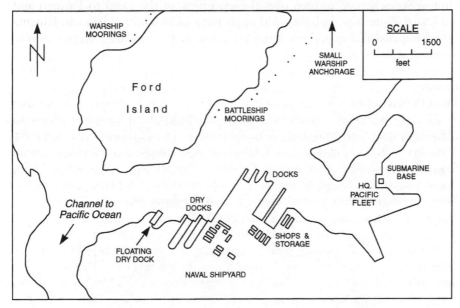

Pearl Harbor in 1941.

In 1915, the navy established a temporary submarine base at Pearl Harbor, and in 1923, it became a permanent base for the submarines of the US Pacific Fleet. The PEARL HARBOR SUBMARINE BASE is located on the Southeast Loch of Pearl Harbor at the east end of the Pearl Harbor Naval Base, and at the time of the Japanese attack on Pearl Harbor in December 1941, the Headquarters of the Commander of the Pacific Fleet was actually situated on the grounds of the Submarine Base. The base currently serves as the home port for twenty-three nuclear submarines of the Pacific Fleet.

The MIDWAY ISLANDS consist of two small islands that are actually an extension of the Hawaiian Island group to the northwest. The Midway Islands were discovered and claimed for the United States by Captain N C Brookes in 1859, and they were formally annexed in 1867. In 1903, the Midway Islands were placed under the control of the US Navy, but it was not until 1940 that the navy began work on a major air base and submarine base on one of the islands. The Midway Islands became the objective of a Japanese invasion fleet in May 1942, but the fleet was savagely attacked by American aircraft operating from US aircraft carriers. After suffering heavy losses, including four aircraft carriers, the Japanese withdrew.

The defeat of the Japanese strike force at Midway proved to be the turning point of the Second World War in the Pacific. The US Navy improved the facilities and defences at the Midway Islands, and Midway continued to be used as a base for the reconquest of the Pacific. After the war, there was little interest in the Midway Islands except as a naval air facility. In 1950, the naval activity was reduced to housekeeping functions, and the main island now serves as the host installation for a Naval Air Activity.

AMERICAN SAMOA consists of five inhabited islands in the eastern section of the Samoan Islands group about 2700 miles southwest of Hawaii. With the advent of steam power, the US Navy began looking for coaling stations throughout the Pacific to support its warships operating in that region. In 1878, the United States obtained from the independent kingdom of Samoa the right to establish a coaling station at Pango Pango (Pago Pago) on the island of Tutuila.

In 1900, the head chiefs of the islands of Tutuila and Aunuu ceded those islands to the United States, and in 1904, the head chief of the islands of Tau, Olosega, and Ofu followed suit. It was not until 1929, however, that Congress formally accepted the annexation of those islands to the United States. The naval base at Pago Pago continued to be used by the US Navy as a refuelling station throughout most of the twentieth century. From 1900, American Samoa was under the control of the US Navy, but in 1951, the administration of that territory fell under the Department of the Interior.

WAKE ISLAND is located about 2500 miles due west of Honolulu, Hawaii. The island was claimed by the United States for use as a cable station in 1899, and in 1934, Wake was placed under the jurisdiction of the US Navy. In 1941, work was begun on an air base and submarine base on Wake, but those facilities were only partially completed by December of that year when a Japanese task force captured the island. After the Japanese surrender in 1945, the navy completed the naval air station on Wake.

GUAM is the largest and most southern island of the Mariana group of islands, and it is located about 1500 miles southwest of Wake and an equal distance east of Manila. Guam was discovered by Ferdinand Magellan, a Portuguese navigator in the service of the Holy Roman Emperor, Charles V, in 1521, just before Magellan went on to discover the Philippine Islands. In the latter part of the seventeenth century, Guam was conquered by Spain, but in 1898, the island was ceded to the United States under the Treaty of Paris after the Spanish-American War. The US Navy began to build a naval station at Guam, but lack of funds and the political climate in the 1930s kept the navy from building a formidable base on the island.

Guam was quickly captured by a small Japanese naval force within a couple of days after the attack on Pearl Harbor in December 1941. During the summer of 1944, Guam, Saipan, and the Tinian Islands in the southern Marianas chain were recaptured by American forces after overcoming strong opposition from the Japanese. Tinian became the main base for the B-29 bomber raids on Japan, which culminated in the dropping of atomic bombs on Hiroshima and Nagasaki in August 1945. Guam now serves as the host installation for the MARIANAS SHIP REPAIR FACILITY as well as the MARIANAS NAVAL STATION, and it is the home base for several auxiliary naval vessels.

ULITHI ATOLL is located in the Yap Islands group of the Caroline Islands chain about 1300 miles east of Manila. The Caroline Islands were discovered by Spanish ships in the sixteenth century, but the islands were not settled by Spain until the nineteenth century. After losing the Philippines and Guam to the United States as a result of the Spanish-American War, Spain decided to pull out of the Pacific region, and therefore she sold the Caroline Islands to Germany in 1898. After the First World War, Germany lost the islands to Japan, which then held them by mandate from the League of Nations.

During the inter-war period, the Japanese built a number of naval and air bases throughout the Caroline Islands, including their main base at Truk. In September 1944, Ulithi was occupied by American forces, and in view of its large deep lagoon that could provide an excellent fleet anchorage, it was quickly turned into a naval base for the US Navy. The atoll became the main base for Fast Carrier Forces, Pacific Fleet (Task Force 38) under Admirals Halsey and Mitscher. Ulithi is now part of the Federated States of Micronesia.

The Philippine Islands were discovered by Magellan in 1521. The first permanent settlement by Europeans was on the island of Cebu in 1565, and from then on, there were increasing settlements by both Portugal and Spain. Although the British and Dutch also had some interest in the islands, the Philippines were eventually conquered by Spain after her settlers achieved dominance in the region. In 1898, the Philippines declared its independence from Spain, but this was overtaken by the Spanish-American war which resulted in the ceding of the Philippines to the United States under the Treaty of Paris.

The Spanish had a naval shipyard at Cavite on a peninsula sticking out into Manila Bay at the south end of the bay across from the city. This shipyard, which had been used to build gunboats and other small craft for the Spanish Navy, was taken over by the US Navy and developed into the CAVITE NAVY YARD, the most important US naval base in the Far East region. The Cavite Navy Yard was heavily damaged by Japanese bombers shortly after the Japanese attack on Pearl Harbor in December 1941, and it quickly fell to Japanese forces when they invaded the Philippines a few weeks later. US forces returned to the Philippines in 1944 and began the process of recapturing the islands. After the Second World War, the Philippines achieved their independence.

The United States occupied Japan after the end of the Second World War, and used its naval bases to support the US Navy in its occupation duties. After Japan again became a free nation in 1952, the US Navy leased the naval shipyards at Yokosuka and Sasebo as naval bases for the Pacific Fleet. The YOKOSUKA NAVAL BASE continues to be used by the US Navy as a ship repair facility, as well as the home port for one aircraft carrier, two guided missile cruisers, two guided missile destroyers, two destroyers, two guided missile frigates, and one amphibious command ship.

The SASEBO NAVAL BASE is also being used as a ship repair facility by the US Navy, but to a lesser degree than Yokosuka. Sasebo serves as the home port for several American amphibious support ships of various types and two mine countermeasures ships.

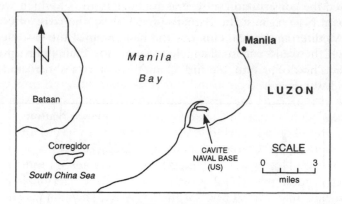

Cavite Naval Base, Manila.

### Indian Ocean

The US Navy currently maintains a naval support facility at Diego Garcia, a small island in the Chargos Archipelago about 1000 miles off the southern tip of India. The DIEGO GARCIA NAVAL SUPPORT ACTIVITY provides logistic support for ships of the navy operating in the Indian Ocean and adjacent areas.

## PRIVATE SHIPYARDS ON THE EAST COAST

Initially, the naval requirements for the Continental Navy of the United States had to be met by private shipyards. By the time of the American Revolution, colonial shipyards had developed to the point of being able to build acceptable warships for the Royal Navy as well as commercial vessels for trade among the colonies. In 1775, the Continental Congress authorised the construction of thirteen frigates for the Continental Navy, including five 32-gun, five 28-gun, and three 24-gun ships. The work was parcelled out among the colonies, two for Massachusetts, two for Rhode Island, two for New York, four for Pennsylvania, and one each for New Hampshire, Connecticut, and Maryland. The selection of the individual shipyards to build those ships was left to each colony

Private shipyards continued to provide warships for the Federal Navy into the early part of the nineteenth century until the Federal navy yards authorised by Congress in 1800 could become fully operational. In 1794, Congress authorised the construction of six new frigates for the Federal Navy, four of which would be 44-gun and the remaining two, 36-gun ships. These frigates were built at private shipyards, one each in New Hampshire, Boston, New York, Philadelphia, Baltimore, and Gosport (Norfolk), and they carried the brunt of fighting against the British during the War of 1812.

Eight additional smaller frigates, ranging from 36-guns down to 24-guns, were built by private shipyards at the turn of the century. In 1803, Congress authorised the construction of several gunboats, some of which were used by the Federal Navy against the Barbary pirates along the coast of North Africa on the Mediterranean Sea. This was the beginning of the so-called 'gunboat navy', which would eventually include some 175 craft built through 1811, mostly by a host of private shipyards along the eastern seaboard and a few even on inland waterways.

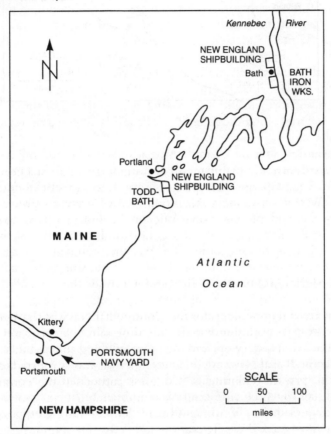

Maine and New Hampshire.

Federal navy yards were given priority for the construction of major warships for the US Navy once they were fully operational, but at times of national emergency, private shipyards were still needed to accommodate the increased warship requirements. Private shipyards were again called upon to build a large number of monitors and gunboats for the Federal Navy during the Civil War period. As with the 'gunboat navy' at the early part of the century, orders for these ships were placed in small quantities spread among nearly fifty private shipyards.

Many of the private yards that built monitors and gunboats during the Civil War were older shipyards that specialised in the construction of wooden sailing ships, including the shipyard of Donald McKay of later clipper ship fame. The advent of steam power and the use of iron in the construction of new ships spawned a new type of shipyard, the iron works. As ships became larger and involved the greater use of iron and steel, these iron works gradually replaced the older shipyards that could not keep pace with the transition to the new technology.

By the end of the century, most of the older shipyards had gone out of business, and the new iron works dominated the shipbuilding industry. Bethlehem Steel Corporation soon entered the shipbuilding field, and it gradually expanded its domain to include several major shipyards on both coasts of the United States. Its major acquisitions included the Fore River Shipbuilding & Engine Co. of Quincy, Massachusetts, the Harlan & Hollingsworth shipyard at Wilmington, Delaware, and Union Iron Works of San Francisco, California. In 1916, the New York firm of Todd Shipyard Corporation was formed, and it soon established a string of shipbuilding and ship repair facilities along the Atlantic, Gulf, and Pacific coastal regions of the United States.

Naval expansion after the Spanish-American War required the assistance of private shipyards to meet the increased requirements for all-steel ships for the 'New Navy'. The navy also used private shipyards to a great extent during the First World War to supplement the production of warships by Federal navy yards. After the end of the war, naval construction reverted back almost exclusively to the navy yards, and it was not until the advent of the Second World War that significant orders for warship construction again began flowing to private shipyards. During the war, private shipyards gradually took over the lion's share of major warship production for the US Navy.

After the end of the war, it became increasingly difficult to justify the retention of Federal naval shipyards for economic and political reasons, so one by one the great naval shipyards were closed. Warship construction declined, and soon the remaining workload was concentrated among a few private yards. By the end of the twentieth century, there were no Federal shipyards and only four private yards engaged in warship production. Newport News Shipbuilding and Dry Dock Company continues to build nuclear-powered aircraft carriers, Bath Iron Works and Ingalls Shipbuilding Company share in the production of guided missile cruisers and destroyers, and the Electric Boat Division still builds submarines for the navy.

## New England

### Bath

BATH IRON WORKS was the major producer of torpedo-boats and destroyers for the US Navy throughout the century. Its yard is located on the west bank of the Kennebec River near its exit into the Atlantic Ocean at the south end of Bath, Maine, about thirty miles northeast of Portland. Bath Iron Works was established in 1884 by Thomas W. Hyde, and four years later the company acquired the Goss Marine Iron Works, which manufactured

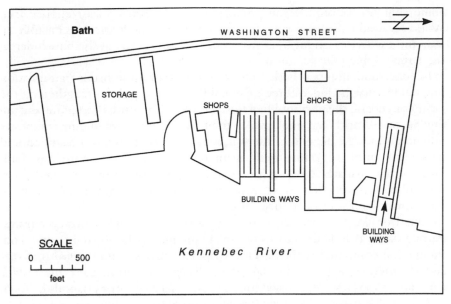

Bath Iron Works in 1945.

steam engines for maritime use. In 1890, Bath launched its first ship, a wooden steamer, but it then received orders to build two 190ft steel gunboats for the US Navy. In 1900, Bath occupied 13 acres of land with a 1000ft waterfront.

In 1900, Bath Iron Works began its long string of torpedo-boat and destroyer production, building two torpedo-boats in that year, and another two in the following year. In 1903, Bath built the cruiser *Cleveland* (C-19), later redesignated as a light cruiser (CL-21). The largest ship built by Bath was the 15,000-ton pre-Dreadnought battleship *Georgia* (BB-15), which was completed in 1906. One year later, Bath launched the scout cruiser *Chester* (CS-1), later redesignated as a light cruiser (CL-1), the first American warship equipped with a reaction type steam turbine.

In 1908, Bath built two 700-ton coal-burning destroyers, and during the period 1911-14, it built four 1000-ton destroyers, including the USS *Wadsworth*, the first US naval vessel with geared turbines. Just prior to the First World War, the workforce at Bath had averaged about 1300 employees, but as war threatened, that figure began to increase as the workload at the yard picked up. During the war, Bath Iron Works designed and built twelve of the famous 4-stacker, flush-deck destroyers that were the mainstay of the fleet throughout the 1920s and early 1930s. At that time, Bath had five slipways, one 600ft long, one 500ft long, and the remaining three all 350ft long.

Employment at Bath Iron Works reached a peak of nearly 2000 workers during the war, but in 1920, the workforce dropped to 650 people as the shipbuilding workload declined. In 1925, the shipyard had to close, but two years later, it opened again with the same name but under new management. The new owners had stripped the yard and installed new facilities and equipment, and it soon began producing luxury yachts. In 1934, Bath Iron Works received an order for the first destroyer to be built after the First World War, the USS *Dewey*, and it built five more destroyers during the remainder of the 1930s.

In 1940, soon after war broke out in Europe, Bath underwent an expansion programme that included three new building berths and the lengthening the fitting out docks, thereby doubling the capacity of the yard. Production during the Second World War included a total of eighty-eight destroyers of six different classes. At the end of the war, naval construction again declined, and it was not until 1953 that Bath again received orders for warships. Bath produced the frigates *Mitscher* (DL-2) and *McCain* (DL-3) in 1953, and those ships were followed by two destroyer escorts in 1957 and nine destroyers of the *Forrest Sherman* class in 1959.

Bath Iron Works then began building a string of guided missile frigates, starting with the *Dewey* (DLG-14) in 1959 and *Preble* (DLG-15) in 1960. Production continued with the *Leahy* (DLG-16) in 1962, the *Yarnell* (DLG-17) and *Worden* (DLG-18), both in 1963, the *Belknap* (DLG-26) in 1964, the *Daniels* (DLG-27) in 1965, the *Wainwright* (DLG-28) and *Standley* (DLG-32), both in 1966, and the *Biddle* (DLG-34) in 1967. Frigates in this latter group, beginning with DLG-13, were later reclassified as guided missile cruisers (CG), but they kept their original numbers. Bath also resumed destroyer production in the same time frame, building four guided missile destroyers in 1961-4 and two more in 1968. The yard also built three guided missile destroyer escorts in 1967.

In 1965, the shipbuilding berths at Bath Iron Works were expanded to 750 × 105ft in size, and the yard was equipped with a 220-ton capacity crane. Bath produced a number of guided missile cruisers of the *Ticonderoga* class, including the *Gates* (CG-51) in 1987, the *Philippine Sea* (CG-58) and *Normandy* (CG-60), both in 1989, *Monterey* (CG-61) in 1990, *Cowpens* (CG-63) and *Gettysburg* (CG-64), both in 1991, the *Shiloh* (CG-67) in 1992, and the *Lake Erie* (CG-70) in 1993. From 1977 to 1989, Bath produced twenty-three guided missile frigates of the *Oliver Hazard Perry* class, and in 1991, it began building eighteen guided missile destroyers of the *Arleigh Burke* class, which are still in production. Bath Iron Works was purchased by General Dynamics in 1995, and it continues to operate as a division of that corporation.

*Boston*
Shipbuilding in the Boston area began early in the eighteenth century, and by the time of the American Revolution, the industry had developed considerably. In 1776, private shipyards at Newburyport, about 40 miles north of Boston, built two of the thirteen frigates authorised by the Continental Congress for the new Continental Navy. The 32-gun frigate *Hancock* was built by JONATHAN GREENLEAF, and the 24-gun frigate *Boston* was built by STEPHEN AND RALPH CROSS. The famous 44-gun frigate USS *Constitution*, which became known as 'Old Ironsides' after her battle with British forces in the War of 1812, was built by GEORGE CLAGHORN of Boston in 1798. In the following year, the HARTT BROS. of Boston built the 28-gun frigate *Boston*.

In 1813, CROSS & MERRILL of Newburyport built the 18-gun sloop-of-war *Wasp* and JOSIAH BARKER built the similar *Frolic*. EDWARD HARTT & JOSIAH BARKER built the 74-gun ship-of-the-line *Independence* at Charlestown across the Charles River from Boston in 1814. When the Boston Navy Yard became fully operational after the War of 1812, little naval construction work was contracted out to local private shipyards. It was not until the Civil War that private shipyards were again called upon to build warships for the navy. From 1862 to 1865, private shipyards in the Boston area produced twelve ironclads and ten monitors for the Federal Navy, but after the war, most of the older shipyards closed down. One of the remaining Boston shipyards, the CITY POINT WORKS, built the protected cruiser *Marblehead* (C-11) in 1894.

*Quincy*

In 1884, a skilled machinist, Frank O Wellington, and an engine designer, L G Wing, founded the F. O. WELLINGTON & CO. in East Braintree on the Fore River branch of the Weymouth River, about ten miles southeast of Boston. The company initially produced a line of marine steam engines under the trade-name of 'Fore River', and in 1894, the name of the company was changed to

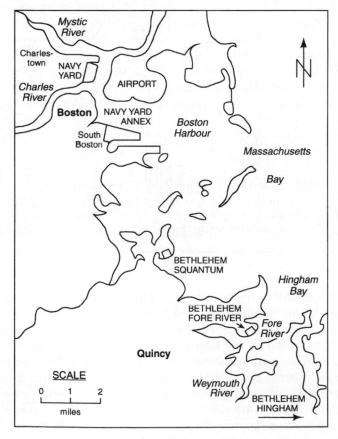

Shipyards in the Boston area.

FORE RIVER ENGINE CO. Two years later, the company began building ships at the site, and in 1898, during the Spanish-American War, it received its first order from the navy for two 500-ton torpedo boat destroyers. A year later in 1899, the yard received an order from the US government to produce a protected cruiser, but the ship could not be built at its existing facility.

The Fore River Engine Co. promptly acquired a 100-acre tract of land two miles to the north at Quincy Point for a shipbuilding centre. In 1901, the new site, with over 10 acres under cover and a river frontage of nearly 6000ft, was opened, and the company changed its name to the FORE RIVER SHIP & ENGINE CO. The yard promptly laid the keel for the protected cruiser *Des Moines* (CL-17), which was completed in 1904. At that time, the yard employed 4000 workers, and during the next year, the yard was improved with higher-capacity cranes and large machine tools. Fore River then built the battleships *New Jersey* (BB-16) and *Rhode Island* (BB-17), both in 1906, the *Vermont* (BB-20) in 1907, and the *North Dakota* (BB-29) in 1910.

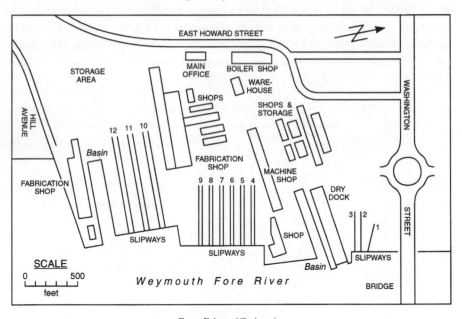

Fore River (Quincy).

Fore River produced the light cruisers *Birmingham* (CL-2) and *Salem* (CL-3), both in 1908, and in 1910, the yard built the battleship *Rivadavia* for the Argentine navy. From 1900 to 1924, Fore River built most of the submarines delivered by the Electric Boat Company to the US Navy under a sub-contract with that company, since Electric Boat did not have its own shipyard until 1924. The submarines produced by Fore River included three 'B' class boats in 1906-07, two 'C' class boats in 1907-09, three 'D' class boats in 1909-10, two 'E' class boats in 1911, and four 'K' class boats in 1913-14. In 1905, Fore River also built five small Holland-type submarines for Japan, which were thereupon taken apart and shipped to Japan for reassembly in shipyards there.

The Fore River shipyard built nine destroyers for the US Navy from 1900 to 1914. In 1913, the Fore River Ship & Engine Co. was taken over by Bethlehem Steel Company, and the shipyard became known as BETHLEHEM QUINCY. By that time, the yard had been expanded to cover 110 acres, and its workforce was nearly 3000 employees. Bethlehem Quincy completed the submarine AA-1 for the US Navy and one additional submarine for Spain in 1915. In 1916, Bethlehem Quincy completed the battleship USS *Nevada* (BB-36), the first oil-burning capital ship in the navy. The *Nevada* may be remembered for her daring escape attempt during the Japanese attack on Pearl Harbor in December 1941, and her subsequent direct support of American ground forces during the invasion of Normandy in June 1944.

Continuing with submarine production, Bethlehem Quincy completed ten 'H' class boats for Britain, Canada, and Chile in 1915-17, eight 'O' class boats in 1917-18, fourteen 'R' class boats in 1918-19, and twelve 'S' class boats in 1918-21 for the US Navy. In 1914, the yard built ten submarines for the Royal Navy, which were prefabricated for assembly in Canada. Naval construction during the First World War also included thirty-six 4-stacker flush-deck destroyers and eight 'O' class and fifteen 'R' class submarines for the US Navy, as well as ten submarines for Great Britain. During the war, the yard had increased its slipways to forty, including twenty for submarines, four for destroyers up to 300ft in length, and one 1000 × 130ft concrete and steel building way. The workforce at Bethlehem Quincy had reached a peak of 15,000 employees in 1916.

Not being able to keep up with the demand for flush-deck destroyers, Bethlehem built another shipyard at nearby Squantum in 1917. The 60-acre BETHLEHEM SQUANTUM yard was completed a year later, and it featured a frontage of 3000ft, ten covered building ways with electric bridge cranes, and six wet slips with cranes up to 25-tons capacity. During the period 1918 to 1920, Bethlehem Squantum had up to 9000 workers. In that period, the yard turned out thirty-five additional flush-deck destroyers, bringing the total number of flush-deck destroyers produced by Bethlehem in the Quincy area to over seventy vessels. Having served its purpose, the Bethlehem Squantum yard was closed down after completing its destroyer production.

When the war ended, work on the battleship *Massachusetts* (BB-54) at Bethlehem Quincy was cancelled. The yard took advantage of the post-war slump in new naval construction by upgrading its facilities to include the building of new slipways for battleships and large merchant ships and the acquisition of a 10,000-ton capacity floating dry dock. Although the First World War was over, the navy authorised the construction of six new 45,000-ton battlecruisers, and in 1921, the keel was laid for the *Lexington* (CC-1) at the Bethlehem Quincy yard. Subsequent Washington Naval Treaty restrictions precluded her completion as a battlecruiser, so the *Lexington* and her sister ship, the *Saratoga* (CC-3), under construction at Camden, New Jersey, were selected for conversion to aircraft carriers.

The aircraft carrier *Lexington* (CV-2) was completed in 1927, the same year that her sister ship, the *Saratoga* (CV-3) was completed at Camden. The ill-fated

*Lexington* became the first carrier lost by the United States during the Second World War, having been sunk by Japanese naval aircraft in the Battle of the Coral Sea in May 1942. In the inter-war period, Bethlehem Quincy built the light cruisers *Raleigh* (CL-7) in 1924 and *Detroit* (CL-8) in 1923. From 1922 to 1924, the yard also completed twenty-six submarines of the 'S 'class, ending its submarine production as the Electric Boat Co. established its own shipyard at Groton, Connecticut in 1925.

By 1930, the workforce at Bethlehem Quincy had dropped to under 5000 employees, but as new orders started to come in during the following year, the downward trend was reversed. Bethlehem Quincy built the heavy cruisers *Northampton* (CA-26) in 1930, *Portland* (CA-33) in 1933, *Quincy* (CA-39) in 1936, and *Vincennes* (CA-44) in 1937. Both the *Quincy* and *Vincennes*, as well as the heavy cruiser *Astoria* (CA-34), were sunk by a force of Japanese cruisers and destroyers during the Battle of Savo Island while protecting the Marine Corps invasion beachhead on the island of Guadalcanal in August 1942.

Bethlehem Quincy built the passenger liners *Mariposa* and *Lurline* for the Matson Lines, as well as the passenger liner *Monterey*, in 1931-3. Resuming warship production, Bethlehem Quincy produced seven destroyers from 1935 to 1937. As the Second World War approached, Bethlehem Quincy began building aircraft carriers, starting with the *Wasp* (CV-7) in 1940. During the war, the yard produced five *Essex* class aircraft carriers, including the *Lexington* (II) (CV-16) (ex-*Cabot*), *Bunker Hill* (CV-17), and *Wasp* (II) (CV-18) (ex-*Oriskany*), all in 1943, the *Hancock* (CV-19) in 1944, and the *Philippine Sea* (CV-47) in 1946. At the time of the Pearl Harbor attack in December 1941, the yard employed 17,000 workers, but that figure nearly doubled to 32,000 personnel in 1943.

Bethlehem Quincy built the battleship *Massachusetts* (BB-59) in 1942 and completed a total of nineteen light and heavy cruisers during the war. Production of the cruisers began in 1942 with two light anti-aircraft cruisers of the *Atlanta* class, the *San Diego* (CL-53) and *San Juan* (CL-54) in 1942. These ships displaced 6000 tons and carried sixteen 5in dual purpose guns in eight twin mounts, three forward, three aft, and one on either side of the ship. The yard went on to produce the larger 10,000-ton light cruisers *Vincennes* (II) (CL-64) (ex-*Flint*) and *Pasadena* (CL-65), both in 1943, the *Springfield* (CL-66) in 1944; the *Topeka* (CL-67) and *Providence* (CL-82), both in 1945, and the *Manchester* (CL-83) in 1946.

In the same period, Bethlehem Quincy also built the heavy cruisers *Baltimore* (CA-68), *Boston* (CA-69), *Canberra* (CA-70) (ex-*Pittsburgh*), and *Quincy* (II) (CA-71) (ex-*St Paul*), all in 1943, the *Pittsburgh* (CA-72) in 1944, the *St. Paul* (CA-73), *Columbus* (CA-74), *Helena* (II) (CA-75), and *Albany* (CA-123) all in 1945, and the *Oregon City* (CA-122) and *Rochester* (CA-124), both in 1946. After the war, the yard completed the heavy cruisers *Des Moines* (CA-134) in 1948 and *Salem* (CA-139) in 1949. Several cruisers built by Bethlehem Quincy were later converted into guided missile cruisers and renumbered accordingly, including the heavy cruisers *Providence* (CG-6), *Albany* (CG-10), and *Columbus* (CG-12) and the light cruisers *Springfield* (CG-7) and *Topeka* (CG-8). Wartime production also included twelve destroyers of various classes from 1941-5.

Upon America's entry into the Second World War, the country did not have an adequate capacity to build all of the warships for which it had requirements. Consequently, Bethlehem built another shipyard at Hingham on Hingham Bay, about six miles east of Quincy in 1942, to increase its production capacity. The new BETHLEHEM HINGHAM shipyard covered nearly 100 acres, and it was equipped with sixteen slipways. The workforce at the Hingham yard reached a peak of nearly 24,000 employees in 1943. During its 40-month existence, Bethlehem Hingham produced over 225 warships for the US Navy, including forty-six destroyer escorts, ninety-five tank landing ships, and forty infantry landing craft, and another forty-six destroyer escorts went to Great Britain. Orders for an additional 115 destroyer escorts and fifty landing craft were cancelled at the end of the war, and no further warships were produced at the yard after that.

During the downsizing that followed the end of the war, Bethlehem Quincy undertook a modernisation programme to include the conversion of many of its slipways into larger but fewer structures, leaving the yard with twelve slipways. Two of the yard's three wet basins were consolidated into one large wet basin at the north end of the yard. Other improvements included a new two bay fabrication shop with a total covered floor space of $250,000 ft^2$ and served by seventeen bridge cranes with lifting capacities up to fifteen tons, as well as a modern $140,000 ft^2$ machine shop. The yard's new $142,000 ft^2$ mould loft was the largest in the country, and its new brass foundry was state-of-the-art.

After the war, Bethlehem Quincy initially reverted to the production of commercial ships, and it completed the 30,000-ton passenger liners *Constitution* and *Independence*, both in 1951. By 1950, the workforce at the yard had dropped to 3800 employees. Bethlehem Quincy resumed warship construction by building the first tactical command ship, the USS *Northampton* (CC-1), in 1954. The yard then went on to produce the frigates *Willis Lee* (DL-4) and *Wilkinson* (DL-5), both in 1954, and five destroyers of the *Forrest Sherman* class in 1959. When anti-aircraft guided missiles were introduced into the navy, Bethlehem Quincy built the guided missile frigates *Farragut* (DLG-6) in 1960 and the *Luce* (DLG-7) and *MacDonough* (DLG-8), both in 1961.

Due to labour problems at Bethlehem Quincy, work on the almost completed conversion of the light cruiser *Springfield* into a guided missile cruiser (CG-7) was cancelled, and the ship had to be towed to the Boston Naval Shipyard for completion. Bethlehem Quincy then completed the first nuclear-powered guided missile cruiser, the USS *Long Beach* (CGN-9) in 1961, and one year later, it built the first nuclear-powered guided missile frigate, the USS *Bainbridge* (DLGN-25). In 1962, the shipyard completed the 150,000-ton tanker *Manhattan*, the largest commercial ship built in the United States up to that time.

In 1964, the shipyard was sold to General Dynamics Corporation, and at that time, the yard covered 180 acres of land and it had a workforce of 1800 employees. GENERAL DYNAMICS QUINCY was closed down for a period of time to make improvements to the slipways, cranes, piers, and wet basin. The most significant improvement was the conversion of six slipways, Nos. 4-9, into three building docks. In the period 1967 to 1970, General Dynamics Quincy built two advanced nuclear attack submarines and one guided missile destroyer of the *Decatur* class. In addition, the yard produced six auxiliary oil replenishment ships in 1966-73 and four dock landing ships in 1970-2.

In the 1970s, the Quincy shipyard had five shipbuilding ways ranging from 550 to 940ft in length, an 880 × 160ft building position, three building docks, one of which was 940ft long and the other two 865ft, and one 465ft floating dock. The yard subsequently built a number of commercial natural gas carriers (LNG) and performed some ship conversion and repair work for naval vessels, but its workload was gradually declining. General Dynamics Quincy was finally shut down in 1986.

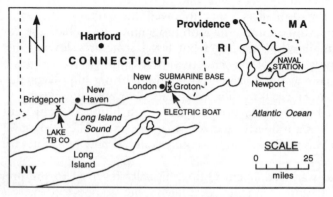

Naval Bases in Connecticut and Rhode Island.

## Rhode Island

Rhode Island has made significant contributions to the US Navy, especially during the earlier years of the nation. Rhode Island was selected as the site for the construction of two of the first thirteen frigates authorised by the Continental Congress in 1775 for the Continental Navy. SYLVESTER BOWERS of Providence built the 28-gun frigate *Providence* in 1776, and BENJAMIN TALMAN of Warren, Rhode Island built the 32-gun frigate *Warren* in 1778. Benjamin Talman later went on to produce another frigate, the 28-gun *General Greene* in 1799.

In 1805, Congress began authorising the construction of the first of 175 gunboats. BENJAMIN MARBLE of Newport, JOHN GLOZIER of Greenwich, and ADAM CROSS of Westerly, Rhode Island each built two gunboats under that authorisation. At the end of the nineteenth century, the HERRESHOFF MANUFACTURING CO. of Bristol, Rhode Island produced three torpedo-boats for the US Navy in 1890-7.

## Groton

Groton, Connecticut is associated almost exclusively with the construction and operation of submarines for the US Navy. In addition to being the site of the New London Submarine Base, it is also the home of the Electric Boat

Company, the primary producer of submarines for the US Navy. It all began in 1875 when John Holland, an American inventor, produced his first practical submarine. It took another twenty years before Holland could show a military application for his invention, and in 1895, he was given an order to produce a submarine for the US Navy. Holland immediately organised the HOLLAND SUBMARINE TORPEDO BOAT CO. to produce this first submarine, the USS *Holland* (SS-1), which was delivered to the Navy in 1900.

With the navy showing an increased interest in submarines, the Holland Submarine Torpedo Boat Co. was reorganised in 1900 into the ELECTRIC BOAT CO. to continue the development and production of submarines. In 1903, the company produced seven 'A'-type boats, based on the original USS *Holland* design, for Great Britain and Japan. Electric Boat then produced three 'B' class boats in 1907, five 'C' class and three 'D' class boats in 1910, and two 'E' class boats in 1912. Actually most of these submarines were subcontracted to the Fore River Ship and Engine Co. to produce the hulls of these boats since Electric Boat did not yet have its own shipyard.

At the beginning of the First World War, Electric Boat delivered three 'H' class boats to the US Navy and a number to foreign customers. Wartime

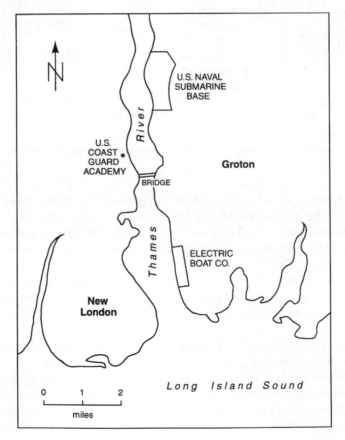

Groton/New London.

production continued with eight 'K' class boats in 1916, eight 'L' class boats in 1917, and a total of thirteen additional submarines of various classes through 1918. Production of submarines slowed down after the end of the First World War, and Electric Boat did not win any more contracts until the 1930s. By 1924, Electric Boat had established its own shipyard on the east bank of the Thames River near its effluence into Long Island Sound at the south end of Groton. In 1934, Electric Boat completed the USS *Cuttlefish*, the first submarine to use welding in its construction. During the 1930s, the yard built an additional thirteen submarines.

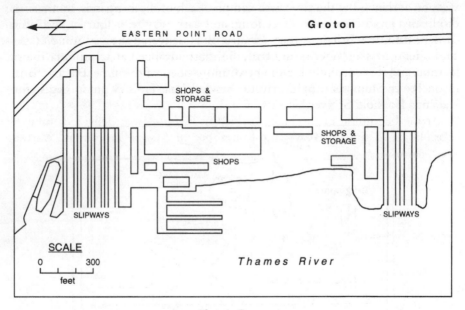

Electric Boat.

As might be expected, submarine production shot up dramatically upon the outbreak of the Second World War. By that time, Electric Boat had expanded to include over twenty building ways, and during the war, it produced a total of seventy-five submarines, including fifty in the year 1945 alone. After the end of the war, submarine production dropped to a trickle, and from 1949 to 1952, Electric Boat built only ten submarines. In 1952, General Dynamics Corporation was formed, and it acquired the Electric Boat company. Electric Boat continues to operate today as a Division of General Dynamics Corporation.

Business picked up in 1954 when Electric Boat built the first nuclear-powered submarine, USS *Nautilus* (SSN-571). From then on, all submarine production by Electric Boat Co. would include nuclear power plants, except for one more conventional type submarine built in 1959. Electric Boat has since built over fifty nuclear attack submarines, including thirty-three of the latest *Los Angeles* class built from 1976 to 1995. In addition, the yard produced thirty-five ballistic missile submarines, starting in 1959-60 with the first two boats of the 6700-ton, 382ft long *George Washington* class, the uss *George Washington* (ssbn-598) and uss *Patrick Henry* (ssbn-599), each of which carried sixteen Polaris missiles. In 1961-2, Electric Boat built two boats of the 7900-ton, 410ft *Ethan Allen* class, each of which carried sixteen Poseidon ballistic missiles.

From 1963-6, the shipyard produced thirteen submarines of the *Lafayette* class, each of which displaced 8250 tons, was 425ft long and carried sixteen Poseidon missiles. In 1981, Electric Boat began its exclusive production of eighteen *Ohio* class submarines, which is the ultimate undersea strategic attack weapon at the end of the twentieth century. Each of these gigantic submarines displaces 18,750 tons, is 560 feet long, and carries twenty-four of the latest Trident ballistic missiles. In 1997, Electric Boat delivered the uss *Seawolf* (ssn-21, under a new numbering system), the most advanced attack submarine of its time, and it is currently building two more boats of this type. Electric Boat in one of the four remaining private shipyards that are still producing major warships for the US Navy.

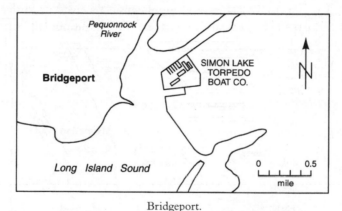

Bridgeport.

## Bridgeport

John Holland was not the only person engaged in submarine development. Another American inventor, Simon Lake, began building submersibles for private use in 1894. In 1897, Lake built the submarine *Argonaut*, which could operate in the open seas, and three years later in 1900, he established a submarine building facility at Bridgeport, Connecticut. The Simon Lake Torpedo Boat Co. was located on the east bank of the Pequonnock River near its exit into the Long Island Sound in the southeastern section of Bridgeport. At the beginning of the twentieth century, Lake produced several submarines for Russia, and it was not until the start of the First World War that the yard began receiving orders for submarines from the US Navy.

Simon Lake built a total of twenty-three submarines for the US Navy during the war, and an additional three submarines after the end of the war. These included two boats of the 'G' class in 1915, the *L-5* in 1917, four boats of the 'N' class and three boats of the 'O' class in 1918, seven boats of the 'R' class in 1919, and finally four boats of the 'S' class in 1923. At the end of the war, the Simon Lake yard had four slipways and seven workshops, and it employed over 2000 workers. The Simon Lake Torpedo Boat Co. went out of business in 1924, shortly after the United States and Japan signed an agreement establishing a moratorium on the further production of submarines.

### Middle Atlantic

*New York*

The large protected harbour of New York provided many excellent sites for shipbuilding, and this encouraged the establishment of numerous shipyards in the region dating back to colonial times. By the time of the Civil War, the New York region had spawned over forty shipbuilding and ship repair yards, including the new breed of iron works that began building steam-powered, ironclad or iron hulled ships. These shipyards extended north along the Hudson (North) River as far as Poughkeepsie, east along the East River, west along the Hackensack River and Newark Bay, and south along the Upper New York Bay.

In 1775, LANCASTER BURLING of Poughkeepsie received an order to build two of the thirteen frigates authorised for the Continental Navy by the

New York and environs.

Continental Congress. Work began on the 28-gun frigate *Congress* and the 24-gun *Montgomery* in 1776, but both vessels had to be destroyed a year later to keep them from falling into British hands when they captured New York. In 1799, FOREMAN CHESSMAN of New York built the 44-gun frigate *President*, one of six frigates authorised by Congress to combat the Barbary pirates of northern Africa who were preying on American merchant ships. Also produced at that time were the 36-gun frigate *New York*, built by PECK & CARPENTER of New York in 1799, and the 28-gun *Adams*, built by JACKSON & SHEFFIELD of Brooklyn in 1800.

From 1805 to 1811, a total of thirty-two gunboats were built by New York private shipyards. These included nine boats built by ECKFORD & BEEDE, nine boats built by CHRISTIAN BERGH, nine boats built by ADAM & NOAH BROWN, and five boats built by CHARLES BROWNE. Adam & Noah Brown also built the 18-gun sloop-of-war *Peacock* in New York in 1813. In 1814, Adam & Noah Brown built the first steam-powered warship in the world, the *Demologos*, which was designed by Robert Fulton for the US Navy. The *Demologos* was a steam-powered vessel that was propelled by the unique means of a single paddle wheel mounted amidships at the centre of the ship. During the Civil War, New York area private shipyards produced twelve ironclads, twelve gunboats, and five monitors.

Of the dozen or more New York shipyards involved in the wartime shipbuilding effort, the most notable were the SECOR CO. of Jersey City, New Jersey and the C.H. DELAMATER IRON WORKS of New York. Another important New York shipyard of the Civil War era was the CONTINENTAL IRON WORKS at Greenport on Long Island. It was here that John Ericsson built the USS *Monitor*, which later saved the day for the Federal fleet at the entrance to the Chesapeake Bay. The ship had two 11in guns in a single turret amidships, and all exposed surfaces were fully protected with iron plates. Also involved in the construction of the *Monitor* were NOVELTY IRON WORKS of New York, which built the turret, and C.H. Delamater Iron Works, which provided the engine.

The Confederate ironclad CSS *Virginia*, which was salvaged from the burned hulk of the Federal frigate *Merrimack* at the Norfolk Navy Yard, began decimating the wooden ships of the Federal fleet blockading Chesapeake Bay on 8 March 1862. The *Monitor* arrived on the scene on the following day, and in the famous Battle of Hampton Roads, it forced the *Virginia* to turn back to Norfolk. Continental Iron Works subsequently built six additional monitors as well as six other types of ironclad vessels for the Federal Navy.

After its establishment in 1916, the TODD SHIPYARD CORPORATION took over a number of private shipyards throughout the United States, including several in the New York area. These included the Robins Dry Dock & Repair Co. at Erie Basin in Brooklyn and the Tietjen & Lang ship repair facilities in Jersey City and Hoboken, New Jersey. While these yards were not involved in naval construction, they did serve the navy by repairing and performing maintenance operations on naval vessels.

*Staten Island*

Most of the old private shipbuilding facilities in the New York area fell by the wayside by the turn of the century. In 1907, UNITED SHIPYARDS, also known as United Dry Docks, acquired the 40-acre shipbuilding facilities of the Port Richmond Iron Works at Mariners Harbor in the northwest corner of Staten Island on the Kill van Kull. The yard was devoted primarily to the construction of cargo vessels, but in the late 1930s, it received an order for naval vessels. United Shipyards completed two destroyers of the *Mahan* class and two destroyers of the *Fanning* class in 1936-7. In 1938, United Shipyards was taken over by Bethlehem Corporation, and it became known as BETHLEHEM STATEN ISLAND.

In 1940, the US Government purchased six additional acres of adjacent land for use by Bethlehem Staten Island to increase its wartime production capacity, giving the 46-acre facility a waterfront of 2500ft. During the Second World War, Bethlehem Staten Island built a total of forty-four destroyers for the US Navy, including twenty of the *Fletcher* class, thirteen of the *Sumner* class, and eleven of the *Gearing* class. Bethlehem Staten Island had a combined wartime workforce of about 10,000 workers at its Mariner Harbor and Port Richmond plants. After the war, Bethlehem Staten Island reverted to the production of merchant ships.

Bethlehem Staten Island had also begun to specialise in the manufacture of ship propellers. In 1950, Bethlehem Staten Island produced the propellers for the passenger liners *Independence* and *Constitution*, both of which were completed at the Bethlehem Quincy yard in the following year. At that time, Bethlehem Staten Island had a workforce of 1300 employees, but that figure began to decline as orders for new work dropped off. In 1962, the Bethlehem Staten Island shipyard was closed due to lack of work, but the foundry and propeller shop remained open until 1971, when those shops were also closed.

*Kearny*

In 1917, Henry Ford leased 80 acres of land in the Kearny meadows near Newark, New Jersey to the US Government for the construction of a shipyard to build ships for the US Navy. The FOUNDATION COMPANY was established for this purpose, and by 1919, it had built thirty cargo ships for the navy. In 1919, the name of the Foundation Company was changed to the FEDERAL SHIPBUILDING AND DRY DOCK CO. The shipyard was located on the west bank of the Hackensack River near its exit into Newark Bay in the eastern end of Kearny about four miles east of Newark. In the 1930s, Federal Kearny began receiving orders for destroyers, and it completed two ships of the *Mahan* class in 1936 and two ships of the *Somers* class in 1937.

As the Second World War approached, Federal Kearny continued its production of destroyers with three ships of the *McCall* class in 1938, two ships of the *Sims* class in 1939, and four ships of the *Benson* class in 1940-1. Among the latter was the USS *Kearny* (DD-432), which was torpedoed and damaged by a German U-boat in the North Atlantic while escorting an Allied convoy to Murmansk in October 1941, two months before America's entry into the

Second World War. Federal Kearny then completed two 6000-ton light anti-aircraft cruisers, the *Atlanta* (CL-51) in 1941 and the *Juneau* (CL-52) in 1942, both of which were lost in action off Guadalcanal in November 1942. The *Juneau* was sunk by a Japanese submarine with the loss of nearly 700 lives, including the five Sullivan brothers.

Warship production continued full blast during the war with Federal Kearny producing seventy-five additional destroyers as well as a sizeable number of fast cargo ships, troopships, tankers, and other naval auxiliary vessels. Federal Kearny also completed the passenger liner *President Roosevelt* in 1944. At the end of the war, many orders for destroyers and other naval vessels were cancelled, but Federal Kearny was permitted to complete the 6000-ton light anti-aircraft cruisers *Juneau* (II) (CL-119), *Spokane* (CL-120), and *Fresno* (CL-121), all in 1946. With no further work in sight, the shipyard was closed down in 1948.

### Newark

Federal operated another shipyard at nearby Port Newark, which was used to supplement the production of its Kearny plant in building destroyers and smaller vessels for the US Navy during the Second World War. From 1942 to 1945, FEDERAL PORT NEWARK built seven destroyers, fifty-two destroyer escorts, forty-two medium landing ships, and thirty-six infantry landing craft. In 1946, Federal Shipbuilding and Dry Dock Co. transferred two partially finished destroyers from the Port Newark facility to the Kearny plant for completion. Having served its purpose as an auxiliary yard for increased warship production, Federal Port Newark was closed down after the war.

Another New York area shipyard was the CRESCENT SHIPYARD at Elizabethport, New Jersey, located just to the south of the Federal Port Newark shipyard. At the beginning of the twentieth century, Crescent built two torpedo-boats and four 'A' class submarines for the US Navy. Crescent then began the construction of the 3200-ton protected cruiser *Chattanooga* (C-16), but it had to close down in 1903 for financial reasons. The *Chattanooga*, which was later reclassified as a light cruiser (CL-18), was then towed to the New York Navy Yard for completion.

The GAS ENGINE & POWER CO. of Morris Heights, New Jersey was also involved in limited naval construction at the turn of the century, building two torpedo-boats in 1901-02 and one destroyer in 1902. That company, however, never developed into a significant naval shipbuilding concern.

## Delaware Valley

### Philadelphia

One of the most important private shipyards in the Delaware Valley region with respect to naval construction was that of William Cramp of Philadelphia. The WILLIAM CRAMP & SONS SHIPBUILDERS was located on the west bank of the Delaware River about four miles northeast of the business centre of Philadelphia. The shipyard was established by William Cramp on a 10-acre

Philadelphia.

tract of land at the foot of Palmer Street in 1830, and it initially built clipper ships and commercial steamers. At the beginning of the Civil War, Cramp received orders for warships for the Federal Navy, and it completed the ironclad warship *New Ironsides* in 1862. Cramp later built the wooden screw-propelled 17-gun frigate *Chattanooga* in 1866.

William Cramp was the only American shipyard that successfully made the transition from wood to iron and from sail to steam. In 1872, the company was incorporated as WILLIAM CRAMP SHIP & ENGINE BUILDING CO., and for the next two decades, it produced forty passenger steamers, seven cargo steamers, and a number of colliers. During the 1870s, the workforce at Cramp averaged about 2000 employees, and that figure reached 3000 during periods of increased activity. In the 1890s, Cramp returned to warship production, starting with the protected cruisers *Baltimore* (C-3) and *Philadelphia* (C-4), both in 1890, and *Newark* (C-1) in 1891. The shipyard went on to build the armoured cruiser *New York* (ACR-2), later renamed *Saratoga*, in 1893 and protected cruisers *Columbia* (C-12) and *Minneapolis* (C-13), both in 1894.

William Cramp then began to produce a string of battleships for the US Navy, including the *Indiana* (BB-1) in 1895, *Massachusetts* (BB-2) in 1896, *Iowa*

(BB-4) in 1897, and *Alabama* (BB-8) in 1900. After the turn of the century, the yard built the battleships *Maine* (BB-10) in 1902, *Mississippi* (BB-23) and *Idaho* (BB-24), both in 1908, *South Carolina* (BB-26) in 1910, and *Wyoming* (BB-32) in 1912. Cramp also produced a number of cruisers during this period, including the armoured cruisers *Brooklyn* (ACR-3) in 1896, *Pennsylvania* (ACR-4), later renamed *Pittsburgh*, and *Colorado* (ACR-7), later renamed *Pueblo*, both in 1905, and *Tennessee* (ACR-10), later renamed *Memphis*, in 1906

In 1900, Cramp purchased the adjacent Charles Hillman Ship & Engine Co. at the foot of Palmer Street, which included one dry dock and several slipways and repair yards. This acquisition increased the total area of the shipyard to 60 acres and increased the yard's capacity to build its own machinery. At that time, the Cramp shipyard employed about 5000 workers. Cramp built fifteen destroyers for the US Navy from 1908 to 1914, and in 1912, Cramp also built one submarine designed by Laurenti of Italy. In addition to producing warships for the US Navy, the yard at the turn of the century also built several naval vessels for foreign governments, with the approval of the US government.

Cramp's foreign orders included the battleship *Retvizan* and the protected cruiser *Varyag* for Russia in 1900. The *Retvizan* was sunk by Japanese forces at Port Arthur in 1905, but it was later salvaged by the Japanese. After renovation at the Sasebo Naval Shipyard, the *Retvizan* was renamed *Hizen* and joined the Japanese fleet. The *Varyag* was sunk by Japanese forces off Korea, but it was also later salvaged by the Japanese and renamed the *Soya*. William Cramp also produced the protected cruiser *Kasagi* for Japan in 1898, the protected cruiser *Medjidieh* for Turkey in 1903, and two light cruisers for Cuba in 1911. The Cramp-built US battleships *Mississippi* (BB-23) and *Idaho* (BB-24) were stricken from the Navy List in 1914, and they were then sold to Greece, where they were renamed *Lemnos* and *Kilkis*, respectively.

William Cramp built the steam turbine-powered passenger liners *Great Northern* and *Northern Pacific* in 1915, and it then produced a total of forty-eight flush-deck destroyers from 1917 to 1920. By the end of the war, the Cramp shipyard covered 175 acres with a water frontage of over 6000ft. The yard featured eight slipways ranging in length up to 850ft, a 430 × 60ft graving dock, a 100-ton floating derrick, a 70-ton hammerhead crane, and a number of other cranes ranging from 5 to 25-tons lifting capacity. In addition to producing ships, Cramp also manufactured marine boilers, marine engines, and other equipment. Cramp's workforce remained at about 5000 employees during the first decade of the twentieth century, but it rose to 7000 workers in 1914 and then reached a peak of 11,000 people in 1917-18.

After the First World War, William Cramp built five light cruisers of the four-stacker *Omaha* class, namely, the *Richmond* (CL-9), *Concord* (CL-10), and *Trenton* (CL-11), all in 1923, the *Marblehead* (CL-12) in 1924, and the *Memphis* (CL-13) in 1925. Cramp also produced four passenger liners and a number of barges up until 1927, when the yard was closed due to lack of work. In 1941, the yard reopened as CRAMP SHIPBUILDING CO. to resume the construction of warships for the US Navy. During the Second World War, Cramp produced five light cruisers of the *Cleveland* class: *Miami* (CL-89) in 1943, the *Astoria* (II) (CL-90) (ex-*Wilkes Barre*) and *Oklahoma City* (CL-91), both in 1944, and the *Little Rock* (CL-92) and *Galveston* (CL-93), both in 1945. Another *Cleveland* class light cruiser, the USS *Youngstown* (CL-94), was laid down in 1944, but construction work was suspended in 1945 at the end of the war. In 1946, the yard was sold to the navy, and it was no longer used for building ships.

Another noted Philadelphia ship and engine building firm was NEAFIE AND LEVY, located just to the south of the William Cramp shipyard on the west of the Delaware River. Their PENN WORKS, which was established around 1840, specialised in the manufacture of marine steam engines, and they pioneered the introduction of screw propellers in the region. Neafie & Levy produced the engines for many naval vessels used by the Federal Navy during the Civil War, and they also provided the engines for a number of ships built by William Cramp. While devoted primarily to the manufacture of marine engines, Neafie and Levy did produce some steamships and small craft for private customers and the US Navy.

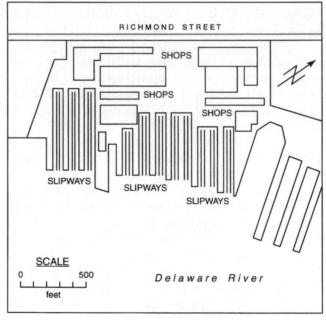

William Cramp in 1945.

At the turn of the century, Neafie & Levy produced three destroyers for the US Navy in 1900. These were followed in 1904 by the protected cruiser *Denver* (C-14), which was later reclassified as a light cruiser (CL-16), and in 1906 by the protected cruiser *St Louis* (C-20), which was later reclassified as a heavy cruiser (CA-18). After William Cramp established its own engine-manufacturing capability, Neafie and Levy began to lose ground in that field, and with few orders for ships being issued by the navy and commercial firms, the Penn Works of Neafie and Levy soon had to close down.

One other private Philadelphia shipyard of note was the AMERICAN INTERNATIONAL SHIPBUILDING CORP. on Hog Island along the west bank of the Delaware River near the mouth of the Schuylkill River. Hog Island is about seven miles southwest of the centre of Philadelphia, and it is now the site of the Philadelphia International Airport. The shipyard, which covered 950 acres of land, was constructed during the First World War, and had some fifty building ways and twenty-five fitting-out basins. Employment at the yard reached 30,000 workers during the war, and American International had the greatest capacity for shipbuilding in the country at that time, exceeding the entire production capacity of Great Britain. After the war, when shipbuilding was in decline, the yard was closed.

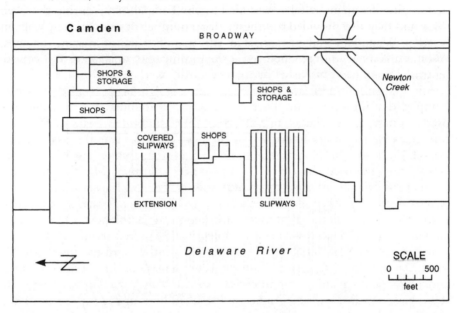

New York Shipbuilding, Camden

## Camden

The NEW YORK SHIPBUILDING & DRY DOCK CO. was founded in 1899 with Henry G Morse, the president of Harlan & Hollingwoth Co. of Wilmington, Delaware, as its first president. Its shipyard was originally intended for Staten Island, New York, hence its name, but a site on the east bank of the Delaware River just to the south of Camden, New Jersey was found to be more suitable. The selected site encompassed over 150 acres of land with a water frontage of 4200ft. At the turn of the century, New York Shipbuilding began producing tankers and cargo ships, and in the following year, it built the 16,000-ton passenger liners *Mongolia* and *Manchuria*. The workforce of the yard then numbered 4000 employees.

New York Shipbuilding began its long association with the US Navy in 1906 when it completed the armoured cruiser *Washington* (ACR-11), later renamed *Seattle*. The shipyard then produced a number of battleships for the

US Navy, including the *Kansas* (BB-21) and *New Hampshire* (BB-25), both in 1907; the *Michigan* (BB-27) in 1910; the *Utah* (BB-31) in 1911; and the *Arkansas* (BB-33) in 1912. In 1910, the yard also built the battleship *Moreno* for the Argentine Navy. It then built the battleships *Oklahoma* (BB-37) in 1916, the *Idaho* (BB-42) in 1919, and the *Colorado* (BB-45) in 1921. The *Oklahoma* was lost at Pearl Harbor in December 1941 when she capsized after being hit by several torpedoes launched by Japanese torpedo bombers.

In addition to the battleships noted above, the New York Shipbuilding & Dry Dock Co. also produced a number of destroyers prior to and during the First World War. These included nine early design destroyers built from 1908 to 1914 and thirty of the famous four-stacker flush-deck destroyers completed in 1917-20. Prior to the First World War, New York Shipbuilding had twelve slipways, including four large slipways that could accommodate ships up to 1000ft long, and two additional large slipways were added during the war. About 7000 workers were employed at the yard in 1917, and its workforce had increased to 19,000 employees by the end of the war.

Another battleship of the *Colorado* class, the USS *Washington* (BB-47) was not completed at the end of the First World War, and its hulk was subsequently used as a naval gunfire target. In 1920, New York Shipbuilding laid the keel for one of six battlecruisers authorised by the navy after the war, the USS *Saratoga* (CC-3). Work on those ships was suspended in 1922 when the Washington Naval Treaty imposed restrictions on the number of capital ships that could be maintained by each of the major naval powers. The *Saratoga* was one of the two battlecruisers that was eventually converted into aircraft carriers, the other being the *Lexington* (CC-1) under construction at Bethlehem Quincy. The aircraft carrier *Saratoga* (CV-3) was completed and entered service in 1927.

In 1920, New York Shipbuilding undertook another yard expansion to the south. An additional four large slipways were constructed, as were new shops and a new power plant. In the inter-war period, New York Shipbuilding built seven passenger liners for the American President lines in 1920-2. In the 1930s, the Camden yard produced the passenger liners *Excalibur* (1930), *Manhattan* (1932), and *Washington* (1933), as well as several smaller passenger liners in the later 1930s.

Building of naval vessels was resumed with the heavy cruisers *Salt Lake City* (CA-25) in 1929, *Chester* (CA-27) in 1930, *Indianapolis* (CA-35) in 1932, and *Tuscaloosa* (CA-37) in 1934. During the late 1930s, the Camden yard also built the light cruisers *Savannah* (CL-42), *Nashville* (CL-43), and *Phoenix* (CL-46), all in 1938, as well as four destroyers of the *Porter* class in 1936-7. New York Shipbuilding continued with the production of light cruisers as the United States entered the Second World War, completing the *Cleveland* (CL-55) and *Columbia* (CL-56), both in 1941, the *Montpelier* (CL-57) and *Denver* (CL-58), both in 1942, and the *Santa Fe* (CL-60) in 1943. Production also included the battleship *South Dakota* (BB-57), which was completed in 1942. New York Shipbuilding won the contract to build all six new battlecruisers of the *Alaska* class, which displaced 27,500 tons and carried nine 12in guns in the traditional arrangement of three triple turrets, two forward and one aft. The Camden yard completed two of these vessels, the *Alaska* (CB-1) and *Guam* (CB-2), both in 1944, and launched the *Hawaii* (CB-3) in 1945, but work was discontinued on the latter at the end of the war. The other three ships of this class, the *Philippines* (CB-4), *Puerto Rico* (CB-5), and *Samoa* (CB-6) were all cancelled in 1943.

New York Shipbuilding also won the contract to build all of the light aircraft carriers to be converted from light cruiser hulls under construction at the yard. In 1943 alone, the Camden yard produced the light carriers *Independence* (CVL-22, ex CL-59), *Princeton* (CVL-23, ex CL-61), *Belleau Wood* (CVL-24, ex CL-76), *Cowpens* (CVL-25, ex CL-77), *Monterey* (CVL-26, ex CL-78), *Langley* (CVL-27, ex CL-85), *Cabot* (CVL-28, ex CL-79), *Bataan* (CVL-29, ex CL-99), and *San Jacinto* (CVL-30, ex CL-100). The yard also continued to produce light cruisers, including the *Wilkes Barre* (CL-103) and *Atlanta* (CL-104), both in 1944, the *Dayton* (CL-105) and *Fargo* (CL-106), both in 1945, and the *Huntington* (CL-107) in 1946.

During the Second World War, employment at New York Shipbuilding reached a peak of 35,000 workers. At the end of the war, New York Shipbuilding completed four heavy cruisers of the *Baltimore* class, the *Bremerton* (CA-130), *Fall River* (CA-131), and *Macon* (CA-132), all in 1945, and the *Toledo* (CA-133) in 1946. The yard also produced two additional light carriers, the *Saipan* (CVL-48) in 1946 and the *Wright* (CVL-49) in 1947, as well as two additional light cruisers, the *Worcester* (CL-144) in 1948 and the *Roanoke* (CL-145) in 1949. In 1953, the Camden yard built the first of a new type of anti-submarine cruiser, the USS *Norfolk* (CLK-1), which was later reclassified as a frigate or destroyer leader (DL-1).

New York Shipbuilding continued to produce frigates for the US Navy, including the guided missile frigates *Dale* (DLG-19) in 1963 and *Turner* (DLG-20) in 1964 and the nuclear-powered guided missile frigate *Truxton* (DLGN-35) in 1967. Post-war production also included three guided missile destroyers in 1960-1 and six guided missile destroyers of the *Adams* class in 1962-4. The Camden yard produced one destroyer escort of the *Dealey* class in 1957, one submarine of the *Barbel* class in 1959, three nuclear-powered submarines of the *Thresher* class in 1965-7, and one nuclear submarine of the *Sturgeon* class in 1969. With shipbuilding workload gradually declining, the shipyard was subsequently closed down in 1969.

*Chester*
During the American Civil War, the firm of REANEY, SON AND ARCHBOLD of Chester, Pennsylvania produced six ironclad warships, three gunboats, and one monitor for the Federal Navy. The Reaney shipyard was located on the west bank of the Delaware River at the northern end of the town of Chester, and it had a water frontage of 1300ft. In 1871, John Roach acquired the shipyard of Reaney, Son & Archbold and operated the facility under the name of the DELAWARE RIVER IRON SHIPBUILDING AND ENGINE WORKS.

From 1870 to 1890, the Roach shipyard was one of the most important yards in the country, and it was also a prime manufacturer of marine steam engines. The yard had excellent foundries, forges, and workshops to facilitate the manufacturing of marine components. During that period, the yard had an steady workforce of 1500 people, which occasionally approached 2000 employees in peak periods. In 1875, Roach built two wooden, screw-propelled sloops-of-war, and in the following year, the yard completed two monitors for the Federal navy.

In 1883, Roach began building the first all-steel warships for the US Navy, including the dispatch boat *Dolphin* in 1884 and the 2300-ton protected cruisers *Atlanta*, completed in 1886, and the *Boston*, completed in 1887. These two ships did not fully meet the navy's expectations, and they were never assigned formal numbers. The Delaware River yard then built the 3500-ton protected cruiser *Chicago* in 1889, and this ship was eventually classified as a heavy cruiser and assigned the number CA-14. Delaware River built two 1500-ton gunboats in 1890, but in view of past problems with the navy, the company decided not to do any more work for the government.

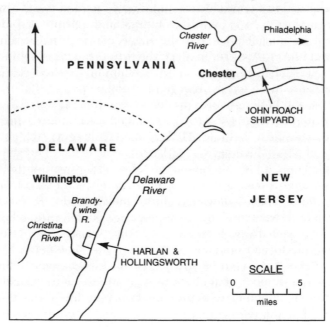

Chester/Wilmington area.

The Delaware River yard then concentrated on the construction of steamships, ferry boats, and other commercial vessels. In 1917, the Sun Oil Co. acquired the Delaware River Iron Shipbuilding and Engine works and established the SUN SHIPBUILDING & DRY DOCK CO. so that it could build its own tankers. The initial workload of the yard consisted mostly of oil tankers, but in 1941, it geared up for war production and built a number of ships for the navy. After the Second World War, Sun produced over thirty tankers and a dozen cargo vessels, including the 500ft roll-on roll-off ship *Comet*. In 1982, Sun Oil Co. decided to discontinue its own shipbuilding efforts, and it sold the facility to another concern.

The new owners renamed the shipyard PHILADELPHIA SHIPBUILDING, and it continued to build oil tankers and cargo ships for a number of different customers. In 1985, Philadelphia Shipbuilding won an order for two Navy oilers with the potential for additional orders if its work was satisfactory. In 1989, the company told the navy that it could not complete the two oilers due to financial problems, and the ships had to be towed to another shipyard for completion. The demise of Philadelphia Shipbuilding spelled the end of shipbuilding at Chester.

## Wilmington, Delaware

Further down the Delaware River at Wilmington, Delaware was the famous HARLAN & HOLLINGSWORTH Co. shipyard. The shipyard began in 1836 under the partnership of Mahlon Betts and Samuel N Pusey, and a year later, Samuel Harlan was admitted into the concern as a partner. At that time the 45-acre facility was engaged in the production of railroad cars, and it had a workforce of forty-five employees. In 1841, Pusey's interest in the firm was sold to Elijah Hollingsworth of Philadelphia, and the name of the firm became BETTS, HARLAN, AND HOLLINGSWORTH. In 1843, the firm turned to shipbuilding, and one year later, it launched its first ship. The shipyard covered more than 40 acres of land and it had a water frontage of 1800ft.

Betts, Harlan, and Hollingsworth produced two ironclad warships and three monitors for the Federal Navy during the Civil War. In 1849, when Mahlon Betts retired, the firm became Harlan and Hollingsworth, and it was incorporated in 1867 as HARLAN & HOLLINGSWORTH Co. The shipyard was improved in 1870 with the construction of a 330 × 90ft dry dock, new building ways, new machinery, and new derricks. The yard then had six acres under cover with a total of nearly forty buildings. In 1876, Harlan & Hollingsworth built one wooden, screw-propelled sloop for the US Navy, and at the turn of the century, the yard produced two 420-ton coal-burning destroyers and one torpedo-boat.

Bethlehem Steel Co. acquired the Harlan & Hollingsworth shipyard in 1904, the first in a number of acquisitions that would soon make Bethlehem Steel the primary shipbuilder in the country. After the yard's takeover by Bethlehem Steel, it was used primarily for the production of merchant ships. By the end of the First World War, the Harlan and Hollingsworth yard had five slips that could accommodate ships up to 15,000 tons displacement, and it possessed modern facilities and equipment. The yard employed 1000 workers at the time, but after the war, that figure dropped as the need for new ships began to disappear. The yard was subsequently phased out by Bethlehem Steel.

Another Wilmington shipyard of note was that of PUSEY & JONES Co., which began in 1848 with the partnership of Joshua Pusey and John Jones. The shipyard produced two ironclads for the Federal Navy during the Civil War, but it then concentrated on the building of river steamers for customers in the United States as well as in Mexico and South America.

Shipbuilding in the Delaware Valley region resumed during the Second World War when the DRAVO CORPORATION, a Pittsburgh-based firm, established a second shipbuilding facility at Wilmington to supplement the wartime production of its Pittsburgh yard. In 1943-4, Dravo Wilmington built six destroyer escorts for the US Navy, six for France, and another three for Brazil. After the war, Dravo discontinued the use of the Wilmington facility in favour of keeping up production at its primary Pittsburgh yard.

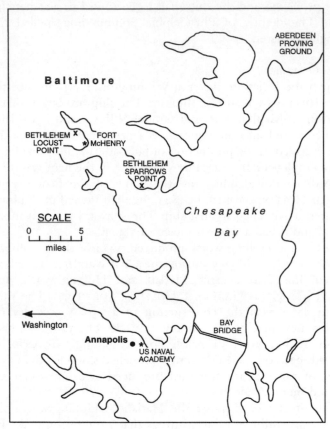

Chesapeake Bay.

### Chesapeake Bay Region

*Baltimore*
Baltimore, located at the mouth of the Patapsco River near the northern end of the Chesapeake Bay, became of the earliest maritime centres of the colonies. Its shipbuilding industry, which began around the middle of the eighteenth century, lasted until after the Second World War. Baltimore was one of the sites chosen to build a total of thirteen frigates for the Continental Navy, as authorised by the Continental Congress in 1775. GEORGE WELLS at Fells Point built the 28-gun frigate *Virginia* in 1776 in response to that order.

In 1797, DAVID STODDER built the famous 36-gun frigate *Constellation*, one of six frigates authorised by Congress to combat the Barbary pirates of northern coast of Africa. The *Constellation* remains today as a naval museum in Baltimore, as does her sister ship, the USS *Constitution*, at the Boston Navy Yard. In 1805, William Price of Baltimore produced one of the 175 gunboats authorised by Congress. FLANNIGAN & PARSONS built the 44-gun frigate *Java* in 1813, and THOMAS KEMP completed two 18-gun sloops-of-war in that same year. During the American Civil War, A. & W. DENMEAD produced two ironclads, one gunboat, and one monitor for the Federal Navy, and three additional gunboats were provided by J. J. ABRAHAMS in that time frame.

The COLUMBIAN IRON WORKS of Baltimore built the protected cruisers *Detriot* (C-10) in 1893 and the *Montgomery* (C-9) in 1894. These ships were followed by five torpedo-boats in 1897-1904. MARYLAND STEEL CO. of Sparrows Point, located on the north bank of the Patapsco River about ten miles southeast of the centre of Baltimore, built three 460-ton destroyers for the US Navy in 1900. Bethlehem Steel Corporation soon came on the scene, taking over the Maryland Steel Co. plant as the BETHLEHEM SPARROWS POINT plant. In addition to the Bethlehem Sparrows Point plant, Bethlehem also operated the BALTIMORE DRY DOCKS WORKS at Locust Point.

## Washington, D.C.

Although selected as a site for one of the first six navy yards, Washington D.C. was really not suitable for shipbuilding, so no private yards of any significance were ever established there. ANNAPOLIS, Maryland is a historic seaport, as well as being the state capital and the home of the US Naval Academy, but it also lacks the features conducive to naval construction.

## Southeastern Region

### Richmond

Although the Confederate Navy Yard at Richmond, Virginia built one ironclad warship for the Confederate Navy during the Civil War, Richmond was not noted for shipbuilding activities. The Richmond firm of WILLIAM R. TRIGG CO., however, did produce two destroyers and three torpedo-boats at the beginning of the twentieth century. Trigg then began building the protected cruiser *Galveston* (C-17), but the company went out of business in 1902 before the *Galveston* could be completed. The *Galveston* was subsequently towed to the Norfolk Navy Yard for completion, and the ship was later reclassified as a light cruiser, CL-19.

### Newport News

The CHESAPEAKE DRY DOCK & CONSTRUCTION CO. was founded by the industrialist Collins P Huntington in 1886. The shipyard was located on the east bank of the James River near its effluence into the harbour of Hampton Roads at the lower end of the Chesapeake Bay just to the south of the town of Newport News. Originally intended as a ship repair facility, the shipyard was expanded in 1889 to include shipbuilding facilities. Improvements also included the construction of the yard's first dry dock, a structure measuring

600ft in length. In 1890, the name of the company was changed to NEWPORT NEWS SHIPBUILDING AND DRY DOCK CO.

During its first decade, Newport News built mostly tugs, freighters, and passenger ships, although in 1893, it received a contract to build three gunboats for the Navy. Major warship production began in earnest at the beginning of the twentieth century when Newport News built the 11,500-ton battleships *Kearsarge* (BB-5) and *Kentucky* (BB-6), both in 1900, and the *Illinois* (BB-7) in 1901. The yard constructed its second dry dock in 1901, and its third dry dock was built in 1908. Newport News went on to produce the even larger battleships *Missouri* (BB-11) in 1903, the *Virginia* (BB-13) and *Louisiana* (BB-19), both in 1906, and the *Minnesota* (BB-22) in 1907

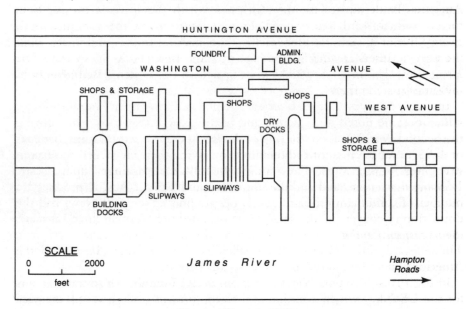

Newport News in 1945.

During the first decade of the twentieth century, Newport News also built several cruisers, including the armoured cruisers *West Virginia* (ACR-5) and *Maryland* (ACR-8) and the protected cruiser *Charleston* (C-22), all in 1905. In accordance with new naval policy to name battleships after states and cruisers after cities, the *West Virginia* was later renamed the *Huntington* and the *Maryland* was renamed the *Frederick*, both being cities in those respective states. Newport News also built six submarines in 1906, one being the experimental *Simon Lake X*. That ship was followed by two more armoured cruisers, the *North Carolina* (ACR-12) and *Montana* (ACR-13), both in 1908. Those ships were later renamed for cities in those states, *ie* the *Charlotte* and *Missoula*, respectively.

In 1910, Newport News built its first Dreadnought-type battleship, the *Delaware* (BB-28), which displaced 20,000 tons and carried ten 12in guns in five twin turrets. During the period from 1910 to 1914, the yard built four

740-ton coal-burning destroyers for the US Navy as well as the submarine *G-1* in 1912. In 1914, Newport News shipyard occupied 100 acres of land with a waterfront length of over 2500ft. At that time, the yard had six large slipways and six dry docks, two of which were over 800ft in length and 80ft wide. Warship production during the First World War era included the battleships *Texas* (BB-35) in 1914, the *Pennsylvania* (BB-38) in 1916, and the *Mississippi* (BB-41) in 1917.

After the war, the workload at Newport News declined, and by 1922, its workforce had dropped to 2000 men. Work began to pick up again after that, and Newport News built the battleships *Maryland* (BB-46) and *West Virginia* (BB-48), both in 1923. With the USS *Colorado* (BB-45), these were the first American battleships to mount 16in guns, which they carried in four twin turrets, two forward and two aft. From 1923 to 1926, the yard produced twenty-five of the famous four-stacker, flush-deck destroyers, and it later built the heavy cruisers *Houston* (CA-30) in 1930 and *Augusta* (CA-31) in 1931. The *Houston* was lost in 1942 while trying to defend the Dutch East Indies from invading Japanese forces.

In 1926, Newport News built the freight and passenger liner *Dorchester*, which became noted for a heroic and historic event that took place during the Second World War. As the ship sank due to enemy action, four chaplains of different religions sacrificed their lives by giving their life jackets to seamen struggling in the water. The yard then built the passenger liner *George Washington* in 1928, and in the late 1920s and early 1930s, it produced a number of combination freight and passenger liners. Newport News had the distinction of converting the huge 58,000-ton former German liner *Vaterland*, the largest ship in the world at that time, to the United States Line's *Leviathan*. The shipyard also converted the smaller ex-German liner *Amerika* to the American liner *America* during the post-war period.

In the 1930s, Newport News began building a long line of aircraft carriers for the US Navy which continues up to the present time. In 1934, the yard build the aircraft carrier *Ranger* (CV-4), the first American warship built from the keel up as an aircraft carrier. The *Ranger* was soon followed by the aircraft carriers *Yorktown* (CV-5) in 1937, the *Enterprise* (CV-6) in 1938, and the *Hornet* (CV-8) in 1941. The *Yorktown* was the only US carrier lost during the Battle of Midway in June 1942 when American naval sank four Japanese carriers and turned back the enemy invasion fleet. The *Hornet*, which was the launching platform for the Army B-25 Mitchell medium bombers that bombed Tokyo in April 1942, was sunk in the Battle of Santa Cruz in October of that year.

In 1942, Newport News built the USS *Essex*, the first of a new class of standard 27,000-ton aircraft carriers that would dominate the American advance across the Pacific to Japan. During the Second World War, the yard produced several additional *Essex* class carriers, including the *Yorktown* (II) (CV-10), *Intrepid* (CV-11), *Hornet* (II) (CV-12), *Franklin* (CV-13), *Ticonderoga* (CV-14), *Randolph* (CV-15), *Boxer* (CV-21), and *Leyte* (CV-32). In 1943, Newport News reached its peak workforce of 31,000 employees. Newport News was chosen to build two of the three new 45,000-ton super aircraft carriers of the

*Midway* class, the *Midway* (CVB-41), completed in 1945, and the *Coral Sea* (CVB-43), completed in 1947. Production also included the 35,000-ton battleship *Indiana* (BB-58) in 1942. Just prior to and during the war, Newport News produced the light cruisers *Boise* (CL-47) in 1938, the *St. Louis* (CL-49) in 1939, the *Birmingham* (CL-62) and *Mobile* (CL-63), both in 1942-3, and the *Biloxi* (CL-80) and *Houston* (II) (CL-81), both in 1943. The shipyard subsequently built the light cruisers *Vicksburg* (CL-86) and *Duluth* (CL-87), both in 1944, and the *Amsterdam* (CL-101) and *Portsmouth* (CL-102), both in 1945. The yard also built two destroyers of the *Sims* class in 1940. In that same year, Newport News completed the 34,000-ton passenger liner *America*, which served as the naval troop transport USS *West Point* (AP-23). After the end of the war, Newport News built its namesake, the 17,000-ton heavy cruiser *Newport News* (CA-148) in 1949.

Newport News then reverted to the construction of merchant ships, including passenger vessels, cargo vessels, and tankers. In 1952, the yard completed the 51,000-ton passenger liner *United States*, which easily captured the Blue Riband for the speediest North Atlantic run. Warship construction resumed with the 60,000-ton aircraft carriers *Forrestal* (CVB-59) in 1955 and *Ranger* (CVA-61) in 1957. In 1958, one of the slipways at the yard had to be extended to 1100ft to accommodate the new class of aircraft carriers on the drawing board. Newport News built the first nuclear-powered aircraft carrier, the huge 88,000-ton USS *Enterprise* (CVAN-65), in 1961. The *Enterprise* was later followed by two conventionally-powered aircraft carriers, the *America* (CVA-68) and *John F. Kennedy* (CVA-69), both in 1968.

In 1968, the Newport News Shipbuilding and Dry Dock Co. was purchased by the Tenneco Corp. In order to accommodate the production of even larger aircraft carriers, Tenneco began to convert the entire northern end of its shipyard for that purpose. The work included the construction of a large building dry dock, Graving Dock No. 12, which measures 2300ft in length and 250ft in width and has sufficient space to accommodate two large vessels at the same time. The dry dock and an adjacent service strip are supported by a 900-ton capacity travelling gantry crane with a span of 500ft. Two older dry docks, Nos. 10 and 11, were filled in to provide the additional space required for the complex. The North Yard was completed in 1976.

The new ship module shop has eight bays for the construction of completely outfitted ship modules, and two large facilities provide pre-fabricated steel components required for those modules. In the meanwhile, Newport News built the amphibious command ship *Mount Whitney* in 1971, and that ship was followed by the nuclear guided missile frigates *California* (DLGN-36) in 1973, *South Carolina* (DLGN-37) in 1974, *Virginia* (DLGN-38) in 1976, *Texas* (DLGN-39) in 1977, and *Mississippi* (DLGN-40) in 1978. These were later reclassified as nuclear guided missile cruisers and renumbered CGN-36 through CGN-40 respectively. The yard then built the nuclear-powered guided missile cruiser *Arkansas* (CGN-41) in 1980.

Newport News also built seventeen nuclear submarines in the 1960s, including ten boats of the *Lafayette* class in 1964-7 and seven nuclear submarines of various classes in the 1970s. The yard built the nuclear submarine USS *Los Angeles*, the first of its class, in 1974, and it went on to produce 28 more of this class through 1996. Newport News built a succession of 91,000-ton nuclear-powered aircraft carriers, including the *Nimitz* (CVAN-66) in 1975, the *Dwight D Eisenhower* (CVAN-69) in 1977, the *Carl Vinson* (CVN-70) in 1982, and the *Theodore Roosevelt* (CVN-71) in 1986. The line of carriers continued with the *Abraham Lincoln* (CVN-72) in 1989, the *George Washington* (CVN-73) in 1992, the *John C Stennis* (CVN-74) in 1995, and the *Harry S Truman* in 1998.

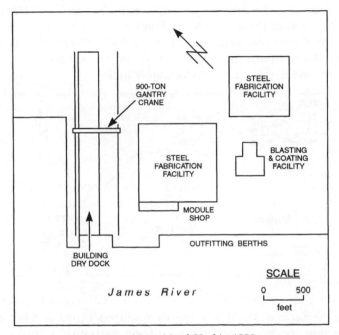

Newport News North Yard in 1980.

Newport News again became an independent shipyard in 1996, and it is one of only four private shipyards that continues to produce major combat vessels for the US Navy. Newport News is now the sole producer of nuclear-powered aircraft carriers and one of only two producers of nuclear-powered submarines, the other being the Electric Boat Division of General Dynamics in Groton, Connecticut.

## PRIVATE SHIPYARDS ON THE GULF COAST

The first coastal section of the Gulf of Mexico that became part of the United States was the Louisiana coastline, which was part of the Louisiana Territory purchased from France in 1803. In 1819, the United States acquired from Spain that portion of the Gulf coastline stretching from Florida westward to Louisiana. The remaining portion of the current US Gulf coastline to the west of Louisiana came under American control with the annexation of the Texas Territory from Mexico in 1845.

*Pascagoula*

The French had been building ships at Pascagoula in the Louisiana Territory since the early part of the eighteenth century, and in 1718, Pascagoula produced its first warship for the French Navy. After the United States acquired the Louisiana Territory from France in 1803, Pascagoula came within the new state of Mississippi. In 1938, INGALLS IRON WORKS CO. of Birmingham, Alabama acquired a 160-acre site on the east bank of the Pascagoula River just to the south of the town of Pascagoula for a shipyard, and in that same year, INGALLS SHIPBUILDING CORP. was incorporated to operate the yard. One year later, the shipyard produced its first ship, the Type C-3 cargo vessel, SS *Exchequer*, the first ship in the world to have an all-welded steel hull.

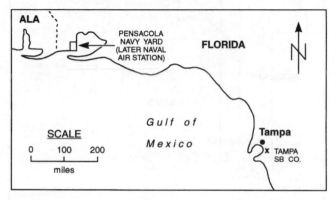

Gulf Coast of Florida

During the Second World War, Ingalls produced a total of forty-three Type C-3 cargo ships, twenty-two combat-loaded transport ships, and a number of auxiliary vessels for the US Navy. The yard also built four escort aircraft carriers for the British navy. After the war, Ingalls continued to specialise in cargo vessels, but in 1953, it produced six tank landing ships, and this was followed by eight dock landing ships in 1954-7. The shipyard then built the large passenger cruise ships *Argentina* and *Brasil*, both completed in 1958. Ingalls constructed two destroyers of the *Forrest Sherman* class in 1959 and one conventional submarine in 1960 for the US Navy.

In 1961, Ingalls Shipbuilding Corp. was acquired by Litton Industries of California, and from 1961 to 1974, Ingalls produced twelve nuclear attack submarines. In that period, the yard also built two 18,000-ton helicopter-carrying amphibious assault ships in 1966-70 and two 17,000-ton amphibious transport dock ships in 1967-8. In 1968, Ingalls began construction of a modern shipyard on a 610-acre tract of land on the west bank of the Pascagoula River, directly across from the original yard. This facility was intended to revolutionise shipbuilding by introducing modular construction techniques. At first, the two shipyards operated independently, but in 1972, they were combined under single management as the INGALLS SHIPBUILDING DIVISION of Litton Industries.

In 1969, Ingalls was awarded a contract to design and build a number of 39,000-ton helicopter-carrying general purpose amphibious assault ships, and the yard completed all five of those *Tarawa* class vessels in 1976-80. Simultaneously, the yard produced thirty-one destroyers of the *Spruance* class from 1975 to 1983 and four guided missile destroyers of the *Kidd* class in 1981-2. With such a large and diverse shipbuilding programme, the workforce at Ingalls reached a peak level of 25,000 employees in 1977. In the 1978, Ingalls became the lead shipyard for the new Aegis-type guided missile cruisers, and the yard completed a total of nineteen such vessels through 1994, including the *Ticonderoga* (CG-47) in 1983, *Yorktown* (CG-48) in 1984, *Vincennes* (CG-49)

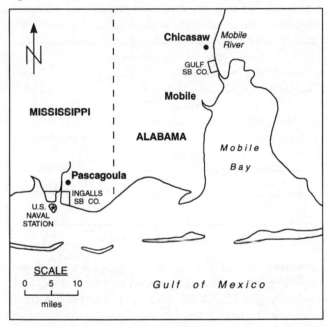

Mobile Bay.

in 1985, the *Valley Forge* (CG-50) and *Bunker Hill* (CG-52), both in 1986, the *Mobile Bay* (CG-53), *Antietam* (CG-54), and *Leyte Gulf* (CG-55), all in 1987, the *San Jacinto* (CG-56) and *Lake Champlain* (CG-57), both in 1988, and the *Princeton* (CG-59) and *Chancellorsville* (CG-62), both in 1989. During the 1990s, Ingalls produced the *Chosen* (CG-65) and *Hue City* (CG-66), both in 1991, the *Anzio* (CG-68) and *Vicksburg* (CG-69), both in 1992, the *Cape St. George* (CG-71) and *Vella Gulf* (CG-72), both in 1993; and the *Port Royal* (CG-73) in 1994.

In 1990, Ingalls began building Aegis-type guided missile destroyers of the *Arleigh Burke* class, and it has completed eleven such ships to date. At the present time, Ingalls has an additional fourteen of this class under contract with the US Navy. The yard has also produced six 40,000-ton *Wasp* class helicopter-carrying multipurpose amphibious assault ships in 1989-98, with one additional vessel currently still under construction. Ingalls remains today as one of only four private shipyards that continues to build major warships for the US Navy.

*New Orleans*

The AVONDALE MARINE WAYS, INC. main shipyard is located on the south bank of the Mississippi River at Westwego, Louisiana about five miles southwest of New Orleans. Avondale began building destroyer escorts for the US Navy in 1960, completing four of them in that year and two more in 1963. The yard then built two guided missile destroyers in 1964 before returning to destroyer escort production. From 1965-74, Avondale completed a total of thirty destroyer escorts, three of the *Garcia* class and twenty-seven of the *Knox* class, all of which were later reclassified as frigates. In addition, eight 15,750-ton dock landing ships of the *Whidbey Island* class were produced by the yard in 1995-8.

The Avondale main yard features a large floating dry dock, which is 900 × 260ft in size and is served by two 50-ton capacity gantry cranes on the dock. This floating dry dock can accommodate ships up to 80,000 tons displacement. The yard also possesses a 20,000-ton capacity floating dry dock, 700 × 120ft in size and with two 25-ton cranes on the dock. Other facilities include a 600-ton floating heavy lift barge, and four gantry cranes, one of 225-ton, one of 160-ton, and two of 50-ton capacity. Together with its Algiers ship repair facility directly across the river from New Orleans, Avondale has a total workforce of over 5000 employees.

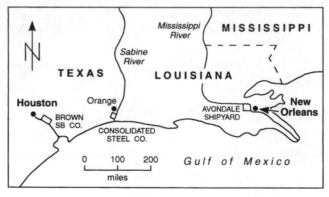

New Orleans and Houston.

*Other Gulf Shipyards*

In addition to the Ingalls shipyard at Pascagoula and the Avondale shipyard at New Orleans, there were several other shipyards along the Gulf Coast that produced warships for the US Navy, especially during the Second World War. The TAMPA SHIPBUILDING & ENGINEERING CO. of Tampa, Florida built nine destroyer escorts for the US Navy in 1943. Further west, the GULF SHIPBUILDING CORP. of Chicasaw, Alabama, located on Chicasaw Bogue about six miles north of Mobile, produced seven destroyers from 1942-4. Two other Gulf Coast yards noted for their contribution to naval shipbuilding were located in Texas.

The CONSOLIDATED STEEL CORP. shipyard at Orange, Texas, located on the Sabine River across from the Louisiana border, produced some forty destroyers and over one hundred destroyer escorts from 1943–5. Another Texas naval shipbuilder was the partnership of the brothers George and Herman Brown of Houston Texas, which was known at various times as either the BROWN ENGINEERING CO. or the BROWN SHIPBUILDING CORP. The Brown shipyard was located on the Houston Ship Channel about twenty-five miles east of the city of Houston. In 1943, the yard produced sixty-one destroyer escorts for the US Navy. In 1949, the Brown shipyard was acquired by Todd Shipbuilding Corp., and it became the HOUSTON DIVISION of Todd Shipbuilding.

## PRIVATE SHIPYARDS ON THE WEST COAST

### California

#### Los Angeles
There were several shipyards located in the San Pedro and Long Beach area just to the south of Los Angeles, but only a few were involved in naval

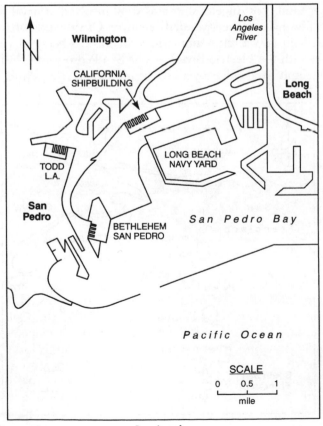

Los Angeles.

shipbuilding. The SOUTHWESTERN SHIPBUILDING CO. began building ships at its Terminal Island facility early in 1918, and its workforce soon reached 9000 men during that year as a result of peak wartime production. Bethlehem Steel Co. acquired the shipyard in 1922, and the company immediately began expanding and modernising the facility. BETHLEHEM SAN PEDRO produced twenty-five destroyers of various classes for the US Navy during the Second World War. Although Bethlehem San Pedro was expanded and modernised in the 1960s, the continued drop in workload and labour disputes caused the closure of the yard in 1980.

TODD SHIPYARDS CORPORATION, SAN PEDRO acquired the Los Angeles Shipbuilding and Dry Dock Co. in 1940, and during the Second World War, it built ten auxiliary vessels for the US Navy. Todd San Pedro continued to produce warships for the US Navy after the war, including the guided missile frigates *England* (DLG-22) in 1963 and *Fox* (DLG-33) in 1966. Both of those ships were later reclassified as guided missile cruisers and renumbered CG-22 and CG-33 respectively. From 1966 to 1971, Todd San Pedro built six destroyer escorts of the *Knox* class, which were subsequently reclassified as frigates. Todd San Pedro later produced seventeen guided missile frigates of the *Oliver Hazard Perry* class from 1977 to 1987.

Two other south Los Angeles shipyards were involved in naval shipbuilding during the first half of the twentieth century. CRAIG SHIPBUILDING CO. of Long Beach built two 'L' class submarines for the US Navy in 1916 under a sub-contract with the Electric Boat Co. The San Pedro yard of WESTERN PIPE & STEEL CO., built twelve destroyer escorts in 1942-3.

San Francisco.

*San Francisco*

The most important shipyard on the West Coast for naval construction was the Union Iron Works of San Francisco. The shipyard was located on a 30-acre tract of land with a water frontage of 1800ft in the Potrero District at the southeast end of the downtown area of the city on San Francisco Bay. Originally established as the Donahue Foundries in 1849, Union Iron Works began shipbuilding in 1883, and it completed the steamer *Arago*, the first steamship built on the West Coast, in the following year. The yard soon received orders for building warships for the US Navy, and it produced the protected cruisers *Charleston* (C-2) in 1889, *San Francisco* (C-5) in 1890, and *Olympia* (C-6) in 1895. Union Iron Works then built the battleship *Oregon* (BB-3) in 1896 and one torpedo-boat in 1899. The shipyard also built the protected cruiser *Chitose* for Japan in 1898.

Both the *Olympia* and *Oregon* achieved fame during the Spanish-American War of 1898. The USS *Olympia*, which was later classified as a heavy cruiser and renumbered CA-15, served as Admiral Dewey's flagship during the Battle of Manila Bay. The battleship USS *Oregon* helped to defeat the Spanish fleet in the Battle of Santiago off the southern coast of Cuba. By the turn of the century,

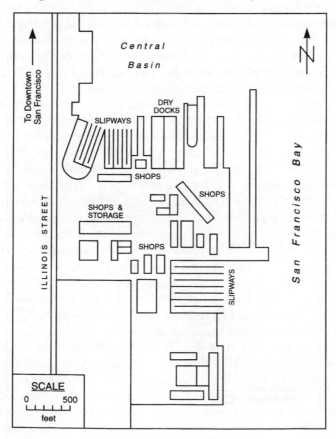

Union Iron Works (Bethlehem).

Union Iron Works had become one of the most important marine engineering facilities in the nation, and it had a workforce of 2500 employees which occasionally rose to 3000 people during periods of peak workload.

Union Iron Works continued to produce warships for the US Navy into the twentieth century, including the battleships *Wisconsin* (BB-9) in 1901 and *Ohio* (BB-12) in 1904. The yard also built the protected cruisers *Tacoma* (C-18) in 1904 and *Milwaulkee* (C-21) in 1906. The *Tacoma* was later reclassified as a light cruiser and given the new designation of CL-20. The yard then produced the armoured cruisers *California* (ACR-6), later renamed *San Diego*, in 1907 and *South Dakota* (ARC-9), later renamed *Huron*, in 1908, as well as three destroyers during that time frame. Union Iron Works also built several submarines for the US Navy, including two 'A' class boats in 1901-03, one 'F' class boat in 1911, two 'H' class boats in 1913, and three 'K' class boats in 1913-14.

In 1914, Union Iron Works had three slipways and three floating dry docks. The largest of the dry docks was 450 × 80ft in size with a lifting capacity of 6500 tons, one was 300 × 70ft in size with a capacity of 2500 tons, and the smallest was 270 × 65ft and had a capacity of 2000 tons. About 1915, the Union Iron Works was taken over by the Bethlehem Steel Corporation, and the yard, which became known as BETHLEHEM SAN FRANCISCO, was enlarged in 1917. Bethlehem San Francisco continued serving the navy by completing the wartime production programme of sixty-six flush-deck, 4-stacker destroyers begun earlier by the Union Iron Works. The shipyard also completed several submarines, including six 'R' class boats in 1918-19 and twelve 'S' class boats in 1919-22.

In addition to its Potrero Works, Bethlehem built the new facility at Alameda across the bay from San Francisco in 1916 to supplement its shipbuilding capacity in the area. The BETHLEHEM ALAMEDA WORKS, originally intended as a shipbuilding facility with its six slipways, became the primary producer of steam engines, steam turbines, and other mechanical equipment for Bethlehem's shipbuilding operations in the San Francisco area. Bethlehem subsequently acquired a facility at the northern edge of Hunters Point on San Francisco Bay, about three miles south of San Francisco. BETHLEHEM HUNTERS POINT had two large graving docks, one 1120 × 150ft and the other 750 × 120ft in size, both of which had been excavated from solid rock and then lined with concrete.

During the period between the two world wars, Bethlehem San Francisco was involved primarily in the production of merchant ships, but that changed as war clouds loomed on the horizon. Production during the Second World War included the four light anti-aircraft cruisers, *Oakland* (CL-95) and *Reno* (CL-96), both in 1943, *Flint* (CL-97) in 1944, and *Tuscon* (CL-98) in 1945. Bethlehem San Francisco also built twelve destroyers and twenty destroyer escorts during the war. The yard, which was used exclusively for building warships for the US Navy during the war, had a peak wartime workforce of 12,000 employees in 1944.

By the end of the war, employment at Bethlehem San Francisco had dropped to 9200 workers, with 2200 people engaged in new construction. Another 5700 workers were then employed repairing ships at the Bethlehem Alameda plant. In the post-war era, Bethlehem San Francisco built two destroyer escorts of the

*Dealey* class in 1957 and two destroyer escorts of the *Garcia* class in 1968, the latter two of which were later redesignated as frigates in 1975. Those ships were the last naval vessels produced by the yard for the US Navy.

The CONTINENTAL IRON WORKS shipyard was located at Vallejo, California, just across the strait from the Mare Island Navy Yard, about 140 miles northeast of San Francisco. Continental produced the iron-hulled, twin screw, double-turreted monitor *Monadnock* in 1883. The *Monadnock* displaced 4000 tons, was over 260ft long, and carried four 10in guns, two in each turret.

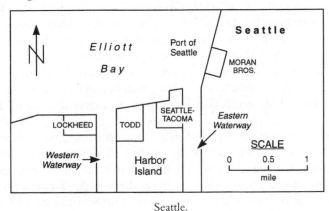

Seattle.

## Pacific Northwest

*Seattle*
One of the early pioneers of private shipbuilding in this area was Robert Moran, who started a ship repair facility at Seattle in 1882. In 1890, Robert Moran and his brother established the MORAN BROTHERS partnership and began to build ships at their shipyard just to the south of the town of Seattle. A few years later, the Moran Brothers was awarded a contract to build a torpedo-boat for the US Navy, and that ship was delivered in 1897. The victories achieved over the Spanish Navy during the Spanish-American War established the United States as a major naval power, and the US Navy began to expand its fleet into a formidable fighting force.

Spreading naval shipbuilding work to all sections of the country, the Federal government selected the Moran Brothers shipyard to build one of the five new 15,000-ton battleships of the *Virginia* class that had recently been authorised by Congress. The USS *Nebraska* (BB-14) was laid down in 1902, launched in 1904, and completed in 1906. Upon completion of the USS *Nebraska*, the Moran Brothers, operating on a shoestring, became insolvent. The shipyard was purchased by a group of investors in 1906 and it was subsequently sold off to the Seattle Construction and Dry Dock Co. in 1911.

The SEATTLE CONSTRUCTION AND DRY DOCK Co., under contract with the Electric Boat Company, built two 'F' class and one 'H' class submarine for the US Navy in 1912-13. In 1911, Seattle Construction began work on two submarines for Chile, but these were subsequently purchased by Canada in 1914 at the beginning of the First World War. In 1916, the newly formed Todd

Shipyards Corporation, a New York-based concern, acquired the Seattle Construction and Dry Dock Co., but the shipyard was allowed to continue operations under its own name for the next two years. During that period, the Seattle Construction & Dry Dock Co. built three 'N' class submarines and one destroyer for the US Navy.

In 1918, the Seattle Construction & Dry Dock Co. was sold off, and Todd established a new shipyard at the northwest corner of Harbor Island about two miles southwest of the centre of Seattle. A new corporation, the TODD SHIPYARDS CORPORATION, SEATTLE DIVISION (Todd Seattle), was formed to operate this new shipyard. At the end of the First World War, the Todd Seattle Division completed one of the famous group of nearly 280 four-stacker, flush-deck destroyers built at that time. In the post-war era, Todd Seattle kept busy with the construction and repair of merchant vessels. In 1939, as war again threatened Europe, the SEATTLE-TACOMA SHIPBUILDING CORP. (Sea-Tac) was established by Todd Shipyards Corporation to accommodate increasing orders for warships.

The Seattle Branch of Sea-Tac was located at a new facility on the northeastern corner of Harbor Island, just to the east of the existing Todd Seattle shipyard. By 1942, the Seattle Branch of Sea-Tac completed twenty-five destroyers of the *Fletcher* class In 1944, the Seattle-Tacoma Shipbuilding Corp. was renamed TODD PACIFIC SHIPYARDS. The Seattle yard of Todd Pacific Shipyards continued to build *Fletcher* class destroyers, producing twenty-one more vessels of that type before the end of the Second World War. In 1947, Todd Pacific Shipyards was liquidated, leaving Todd Seattle as the only Todd facility to continue the construction and repair of ships in the Puget Sound region.

During the period 1959-66, Todd Seattle built five guided missile destroyers, and one destroyer. From 1969 to 1974, Todd Seattle produced eight destroyer escorts of the *Knox* class, which were later reclassified as frigates. Those ships were followed by eight guided missile frigates of the *Oliver Hazard Perry* class in 1977-89.

The PUGET SOUND BRIDGE & DRY DOCK CO. was established in 1916 on the southwestern coast of Elliot Bay about three miles southwest of Seattle. For most of its existence, the Puget Sound Bridge & Dry Dock Co. was involved in ship repair and the production of small merchant vessels. From 1960-64, the yard produced three *Adams* class guided missile destroyers for the US Navy. In 1965, the Puget Sound Bridge & Dry Dock Co. was taken over by the Lockheed Corporation, and it became the LOCKHEED SHIPBUILDING AND CONSTRUCTION CO. From 1967-74, Lockheed Shipbuilding produced seven destroyer escorts, which were later reclassified as frigates, and three guided missile destroyer escorts, later reclassified as guided missile frigates. In 1985, Lockheed Shipbuilding ceased to operate.

*Tacoma*

In 1918, the TODD DRY DOCK & CONSTRUCTION CO. was established to operate a Todd shipyard on Commencement Bay, about three miles northeast of

Tacoma, in addition to its Seattle yard. In the post-war period, the Todd Tacoma yard built the light cruisers *Omaha* (CL-4), *Milwaukee* (CL-5), both in 1923, and *Cincinnati* (CL-6) in 1924, but in 1925, the Tacoma yard was deactivated due to lack of work. In 1939, as the Second World War was threatening in Europe, the SEATTLE-TACOMA SHIPBUILDING CORP. (Sea-Tac), a Todd Shipyards subsidiary, was formed with branches in Seattle and Tacoma. The Tacoma Branch of Sea-Tac was established at the same site as the original Todd Dry Dock and Construction Co. During the war, the Tacoma yard concentrated on the construction of Type C-1 cargo ships for the Merchant Marine.

In 1944, the Seattle-Tacoma Shipbuilding Corp. was renamed TODD

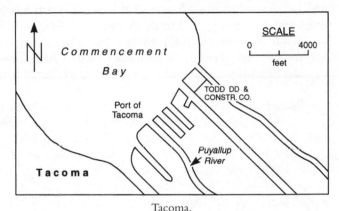

Tacoma.

PACIFIC SHIPYARDS. The Tacoma yard of Todd Pacific Shipyards, in addition to the Seattle yard, began to build *Fletcher* class destroyers, completing nineteen of those ships by the end of the war. The Tacoma yard also launched nineteen escort carrier hulls, and it completed twelve of them, with the remaining seven hulls going to other shipyards for completion. In addition, the Tacoma yard built seven escort carriers at the end of the war. In 1947, Todd Pacific Shipyards was liquidated, and the Tacoma yard was closed in favour of consolidating Todd shipbuilding and repair activities at the Seattle facility.

## PRIVATE SHIPYARDS INLAND

### Great Lakes

At the beginning of the nineteenth century, American relations with Great Britain began to deteriorate as a result of Britain's proclaimed right to search neutral American shipping during Britain's wars with other nations. This practice, and the impressment of American seamen by the British during that period, eventually led to the War of 1812. Anticipating the possibility of military actions along the border with British Canada, the American Congress authorised the construction of a number of warships by American shipyards in the Great Lakes region.

While most of the naval actions during the War of 1812 took place along the eastern coast of the United States, the Great Lakes did become the scene of several naval battles with British forces. Admiral Oliver H Perry's victory on Lake Erie in 1813 secured that region for the Americans, as did Commodore Macdonough's victory at Plattsburg on Lake Champlain in the following year. The battle for Lake Ontario ended in a stalemate with neither side achieving any decisive victory. Naval shipbuilding on the Great Lakes ceased after the War of 1812, and it was not until the Second World War that shipyards on the Great Lakes were again called upon to provide warships for the US Navy in time of a national emergency.

Three names dominated shipbuilding on Lake Ontario at the beginning of the nineteenth century, namely, Eckford, Brown, and Bergh. In 1809, the partnership of HENRY ECKFORD AND CHRISTIAN BERGH built a 14-gun brig at Oswego, New York at the eastern end of Lake Ontario. After dissolving his

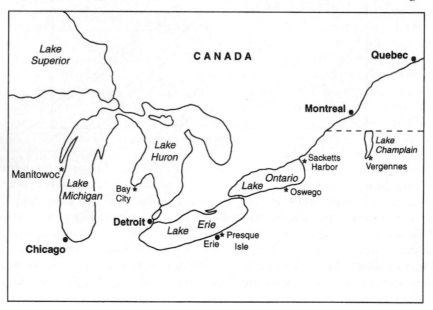

The Great Lakes.

partnership with Christian Bergh, HENRY ECKFORD went on to build a number of warships at his Sackets Harbor shipyard near Watertown, New York in the northeastern corner of Lake Ontario. These ships included the 44-gun frigate *Superior* (1815), the 32-gun frigate *Mohawk* (1814), one 24-gun corvette, one 20-gun sloop-of-war, three 14- to 18-gun brigs, two schooners, and a number of gunboats between 1812 and 1815.

ADAM & NOAH BROWN built the 44-gun frigate *Plattsburg* at their Sackets Harbor shipyard in 1815, and during that same year, they laid down two 74-gun ships-of-the-line, the *New Orleans* and the *Chippewa*. At the end of the War of 1812, construction on those ships was terminated while they were still on their stocks, and they were later destroyed. Adam & Noah Brown dominated shipbuilding on Lake Erie with their other shipyard on Presque Isle near Erie, Pennsylvania. There in 1813, Adam & Noah Brown built two 18-gun brigs and a schooner for the Federal Navy. On Lake Champlain, the Adam and Noah Brown's third shipyard at Vergennes, Vermont at the southern tip of Lake Champlain built a 24-gun corvette and an 18-gun brig in 1814.

The Second World War brought renewed interest in using Great Lake shipyards to increase the war production of fighting ships for the Navy. In 1943, the DEFOE SHIPBUILDING CO., located at Bay City, Michigan at the lower end of Saginaw Bay, built a total of 28 destroyer escorts for the US Navy. After the end of the war the Defoe Shipbuilding Co. continued to produce warships for the navy, including two destroyer escorts in 1957, two guided missile destroyers in 1961, and three more destroyer escorts, later reclassified as frigates, in 1968.

During the Second World War, the MANITOWOC SHIPBUILDING CO. of Manatowoc, Wisconsin built some thirty submarines for the US Navy, under the supervision of the Electric Boat Co. The Manitowoc shipyard was located on the west shore of Lake Michigan at the mouth of the Manitowoc River about 60 miles north of Milwaukee. The yard used the unusual technique of launching its ships sideways into the Manitowoc River since the river was not broad enough to accommodate lengthwise launchings. Completed submarines were then placed on shallow-draught barges and floated down to sea via the Chicago Sanitary and Ship Canal and the Des Planes River to Joliet, Illinois, the Illinois River to St. Louis, and finally the Mississippi River to the Gulf of Mexico.

*Inland Waterways*
Due to their shallow depths, America's inland rivers provided limited capability for shipbuilding, especially the construction of warships. There were, however, occasions when inland rivers were able to make a naval contribution to the American war effort. Some inland rivers were within the boundaries of the original thirteen colonies, but unless they flowed eastward toward the Atlantic Ocean, they could not be used for anything but local trading. The Treaty of 1783 with Great Britain following the American Revolutionary War gave the United States additional territory west of the colonial borders to the Mississippi River. The Louisiana Purchase of 1803 opened the way for access from these inland rivers down the Mississippi River to the Gulf of Mexico.

At the beginning of the nineteenth century, Congress authorised the construction of a large number of shallow draught gunboats intended for use against the Barbary pirates of northern Africa. Several orders for these gunboats went to shipyards on the Ohio River, including yards at Cincinnati, Ohio and at certain Kentucky locations. During the Civil War, some thirty ironclads were built for the Federal Navy on inland rivers, mostly at Cincinnati and St. Louis. During the Second World War, the Pittsburgh shipyard of DRAVO CORPORATION produced thirteen destroyer escorts for the US Navy. In addition, the AMERICAN CORPORATION shipyards at Cleveland and Lorain, Ohio built thirteen patrol frigates for the navy from 1943-5.

# 4 France

The French government recognised early on the importance of exercising direct control over the construction of their warships to achieve quality and standardisation. The French navy was founded in

France

1624 after Cardinal Richelieu became the prime minister of France. In 1636, France established a marine arsenal (naval shipyard) at its naval base at Toulon on the Mediterranean coast. Later in the seventeenth century, Jean-Baptiste Colbert, Minister of Marine under Louis XIV, reorganised the French naval establishment and founded the naval shipyard at Rochefort. Naval shipyards were then established at Brest and at several other locations on the Atlantic coast and on the northern coast of France along the English Channel.

France began to produce outstanding warships during the middle of the eighteenth century, and at that time, her ships-of-the-line and frigates were considered to be among the best in the world. With a progressive naval construction programme, France gradually increased the strength of her fleet during the remainder of the eighteenth century. A French squadron was able to block British reinforcements from reaching Yorktown, and thereby help to secure American independence in 1781. The French fleet reached its peak at the end of the eighteenth century, but after naval defeats at the Battles of the Nile in 1798 and at Trafalgar in 1805, it declined to become a secondary naval power.

During the twentieth century, France maintained a formidable navy, but it never again reached a level of major significance in the world. The Washington Naval Treaty of 1922 relegated France to become a third-rate naval power by allowing France, as well as Italy, to possess a fleet of only 20 per cent of the strength of the  navies of Great Britain or the United States. Japan, on the other hand, could maintain a fleet up to 60 per cent of the strength of the British Royal Navy and the US Navy under the famous 5:5:3:1:1 ratio.

## NAVAL SHIPYARDS

### Brest

The ARSENALE DE BREST (Brest Naval Arsenal) is the most important French naval shipyard on the Atlantic coast. It is located in the protected harbour of the town of Brest at the northwestern tip of France. The history of Brest as a naval base dates back to 1631 when it was declared to be a royal port by Cardinal Richelieu. In the late 1650s, the construction of a naval shipyard was begun at Brest, and in 1661, the yard completed its first vessel, the 40-gun ship *Infante*. From 1664 to 1699, Brest produced ninety-four warships, including thirty-eight ships-of-the-line with 48 guns or more. Among the ships-of-the-line were the 110-gun *Royal Duc* in 1668, the 120-gun *Soleil Royal* in 1669, the 100-gun *Formidable* in 1691, the 102-gun *Soleil Royal II* in 1692, and the 100-gun *Foudroyant* and *Terrible*, both in 1693.

Around the turn of the century, the Brest Arsenal was improved by Colbert, the navy Minister to Louis XIV, and further fortified by Marshal Vauban, the French fortifications expert. From 1700-49, Brest built sixty-seven warships, including thirty-two ships-of-the-line mounting fifty guns or more and ten frigates. The ships-of-the-line included the 110-gun *Foudroyant* in 1724 and

*Royal Louis* in 1740, one 80-gun, and seven 74-gun ships. After 1750, there was a resurgence in naval construction, and Brest produced eighty-nine warships, including fifty ships-of-the-line with fifty or more guns. Among those ships-of-the-line were the 116-gun *Royal Louis* in 1759, the 110-gun *Bretagne* in 1766, the 100-gun *Royal Louis* in 1780, and the 120-gun *Les Etats de Bourgogne* in 1790, four 80-gun ships, and twenty-three 74-gun ships.

Two of the above mentioned ships, the 74-gun *Duguay Trouin* built in 1788 and the 80-gun *Indomptable* built in 1790, participated in the Battle of Trafalgar in 1805. From 1800-47, Brest completed sixty-nine warships, but only nine ships-of-the-line, including the 118-gun *Vengeur* in 1803 and the 120-gun *Valmy*, the last sailing warship produced for the French navy, in 1847. During that period, the shipyard also built nine frigates in addition to a host of smaller warships. In 1850, Brest began to convert from the production of wooden sailing vessels to steam-powered vessels with ironclad hulls. From 1850-64, the shipyard built four screw-propelled ships-of-the-line and eight screw frigates. Brest also produced seven ironclad steam frigates and six unprotected cruisers from 1862-9.

By 1870, the workforce at the Brest shipyard was up to 7000 employees. Brest produced an additional eleven unprotected cruisers from 1870 to 1884, and four barbette ships in 1887-92. The yard built the armoured cruiser *Dupuy de Lôme* in 1895 and the protected cruisers *Sfax* in 1887, *Isly* in 1893, and *Friant* in 1895. Brest then began producing a series of battleships, including the *Charles Martel* (1897), *Charlemagne* (1899), and *Gaulois* (1899). At the beginning of the twentieth century, Brest continued building battleships such as the *Iéna* (1902), *Suffren* (1903), *Republique* (1906), *Democratie* (1908), and *Danton* (1911). During this period, Brest also built the armoured cruisers *Marseillaise* (1903), *Léon Gambetta* (1905), and *Edgar Quinet* (1911).

In 1908, a large 160-ton capacity electric crane was installed at the fitting-out quay of Brest. Excavation for a new 820ft long, 118ft wide dry dock was begun in 1910, and the dock was completed in 1916. Although the workforce averaged 7000 workers from 1870-1910, the number of employees rose to nearly 8500 in 1913 as the First World War approached. Brest went on to produce the Dreadnought battleships *Jean Bart* in 1913 and the *Bretagne* in 1915. The shipyard laid down the battleship *Flandre* in 1913, but she was cancelled after the ship had been launched in 1914. Another battleship, the *Duquesne*, was cancelled in 1914 before it was even laid down.

After the war, Brest produced the heavy cruisers *Suffren* (1927), *Duquesne* (1928), *Colbert* (1931), *Foch* (1931), *Dupleix* (1932), and *Algérie* (also in 1932). During that period, the yard also built the light cruisers *Duguay-Trouin* (1926), *Primauguet* (1926), and *La Galissonnière* (1935). In addition, Brest produced nine submarines in 1924-31. Brest then built the 26,500-ton battleship *Dunkerque* in 1937 and the 35,000-ton battleship *Richelieu* in 1939. The *Dunkerque* was heavily damaged by British naval forces at the French naval base of Mers-el-Kebir near Oran on the coast of Algeria in July 1940, shortly after the fall of France. The ship was later scuttled at Toulon in November 1942 to keep it from falling into German hands.

In 1942, two years after the fall of France, the Germans built a concrete U-boat bunker at Brest to protect their U-boats from Allied bombing raids while they were in port. The base by that time had become the headquarters of the German 9th U-boat Flotilla. During the German occupation, Brest also served as a major ship repair yard for the German naval forces operating in the Atlantic. After the war, the Brest Naval Arsenal was kept busy by building the passenger liner *Antilles* in 1952. The yard resumed the production of warships with six destroyers in 1956–8 and the 27,000-ton aircraft carrier *Clemenceau* in 1961. Brest then built the helicopter carrier *Jeanne d'Arc* in 1964, two submarines in 1969–70, and one guided missile destroyer in 1970.

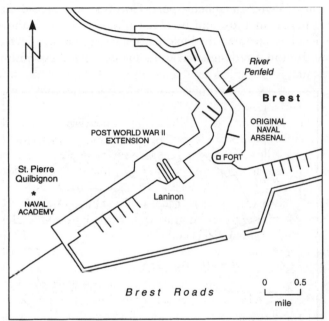

Brest Dockyard in 1990.

From 1979 to 1990, Brest built seven additional guided missile destroyers and two submarines. Brest produced the 38,000-ton nuclear-powered aircraft carrier *Charles de Gaulle* in 1994, and it currently has four destroyers under construction. Brest is the most important facility under the Direction des Constructions Navales (DCN). In addition to continuing naval construction, DCN Brest is also responsible for maintaining the Force Océanique Stratégique (FOST), the French ballistic missile submarine force, in an operationally ready condition. The naval base at Brest is also the headquarters of the Région Maritime Atlantique (Atlantic Maritime Region), which has operational control of all French naval forces in the Atlantic Ocean. That command has responsibility for the French coastline from the Belgian border westward to Brest and then southward to the Spanish border.

Brest is the current location of the Ecole Navale (French Naval Academy), which had originally been established at Rochefort, but was later transferred to Brest in 1830. In 1928, a new Naval Academy was constructed at Quatre Pompes, a small bluff overlooking the western end of the shipyard near St Pierre Quilbignon.

*Toulon*
The ARSENALE DE TOULON (Toulon Naval Arsenal) is the second most important naval facility in France, serving as the main base of the French Mediterranean Fleet. Toulon is located on the Mediterranean coast about 35 miles east of Marseilles and only 100 miles west of the Italian border. The history of Toulon as a naval base dates back to 1589 when King Henri IV established the town as a military port. Construction of the Toulon Naval Arsenal was begun in 1595, and in 1610, it was set up to construct galleys. Cardinal Richelieu favoured the building of a strong French fleet, and in 1636 at his behest, Toulon was designated as the primary naval establishment on the Mediterranean.

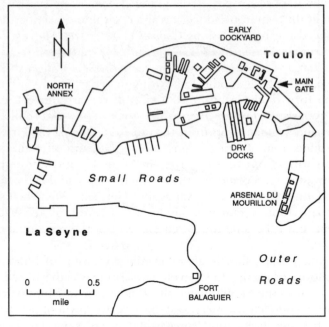

Toulon.

In 1638, Toulon completed its first warship, the galliot *Eclatante*. In 1650, the arsenal was expanded and improved, and in 1666, Colbert constructed a ropery and foundry at the arsenal. Further improvements were made at the arsenal during the last two decades of the seventeenth century. From 1638 until the end of the century, the shipyard produced 124 ships, including fifty ships-of-the-line with fifty or more guns, four frigates, and numerous smaller warships. The First Rate *Royal Louis*, built in 1668, was the pride of the French navy at that time. From 1700-49, Toulon built sixty naval vessels, including twenty ships-of-the-line with fifty or more guns and seven frigates. During the middle of the eighteenth century, Toulon had a workforce of about 2000 men.

From 1750-99, Toulon built ninety warships, including twenty-five ships-of-the-line and twenty-seven frigates. Among the ships-of-the-line were the First Rates *Foudroyant* in 1750 and *Terrible* in 1780, as well as the *Indomptable* (1751), *Redoubtable* (1752), *Souverain* (1757) and *Dauphin-Royal* (1791). Few warships were constructed during the French Revolution, but after that there was a resurgence in naval shipbuilding. From 1800-47, Toulon produced another 100 naval sailing vessels, including twelve ships-of-the-line and nine frigates. Among the ships-of-the-line were the 74-gun *Neptune* built in 1803 and the 80-gun *Pluton* completed in 1805, both of which participated in the Battle of Trafalgar in 1805. The huge 120-gun *Souverain* was built in 1819.

Over the years, the Toulon Arsenal was subject to continuous improvements and modernisation. During the mid-nineteenth century, Toulon converted to the construction of steam-powered and ironclad warships. From 1860 to 1886, the yard built thirteen ironclad frigates and eight unprotected cruisers. Toulon then produced the barbette ships *Caiman* in 1888 and *Magenta* in 1893, the protected cruisers *Davout* in 1891, *Suchet* in 1894 and *Pascal* in 1897, and the battleship *Lazare-Carnot*, also in 1897. In 1888, Toulon built its first submersible, and it built another submarine in 1893.

After the turn of the century, Toulon built the armoured cruisers *Jeanne d'Arc* in 1902 and *Dupetit-Thouars* in 1905. The yard built twenty-six submarines and five destroyers from 1903 to 1913. During the First World War, Toulon produced an additional nine submarines, and after the war it built twelve submarines from 1925 to 1939. The Second World War began with the German invasion of Poland in 1939, and Britain and France immediately responded with a declaration of war against Germany. After the fall of France in June 1940, Toulon remained under the control of the Vichy French government, and it became the haven for most of the remaining units of the French Fleet.

In November 1942, shortly after the Allied invasion of North Africa, the Germans moved to occupy the remainder of France. As they raced for Toulon, hoping to capture the French Fleet, all of the major warships were blown up or scuttled by their crews, including the modern battleships *Dunkerque* and *Strasbourg*, the old battleship *Provence*, the heavy cruisers *Algérie*, *Colbert*, *Dupleix*, and *Foch*, the light cruisers *La Galissonnière*, *Jeanne de Vienne*, and *Marseillaise*, eighteen super-destroyers; twelve destroyers, four torpedo-boats, sixteen submarines; and the seaplane tender *Commandant Teste*. Toulon was liberated on 28 August 1944, shortly after the Allied invasion of southern France.

The Toulon naval shipyard discontinued the construction of warships after the war. During its long history, Toulon produced over 500 warships of various types for the French navy. Today, it operates under the Direction des Constructions Navales de Toulon (DCN Toulon), and it is responsible for the maintenance, repair, and refit of some seventy French warships, including two aircraft carriers. The yard supports French naval forces in the Mediterranean Sea and in certain limited overseas areas, representing about 60 per cent of the French fleet. DCN Toulon is also responsible for ammunition maintenance, engineering support, and logistics support for naval activities. The shipyard currently has nearly 4300 employees.

### Cherbourg

The ARSENALE CHERBOURG, located at the northern tip of the Cotentin Peninsula, was not among the early naval arsenals founded by the French crown. It was established in the nineteenth century to supplement the capacity of other French naval shipyards in producing steam-powered warships for the French navy. From 1862 to 1889, Cherbourg built six ironclad frigates, twelve unprotected cruisers, and the barbette ships *Vauban* (1885) and *Furieux* (1887). The shipyard then built the protected cruisers *Surcouf* (1890), *Alger* (1891), *Chasseloup-Laubat* (1895), *Bugeaud* (1896), *Cassard* (1898), and *Du Chayla* (also in 1898). After the turn of the century, Cherbourg produced the battleship *Henri IV* in 1903 and the armoured cruiser *Jules Ferry* in 1905.

Cherbourg began to specialise in the construction of submarines, and before the outbreak of the First World War, it had completed eleven submersibles for the French navy. After the war, Cherbourg resumed submarine production, completing ten boats from 1924 to 1934. One of the submarines built during this period was the unique cruiser submarine *Surcouf* (1929), which displaced 2900 tons surfaced and 4300 tons submerged. In addition to ten 21in torpedo tubes, the *Surcouf* carried two 8in guns in a turret directly in front of the conning tower. It could travel at 18kts on the surface and 10kts submerged. During the German occupation, Cherbourg was not extensively used due to its vulnerability to British air attacks.

After the Second World War, Cherbourg renewed submarine production, building eight submarines in 1957-60 and another twenty-four boats in the period from 1971-9. In addition, Cherbourg completed two more nuclear strategic missile submarines of *L'Inflexible* class in 1980-5 and six nuclear attack submarines in 1983-93. Two nuclear strategic missile submarines of the *Le Triomphant* class were built in 1997-9 and one additional submarine of that class is currently under construction with delivery scheduled for 2003. Cherbourg falls under the Direction des Constructions Navales (DCN) of the French naval establishment, and it now specialises in the production of nuclear submarines and their engines. The yard currently employs about 4150 personnel.

### Lorient

The ARSENALE LORIENT, another important French naval shipyard on the Atlantic coast, is located about 70 miles south of Brest. Like Cherbourg, Lorient was established in the nineteenth century to supplement the capacity of other naval shipyards. From 1862 to 1882, the shipyard produced ten ironclad frigates and seven unprotected cruisers. Lorient then built the barbette ships *Turenne* (1882), *Indomptable* (1887), *Formidable* (1889), and *Hoche* (1890). Those ships were followed by the battleships *Amiral Tréhouart* (1896), *Brennus* (also 1896), *Bouvet* (1890), and *St. Louis* (1900).

After the turn of the century, Lorient produced the protected cruiser *La Gravière* in 1903 and the armoured cruisers *Gueydon* (1903), *Conde* (1904), *Gloire* (1904), *Victor Hugo* (1907), *Jules Michelet* (1908), *Mirabeau* (1911), and *Waldeck-Rousseau* (also in 1911). The yard then built the Dreadnought battleships *Courbet* and *Jean Bart*, both in 1913 and the *Provence* in 1915. Lorient began work on the battleship *Gascogne* in 1913, but the programme was cancelled soon after the ship was launched in 1914.

After the First World War, Lorient built the heavy cruiser *Tourville* in 1928 and the light cruisers *Primauguet* in 1926, *La Tour d'Auvergue* (ex-*Pluton*) in 1929, and the *Jeanne de Vienne* in 1937. The shipyard also produced seven destroyers from 1926 to 1940 and three submarines in 1928-31. During the Second World War, the Germans used Lorient as a submarine base, and they built large concrete bomb-proof U-boat pens to protect the submarines while being repaired and serviced between patrols.

After the war, Lorient completed the light (anti-aircraft) cruiser *De Grasse*, which had been laid down in 1938. It also resumed the production of destroyers, completing seven in 1955-8, eleven in 1979, and two in 1998. As a key activity under the Direction des Constructions Navales (DCN), Lorient now specialises in the maintenance of naval surface vessels. Over 3100 workers are currently employed by the Lorient shipyard.

*Rochefort*
ARSENALE DE ROCHEFORT was founded 1670 by Jean-Baptiste Colbert, the navy and Finance Minister under Louis XIV. He also established the French naval college there, but it was later transferred to Brest in 1830. From 1862 to 1884, Rochefort built five ironclad frigates and six unprotected cruisers. It then produced the barbette ships *Tonnant* in 1884 and *Duguesclin* in 1886, the protected cruisers *Forbin* (1889), *Jean Bart* (1891), *Galilée* (1897), *Lavoisier* (1898) and *D'Estrées* (1899), and the armoured cruisers *Amiral Charner* (1894), *Bruix* (1896), and *Dupleix* (1903). Rochefort built twenty-four destroyers and one submarine before the First World War, but after building just one submarine after the war, it was phased out as a naval shipyard.

## NAVAL BASES

France had a number of naval bases of varying degree of importance along its coastline and at its one-time colonial possessions. On its northern coastline, France had bases at Ostende, Calais, Dieppe, Le Havre, Rouen, Caen, Cherbourg, and St. Malo. On its west (Atlantic) coast, it had bases at Lorient, St. Nazaire, Nantes, La Rochelle, Gironde, Bordeaux, and Bayonne in addition to its major base at Brest. On the Mediterranean, it had bases at Marseilles, Nice, and Cannes in addition to its major naval base at Toulon.

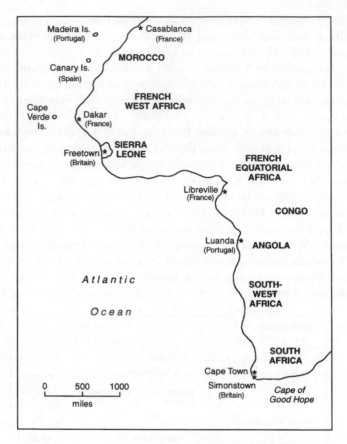

West Africa in 1940.

Across the Mediterranean on the northern coast of Africa, France had several naval bases including Bizerte in Tunisia and Algiers, Oran, and Mers-el-Kebir in Algeria. On 3 July 1940, the British Force H, operating out of Gibraltar, attacked the French Fleet at Mers-el-Kebir to keep its warships from falling into the hands of the Germans after the fall of France. Led by the battlecruiser *Hood*, the British squadron destroyed the old battleships *Provence* and *Bretagne* and severely damaged the battleship *Dunkerque* and destroyer *Mogador*. The battleship *Strasbourg* and several destroyers were able to escape and make their way Toulon.

In addition to its Mediterranean bases, France had a naval base at Casablanca on the Atlantic coast of Morocco, about 200 miles southwest of Gibraltar. On 8 November 1942, American and British forces attacked French naval units there during the Allied invasion of North Africa. The battleship *Jean Bart*, which was not yet fully operational, was damaged, and several destroyers and submarines at the base were sunk or severely damaged.

France also had a naval base at Dakar in French West Africa, 1600 miles further down the coast from Casablanca. On 23 September 1940, three

months after the fall of France, a joint British-Free French force attacked
Dakar, which had remained loyal to the Vichy government. The attack was
successfully repulsed by the garrison and units of the French fleet at the base,
including the battleship *Richelieu*. Upon the German occupation of the south
of France and the scuttling of the French fleet at Toulon in November 1942,
the *Richelieu* and other surviving units of the French fleet joined the Free-
French forces.

Other significant French naval bases included Libreville on the coast of
French Equatorial Africa (now Gabon), Diego Suarez on the northern tip of
Madagascar, Djibouti on the coast of French Somaliland in northeast Africa,
Beirut on the coast of Lebanon, and Saigon on the coast of French
Indochina (now Vietnam). France had naval stations elsewhere in French
Indochina, including Haiphong and Tonkin, as well as at some of its other
Pacific island possessions, such as Réunion, New Caledonia, New Hebrides,
and Tahiti. France also had naval stations in French Guiana on the northern
coast of South America and at Fort-de-France on the island of Martinique,
one of the Windward Islands in the Lesser Antilles at the eastern end of the
Caribbean.

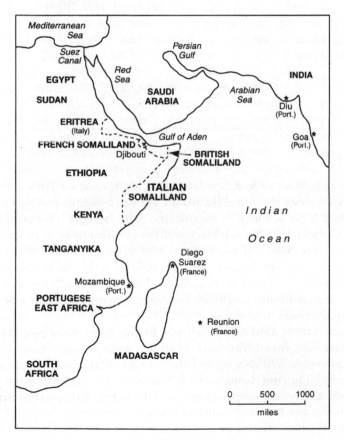

East Africa in 1940.

## PRIVATE SHIPYARDS

### Channel Coast

*Dunkerque*
The northern Channel coast of France extends from Dunkerque (Dunkirk) near the Belgian border, westward along the English Channel, and to the northwestern tip of France above Brest. The ATELIERS ET CHANTIERS DE FRANCE at Dunkerque built the passenger liner *Colombie* in 1931, and it produced five destroyers from 1924 to 1940. In 1952, the Dunkerque shipyard completed the 20,500-ton cruise-liner *Flandre*, but it built no major warships after the Second World War.

*River Seine*
The towns of Le Havre and Rouen at the mouth of the River Seine represent the most important French shipbuilding region on the English Channel coast. Le Havre, the second largest seaport in France, after Marseilles, is located about 150 miles northwest of Paris. Le Havre was an important seaport as early as the late sixteenth century, when it received the attention of Cardinal Richelieu, and Marshal Vauban as a potential stronghold. Action was thereupon taken to improve its harbour and fortifications. Le Havre was eventually established as a naval base by Napoleon I early in the nineteenth century.

The AUGUSTIN NORMAND ET CIE shipyard, which produced mostly torpedo-boats, destroyers, and submarines for the French navy, is located at Le Havre. The yard built three unprotected cruisers in 1863-9 and four sloops in 1874-8. Normand also produced one unprotected cruiser for Russia in 1881 and two protected cruisers for Portugal, both in 1898. The shipyard produced some 100 torpedo-boats and fourteen destroyers before the outbreak of the First World War, as well as five additional destroyers built for the Imperial Russian navy. After the war, Normand built three destroyers, but by that time it had begun to construct submarines. The shipyard completed twelve submarines from 1925 until 1940, when France was invaded by the Germans. After the Second World War, Normand built five more submarines from 1946-79.

The FORGES ET CHANTIERS DE LA MEDITERRANÉE, whose main yard was at La Séyne near Toulon on the Mediterranean coast, also had a small shipyard at Le Havre. The shipyard was involved primarily with the production of commercial vessels, but it did produce five destroyers for the French navy prior to the First World War and four more in 1925-32.

The CHANTIERS WORMS, later CHANTIERS DE LA SEINE, is located at Rouen, about 50 miles upriver (east) of Le Havre. That firm produced six destroyers and eight submarines from 1930 to 1940. After the Second World War, Chantiers de la Seine built four submarines from 1948-79. The CHANTIERS NORMANDIE, also at Rouen, had been absorbed by Chantiers de Penhoët in 1901, and it built two destroyers for the French navy before the First World War.

*Other Channel Shipyards*

The FORGES ET CHANTIERS DE LA MÉDITERRANÉE, in addition to its shipyards at La Seyne and Le Havre, also had a shipyard at Granville on the western coast of the Cotentin Peninsula, about 60 miles south of Cherbourg. Granville produced the battleships *Hydra* and *Psara* for Greece in 1891 and 1892, respectively. The yard also produced two destroyers for the French navy prior to the First World War. The CHANTIERS NAVALES DE FRANÇAIS at Blainville produced nine destroyers and two submarines for the French navy between 1924-33. Neither yard built any major naval vessels during or after the Second World War.

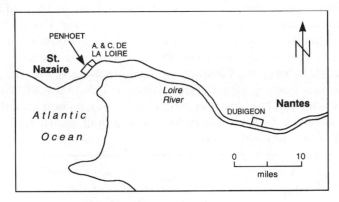

The Loire.

## Atlantic Coast

*River Loire*

The most important private shipbuilding area on the western Atlantic coast of France is at the mouth of the Loire River, about 60 miles south along the coast from Lorient. The Loire maritime region encompasses the historic towns of St. Nazaire and Nantes. The CHANTIER DE PENHOËT (also known as CHANTIERS DE LA ST. NAZAIRE) was founded in 1861 by the Compagnie Général Transatlantique, the steamship company that later became popularly known as just the French Line. The shipyard began with 27 acres of land and 2300ft of waterfront. Within four years, Penhoët had built four steel-hulled passenger liners for the North Atlantic trade.

Penhoët began building warships late in the nineteenth century. The shipyard built the coastal defence battleship *Spetsai* for Greece in 1891, and then it produced the protected cruiser *Coetlogon* in 1894 and the armoured cruiser *Ernest Renan* in 1909 for the French navy. Penhoët built the pre-Dreadnought battleships *Condorcet* and *Diderot*, both in 1911, and the Dreadnought battleship *Lorraine* in 1916. The yard began construction on the battleship *Normandie* in 1913, but she was cancelled before completion. Another battleship, the *Lyon*, was cancelled before the keel was even laid. Prior to the First World War, Penhoët also produced two destroyers for the French navy.

The Penhoët shipyard became famous for its construction of passenger liners of increasing size, speed, and luxury, including the *La Savoie* (1901), *La Provence* (1906), *Rochambeau* (1911), and *France* (1912). After the First World War, Penhoët resumed the construction of passenger liners with the *Ile de France* in 1927 and then the magnificent 83,500-ton *Normandie* in 1935. The *Normandie* was damaged beyond repair by a fire that broke out while the ship was being converted into a troopship by the US Navy in New York in 1942. Penhoët also produced the liners *Ville d'Alger*, also in 1935, and *Pasteur* in 1939. The *Pasteur* was later sold to the North German Lloyd Line in 1957 and renamed the *Bremen* after its namesake that was lost during the war.

Penhoët produced the training cruiser *Jeanne d'Arc* in 1931 and the light cruisers *Emile Bertin* in 1933 and *Georges Leygues* in 1937. The yard then built the 26,500-ton battleship *Strasbourg* in 1938 and the 35,000-ton battleship *Jean Bart* in 1940. Penhoët also produced five destroyers and one submarine from 1924 to 1931. In 1955, the Chantiers de Penhoët merged with the Ateliers et Chantiers de la Loire to form the CHANTIERS DE L'ATLANTIQUE. The shipyard built the 65,000-ton liner *France* in 1962, and in 1963, it completed the 30,000-ton aircraft carrier *Foch*, the last major warship built at that yard during the latter half of the twentieth century.

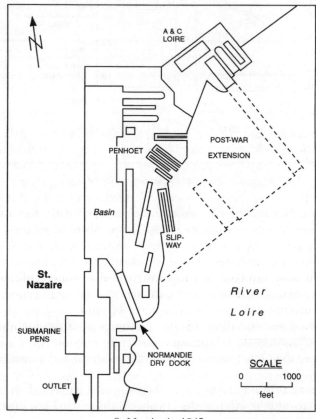

St Nazaire in 1945.

In 1969, Chantiers de l'Atlantique established a ship assembly area in a new two-section building dock, 3000ft long and 275ft wide, that can accommodate ships up to 500,000 tons displacement. A 150ft wide preassembly area adjacent to the building dock and extending along its entire 3000ft length allows ship modules to be assembled there before being installed on the ship under construction. The building dock and preassembly area are both served two travelling gantry cranes spanning both facilities, one of 750-ton capacity and the other of 250-ton capacity. That shipbuilding facility was followed in 1972 by a new 1500 × 310ft outfitting dock.

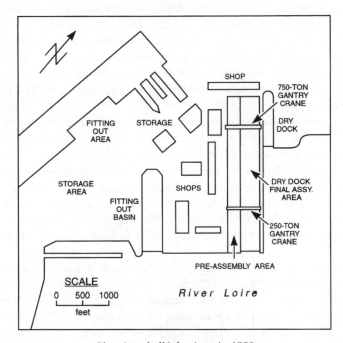

Chantiers de l'Atlantique in 1990.

In 1976, the Chantiers de l'Atlantique merged with the international Alsthom Group to form ALSTHOM ATLANTIQUE. Alsthom merged with GEC Power Systems in 1989 to form G.E.C. Alsthom with the Chantiers de l'Atlantique as its affiliated naval construction branch. Chantiers de l'Atlantique is now involved in the construction of super-tankers, LPG and methane gas carriers, container ships, car ferries, and large cruise liners. The shipyard is currently situated on 320 acres of land, 82 acres of which are covered. Its modern workshops feature machines with the highest degree of automation. Chantiers de l'Atlantique currently employs over 4400 people, including more than 2700 workers and 1700 technical and administrative staff members.

The ATELIERS ET CHANTIERS DE LA LOIRE, was established in 1881 at St. Nazaire just to the north of the Penhoët shipyard. The yard built one unprotected cruiser in 1885, and that ship was followed by the protected cruisers *Tage* (1890), *Descartes* (1896), *D'Assas* (1898), and *Guichen* (1899). A & C de la Loire began producing coastal defence battleships late in the nineteenth century with the *Jemmapes* and *Valmy*, both built in 1894, and the *Masséna* in 1898. The shipyard then built the armoured cruiser *Desaix* in 1904, the pre-Dreadnought battleship *Liberté* in 1908, and the Dreadnought battleship *France* in 1914. A & C de la Loire built three torpedo-boats in 1886 and one destroyer prior to the First World War.

After the First World War, A & C de la Loire built the light cruiser *Marseillaise* in 1937, thirteen destroyers from 1924 to 1939, and seven submarines in 1925-31. In 1955, the Ateliers et Chantiers de la Loire merged with the Chantier de Penhoët to combine their resources and form CHANTIERS DE L'ATLANTIQUE (see above). The Ateliers et Chantiers de la Loire also had a shipyard at Nantes, about 40 miles upstream (east) of St Nazaire on the River Loire. That yard produced twelve torpedo-boats from 1887 to 1900 and one destroyer prior to the First World War, but that was the extent of its naval construction.

The ATELIERS ET CHANTIERS DE BRETAGNE, also located at Nantes, was established in 1909 from the former Brosse et Fouchet establishment. The yard built fourteen destroyers prior to the First World War, and after the war, it produced eight destroyers from 1924 to 1940. After the Second World War, Bretagne built five additional destroyers in 1955-8. In 1962, the Ateliers et Chantiers de Bretagne became the ATELIERS ET CHANTIERS DE NANTES. A & C de Nantes built four frigates for the Portuguese navy in 1967-9. In 1969, the firm merged with Anciens ETA.t Dubigeon to form DUBIGEON S.A.

CHANTIERS DUBIGEON was originally established at Nantes in 1760, and it was incorporated as ANCIENS ETA.t DUBIGEON in 1912. Dubigeon built three destroyers in 1925-9, and those were followed by eight submarines from 1928 to 1940. In 1964, Dubigeon completed one submarine for the French navy and three submarines for Portugal in 1967-9. In 1969, Chantiers Dubigeon merged with Ateliers et Chantiers de Bretagne to form DUBIGEON S.A. Dubigeon build one destroyer for the French navy in 1979 before coming under the Alsthom Atlantique Group in 1983. The Dubigeon shipyard at Nantes was closed in 1987, and its resources were consolidated with other Alsthom facilities at St. Nazaire.

*Bordeaux*
The FORGES ET CHANTIERS DE LA GIRONDE, located at the lower end of an inlet near the mouth of the Garonne River at Bordeaux, was another important shipyard on the Atlantic coast. Gironde built the barbette ship *Requin* in 1888 and the protected cruisers *Lalande* (1890), *Cosmao* (1891), *Troude* (1891), *Protet* (1899) and *Infernet* (1900). The yard built the armoured cruisers *Chanzy* in 1894 and *Kléber* in 1904, and these were followed by the battleships *Vérité* in 1908 and *Vergniard* in 1911. Gironde began construction on the Dreadnought battleship *Languedoc* in 1913, but the programme was cancelled after the ship was launched in 1915.

The launch of the three-decker ship-of-the-line HMS *Prince of Wales* at Portsmouth Dockyard in 1794. (U.S. Naval Historical Center: NH 57196)

The U.S. gunboat USS *Seneca* under construction at the J Simonson Yard, New York, in 1861. (U.S. Naval Historical Center: NH 59372)

The French battleship *Marceau* and (foreground) the torpedo-boat *No. 103* on the building ways of Forges et Chantiers de la Mediterranée, La Seyne, in 1887. (U.S. Naval Historical Center: NH 74855)

Brest Navy Yard photographed during the mid-1880s, looking inland up the Penfeld River. (U.S. Naval Historical Center: NH 74895)

The launch of the Russian armoured cruiser *Vladimir Monomakh* at the Baltic Works, St Petersburg, in 1882. (U.S. Naval Historical Center: NH 90580)

The launch of the Austro-Hungarian protected cruiser *Kaiser Franz Josef I* at Stabilimento Tecnico Triestino, Trieste, on 18 May 1889. The motto of the Austro-Hungarian Empire, 'Viribus Unitis', can been seen on the side of the ship. (U.S. Naval Historical Center: NH 88932)

(Above) The American battleship USS *Connecticut* having her 12in guns installed in her forward turret at the New York Navy Yard, 31 January 1906. (U.S. Naval Historical Center: NH 78359)

(Right) USS *Idaho* (BB-42) fitting out at the New York Shipbuilding Corp. yard, Camden, in 1919. (U.S. Naval Historical Center: NH 60221)

The British battleship HMS *Nelson* fitting out at Armstrong High Walker shipyard, Newcastle-upon-Tyne, in 1926. Note the cantilever crane in the background. (U.S. Naval Historical Center: NH 57530)

Two British light cruisers, HMS *Neptune* (foreground) and *Amphion*, fitting out at Portsmouth Dockyard in 1936, with a hammerhead crane in the background. (U.S. Naval Historical Center: NH 50142)

The heavy cruiser USS *Chicago* on the building way at Mare Island Navy Yard, Vallejo, in 1930. (U.S. Naval Historical Center: NH 70787)

The destroyer leader USS *Luce* prior to launching at Fore River Shipyard, Quincy, in 1958. (U.S. Naval Historical Center: NH 51452)

Boiler shop at Chantiers de Penhoët, St Nazaire, in 1932. (Chantiers de l'Atlantique)

Machine shop at Chantiers de Penhoët, St Nazaire, in 1932. (Chantiers de l'Atlantique)

(*Above*) Submarines under
construction at the RDM
Shipyard, Rotterdam, in
1931. (RDM Submarines)

(*Right*) Installation of a
diesel engine in a Dutch
submarine at the RDM
Shipyard, Rotterdam,
1960. (RDM Submarines)

The German heavy cruiser *Admiral Hipper* at the Blohm & Voss shipyard, Hamburg, 1939.
(Blohm + Voss)

Launch of the Japanese heavy cruiser *Myoko* at Yokosuka Navy Yard on 16 April 1927.
(U.S. Naval Historical Center: NH 48396)

The battleship *Bismarck* under construction at the Blohm & Voss shipyard, Hamburg, in 1939.
(Blohm + Voss)

The Italian *Littorio* class battleship *Impero* on the building way at the Ansaldo shipyard, in 1939. She was in fact never completed and was broken up on the stocks between 1948 and 1950. (U.S. Naval Historical Center: NH 86123)

The Japanese battleship *Yamato* fitting out at the Kure Navy Yard in 1941. Note the three 18.1in guns in the after turret, the most powerful main armament ever carried by a battleship. (U.S. Naval Historical Center: NH 63433)

U-boats under construction at the Blohm & Voss shipyard, Hamburg in 1915. The yard built nearly 100 submarines during the First World War. (Blohm + Voss)

Incomplete Type XXI U-boats on the building ways at the Deschimag Shipyard, Bremen, at the end of the Second World War. (U.S. Naval Historical Center: SC 290914)

The Chantiers de Penhoët shipyard, St Nazaire, in the late nineteenth century. (Chantiers de l'Atlantique)

The same shipyard, now Chantiers de l'Atlantique, in 1971, with a gantry crane in the centre of the picture. (Chantiers de l'Atlantique)

Aerial view of Swedish Karlskronavarvet with new shipbuilding shed in 1995. (Kockums AB)

Small Swedish warships under construction in the new shipbuilding shed at Karlskronavarvet. From the left, two *Göteborg* class corvettes, and a *Landsort* class mine countermeasures vessel. (Kockums AB)

Aerial view of the North Yard at Newport News Shipbuilding in 1996, with a nuclear-powered aircraft carrier under construction in the foreground, and two more in the background. (Newport News Shipbuilding)

A gantry crane used in the construction of aircraft carriers at Newport News. (Newport News Shipbuilding)

*(Left)* The *Nimitz* class aircraft carrier USS *Harry S Truman* (CVN-75) under construction at Newport News in 1995. (Newport News Shipbuilding) *(Right)* The prefabricated island superstructure of the *Harry S Truman* being lifted into position. (Newport News Shipbuilding)

The *Harry S Truman* fitting out at Newport News in 1997. (Newport News Shipbuilding)

Gironde produced four torpedo-boats in 1892-7, and it completed two destroyers prior to the First World War. After the First World War, the shipyard produced ten destroyers from 1925 to 1940, and it built the 10,000-ton seaplane tender *Commandant Teste* in 1929. The *Commandant Teste* was a ship of unique design with four catapults, two on either side of the ship, and she carried a total of twenty-six aircraft. Gironde then built the light cruiser *Gloire* in 1937. After the Second World War, the shipyard produced four destroyers in 1955-8 and two more in 1979.

Another Bordeaux shipyard, M. ARMAN, was noted more for its production of warships for foreign customers than those for the French navy. Arman produced eight gunboats for the French navy in 1862-8, and during this period, it also built two wooden, steam-powered corvettes for Prussia in 1864 and the ironclad rams *Prinz Adalbert* for Prussia in 1865, and the *Stonewall* for the Confederate navy in 1865. Arman built the coastal defence battleship *Silvado* for Brazil in 1866, but it was not involved in any significant naval construction after that time.

The shipyard of DYLE ET BACALAN, also of Bordeaux, built four destroyers prior to the First World War and two more destroyers in 1925-9, but no major warships were produced by the yard after that period.

### Mediterranean Coast

The main shipyard of the FORGES ET CHANTIERS DE LA MEDITERRANÉE is located at La Seyne, just three miles southwest of the naval shipyard at Toulon on the Mediterranean coast. Popular with foreign governments, La Seyne built several ironclad frigates for other countries, including four for Italy in 1861-4, one for Spain in 1863, one for Prussia in 1867, and two for Turkey in 1868, as well as a turret ram for the Netherlands in 1868. The yard then built an armoured cruiser for Greece in 1879 and two protected cruisers for Chile in 1890.

Turning to capital ship construction, La Seyne built the battleship *Pelayo* for Spain in 1887, the battleship *Capitan Prat* for Chile in 1890, the battleships *Marshal Floriano* and *Marshal Deodora* for Brazil, both in 1899, and the battleship *Tsessarevitch* for Russia in 1904. La Seyne also produced one armoured cruiser for Greece in 1879, two protected cruisers for Chile in 1890, and two armoured cruisers for Russia in 1903-08.

For the French navy, La Seyne produced one unprotected cruiser in 1877, the protected cruisers *Amiral Cécille* (1890), *Linois* (1895), *D'Entrecasteaux* (1899) and *Châteaurenault* (1902), and the armoured cruisers *Montcalm* in 1902 and *Sully* in 1903. During that period, the yard also built the barbette ships *Amiral Duperié* in 1883 and *Marceau* in 1891. La Seyne then built the coastal defence battleship *Bouvines* in 1894, and this was followed by the pre-Dreadnought battleships *Jauréguiberry* (1897), *Patrie* (1906), *Justice* (1908), and *Voltaire* (1911).

La Seyne built the Dreadnought-type battleship *Paris* in 1914, and it began work on the battleship *Béarn* in that same year. The ship was cancelled during the First World War before the she was even launched, and her hull was later converted into an aircraft carrier which was finally completed in 1927, retaining the original name. La Seyne also produced seven destroyers prior to the First World War, and after the war, it built the light cruiser *Montcalm* in 1937, as well as one destroyer in 1933. La Seyne laid down six more destroyers of the *Hardi* class in 1938-9, but these had not been completed by the time of the German invasion in 1940. Its last major shipbuilding project was the liner *Sagafjord*, built for Norway in 1965.

CHANTIERS SCHNEIDER was actually not located on the Mediterranean coast, but rather deep inland at Chalon-sur-Saône on the River Saône in the eastern part of France, about 40 miles south of Dijon. Ships built by Schneider were sailed down the River Saône to Lyon, and from there down the River Rhône to the Mediterranean Sea, about 25 miles west of Marseilles. Schneider built three destroyers prior to the First World War, and after the war, it built eight submarines from 1925 to 1940. The yard did not build any major naval vessels after that period.

The CHANTIERS ET ATELIERS DE PROVENCE at Port de Bouc, about 20 miles west of Marseilles, built smaller naval vessels for the French navy as well as merchant vessels. Among the passenger liners that the yard built were the *Espagne* in 1910 and *Lafayette* in 1915. The yard has not produced any major naval vessels in recent times.

# 5 Japan

I t was not until the 1850s that Commodore Matthew Perry and Consul
General Townsend Harris opened Japan to the West with trade
agreements. The Japanese were quick to learn Western methods and
technology, including naval science. In 1866, the first warship built in Japan
was a gunboat produced by the private shipyard of Ishikawajima on the
outskirts of Tokyo. In 1865, construction of a naval shipyard began at Yokosuka
on the western shore of Tokyo Bay about 30 miles south of the capital. This
was followed eleven years later by the establishment of a naval base at Kure in
1886. In 1896, a third naval base was established at Sasebo on Kyushu Island,
and in 1902, Japan's fourth naval base was established at Maizuru on the
northern coast of Honshu.

Japanese naval and private shipyards gradually improved their capability for
producing warships with the construction of larger and larger vessels.
Beginning with gunboats and sloops, they advanced to unprotected cruisers
and then to protected cruisers in the late nineteenth century. Not yet having
the equipment and skills to construct major warships on their own, the
Japanese began building a fleet through the acquisition of warships from
foreign shipyards, primarily British. Japan obtained ten armoured cruisers from
various foreign yards in 1890-1904, and during this period, the nation also
turned to battleships. Japan acquired the battleships *Fuji* (1897) and *Shikishima*
(1900) from the Thames Iron Works, the *Asahi* (1900) from Clydebank, and
the *Mikasa* (1902) from Vickers, Barrow. The *Mikasa* later served as the flagship
of Admiral Togo at the Battle of Tsushima.

When the Russians occupied the Chinese fortress of Port Arthur on
the tip of the Lioantung Peninsula in February 1904, the Japanese felt that
they were strong enough to challenge the Russian move, and they
blockaded the port. Elements of the Russian Far East Squadron, normally
based at Vladivostok, then tried to break out of the blockade, but they were
turned back by the Japanese force, and their commander was killed in the
process.

Japan.

Tsar Nicholas II ordered the Russian Baltic Fleet to the Far East to teach these upstart orientals a lesson. The fleet sailed in October 1904 with four new battleships, the *Orel*, *Alexandr III*, *Borodin*, and *Suvaroff* (flagship), under the command of Admiral Rojdestvensky. Going around the Cape of Good Hope, the fleet did not arrive at Madagascar until early in 1905. There, the fleet was reinforced by a squadron of three older battleships under Rear-Admiral Nebogatoff flying his flag in *Nikolai I*. The combined force then sailed for Singapore and proceeded up along the coast of French Indo-China to Shanghai.

Dropping off their auxiliary vessels at Shanghai, the Russians headed for their base at Vladivostok through the Straits of Tsushima, a 50-mile wide strait that separated Tsushima, a small cluster of islands, from Honshu, the main island of Japan. On the morning of 27 May 1905, Admiral Togo, flying his flag in the battleship *Mikasa*, manoeuvred the Japanese fleet across the front of the Russian squadron and utterly devastated the oncoming column of ships. The Russian flagship, *Suvaroff*, and the older *Oslyabaya* were quickly knocked out of action, and the remaining elements of the fleet soon surrendered.

As a result of the Russo-Japanese War, Japan acquired several Russian battleships as war prizes. Most of those vessels were older ships, such as the

*Imperator Nikolai I* (1893), but the war prizes did include two ships of later vintage, the *Orel* (1904), renamed the *Iwami,* and the American-built *Retvizan* (1902), renamed *Hizen.* Although these acquisitions provided the fledgling sea power with a sizeable fleet, they did not contribute to Japan's goal of self-sufficiency in naval construction. Turning from foreign sources for its warships, Japan built four armoured cruisers in its own shipyards in 1905-11.

By 1907, the Kure Naval Shipyard had produced the first home-built battleship for the Japanese Navy. Japanese shipyards built five additional pre-Dreadnought battleships by 1911 and two Dreadnoughts in 1912. In 1913, the Japanese Navy acquired the battlecruiser *Kongo* from Vickers-Barrow, and it then proceeded to build three sister-ships in Japanese yards. From that time on through to the end of the Second World War, all major Japanese warships were built in Japan. Japan entered the First World War on the side of the Allies, and was therefore awarded the former German-held Caroline Islands in the Pacific Ocean after the war. This included the strategic base at Truk, which the Japanese later developed into a major naval base for the Japanese Fleet.

Japan continued to build up its fleet during and after the war, and was recognised as a major naval power, third only after Great Britain and the United States. Under the Washington and London Naval Treaties, Japan was allowed to maintain its fleet up to 60 per cent of the strength of the Royal Navy and that of the United States Navy (the famous 5:5:3 ratio). With Great Britain and the United States each retaining fifteen battleships with a total displacement of 500,000 tons, Japan was able to maintain a force of ten battleships with a total displacement of 300,000 tons.

In compliance with the London Naval Treaty of 1930, Japan in the early 1930s began construction of four light cruisers of the *Mogami* class with fifteen 6in guns in five triple turrets. However, these ships were designed to also accept twin 8in turrets, and after the Second World War broke out in 1939, all four ships were converted into heavy cruisers by merely replacing their 6in gun with the 8in ones. This conversion increased the firepower of each ship by more than 60 per cent. Two additional ships originally designed as light cruisers were completed as heavy cruisers during the war.

In the late 1930s, as the London Naval Treaty was approaching expiration, Japan undertook a programme to design and build the most powerful class of battleships in the world, the *Yamatos.* Each of these ships would have a standard displacement of 65,000 tons and be over 860ft long. They would also carry nine 18.1in guns in three triple turrets, two forward and one aft, the largest-calibre guns ever mounted on a capital ship. The *Yamato* was commissioned in December 1941, shortly after the outbreak of the Pacific war, and the *Musashi* entered service in August 1942.

After the Japanese attack on Pearl Harbor in December 1941, the Japanese fleet swept far and wide to support its invasion operations throughout southeast Asia. It was not until the Battle of Midway in June 1942, when American naval forces defeated a Japanese invasion fleet, that Japanese expansion was brought to a halt. From there it was a struggle lasting three more years before Allied forces invaded Okinawa near Japan and the Japanese

Navy was finally destroyed as a fighting force. At the end of the war, Japan was occupied by mostly American forces, and all surviving units of the Imperial Japanese Navy were surrendered to the Allies.

In 1952, Japan became a free nation again as a result of the San Francisco Peace Treaty Conference, which had begun in late 1951. Under the treaty, Japan was given the right of individual or collective self-defence, and it subsequently established a Maritime Self Defence Force. Initially, it acquired several surplus American destroyers, destroyer escorts, and patrol craft, but it soon began a naval construction programme for destroyers, frigates, and smaller vessels in 1954. Japan currently builds its own guided missile destroyers, guided missile frigates, conventional attack submarines, and other types of naval vessels

## NAVAL SHIPYARDS

*Yokosuka*

In 1865, construction began on the YOKOSUKA IRON WORKS, an iron foundry and shipbuilding yard, on a 20-acre tract of land on the southwestern shore of Tokyo Bay. The facility was transferred to the Japanese Navy in 1868 for the purpose of producing warships. At that time, Yokosuka had three wooden slipways, and in 1871, those facilities were augmented by the construction of its first dry dock, a stone structure measuring 400 × 90ft and capable of accommodating ships up to 5000 tons displacement. In that same year, the yard was renamed the YOKOSUKA SHIPYARDS. In 1874, a second stone dry dock was built at the yard, a 490 × 95ft structure that could be used for ships up to 10,000 tons displacement.

Yokosuka built the first modern warship constructed in Japan, a 900-ton gunboat, in the early 1870s, and in 1877, Yokosuka was designated as an Imperial Naval Port. A third but smaller stone dry dock, measuring only 310 × 50ft, was built in 1884, and in 1886, the shipyard was renamed YOKOSUKA NAVAL SHIPYARD. After building several corvettes and dispatch vessels from 1876 to 1885, Yokosuka produced three unprotected cruisers in 1887-9, and those ships were followed by the protected cruisers *Hashidate* (1894), *Akitsushima* (1894), *Suma* (1896), and *Akaski* (1899). After the turn of the century, Yokosuka produced one unprotected cruiser in 1901, the protected cruisers *Niitaka* and *Otowa*, both in 1904, and the armoured cruiser *Kurama* in 1911.

Early in the twentieth century, Yokosuka also produced eight torpedo-boats in 1900-03 and eight destroyers in 1903-06. In 1905-06, the shipyard underwent a major improvement programme that included the construction of a fourth dry dock, which measured 780 × 90ft in size and was able to accommodate ships up to 25,000 tons displacement. Slipway No. 1 was put out of service, but slipways Nos. 2 and 3 were modernised, to include the installation of gantry cranes. The shipyard was extended to over 330 acres in 1907. Graduating to the construction of capital ships, Yokosuka built the pre-

Dreadnought battleship *Satsuma* in 1909 and the Dreadnought battleship *Settsu* in 1912.

Further improvements were made to the Yokosuka Naval Shipyard prior to and during the First World War, consisting of the installation of a 200-ton capacity hammerhead crane at the fitting-out pier in 1911 and upgrading the slipway cranes to ones of greater capacity in 1913. In 1915, a huge 1060 × 125ft dry dock, the yard's fifth, was constructed at Yokosuka. During the war, Yokosuka built the battleships *Hiei* in 1914 and *Yamashiro* in 1917, as well as one destroyer in 1918. The shipyard completed the battleship *Mutsu* in 1921 after the war, but the battlecruiser *Amagi* was cancelled.

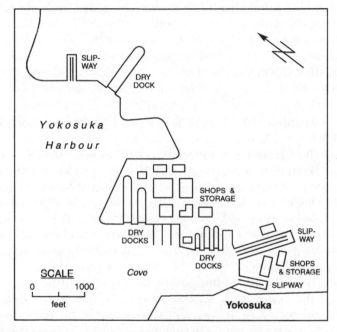

Yokosuka in 1945.

In the inter-war period, Yokosuka completed the light cruiser *Tenryu* in 1919, four destroyers in 1918-20 and six submarines in 1922-30. Yokosuka was heavily damaged during the 1923 earthquake, but it soon recovered and resumed naval shipbuilding. The yard subsequently built the heavy cruisers *Myoko* in 1929 and *Takao* in 1932, as well as the light cruiser *Suzuya* in 1937, which was later converted into a heavy cruiser with 8in guns (see above).

Turning to aircraft carrier production, the shipyard built the carriers *Hiryu* (1939), *Shokaku* (1941), *Ryuho* (1942), *Chiyoda* (1943), *Shinano* (1944), and *Unryu* (1944). The 72,000-ton *Shinano* was Japan's largest aircraft carrier, having been converted after the Battle of Midway from the hull of the third battleship of the *Yamato* class. A sixth and larger dry dock, measuring 1100 × 165ft in size, had to be constructed in 1940 to accommodate the building of this huge ship. The *Shinano* was sunk on its maiden voyage while en route to the Kure Naval Base by an American submarine in November 1944.

During the Second World War, Yokosuka also built twenty submarines and fourteen destroyers, with two more destroyers having been launched and three more just laid down in 1945. Heavily damaged in American air raids, Yokosuka Naval Shipyard was taken over by the United States Navy at the end of the war, and it is still utilised as a base and ship repair facility for American naval forces in that region.

## Kure

Kure, in a remote and protected location in southwestern Honshu, about twelve miles southeast of Hiroshima, became a military port in 1887, and in the following year, a naval base was established at that location. Kure began building ships late in the nineteenth century, completing one light cruiser in 1890, after the shipyard's first dry dock was constructed. The yard's first slipway was built in 1892, and the second slipway followed three years later. In 1898, the KURE NAVAL SHIPBUILDING FACTORY was established, and it built nine torpedo-boats in 1902-04. The third slipway at the yard was completed in 1904. Kure then produced the protected cruiser *Tsushima* in 1904, two destroyers in 1905, and the armoured cruisers *Tsukuba* (1907), *Ikoma* (1908), and *Ibuki* (1911).

In 1908, two additional dry docks were built at the Kure Naval Shipyard. Advancing to the production of capital ships, Kure built the pre-Dreadnought battleship *Aki* in 1911 and the Dreadnought battleship *Kawachi* in 1912. Warship production at Kure during the First World War included the battleships *Fuso* in 1915 and *Nagato*, completed in 1920. as well as seven destroyers in 1915-20 and eight submarines in 1916-22. Two battleships were cancelled at the end of the war. The hull of one battleship, laid down in 1920, was subsequently completed as the aircraft carrier *Akagi* in 1927, in accordance with the terms of the Washington Naval Treaty.

Kure built the heavy cruisers *Nachi* in 1928 and *Atago* in 1932, the light cruiser *Mogami* in 1935, the aircraft carrier *Soryu* in 1937, and sixteen submarines from 1922 to 1938. The *Mogami*, originally equipped with fifteen 6in guns in five triple turrets, was later converted into a heavy cruiser with twin 8in turrets.

Kure had been designated to build the first of the super battleships planned for the Imperial Japanese Navy. The mighty *Yamato*, which was laid down in 1937, launched in 1939, and completed in 1941, displaced 70,000 tons and carried nine 18.1in guns, the largest guns ever installed as the main armament of a capital ship. She was sunk by US naval aircraft in the Bongo Strait on 7 April 1945 while en route from the Japanese Inland Sea to attack American forces invading Okinawa. Other wartime production at Kure included the aircraft carrier *Katsuragi* in 1944, light cruiser *Oyodo* in 1943, twenty-nine submarines, and three escort carriers converted from merchant ships.

The Kure Naval Shipyard was heavily bombed in March and again in July of 1945, bringing naval shipbuilding at the facility almost to a halt. The shipyard was initially occupied by American naval forces in October 1945 after the Japanese surrender, and it was used as a naval base by the US Navy during

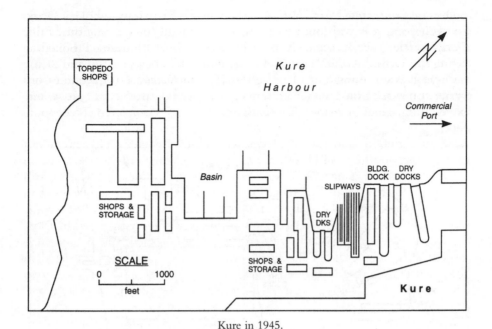

Kure in 1945.

the Korean War. The shipyard was later turned over to the Japanese Maritime Self Defence Force and it continues to serve as a naval base.

### Sasebo

Sasebo, located near the mouth of Omura Bay on Kyushu Island about 30 miles north of Nagasaki, was opened as a naval port in 1886. The base gradually developed into a shipbuilding facility with the construction of its first dry dock in 1895. One year later, the facility was established as the SASEBO NAVAL SHIPYARD in 1896. With two new slipways installed in 1898 and in 1902, and a another dry dock built in 1905, Sasebo soon began to increase its production of warships. The yard built four destroyers in 1905-06, the protected cruiser *Tone* in 1910, and the light cruiser *Chikuma* in 1912. Two additional dry docks were completed prior to the outbreak of the First World War.

During the war, Sasebo built four destroyers in 1915-18. In that period, the yard completed three additional dry docks and constructed a 1900 × 1200ft fitting-out basin with a 250-ton capacity hammerhead crane. That gave Sasebo a total of six dry docks, ranging in length from 500 to 1300ft, in addition to its nine shipbuilding berths. During the inter-war years, the yard produced the light cruisers *Tatsuta* (1919), *Kuma* (1920), *Kitakami* (1921), *Nagara* (1922), *Yura* (1923), and *Yubari* (1923). Sasebo also constructed fourteen destroyers and ten submarines from 1920 to 1939. In 1923, action was taken to increase the size of the yard's fourth dry dock to over 1300ft to accommodate larger vessels.

From 1931 to 1937, several new factories were built at the Sasebo Naval Shipyard to produce warship components and armaments. In 1934-6, Sasebo modernised the aircraft carrier *Kaga*, originally built by Kawasaki Dry Dock Co. Kobe, and this was followed in 1936-8 with the modernisation of the aircraft carrier *Akagi*, originally built by Kure Naval Shipyard. Production during the Second World War included the light aircraft carrier *Chitose* (1944), the light cruisers *Agano* (1942), *Yahagi* (1943) and *Sakawa* (1944), one escort carrier converted from a merchant ship in 1941, four destroyers in 1940-5, and sixteen submarines in 1940-5. A seventh dry dock was completed at Sasebo in 1941.

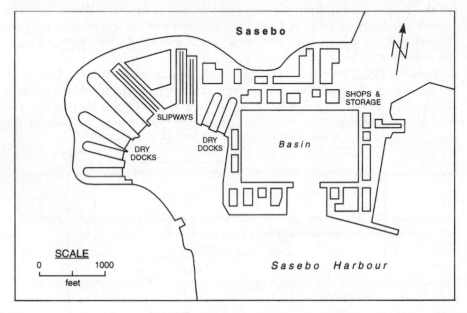

Sasebo in 1945.

The Sasebo Naval Shipyard was severely damaged in bombing raids during the last year of the war. The naval headquarters at the base was dissolved at the end of the war, and the base was evacuated at the end of August 1945. Sasebo was subsequently occupied by American forces after the Japanese capitulation, and it is still being operated as a support base for the US Navy.

## Maizuru

The MAIZURU NAVAL SHIPBUILDING WORKS was established at the Maizuru naval base on the northern coast of Honshu, about 60 miles north of Kobe, in 1902. The facility was renamed the MAIZURU NAVAL SHIPYARD two years later in 1904, and it soon began producing warships for the Imperial Japanese Navy. Maizuru built eight destroyers from 1906 to 1912 and four more during the First World War. After the war, Maizuru continued to produce destroyers, completing twenty-three from 1920 to 1939. Production during the Second World War consisted of twenty-six additional destroyers, with another two left incomplete at the end of the war.

## NAVAL BASES

Japan had naval bases to support the operation of its fleet units at many locations among the home islands, including Kobe, Nagasaki, Takeshiki, Matsumi, and Ominato. Beyond the home islands, Japan had naval bases at Masanpo and Chinkai in Korea and at Maku on the Pescadore (Penghu) Islands in the Formosa Strait west of Taiwan. Truk Atoll was developed into an strong naval base after Japan acquired the Carolina Islands, in the western half of the Pacific Ocean, from Germany at the end of the First World War. The primary military facilities at Truk were concentrated on several islands in the eastern half of the atoll, which is roughly circular-shaped with a circumference of about 125 miles.

Japan also took over the naval facilities that it captured from the Allies early in the Pacific War, including Singapore at the tip of British Malaya, Hong Kong, Batavia (Jakarta) and Surabaya on Java in the Dutch East Indies, and Cavite near Manila. Those facilities were later restored as a result of the Japanese capitulation in August 1945.

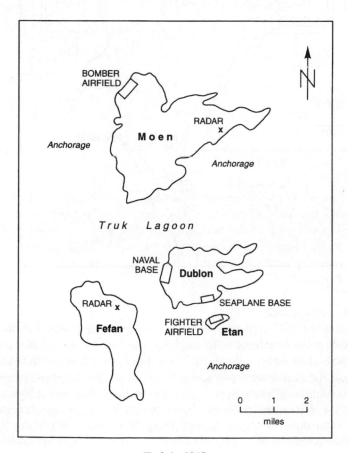

Truk in 1945.

## PRIVATE SHIPYARDS

The two most important Japanese private shipyards were Mitsubishi (Nagasaki) and Kawasaki (Kobe), both of which were classified as naval shipyards. As such, they shared in the naval construction programme with Kure and Yokosuka naval shipyards in the production of major warships for the Imperial Japanese Navy.

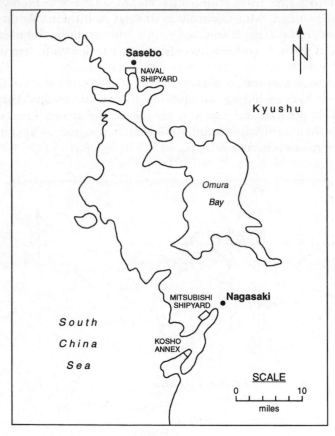

Kyushu.

### MITSUBISHI NAGASAKI

Construction of the MITSUBISHI NAGASAKI shipyard began in 1857, and it built mostly merchant vessels throughout the remainder of the nineteenth century. Mitsubishi Nagasaki became an Imperial Shipyard in 1900, and it soon began the construction of torpedo-boats, producing three of those craft in the following year. The shipyard built the protected cruiser *Mogami* in 1908, produced six destroyers in 1907-11, and it then built the light cruiser *Yahagi* in 1912. During the First World War, Mitsubishi Nagasaki built the battlecruiser *Kirishima* in 1915 and the battleship *Hyuga* in 1918, as well as two destroyers in 1915. Mitsubishi Nagasaki laid down the battleship *Tosa* in 1920, but the programme was cancelled before the ship was even launched. Two other battleship programmes were also cancelled at the end of the war.

In the inter-war years, Mitsubishi Nagasaki produced the light cruisers *Tama* (1921), *Kiso* (1921), *Natori* (1922), and *Sendai* (1924), as well as seven destroyers in 1920-3. Turning to the production of larger ships, the shipyard built the heavy cruisers *Furutake* (1926), *Aoba* (1926), *Haguro* (1929), and *Chokai* (1932). In 1935, the yard completed the light cruiser *Mikuma*, but in 1939, that ship was converted into a heavy cruiser by replacing its five triple 6in gun turrets with twin 8in turrets. Mitsubishi Nagasaki then built the heavy cruisers *Tone* (1938) and *Chikuma* (1939), both of which had originally been designed as light cruisers with twelve 6in guns in four triple turrets, but they were completed as heavy cruisers with twin 8in gun turrets.

As only one of three shipyards capable of building battleships of the *Yamato* class, Mitsubishi Nagasaki was chosen to construct the mighty *Musashi*. With two 1060ft slipways, the yard could easily accommodate the 70,000-ton, 862ft ship. The *Musashi* was laid down in 1938, launched in 1940, and completed in 1942. The ship was subsequently sunk by US naval aircraft in the waters of the central Philippine Islands in October 1944.

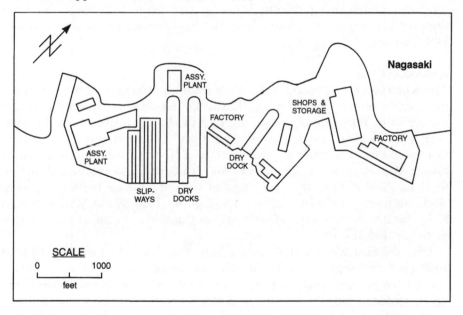

Mitsubishi Nagasaki in 1990.

Wartime construction by Mitsubishi Nagasaki included the aircraft carriers *Junyo* (converted from a large merchant vessel) in 1942 and the *Amagi* in 1944, as well as five destroyers in 1942-5. The yard also completed two large ocean liners, which were subsequently converted into escort aircraft carriers at naval shipyards, the *Taiyo* at Sasebo Naval Shipyard in 1941 and the *Unyo* at Kure Naval Shipyard in 1942. Work on the aircraft carrier *Kasagi* was cancelled early in 1945 after the ship had been launched. In addition, one heavy cruiser had been laid down in June 1942, but the programme was cancelled one month later. The shipyard was severely damaged by the atomic bomb dropped on Nagasaki in August 1945.

The shipyard reopened in 1950 as the MITSUBISHI ZOSEN CO., and it renewed its construction of warships for the Japanese Maritime Self Defence Force after Japan regained its right to self-determination in 1952. Mitsubishi Nagasaki built three destroyers in 1956-9, one frigate in 1960, and seven additional destroyers in 1960-79. The yard built eight guided missile destroyers from 1976 to 1996, and it has two additional guided missile destroyers programmed for completion by the year 2000. Since Mitsubishi reopened the yard in 1950, it has undergone major improvements during the intervening years. It now has two large building docks, one 1230ft long and the other 1150ft long, as well as several component assembly plants.

In addition to its main shipyard, Mitsubishi also has a large shipyard annex across the bay at Kosho, about five miles to the southwest of the main yard. The Kosho complex features a huge 3250ft long, 300ft wide construction dock served by two 800-ton travelling gantry cranes. Other facilities at Kosho include a 1300ft repair dock, a boiler factory, and several other modern manufacturing plants. Whereas the main Mitsubishi Nagasaki shipyard has about 200 acres of land, the Kosho Annex is double that size with 400 acres.

## KAWASAKI KOBE

The KAWASAKI DOCKYARD CO. LTD. was established at Kobe at the end of the nineteenth century by Shouzou Kawasaki, founder of Kawasaki Heavy Industries in Tokyo in 1879. The shipyard produced thirteen torpedo-boats from 1899 to 1904, two destroyers in 1905, and two submarines in 1906, the first submarines ever built in Japan. Kawasaki Kobe then built the protected cruiser *Yodo* in 1908, the light cruiser *Hirado* in 1912, and another submarine in 1912. At that time, the yard featured six shipbuilding berths, a graving dock, and other support facilities. During the First World War, Kawasaki Kobe built the battleships *Haruna* in 1915 and the *Ise* in 1917, and two destroyers in 1915-17.

After the First World War, Kawasaki Kobe laid down the battleship *Kaga* in 1920, but the ship was subsequently converted into an aircraft carrier (completed in 1928) under the terms of the Washington Naval Treaty. Three other battleship projects awarded to Kawasaki Kobe were also cancelled as a result of the naval limitations imposed in 1922. In the inter-war years, the shipyard built the light cruisers *Oi* (1921), *Kinu* (1922), and *Jintsu* (1925), eight destroyers in 1919-22 and nine submarines in 1920-3. Kawasaki Kobe then built several heavy cruisers, including the *Kako* in 1926, *Kinugasa* in 1926, *Ashigara* in 1929, and *Maya* in 1932.

Kawasaki Kobe completed the light cruiser *Kumano* in 1937 with fifteen 6in guns in five triple turrets, but the ship was subsequently converted into a heavy cruiser by replacing its turrets with a like number of twin 8in turrets. The yard also completed three additional destroyers in 1935-8 and another nine submarines from 1929 to 1938. At that time, Kawasaki Kobe had seven slipways ranging in size from 4000 tons to over 90,000 tons capacity and four dry docks ranging in size from 15,000 tons to 60,000 tons capacity. Naval construction at Kawasaki Kobe during the Second World War centred on aircraft carriers, with the yard building the carrier *Zuikaku* in 1941, the *Hiyo* (a converted liner) in 1942, and the *Taiho* in 1944.

Another carrier, the *Ikoma*, was laid down in 1943, but the programme was cancelled before the end of the war. Other wartime production included two destroyers in 1940-5 and a total of thirty-five submarines in that same period. Kawasaki Kobe was heavily damaged by bombing raids during the war, and it was not until the mid-1950s that the yard resumed the production of warships. As the KAWASAKI JYUKO CO., the yard built one frigate in 1956, one destroyer in 1958, and eight attack submarines from 1981 to 1995. The Kawasaki Kobe yard also has orders for two more attack submarines to be delivered by the year 2000.

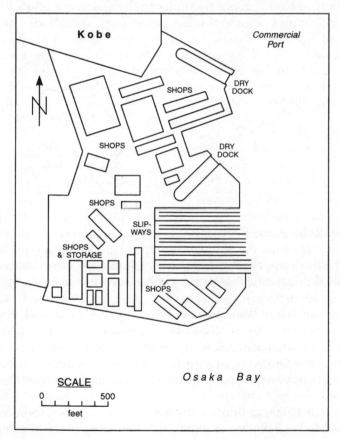

Kawasaki Kobe in 1990.

### Other Honshu Shipyards

Kawasaki's arch rival, Mitsubishi, also established a shipyard at Kobe in 1906. MITSUBISHI KOBE was most noted for its submarine production, building twenty of these craft from 1920 to 1940. During the Second World War, the shipyard produced a grand total of 120 submarines for the Imperial Japanese Navy. At the time, the yard had four slipways, ranging in length from 300 to 900ft, and four dry docks of similar lengths.

Mitsubishi Kobe, like all Japanese industrial activities, suffered heavy bomb damage during the war, and it was not until the mid-1950s that the yard could resume naval construction. The shipyard built three destroyers in 1956-60, and in 1980, it resumed submarine construction, producing nine submarines from 1980 to 1997. Mitsubishi Kobe currently has orders for two additional attack submarines to be completed by the year 2001.

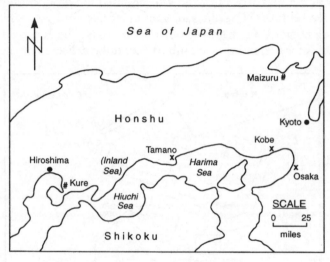

Honshu.

An early Kobe shipyard, ONOHAMA, built a light cruiser in 1887 and three gunboats in 1887-92. At its Nagasaki yard, the company produced one torpedo-boat in 1895. Onohama was not a significant producer of naval vessels in the twentieth century. The FUJINAGATA shipyard at Osaka was noted for its production of destroyers prior to and during the Second World War. Fujinagata built twenty-one destroyers from 1921 to 1940, and an additional fourteen destroyers in 1942-5. Two further destroyers were laid down in 1945, but were not completed before the end of the war. After the war, naval construction was limited to two patrol craft in 1957. Another Osaka shipyard, TEKKOSHO, built two destroyers in 1906-07, but no major naval vessels after that period.

The MITSUI TAMANO shipyard, located on the southern shore of Honshu Island, about 80 miles west of Kobe, began building major warships for the Imperial Navy during the Second World War, completing five submarines in 1944. After the war, the shipyard was taken over by the MITSUI ZOSEN CO., which produced two destroyers and two frigates in 1956-60. The Tamano shipyard built an additional two destroyers in 1966-8 and seven frigates in 1972-7. In the period 1982-91, Mitsui Tamano produced three guided missile destroyers and two guided missile frigates. The shipyard then had five slipways of various lengths up to 925ft and three dry docks, one of which was also 925ft in length, and the other two averaging 650ft in length.

The IINO HEAVY INDUSTRIES AND ENGINEERING CO. was established at Maizuru after the Second World War, and its shipyard produced two patrol craft in 1957 and one destroyer in 1960. The MAIZURU CO. built one frigate in 1964 and one destroyer in 1970.

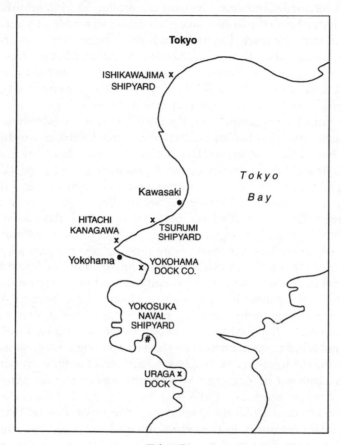

Tokyo Bay.

### Tokyo Bay

Beginning at the southern suburbs of the capital city of Tokyo, a string of shipyards was established over the years along the west and south banks of Tokyo Bay. ISHIKAWAJIMA HARIMA HEAVY INDUSTRIES shipyard was established in 1853 at Ishikawajima just to the south of Tokyo. The yard built two gunboats for the Imperial Japanese Navy during the latter half of the nineteenth century. Ishikawajima produced eleven destroyers from 1920 to 1930 and two torpedo-boats in 1936-7.

Wartime naval construction was limited at Ishikawajima, and the yard was involved mostly in ship repair and maintenance activities. The yard renewed warship construction in the mid-1950s, building three frigates in 1954-6 and three destroyers in 1959-60. The shipyard then had two slipways and two dry docks, all ranging from 400ft to 600ft in length. Ishikawajima built an additional three destroyers and two frigates from 1964 to 1981, and it then produced nine guided missile destroyers through 1998.

The ASANO SHIPBUILDING CO. was established in 1887 at Tsurumi, about 14 miles south of Tokyo. In 1922, Asano completed the aircraft carrier *Hosho*, which was originally laid down in 1919 as a tanker. The HITACHI KANAGAWA shipyard, located about 16 miles south of Tokyo, was built in 1901. The yard completed one destroyer in 1915, and then began the construction of submarine chasers. The Kanagawa shipyard produced thirteen submarines in 1945, completing a total of forty-six warships for the Imperial Japanese Navy before the end of the Second World War. The yard reopened in 1946, but it did not build any major warships after that time.

A little further south, about 20 miles from Tokyo, is the important port city of Yokohama, which has two shipyards that produced warships for the Imperial Japanese Navy. The YOKOHAMA DOCK CO. built one destroyer in 1928, and this was followed by the aircraft carrier *Ryujo* in 1931 and a torpedo-boat in 1936. The MITSUBISHI YOKOHAMA shipyard built one destroyer in 1915 and the light cruiser *Naka* in 1925. During the Second World War, the yard built the light cruisers *Katori* and *Kashima*, both in 1940, and the *Kashii* in 1941. Mitsubishi Yokohama had begun work on the light cruiser *Kashiwara* in 1941, but the programme was cancelled before the ship was even launched.

The URAGA DOCK CO., located on the southern shore of Tokyo Bay about 40 miles south of Tokyo, was an important shipyard in providing naval vessels for the Imperial Japanese Navy prior to and during the Second World War. The shipyard was established in 1853, and in 1872 it built its first warship, the armoured corvette *Ryojo*. Although closed in 1876, the shipyard was reopened in 1894, and it built two destroyers in 1906-07 and one additional destroyer in 1915. During the inter-war years, Uraga Dock built the light cruisers *Isuzu* in 1923 and *Abukuma* in 1925 and twenty-one destroyers between 1920 and 1937.

Naval construction at Uraga Dock during the Second World War consisted of twelve more destroyers. In this period, Uraga Dock had three slipways, one of which was later converted into a 400ft dry dock to match the existing dry dock on the site. The shipyard was closed at the end of the war, but it reopened in the 1950s as the URAGA SHIPBUILDING CO. In 1957, Uraga built two patrol craft, and this was followed by a destroyer in 1959. In 1966, the shipyard became SUMITOMO URAGA under Sumitomo heavy industries. Uraga produced seven more destroyers from 1966 to 1978, after which it built two guided missile frigates in 1983. Then the yard produced five guided missile destroyers from 1983 to 1990. Now part of Marine United, Uraga is currently under contract to build one more destroyer.

# 6 Germany

Germany did not exist as a unified nation until 1871 when the new German Empire (Deutsches Reich) was established from the North German Confederation and the Kingdom of Prussia after the Franco-Prussian War. In ancient times, the area later known as Germany was occupied by various tribes which banded together only in their defence against common foes, including Roman legions invading their homelands from the south. These tribes were later incorporated into the Holy Roman Empire under the Frankish king, Charlemagne, in AD 600. After the empire's division into the western kingdom (France) and the eastern kingdom by Charlemagne's heirs, the German tribes of the eastern kingdom were again united under the restored Holy Roman Empire of Otto I in AD 962.

The Holy Roman Empire evolved into a loose confederation of several Germanic states and free cities that controlled their respective areas of interest in the name of the emperor. Around the twelfth century, as trade was beginning to flourish in western Europe, several free cities along or near the North Sea and Baltic Sea coasts united into the Hanseatic League of merchants to further promote and control trade in the region. This increased trade resulted in the construction of many sea-going 'cogs', and the key Hanseatic cities of Hamburg, Bremen, Lübeck, and Danzig soon developed into major shipbuilding centres. The league maintained a small fleet of armed merchant ships to protect its shipping interests, and these ships also served as the Empire's navy.

The Mark of Brandenburg, a eastern border province of the Holy Roman Empire, began to establish a small navy in the seventeenth century. In 1638, Brandenburg's first warship, the armed schooner *Samson*, was built at Pillau on the Baltic. Pillau later became a naval base and shipyard in 1680. By 1656, at the beginning of Brandenburg's war with Sweden and Poland, the Brandenburg navy had only three warships with a total of thirty-four cannons, but in 1672, it acquired a further ten frigates. Brandenburg subsequently established a naval squadron at Emden at the mouth of the Ems River, and

Emden became Brandenburg's naval strong point on the North Sea in 1682. At about that time, naval colleges were established at Emden, Berlin, and Königsberg.

When Brandenburg merged with the Kingdom of Prussia early in the eighteenth century, the new state became very important in the Empire. As its power grew during the century, Prussia became increasingly interested in maintaining a suitable navy at the eastern end of the Baltic Sea. At the turn of the century, Prussia began to acquire a number of warships from foreign sources. Napoleon overran Prussia and occupied Berlin in 1806, but Prussia's independence was restored in 1814 when the Prussians assisted the Russians in driving the French out of eastern and central Europe. In 1827, Prussia set up a naval establishment, and in 1840, it founded a Navigation School at Danzig to provide navigational training to its seamen.

After Napoleon's defeat in 1814, most of the former states of the Holy Roman Empire formed an economic alliance that became the North German Confederation in 1848. In that same year, the Confederation established a German Federal Navy and authorised the establishment of a naval base and training centre at Bremerhaven. By the following year, the navy consisted of nine paddle wheel warships and two sailing frigates, all acquired from foreign sources. Interest in the Federal Navy soon began to wane, and the fleet was disbanded just three years later in 1852.

In the meantime, Prussia continued to move ahead in establishing a sound naval programme. The effective Danish blockade of Prussian ports from 1848 to 1850 prompted serious consideration for a strong navy to resist such activities in the future. In 1848, Prince Adalbert of Prussia began to plan the development of a strong Prussian fleet, and for the next two decades, steady progress was achieved toward that end. Prussia had been obtaining its warships from various Dutch, French, and British shipyards, but it then decided to start building its warships in-house. In 1850, a Royal Shipyard (Königliche Werft) was established at Danzig, and in 1853, Prussia formally established an Admiralty to manage its naval affairs. In the early 1860s, several steam-driven gunboats were produced by Prussian shipyards at Danzig, Elbing, Stettin, and Wolgast.

Under King Wilhelm I and Chancellor Otto von Bismarck, Prussia began to assert itself over other nations during the next decade. In 1864, Prussia attacked Denmark and thereby acquired the provinces of Schleswig and Holstein. This gave Prussia the lower section of the Danish peninsular, including the important port city of Kiel on the Ostsee at the western end of the Baltic Sea. Prussia soon established a naval base at Kiel in 1865, and in 1867, a Royal shipyard was constructed there. This was followed by another naval base at Wilhelmshaven on the Jade Bay off the North Sea coast in 1867, and in 1870, that facility also became a Royal shipyard.

In 1867, Prussia and the North German Confederation decided to combine their respective fleets into a single national fleet. After defeating the French in the Franco-Prussian War in 1871, Prussia finally agreed to the unification of the German states into the new Deutsches Reich (German Empire), with Wilhelm I of Prussia becoming Kaiser (emperor) Wilhelm I of Germany. The combined national fleet now became the Imperial German Navy, and the Royal Shipyards at Danzig, Kiel, and Wilhelmshaven were each redesignated as an Imperial Shipyard (Kaiserlichewerft). At that time, the German Navy consisted of eight ironclad frigates, six ironclad corvettes, twenty cruisers, twenty-five gunboats, and twenty-eight torpedo craft.

In 1872, the German Naval Academy was established at Kiel to impart knowledge of naval doctrine and leadership to naval officers. The completion of the Kiel Canal in 1895 greatly enhanced the importance of Kiel and Wilhelmshaven as operational bases for the Imperial German Navy by allowing easy and quick passage of warships back and forth between the North Sea and the more protected Baltic Sea. Upon the death of Wilhelm I in 1888, and the subsequent death of his son, Friedrich III, a few months later, his grandson, the young Wilhelm II, ascended to the imperial throne. A keen naval enthusiast, Wilhelm II immediately undertook a naval construction programme that would challenge Britannia's 'ruling the waves'.

In 1898, the German Reichstag authorised the expansion of the navy, and two years later, it granted further authorisation to build a fleet of thirty-eight battleships. This naval programme was engineered by Admiral Alfred von Tirpitz, who built a small coastal defence force into the mighty German High Seas Fleet, second only to the Royal Navy in strength, in only fifteen years. German shipyards began turning out battleships, cruisers, destroyers, and submarines almost as fast as the shipyards of Great Britain. In addition to the output of the imperial naval shipyards, many warships were produced by private shipyards, such as Krupp Germania at Kiel, Blohm & Voss at Hamburg, AG Weser at Bremen, Vulkan at Stettin, and Schichau at Elbing and Danzig.

The German–British naval competition created an explosive situation as relations between those two powers steadily deteriorated. In August 1914, the assassination of Archduke Franz Ferdinand, heir to the Austrian imperial throne, provided the spark that erupted into the First World War. Two years later, at the end of May 1916, the grand fleets of both powers were finally engaged in the North Sea in the famous Battle of Jutland. While the British lost more ships than the Germans, they achieved a strategic victory and kept the High Seas Fleet in its home bases for the remainder of the war.

After the defeat of Germany in 1918, the major units of her High Seas Fleet sailed to the British naval base at Scapa Flow in the Orkney Islands off the northern coast of Scotland for internment. Fearful that the British would take over the ships before a peace treaty had been signed, the German crews scuttled their ships at anchor in June 1919. Under the Treaty of Versailles, Germany was allowed to keep six old battleships for coast defence purposes, six light cruisers, twenty-four torpedo-boats, and a number of lighter craft, but no submarines. New construction of capital ships was limited to ships of 10,000 tons displacement and with a main armament of guns not to exceed 11in in calibre.

In 1925, Germany began the construction of new warships with the 6000-ton light cruiser *Emden*, which carried eight 6in guns in single mounts. The

Northwestern Germany.

*Emden* was followed over the next few years by five light cruisers of 7000 tons displacement and with nine 6in guns in three triple turrets, one forward and two aft. Germany solved the problem of capital ship restrictions by building a new type of warship, which they called merely 'Panzerschiff' (armoured ship), but which became known internationally as the 'Pocket Battleship'. These ships were nominally of 10,000 tons displacement (actually closer to 12,000 tons), mounted six 11in guns in two triple turrets, one forward and one aft, and were driven by diesel engines at a speed of 28kts.

Soon after coming into power in 1933, Adolf Hitler denounced the Versailles Treaty and initiated a major naval construction programme that included two new 32,000-ton battleships mounting nine 11in guns in three triple turrets, two forward and one aft. Giving up on the unique design of the Panzerschiff, Germany began the construction of conventional heavy cruisers of 10,000 tons displacement and carrying eight 8in guns in four twin turrets, two forward and two aft. To round out the fleet, the construction of a number of destroyers was undertaken, and submarine production was instituted for the first time since the First World War.

German naval construction reached a climax in the Third Reich with the building of the mighty battleship *Bismarck* and her sister ship, the *Tirpitz*, early in the Second World War. These ships, while theoretically within the 35,000-ton treaty limitation, actually displaced 42,000 tons, and they carried eight 15in guns in four twin turrets, two forward and two aft. The *Bismarck* was destroyed by the Royal Navy in the North Atlantic soon after it sank the British battlecruiser *Hood* in May 1941. Naval construction in Germany ceased at the end of the war, but it was allowed to resume after West Germany became an independent nation again. Warship production is now concentrated on destroyers and smaller frigates as well as a number of auxiliary naval vessels.

## NAVAL SHIPYARDS

*Danzig*
Danzig, one of the four key Germanic towns of the Hanseatic League, had a varied history, becoming alternately a part of Poland, a part of Prussia, and a free city during much of the second millennium. In the twentieth century, it was part of Germany until the end of the First World War when it again became a free city. Re-occupied by the Germans in 1939, it remained as part of the Third Reich until after the war. Danzig was then ceded to Poland, and is now known as Gdansk.

The DANZIG ROYAL SHIPYARD (Königliche Werft) was established by the King of Prussia in 1850 to reduce Prussia's reliance on foreign shipbuilders. Ships produced by these foreign yards included primarily wooden screw-propelled corvettes, early ironclad warships, and armoured frigates. Production of warships at Danzig began with the paddle wheel corvette *Danzig* in 1851 and the schooner *Helga* in 1854. Those ships were later followed by five wooden screw-propelled frigates in 1859-69, as well as a number of wooden screw corvettes in that same time frame.

Upon the establishment of the new German Empire in 1871, the Danzig shipyard took on the title of KAISERLICHE WERFT (Imperial Shipyard). The Danzig Imperial Shipyard then produced one central battery ironclad in 1872, four unprotected cruisers in 1889-93, and the protected cruiser *Freya* in 1898, as well as a number of ironclad corvettes. At the beginning of the twentieth century, the shipyard produced the unprotected cruisers *Thetis* (1901), *Berlin* (1904), *Danzig* (1907), and *Emden* (1908). The *Emden* achieved fame as a raider during the First World War when she sank or captured a number of Allied warships and merchantmen in the Indian Ocean before being defeated by the Australian cruiser HMAS *Sydney* at the Cocos Islands off the western coast of Sumatra.

Danzig became a free city after the end of the war, but upon Germany's invasion of Poland in September 1939, Danzig was occupied and incorporated into the German Reich. During the Second World War, the shipyard was used to produce forty-two Type VII-C U-boats for the Kriegsmarine. After the end of the war, Danzig became part of Poland, and it is now known as Gdansk.

The Gdansk shipyard continues to build ships for the Polish navy and merchant marine as well as for foreign customers.

### Kiel

The port city of Kiel and the surrounding area were acquired by Prussia in 1864 as part of the province of Schleswig-Holstein ceded by Denmark after the Danish-Prussian War. Kiel is located at the lower end of the Kiel Fjord on the western shore of the Ostsee, an arm of the Baltic. Prussia immediately established a naval base at Ellerbek, just across the harbour from the town. The naval base served as an operational and logistics base, training centre, and fleet headquarters for the German Imperial Navy prior to and during the First World War. A Royal shipyard was subsequently established as part of the naval base in 1867.

In 1877, the KIEL KAISERLICHE WERFT (imperial shipyard) completed its first ship for the Imperial German Navy, the ironclad frigate *Friedrich der Grosse*, and this was followed by two additional ironclad frigates in 1882-3. The Kiel Imperial Shipyard built the unprotected cruiser *Falke* in 1891, and it then produced the battleships *Hildebrand* (1893), *Hagen* (1894), and *Aegir* (1896). The shipyard went on to build the armoured cruisers *Fürst Bismarck* (1897), *Prinz Heinrich* (1900), *Prinz Adalbert* (1903), *Roon* (1905), and *Blücher* (1909), as well as the battleship *Kaiser* in 1912.

During the early part of the twentieth century, the Kiel Imperial Shipyard also produced the light cruisers *Königsberg* and *Nürnberg*, both in 1908, the *Augsburg* in 1910, and the *Grandenz* in 1914. The *Nürnberg* was one of the cruisers of Admiral von Spee's Far East Squadron based at Tsingtao at the

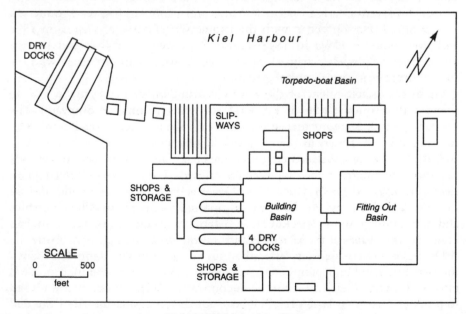

Kiel Naval Shipyard in 1914.

beginning of the First World War. The ship participated in the German naval victory at Coronel, but it was subsequently sunk in the Battle of the Falkland Islands in December 1914.

With the abolition of the monarchy in 1918 at the end of the war, the Kiel naval shipyard lost its imperial title, and it became known as the KIEL REICHSWERFT (national shipyard). In 1919, the shipyard was privatised, and in 1925, the shipyard, together with the nearby FRIEDRICHSORTER TORPEDOWERKSTATT (Torpedo Factory), was sold to DEUTSCHE WERKE AG of Berlin, a firm that continued to build warships at Kiel for the German Navy throughout the Second World War.

The naval base at Kiel was also the home of the MARINEAKADEMIE (German Naval Academy) from the time of its inception in 1872 until its transfer to Berlin in 1926. The Naval Academy was subsequently returned to Kiel in 1931, and it remains in service throughout the Second World War. In this period, the Kiel naval base was also the headquarters of the German Fleet, the German Naval Reconnaissance Forces, and the U-boat Fleet, and it was the home base for many major naval units. Being further away from British airfields than Wilhelmshaven, Kiel was better able to operate without the constant threat of air attacks. Just to the north of Kiel on the shore of the Ostsee is the famous 280ft-high Naval Monument constructed in 1930 as a memorial to the ships and seamen lost at sea during the First World War.

## Wilhelmshaven

The town of Wilhelmshaven on the North Sea coast and the surrounding area were acquired by Prussia from the Kingdom of Hanover in 1854. The construction of a commercial harbour was begun in 1855, and it was opened in 1869. The WILHELMSHAVEN KÖNIGLICHEWERFT was established in the harbour area southeast of the city in 1870, just before the formation of the German Empire in 1871. Redesignated as the WILHELMSHAVEN KAISERLICHE WERFT in 1871, it built its first warship, the ironclad frigate *Grosser Kurfürst*, in 1878. The shipyard then built the corvette *Charlotte* in 1886, the unprotected cruiser *Schwalbe* in 1887, and a torpedo-boat in 1889.

Near the turn of the century, the Wilhelmshaven Imperial Shipyard began producing a series of battleships, including the *Heimdall* (1894), *Kurfürst Friedrich Wilhelm* (1894), *Kaiser Friedrich II* (1898), *Kaiser Wilhelm II* (1899), *Wittelsbach* (1902), *Schwaben* (1903), and *Hannover* (1907). The *Kurfürst Friedrich Wilhelm* was sold to Turkey in 1910, and it became the *Hairreddin Barbarousse* in the Turkish Navy. The Wilhelmshaven Imperial Shipyard then built the Dreadnought battleships *Nassau* (1909), *Ostfriesland* (1911) and *König* (1914), and the battlecruiser *Hindenburg* (1917). The yard had begun work on the battlecruiser *Ersatz Friedrich Carl* (substitute for *Friedrich Carl*), which was laid down in 1915, but work was suspended on her and her sister-ships in 1917.

Several of these battleships were interned at Scapa Flow, the British naval base in the Orkney Islands off the northern coast of Scotland, at the end of the war. The *Ostfriesland* was turned over to the United States where the US Navy used her as a gunnery target, and received considerable notoriety when

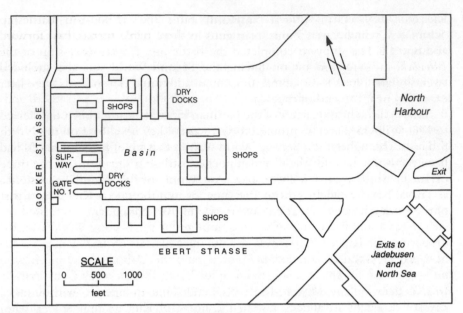

Wilhelmshaven.

she became the first battleship to be sunk by air power. In a demonstration held by Brigadier General William 'Billy' Mitchell in 1921, US Army bombers successfully attacked and sank the *Ostfriesland* with 2000lb bombs in a little over 20 minutes.

Wilhelmshaven also served as a naval base for the Imperial German Navy, and early in the twentieth century, it became the headquarters of the German Fleet. It was from here that both Vice-Admiral Reinhard Scheer's High Seas Fleet and Vice-Admiral Franz Hipper's battlecruisers sailed to do battle with the British Fleet off Jutland in May 1916. It was also here to which the fleet returned after the battle and where many ships were repaired after suffering damage in that engagement. Many warships of the Imperial German Navy sailed from Wilhelmshaven to be interned at the British naval base at Scapa Flow.

The Wilhelmshaven Imperial Shipyard lost its imperial title at the end of the war when Germany became a republic, and it then became known as the WILHELMSHAVEN REICHSMARINEWERFT (National Marine Shipyard). Wilhelmshaven was chosen to begin the new post-war German naval construction programme by building the light cruiser *Emden* in 1925. This was followed by seven destroyers in 1926-7 and twelve torpedo-boats in 1928-9. Wilhelmshaven then build three of the remaining five light cruisers allowed by the Treaty of Versailles, the *Königsberg* (1929), *Köln* (1930), and *Leipzig* (1931).

Wilhelmshaven produced the pocket battleships *Admiral Scheer* in 1933 and *Admiral Graf Spee* in 1934. The *Admiral Graf Spee* was intercepted by British cruisers and was scuttled by her crew in the harbour of Montevideo, Uruguay in December 1939. In 1936, the renamed WILHELMSHAVEN

KRIEGSMARINEWERFT (Naval Shipyard) built the 32,000-ton battleship *Scharnhorst*, which carried nine 11in guns in three triple turrets, two forward and one aft. The shipyard completed the battleship *Tirpitz*, sister-ship of the *Bismarck*, in 1942. Production during the Second World war also included twenty-eight Type VII–C submarines, but an additional eleven boats were later cancelled near the end of the war.

Although the headquarters of the German Fleet had earlier been transferred to Kiel, Wilhelmshaven continued to serve as the key naval base on the North Sea coast throughout the Second World War. At that time, Wilhelmshaven had been the home base for the German pocket battleship squadron. Of the three original naval shipyards, Wilhelmshaven is the only one that is still in existence as a naval base. Danzig is now in Polish hands, and the one at Kiel is now part of the Howaldtswerke Deutsche Werft AG (HDW) complex.


## NAVAL BASES

In addition to its main naval bases at Kiel and Wilhelmshaven, Germany had a number of smaller naval bases scattered along its coastline to support local naval operations in nearby waters. These included the North Sea bases of Cuxhaven and Wesermünde (Bremerhaven). The naval base at Flensburg was located at the western end of the Ostsee near the German border with Denmark, about 50 miles northwest of Kiel. Other naval bases included Stralsund on the Ostsee and Sweinemünde, Stettin, and Pillau, all located on the Baltic Sea.

Mürwik, a suburb of Flensburg, is the home of the MARINESCHULE (German Naval School), which was established in 1910. Closed at the end of the First World War and occupied by British forces until 1920, the school was reclaimed that year by the Reichsmarine (National Navy). Early in 1945, Mürwik became a military hospital, and for a short time, it was the seat of the national government of the Third Reich during the brief regime of Admiral Dönitz between the death of Adolf Hitler and the German capitulation on 8 May 1945. After the war, the facilities at Mürwik served a number of functions, and in 1956 it was again taken over by the German Bundesmarine (National Navy) as a naval school.

During the Second World War, Germany maintained several bases in occupied countries. The Germans had two bases in Poland at the eastern end of the Baltic Sea. One was at the former free port city of Danzig, which was the site of the one time Imperial Naval Shipyard, and the Schichau Danzig shipyard. Both of those yards could be used for ship repairs and possibly minor ship construction. The other base was the Polish port of Gdynia, which the Germans renamed 'Gotenhafen' during their occupation of that country, and it served as the primary base for the battleship *Bismarck* and other German warships using the Baltic Sea for sea trials, gunnery practice, and overall crew training.

In Norway, the Germans had a string of naval bases stretching westward from Oslo along the southern coast of Norway and then northward up to Narvik, including Stavanger, Bergen, and Trondheim. These bases could

Norway 1940.

provide support in the way of refuelling, resupply, and a variety of other services. Bergen served as the stopover point for the battleship *Bismarck* and the heavy cruiser *Prinz Eugen* during their sortie into the North Atlantic in May 1941. In addition to their logistics functions, Bergen and Trondheim also had naval shipyards, and Narvik had a repair and fitting-out base. The Narvik Fjord was the scene of a savage naval battle between British and German destroyers during the invasion of Norway in April 1940, in which the Germans lost ten destroyers against two British destroyers sunk.

While the Germans used the French port facilities along the English Channel for naval activities, they were too close to RAF bases to risk using them to support major German naval units. That left the facilities along the Atlantic coast of France. For surface ships, the most important facilities were those at Brest and St. Nazaire, both of which could provide repair as well as logistics support. The French liner *Normandie* (83,000 tons) was built at St. Nazaire, and its huge dry-dock and other marine facilities could easily accommodate warships as large as the battleship *Bismarck*. Other important German naval and submarine bases on the west coast of France included Lorient and La Rochelle, and Bordeaux.

In the Far East, Germany acquired the coastal town of Tsingtao and the surrounding area from China in 1897 on a 99-year lease. The Germans built a magnificent harbour, which served as the home base for its Far East Cruiser Squadron. It was from here that the Cruiser Squadron, including the light cruiser *Emden*, sailed to begin raiding operations against the Allied shipping in the Pacific Ocean at the beginning of the First World War. Tsingtao was soon blockaded by the Japanese, and it was captured by joint British-Japanese land and naval forces late in 1914. Japan retained Tsingtao until 1922 when it was returned to China by international agreement.

Germany began its colonial expansion in 1884 when it acquired the African territories of Togoland, the Cameroons, and German Southwest Africa (now Namibia). Germany then acquired the Caroline Islands by purchase from Spain in 1898 after the Spanish-American War, and it established a naval station at Truk Atoll. Truk became the rendezvous point for the German Far East Cruiser Squadron after it left Tsingtao to begin its raiding operations against Allied shipping at the beginning of the First World War. Japan seized the Caroline Islands during the war, and they were ceded to Japan under the peace treaty. Japan developed Truk Atoll as a major naval base, and it became the most important naval base for the Imperial Japanese Fleet in the mid-Pacific during the Second World War.

## PRIVATE SHIPYARDS

Like most nations, the Germans also utilised privately-operated shipyards to contract out shipbuilding projects that were beyond the capacity of their naval shipyards, especially during national emergencies. Some of these shipyards were located on two of the largest rivers in western Germany, the Elbe and the Weser, both of which flow into the North Sea, and along the coast of the North Sea itself. Other German private shipyards were located on the Ostsee and the Baltic Sea coasts.

### *Elbe River*

BLOHM & VOSS
Perhaps the most famous German private shipyard is that of BLOHM & VOSS, which is located at Steinwerder on the south bank of the Elbe River just across from the major port city of Hamburg. The Blohm & Voss shipyard was founded in 1877 by Herman Blohm and Ernst Voss as joint partners. By 1879, the firm, with a workforce of 800 men, had completed its first ship, a paddle-wheel steamer. Having to use the nearby Stülcken floating dry dock for several years, Blohm & Voss began designing and building its own floating dry docks in 1881, the first being of 3000-ton capacity. In 1887, the shipyard was substantially enlarged from its original 5 acres of land to 13 acres, and its workforce had increased to 1200.

In 1891, Blohm & Voss was incorporated as BLOHM & VOSS AG, and the shipyard was further expanded to 23 acres. During that year, the yard built its

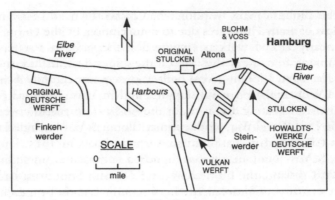

Elbe River.

second floating dry dock, one with a capacity of 2400 tons, and by that time, the company had 2500 employees. In 1892, the Blohm & Voss shipyard built its first warship for the Imperial German Navy, the light cruiser *Condor*, and by 1894, it had completed its 100th vessel. Floating dry docks III and IV, each with a capacity of 17,000 tons, were built at the yard in 1897 and 1902, respectively, and by 1902 the workforce had grown to over 4000 men.

Initially, Blohm & Voss was primarily the builder of merchant ships, and it completed the large passenger liners *Barbarossa* in 1896, *Rhein* in 1899, *Potsdam* in 1900, *Main* in 1900, *Stockholm* (for Sweden) in 1900, and *Suffren* for France in 1901. After the turn of the century, Blohm & Voss turned to the production of warships. The shipyard built the battleship *Karl der Grosse* in 1902, and this was followed by the armoured cruisers *Friedrich Carl* in 1903 and *Yorck* in 1905.

In 1905, the shipyard was further expanded by the acquisition of additional land, making it the largest shipyard in the world with an area of nearly 140 acres and a waterfront 2 miles long. Further improvements were made in 1905 with the installation of a frame structure over the existing slipways to support overhead travelling cranes. Slipways Nos. 6, 7, and 8 were added to the shipyard in 1907, and slipways Nos. 9 and 10 were constructed in 1910. Floating dry dock V, then the largest in the world with a lifting capacity of over 45,000 tons, was built at the yard in 1908.

Blohm & Voss built the armoured cruiser *Scharnhorst* and the light cruiser *Dresden*, both in 1907. The *Scharnhorst* was the flagship of Admiral von Spee's Far East Cruiser Squadron at the beginning of the First World War, and after participating in the German naval victory at Coronel, she was sunk in the Battle of the Falkland Islands in December 1914. The *Dresden*, also part of that squadron, escaped from the Falkland Islands, but she was later scuttled. Blohm & Voss continued building warships with the battlecruisers *Von der Tann* (1910), *Moltke* (1911), *Goeben* (1911), *Seydlitz* (1913), and *Derfflinger* (1914). The *Von der Tann*, *Seydlitz*, and *Derfflinger* were all veterans of the Battles of Dogger Bank and Jutland, and the *Goeben* was later turned over to Turkey to become the *Yavuz Sultan Selim*.

In 1912, the Blohm & Voss workforce had grown to nearly 8000 men, and despite the loss of many employees due to conscription, by the end of the war, there were nearly 14,000 workers employed at the yard. In 1913, a 250-ton capacity hammerhead crane was installed at the shipyard to facilitate the fitting-out of ships. In 1913, Blohm & Voss built a 40,000-ton capacity floating dry dock for the Wilhelmshaven naval shipyard, and in 1915, the yard produced another 40,000-ton floating dry dock for the Austro-Hungarian government.

During the First World War, production at Blohm & Voss included the light cruiser *Cöln* completed in 1918 and six torpedo-boats in 1915. During the war, Blohm & Voss built nearly one hundred submarines, including some thirty UB-type boats and fifty UC-type U-boats. The firm had begun construction on three additional battlecruisers, the *Mackensen*, *Ersatz Freya* (replacement for *Freya*), and *Ersatz Scharnhorst* (replacement for *Scharnhorst*), but these could not be completed before the end of the war. The first two were launched in 1917, but the *Ersatz Scharnhorst*, laid down in 1916, could not even be launched.

In 1914, Blohm & Voss completed the huge 54,000-ton passenger liner *Vaterland* for the Hamburg-America Line. Stranded in New York at the beginning of the First World War, after only its second transatlantic crossing, the largest ship in the world was interned by the United States. When America entered the war in 1917, the *Vaterland* was confiscated and converted into a troopship. Renamed the *Leviathan*, it was used to transport American troops to Europe during the last year of the war. The United States retained the *Leviathan* as part of Germany's war reparations after the war, and it saw several years of transatlantic service with the United States Lines. In 1920, Blohm & Voss delivered a 40,000-ton capacity floating dry dock to the Wilton shipyard in Rotterdam.

Soon after the war, Blohm & Voss resumed the construction of merchant vessels, completing the large passenger liners *Bismarck* in 1922, *Albert Ballin* in 1923, *New York* in 1927, and the *Kungsholm* for Sweden in 1928. The 56,000-ton *Bismarck* was ceded to Britain as part of Germany's war reparations, and she was put into transatlantic service as the Cunard-White Star liner *Majestic*. The Blohm & Voss-built *Leviathan* and *Majestic* remained the largest ships in the world for twenty-five years until overtaken by the French liner *Normandie* (83,000 tons) in 1935. In 1930, Blohm & Voss completed the famous 50,000-ton liner *Europa*, which promptly won the transatlantic Blue Riband for speed with an average speed of 28kts.

In 1922, Blohm & Voss still had over 11,000 workers, but by 1933, the yard's workforce had dropped to 2300, with most of the workers engaged in the breaking-up of surplus vessels. During this slack period, the shipyard produced its sixth floating dry dock, which had a capacity of 46,000 tons. Blohm & Voss did not build any warships in the 1920s, but in the 1930s, it completed five sail-training ships, two for foreign nations. One of these ships produced for the German Navy was the *Horst Wessel*, which later became the US Coast Guard training ship *Eagle* when it was turned over to the United States for war reparations after the Second World War.

As Germany began to rearm under the Nazi regime, the Blohm & Voss workforce grew to 14,000 by 1937. In 1938, Blohm & Voss built three destroyers for the new German Navy (Kriegsmarine), and this was followed by the 14,000-ton heavy cruiser *Admiral Hipper*, which was delivered in 1939. One year later in 1940, Blohm & Voss completed the mighty 42,000-ton battleship *Bismarck*. Although Blohm & Voss specialised in the construction of large surface vessels, the *Bismarck* was the only surface warship built by the firm during the Second World War. Instead, the German Navy established Blohm & Voss as a centre for producing submarines, including the assembly point for submarine sections built in other nearby yards. During the war, Blohm & Voss produced a total of 256 submarines, nearly 200 of which were of the VII-C type.

In 1940, Blohm & Voss launched the new 41,000-ton passenger liner *Vaterland*, but work on the vessel was soon terminated in favour of warship construction. In 1942, the yard completed the permanent dry dock 'Elbe 17', which at the time was the largest graving dock in the world. At the end of the war, Blohm & Voss had a workforce of nearly 20,000 people, most of whom were engaged in submarine construction. Nearly all of them were let go as the shipyard was closed down, and less than 150 remained in 1950. The shipyard was systematically dismantled, first by blowing up the slipway frames in 1946 and finally by blowing up the 'Elbe 17' graving dock in 1950, after all useable equipment had been removed from the yard.

It was not until 1954 that the shipyard was allowed to reopen and work began on restoration. One year later, the tower crane had been rebuilt and two floating dry docks had been returned to the shipyard. At first, only ship repairs

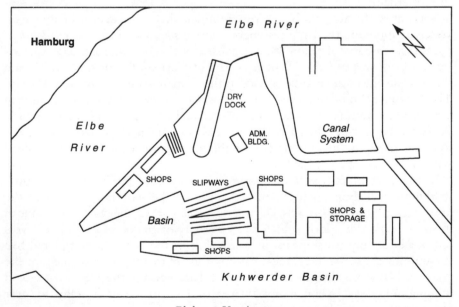

Blohm & Voss in 1945.

could be performed, but then the construction of coastal steamers and finally seagoing ships was permitted. The new corporation of BLOHM & VOSS AG was founded in 1955, and the shipyard began producing passenger ships, cargo ships, bulk carriers, container ships, and a variety of speciality ships. By 1957, the workforce had reached nearly 4000. From 1961-3, Blohm & Voss built six 2100-ton frigates for the German Federal Navy, and this was followed by four 3600-ton guided missile destroyers in 1964-8. In 1966, the corporate name of Blohm & Voss was changed to BLOHM + VOSS with the substitution of the plus sign (+) for the ampersand (&).

In 1966, Blohm + Voss acquired the adjacent shipyard of H.C. Stülcken Sohn and its subsidiary, the Ottensener Eisenwerke GmbH (Iron Works Corp.). By this acquisition, Blohm + Voss increased its land area to over 165 acres and increased its workforce to nearly 7400 people. In 1967, the 'Elbe 17' graving dock had finally been repaired, and in 1972, the dock was lengthened to accommodate ships displacing up to 300,000 tons. While its production consisted mainly of large bulk carriers, cargo ships, and tankers, Blohm + Voss also built smaller warships, not only for the German Federal Navy, but also for foreign navies. The shipyard produced twenty patrol boats for the Argentine Coast Guard and two MEKO 360-type frigates for the Argentine Navy in 1979-80.

In 1980-1, Blohm + Voss built two Class 122 frigates for the German Navy, as well as one MEKO 360-type frigate for Nigeria. In 1986, Blohm + Voss acquired the Hamburg shipyard of the Kiel-based Howaldtswerke Deutsche Werft (HDW), further increasing its holdings and workforce. Continuing with both commercial and warship production, Blohm + Voss produced two Class 123 frigates for the German Navy in 1992-4. The yard also produced four MEKO 200-type frigates for foreign navies, one for Turkey in 1987, one for Greece in 1991, and two more for Turkey in 1995-6. Blohm + Voss is now part of the Thyssen Industrie Group.

VULKAN HAMBURG

VULKAN HAMBURG was established in 1909 on the Elbe River near the port city of Hamburg. The yard produced a number of merchant vessels before completing the 52,000-ton passenger liner *Imperator* in 1912. The *Imperator* was later turned over to Great Britain for war reparations under the Treaty of Versailles, and it became the Cunard White Star liner *Berengaria*, which was subsequently placed in transatlantic service from 1921 until 1938. Turning to warship production, Vulkan Hamburg built the Dreadnought battleships *Friedrich der Grosse* in 1912 and *Grosser Kurfürst* in 1914.

Vulkan Hamburg launched the battleship *Württemberg* in 1917, but the ship could not be completed before the end of the war. Similarly, the battlecruiser *Ersatz Yorck* (replacement for the *Yorck*) was laid down in 1916, but was never even launched. During the First World War, Vulkan Hamburg also built thirteen standard U-boats, three U-boat cruisers, twenty-four Type UB III boats, and thirty Type UC boats for the Imperial German Navy. Orders for an additional sixty-four Type UB III boats were cancelled at the end of the war.

Vulkan Hamburg, together with the shipyard of Janssen & Schilinski, was taken over by Howaldswerke Kiel in 1930, and the shipyard became known as HOWALDTSWERKE HAMBURG. During the Second World War, Howaldtswerke Hamburg completed thirty-three Type VII-C U-boats, but orders for an additional seventeen had to be cancelled as the war drew to a close. In 1968, the shipyard came under the new corporate name of HOWALDTSWERKE DEUTSCHE WERFT AG (HDW) after the merger of Howaldswerke Kiel with Deutsche Werft Hamburg

## DEUTSCHE WERFT HAMBURG

DEUTSCHE WERFT HAMBURG was established in 1920 when the Hamburg-Amerikanische Packetfahrt Aktien Gesellschaft (HAPAG) took over an iron works factory on the south bank of Elbe River in the Finkenwerde district southwest of Hamburg and expanded it into a shipyard. During the period between the world wars, Deutsche Werft (not to be confused with Deutsche Werke of Kiel) became one of the foremost builders of merchant ships in the world. Turning to war production in 1939, the yard built sixty-five Type IX-C U-boats for the German Navy during the Second World War, and had orders for thirty-five more such vessels, but these orders were cancelled late in the war.

Deutsche Werft returned to the construction of merchant ships after the war. In 1968, Deutsche Werft merged with Howaldtswerke to form HOWALDTSWERKE DEUTSCHE WERFT AG (HDW), then becoming the largest shipbuilding concern in Germany. The Deutsche Werft shipyard produced large tankers for the German Navy and submarines mostly for export, and it performed extensive ship repair and maintenance work. In 1986, the HDW Hamburg shipyard was taken over by Blohm + Voss.

## STÜLCKEN

In 1839, Johann Friedrich Stülcken, who was then the foreman of a small shipyard in the Billweder district of Hamburg, decided to go out on his own. He established the STÜLCKENWERFT (shipyard) at Altona on the northern bank of the Elbe River a little over two miles west of Hamburg. In 1845, Stülcken obtained two and a half acres of land on the east side of Steinwerder Island on the south bank of the Elbe River just across from Hamburg, and he thereupon transferred his shipyard to that site. There he was joined by his son, Heinrich Christopher, and they ran the shipyard together for the next nine years. In 1854, Johann Friedrich retired, and his son took over the operation of the shipyard under the name of H.C. STÜLCKEN SOHN.

In 1858, Stülcken build the first floating dry dock in Hamburg, and it was used by the adjacent Blohm & Voss shipyard until that firm could build floating dry docks of its own. In 1865, the shipyard was expanded, and a new slipway was installed. Heinrich Christopher died in 1873, and the shipyard was taken over by his widow, Anna Dorothea Stülcken. H.C. STÜLCKEN WWE. (widow) continued to build sailing ships until 1883, when it built its first iron, screw-propeller ship. Two years later in 1885, the shipyard began producing steel steamships. Anna Dorothea died in 1892, and her son, Julius Caesar Stülcken assumed control of the shipyard under its previous name, H.C. STÜLCKEN SOHN. During the First World War, Stülcken produced a number of patrol boats and minesweepers.

In 1919, Julius brought two of his nephews into the company as partners, and when Julius died in 1925, one of his nephews, Heinrich von Dietlein, took over the shipyard, but retained the name of the company. In 1935, Stülcken developed the popular Type 35 minesweeper, and the company received many orders for this type of vessel. By 1939, the size of the workforce had increased to 3000, and in 1940, the shipyard was further expanded and modernised. During the Second World War, Stülcken built twenty-six Type VII-C U-boats for the German Navy and had orders for twenty more, but these were cancelled before the end of the war. The yard also produced a number of sections of the Type XXVI U-boats, which were subsequently assembled by Blohm & Voss.

The Stülckenwerft was severely damaged by bombing raids in 1944-5, and the yard was eventually closed down by the Allied Industrial Control Council in 1946. In 1948, Stülcken was allowed to resume the construction of fishing vessels, and two years later in 1950, permission was granted for the construction of larger vessels. By 1954, Stülcken had produced a total of fifty-two freighters, tankers, and refrigeration ships. Returning to warship production, Stülcken produced six frigates for the German Navy in 1961-3 and four *Hamburg* class destroyers in 1964-8. Although still working on orders for the German Navy, Stülcken was beset by financial difficulties, and in 1966, the company and its subsidiary, Ottensener Eisenwerke GmbH (ironworks), was taken over by Blohm + Voss.

### Weser River

AG 'WESER'
Carsten Waltjen and his friend, Heinrich Leonhardt, established the iron foundry and machine works of WALTJEN & LEONHARDT in 1843. The facility was located on the Stefanikircheweider on the north bank of the Weser River at the west end of the port city of Bremen. Turning to shipbuilding, the yard completed its first ship, the paddle wheel river steamer *Roland*, in 1846. In that same year, Heinrich Leonhardt left the company, and it became C.WALTJEN & CO. By 1852, the shipyard was employing one hundred workers, but after the new German Empire was established in 1871, the yard soon began to receive orders for the construction of warships for the Imperial German Navy.

In 1872, the Waltjen shipyard was taken over by a group of Bremen merchants and incorporated as AG 'WESER'. AG Weser produced two armoured ships in 1873 and thirteen gunboats in 1876-84 for the Imperial German Navy. In 1882 the yard began building torpedo-boats, and it completed thirteen such craft by 1884. Before the turn of the century, AG Weser had built the battleships *Beowulf* in 1892 and *Frithjof* in 1893, as well as the protected cruiser *Victoria Louise* in 1898. AG Weser then built a string of

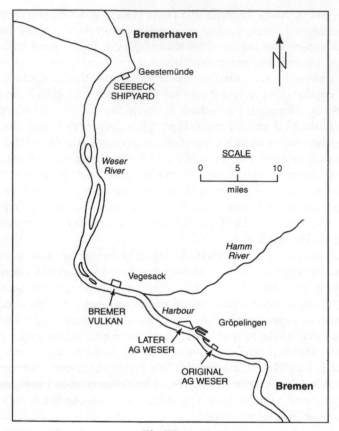

The Weser.

eight light cruisers at the average rate of over one per year from 1901–06. In 1900, AG Weser acquired a 115-acre plot of land with a 1000ft river frontage at Gröpelingen, on the north bank of the Weser River, about seven miles northwest of Bremen, for a new shipyard.

AG Weser moved into the new and larger facility in 1905. The new shipyard, which is now the site of the Industriehafen (commercial harbour) of Bremen, featured five slipways and a number of new electric cranes. In 1907, AG Weser built the armoured cruiser *Gneisenau*, which with the light cruiser *Leipzig* was part of Admiral von Spee's Far East Cruiser Squadron at the beginning of the First World War. Both participated in the German naval victory at Coronel, and both were subsequently sunk at the Battle of the Falkland Islands in December 1914. AG Weser completing the passenger liner *Berlin* in 1908 before resuming warship production. The yard then built the Dreadnought battleships *Westfalen* in 1909 and *Thüringen* in 1911 and the light cruisers *Magdeburg* and *Stralsund*, both in 1912.

Warship production during the First World War included the battleship *Markgraf* in 1914 and the light cruisers *Regensburg* (1914), *Königsberg* (1916), *Emden* (II) (1916) and *Leipzig* (II) (1917). AG Weser began building submarines in 1916, and it completed thirty-eight standard U-boats, three U-boat cruisers, eighty-five Type UB boats, and fifteen Type UC boats by the end of the war. Shipbuilding dropped off after that, but it soon resumed with the production of merchant vessels, and by 1922, the workforce had again risen to 7000 employees. In 1923, the facilities at the yard included three floating dry docks. In 1926, AG Weber merged with G. Seebeck AG and J.C. Tecklenborg, both of Bremerhaven, to form the DEUTSCHE SCHIFFS- UND MACHINENBAU AG (Deschimag) (German Shipbuilding and Machinery Works, Inc.).

Deschimag (Bremen) built the famous passenger liner *Bremen* in 1929, which won the transatlantic Blue Riband on her maiden voyage, giving it up only briefly to her sister-ship, the *Europa*, and then held it until 1937, when it was taken by the Italian liner *Rex*. In September 1939, at the onset of the Second World War, the *Bremen* made a spectacular escape from New York to Germany via Murmansk, Russia and along the Norwegian coastline to avoid British warships waiting to seize her. In 1929, Deschimag (Bremen) had 12,000 workers, but over 5000 were laid off after the liner *Bremen* had been completed. By 1932, the workforce was down to less than 400 employees, and no ships were built in 1932-3.

In 1933, Deschimag (Bremen) hired 200 workers as orders were received for new ships under the industrial revitalisation programme of the Third Reich, and by the end of 1934, the workforce had increased to 3000 employees. Deschimag (Bremen) built the passenger liners *Gneisenau* and *Scharnhorst*, both in 1935, and the *Oslofjord* (for Sweden) in 1938. Deschimag (Bremen) became the most prolific builder of destroyers and submarines for the German Navy prior to and during the Second World War. In 1935-6, the yard built two Type I-A submarines, the only submarines of this type built for the Kriegsmarine, to be used as a test bed for further development. In 1938, Deschimag (Bremen) built four destroyers, and this was followed by six torpedo-boats in 1939-40.

Before the start of the Second World War, Deschimag (Bremen) had begun and launched the heavy cruiser *Seydlitz*, but the hull was later turned over to the Soviet Union as part of an agreement with that country while Germany and the Soviet Union were still bound by a non-aggression pact. In 1942, Deschimag (Bremen) was subjected to air raids of increasing severity, and this led to the construction of the concrete U-boat bunker 'Weser I' to protect the boats while they were being repaired and provisioned. In addition to the bunker, the shipyard was further expanded and improved by the lengthening of four slipways to accommodate larger vessels and the construction of a 1180 × 200ft dry dock. Deschimag (Bremen) then had a total of sixteen slipways for the construction of U-boats.

The workforce at Deschimag (Bremen) had grown from 16,000 employees in 1939 to nearly 20,000 employees by the end of the war. The facility at that time had expanded to 140 acres with a waterfront of 1400ft. During the war, Deschimag (Bremen) built a total of twenty destroyers, with orders for six more being cancelled at the end of the war. The shipyard also produced six Type VII U-boats and 118 Type IX U-boats. Orders for 200 Type VII boats, 100 Type IX boats, 200 Type XX boats, and over 400 Type XXI

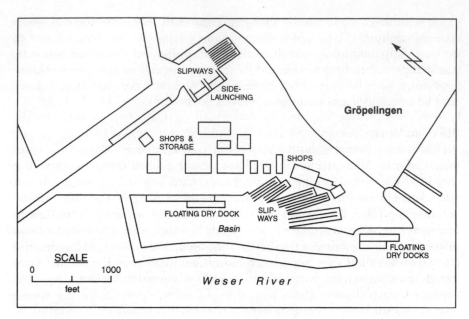

AG Weser in 1945

boats were cancelled at the end of the war. In 1941, management of the Deschimag (Bremen) shipyard was taken over by the Friedrich Krupp Concern, but in 1945 after the war, the name of the corporation reverted back to AG WESER.

The AG Weser shipyard was closed at the end of the war, but 1500 workers were retained to clean up the debris remaining from the devastating wartime air raids. A shipbuilding ban was imposed by the Allied Industrial Control Council, and in 1948, the slipway structures were blown up. The shipyard was reduced to 120 acres by the return of some 20 acres of land along the northwestern side of the yard for use by the commercial harbour. Also in that year, two subsidiary organisations of AG Weser were formed, WERK BREMEN, which encompassed the original Bremen shipyard, and WERK SEEBECK, the Bremerhaven shipyard.

The ban on shipbuilding was lifted in 1949, heralding a new beginning for the shipyard, but initially only ship repair work could be performed by the facility. One year later in 1950, Werk Bremen was permitted to resume the construction of ocean-going vessels, and the shipyard increased its workforce to 2000 employees. The yard then produced a number of freighters, tankers, and a variety of other types of commercial vessels. In the 1960s, four slipways were torn down at Werk Bremen to make room for two new building docks, each with a capacity for ships up to 150,000 tons displacement.

A few years later, the huge 1230 × 215ft building dock 'Alfried' was constructed at the yard. The new dock could accommodate vessels up to 400,000 tons displacement, and it was served by a 780-ton capacity travelling gantry crane spanning the entire width of the dock. The crane, which had a

250ft span and a clearance of 230ft, supplemented an earlier 500-ton gantry crane at the yard. In 1974, the effects of the world-wide oil crisis caused the reduction of 1000 workers at the Werk Bremen shipyard. The workload at the yard continued to decline over the next few years, and in 1983, its workforce was down to 2000 employees. In that year, Werk Bremen was closed down, and its machinery and facilities were sold off.

BREMER VULKAN

In 1803, the JOHANN LANGE WERFT (shipyard) was established on the north bank of the Weser River at Vegesack, about fifteen miles northwest of Bremen. The initial production of the shipyard was sailing vessels, but in 1817, it built the first German steamship, *Die Weser*. In 1849, the shipyard became the CARL LANGE WERFT, and it continued building steamships for the next forty-four years. The nearby Werft Herman F. Ulrich was established in 1844, and it became the Bremer Schiffbaugesellschaft (shipbuilding firm) in 1883. In 1892 the Lange and Ulrich companies merged and were taken over by Bremen merchants who then established BREMER VULKAN. In 1895, Bremer Vulkan constructed a new shipyard on the grounds of the former Ulrich shipyard.

In 1900, the Bremer Vulkan yard was expanded to include seven slipways, and by 1901, its workforce had grown to 2600 employees. Up until the beginning of the First World War, the shipyard produced mostly cargo and passenger steamships, and it became the home yard of the Norddeutsche Lloyd steamship Co. Bremer Vulkan completed the passenger liner *Dresden* in 1915 and during the war, it produced a total of forty-one submarines for the Imperial German Navy. After the war, Bremer Vulkan reverted to the construction of merchant ships, building the passenger liners *Sardegna* (for Italy) in 1923, *Sierra Cordoba* in 1924, and *Berlin* in 1925.

By 1926, there was a shipbuilding crisis in Germany and throughout the rest of the world, and production dropped drastically. In 1933, with the emphasis on increased industrial production under the Third Reich, shipbuilding began to pick up at the yard, and the yard produced several merchant vessels through 1938. In 1939, Bremer Vulkan and other German shipyards were ordered to produce submarines for the Kriegsmarine. After a massive air raid in March 1943, work was begun on the huge concrete U-boat bunker for protection against bombs. The bunker, named 'Valentin', was completed in 1944, and it could accommodate up to a dozen U-boats while in port for replenishment of supplies and repairs.

The workforce at Bremer Vulkan was 5000 employees in 1943, but it was soon expanded with over 10,000 slave labourers from Russia, France, Belgium, and Greece. During the war, Bremer Vulkan completed seventy-four Type VII-C boats for the Kriegsmarine, and orders for another twenty-one Type VII-C boats had to be cancelled near the end of the war. Bremer Vulkan was occupied by British troops at the end of the war, and a shipbuilding ban was imposed at that time by the Allied Industrial Control Council. In 1951, the shipbuilding ban was lifted, and Bremer Vulkan again began to produce cargo and passenger ships. By 1958, Bremer Vulkan employed over 6000 workers as its shipbuilding workload increased.

In 1960, Bremer Vulkan began to produced a series of standard 14,000-15,000-ton cargo ships patterned after the American 'Liberty' ships of wartime fame. By 1969, the Bremer Vulkan shipyard had become one of the busiest in the world, and it was involved primarily with the construction of large tankers. In 1980, the capacity of the shipyard was increased by the addition of a new 1075ft building dock that could accommodate ships up to 250,000 tons. Bremer Vulkan then began to build container ships and large cruise ships. In 1984, Bremer Vulkan merged with Lloyd Reparaturbetriebe (repair works) to form the VULKAN LLOYD Unternehmungsverband (Association). Soon thereafter, the workload of the shipyard began to drop, and it is no longer a significant producer of naval vessels.

### ATLAS WERKE

ATLAS WERKE AG (Atlas Works, Inc.) established a shipyard in 1911 at the site of the former Norddeutsche Maschinen und Armaturen Fabrik (North German Machine and Armature Factory) of Bremen. The shipyard was located on the Weser River near the river port city of Bremen. During the First World War, Atlas Werke AG received orders for ten submarines for the Imperial German Navy, but these orders were subsequently cancelled as the war came to a close. Atlas Werke AG continued producing small ships and marine equipment after the war, but it was finally closed in 1969.

### SEEBECK

The G. SEEBECK shipyard is located at the mouth of the Weser River at Geestemünde (Wesermünde) near the important port city of Bremerhaven. The G. Seebeck shipyard was founded in 1876, and after its merger with Carl Lange and H. F. Ulrich in 1895, it was incorporated as G. SEEBECK AG. Early in the twentieth century, G. Seebeck also absorbed the nearby F. W. Wenke shipyard, making it a sizeable enterprise. In 1926, G. Seebeck became part of Deutsche Schiffs- und Machinenbau AG 'Deschimag' (the German Shipbuilding and Machinery Works), but it continued to operate under its original name.

G. Seebeck is most noted in the field of naval construction by its production of sixteen Type IX-C Type submarines from 1939 to 1944. An additional fourteen U-boats were ordered from G. Seebeck, but were cancelled at the end of the war. In 1945, the G. Seebeck shipyard was absorbed by AG 'Weser', but in 1948, it became WERK SEEBECK as one of two subsidiary works under AG 'Weser'. In 1983, Werk Bremen, the other works under AG 'Weser', was closed, and in 1986, Werk Seebeck was consolidated with Vulkan Lloyd Schichau Unterweser AG to become VULKAN LLOYD SUAG SEEBECK.

### TECKLENBORG

J C Tecklenborg was founded in 1841, and in 1897, it was incorporated as J. C. TECKLENBORG AG. The Tecklenborg shipyard was located at

Geestemünde (Wesermünde) at the mouth of the Weser River near the important port city of Bremerhaven. Tecklenborg was primarily a builder of merchant ships, and in 1908, it built the passenger liner *Prinz Friedrich Wilhelm*. During the First World War, it received an order to build twenty-four submarines for the German Navy, but these orders were later cancelled as the war drew to a close. In 1926, J.C. Tecklenborg became part of the Deutsche Schiffs- und Maschinenbau AG 'Deschimag' (German Shipbuilding and Machinery Works, Inc.).

### North Sea

The NORDSEEWERKE EMDEN WERFT UND DOCK AG (North Sea Works Emden Shipyards and Dock Co.) was established in 1903, partly to take advantage of the opening of the Dortmund-Ems Canal in 1899. That canal connected the Ruhr industrial basin with the Ems River, which emptied into the North Sea, and the increase in trade by that route prompted new shipbuilding. The Nordseewerke shipyard is located near the town of Emden at the mouth of the Ems River about 40 miles west of Wilhelmshaven. The original shipyard was built on 50 acres of land and had one 740ft long side-

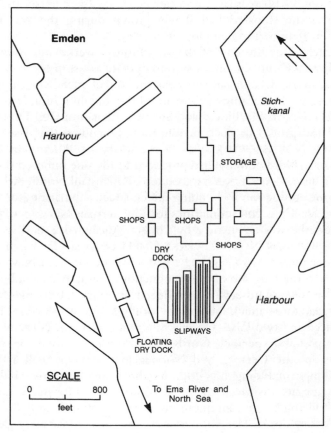

Nordseewerk Emden.

launching slipway. In 1911, Nordseewerke becoming a branch of the DEUTSCH-LUXEMBURGISHE BERGWERK UND HÜTTEN AG (German-Luxemburg Mining and Iron and Steel Works Co.).

In 1912, Nordseewerke purchased another 400 acres of adjoining ground, and it began expanding its shipyard with the construction of four end-launching slipways. One year later in 1913, the yard constructed a huge sea lock 850ft long and 130ft wide to accommodate the dry docking of large ships. Nordseewerke began limited naval construction in 1914, but it was used mostly for ship repair and maintenance work during the First World War. By that time its workforce had grown to 1000 men.

In 1926, Nordseewerke came under the VEREINIGTE STAHLWERKE AG (United Steel Works Co.) Düsseldorf, but due to the depression, it was closed down in that year, leaving only a small ship repair operation still open. The shipyard reopened in 1933 with less than 150 workers, and in 1934, it received a new corporate name of NORDSEEWERKE EMDEN AG, an operating branch of Vereinigte Stahlwerke AG Essen. Nordseewerke built mostly merchant vessels up until 1939. During the Second World War, the shipyard produced thirty Type VII-C submarines for the German Navy, and it had orders for an additional ten U-boats that were cancelled at the end of the war. The workforce at the shipyard had slowly grown during the war from 1000 employees in 1939 to 1200 employees in 1945.

Immediately after the end of the war, Nordseewerke was allowed by the Allied Industrial Control Commission to operate as a ship overhaul and repair facility, and in 1948, it began the construction of merchant ships again. In 1952, Nordseewerke became a subsidiary of Rheinstahl Union Maschinen and Stahlbau AG (Union Machinery and Steel Construction Co.) Düsseldorf. The workforce had grown to 5000 people in 1957, and in that year, it became RHEINSTAHL NORDSEEWERKE AG, a subsidiary of Rheinstahl Stahlwerke Essen. By 1960, Nordseewerke had produced nearly one hundred ships with an aggregate displacement of over 750,000 tons. Rheinstahl Nordseewerke renewed submarine production by building fifteen attack submarines for Norway in 1964-7 and ten Class 206 submarines for the German Navy in 1970-5.

Nordseewerke was taken over by Thyssen AG in 1974, and its name was changed to THYSSEN NORDSEEWERKE GMBH two years later in 1976. Nordseewerke completed two Class 122 frigates for the German Navy in 1980-2, and then it turned to submarine production, building two submarines for Argentina in 1985. Nordseewerke produced six attack submarines for Norway in 1989-93 and three attack submarines for Denmark in 1989-92. The shipyard also produced and two Class 123 frigates for the German Navy in 1994-6.

In the post-war period, Nordseewerke built a total of twenty-five submarines for the German and Norwegian Navies, as well as nearly 200 merchant ships, including fifty-four freighters and forty-five bulk carriers, with an aggregate displacement of 5,000,000 tons. Nordseewerke now has three shipbuilding berths ranging up to nearly 1000ft in length, one dry dock, and two floating docks. The shipyard also has a 450-ton capacity gantry crane, and it is currently served by a workforce of 4000 people.

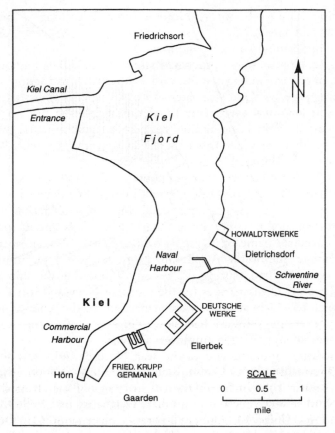

Kiel.

### Kiel-Flensburg

The city of Kiel is located at the southern end of Kiel Fjord on the eastern coast of the Danish Peninsula, about 60 miles due north of Hamburg. The Kiel Fjord is an inlet off the Kieler Bucht (Kiel Bay), which is an arm of the Ostsee (East Sea) at the western end of the Baltic Sea. The Kiel Naval Base and the three major shipyards associated with construction of warships for the German Navy are located on the southeastern end of the fjord across the harbour from the city of Kiel. The eastern terminal of the Kiel Canal, which was completed in 1895 to connect the East Sea with the North Sea, is at the northern end of the Kiel Fjord.

### KRUPP GERMANIA

The Krupp Germania shipyard was the southernmost of the three adjacent shipyards located at the southeastern end of the Kiel Fjord in the Gaarden district of Kiel. The shipyard was founded in 1872 as the NORDDEUTSCHE SCHIFFBAU AG by a group of Berlin financiers. Ten years later in 1882, the shipyard was taken over by the Fried. Krupp concern and renamed the SCHIFF- UND MASCHINENBAU 'GERMANIA' AG (Shipbuilding and Machinery

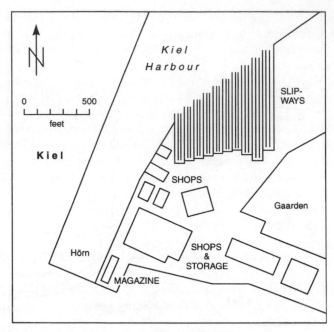

Krupp Germania, Kiel.

Works 'Germania', Inc.). Under Krupp, the shipyard soon began building torpedo-boats for the Imperial German Navy in addition to merchant vessels. By the end of the nineteenth century, Germania had built the protected cruisers *Prinz Wilhelm* (1889) and *Kaiserin Augusta* (1892), the battleships *Siegfried* (1890), *Worth* (1893), and *Kaiser Wilhelm der Grosse* (1899), the light cruiser *Gazelle* (1898), and eight torpedo-boats.

After the turn of the century, Germania built the armoured cruiser *Askold* for Russia in 1901. The yard continued building warships for the Kaiser, including the battleships *Zähringen* (1902), *Braunschweig* (1904), *Deutschland* (1906), *Schleswig-Holstein* (1908), *Schlesien* (1908), *Posen* (1910), *Prinzregent Luitpold* (1912) and *Kronprinz* (1914). During that period, Germania also completed four light cruisers from 1901-13, and forty-six torpedo-boats before the end of the First World War, including two that were delivered to Russia before the outbreak of war. In 1906, Germania built the first German-built submarine, the *U-1*, and from then until the end of the First World War, it produced 122 more U-boats, including seven submarine-cruisers displacing over 2000 tons

During the war, Germania had begun work on the battleship *Sachsen* and the battlecruiser *Ersatz Gneisenau* (replacement for *Gneisenau*), but work could not be completed on these ships before the end of the war. The *Sachsen* had already been launched in 1916, but the keel of the *Ersatz Gneisenau* was only laid down in that year, and work was suspended on both in 1917. The *Schleswig-Holstein* and *Schlesien*, both completed by Germania in 1908, were allowed to be retained by Germany after the war, and they were used as training vessels for the post-war German Navy. The *Schleswig-Holstein* had the distinction of firing the first shots of the Second World War when she bombarded the Polish fortress of Westerplatte near Danzig on the morning of 1 September 1939.

Germania Werft resumed the construction of warships for the German Navy in the mid 1930s, building fourteen Type II coastal submarines in 1935-6, fifteen Type VII U-boats in 1936-9, and five destroyers in 1938-9. In 1940, Germania Werft produced the heavy cruiser *Prinz Eugen*, which later accompanied the battleship *Bismarck* during its famous sortie into the North Atlantic in May 1941. Three additional destroyers were built in 1942-3, and a total of 200 submarines were completed during the Second World War. Submarine production included seventy-five Type VII boats, eight Type X-B mine laying U-boats, and 100 Type XXVII 'Seehund' midget submarines. Cancelled orders at the end of the war amounted to over 500 more U-boats.

Germania Werft, which had been severely damaged by British bombing raids, was closed at the end of the war, and in 1953, the Krupp concern gave up the shipyard. The shipyard was subsequently acquired by Howaldtswerke, giving that firm the entire stretch of shipbuilding facilities at the southeastern end of the Kiel Fjord.

## DEUTSCHE WERKE

The DEUTSCHE WERKE KIEL AG (Kiel German Works, Inc.) shipyard was established in 1925 from the consolidation of the former Kiel Imperial Naval Shipyard and the Friedrichsorter Torpedo Factory. The shipyard was located at the centre of three adjacent shipyards on the southeastern coast of the Kiel Fjord. Deutsche Werke soon began building warships for the new post-war German Navy, including the light cruisers *Karlsruhe* (1929) and *Nürnberg* (1935). In 1931, Deutsche Werke built the first Panzerschiff (pocket battleship), the *Deutschland*, later renamed the *Lützow*, and in 1936, it produced the battleship *Gneisenau*. In 1937, Deutsche Werke came under the operational control of the adjacent Howaldtswerke.

In 1937, Deutsche Werke completed the first three new modern destroyers for the German Navy, the *Z-1* to *Z-3*. Deutsche Werke launched the aircraft carrier *Graf Zeppelin* in 1938, but the ship was never completed. In 1939, Deutsche Werke completed the heavy cruiser *Blücher*, which was later sunk by Norwegian coastal batteries near Oslo during the invasion of Norway in 1940. Deutsche Werke also produced a total of seventy-two submarines prior to and during the Second World War, including thirty-two Type II coastal U-boats, twenty-eight Type VII U-boats, and ten Type XIX U-boats. An additional seven U-boats were cancelled at the end of the war. At the end of the war, the Deutsche Werke shipyard was absorbed by Howaldtswerke.

## HOWALDTSWERKE KIEL

Howaldtswerke was the third and northernmost of the three adjacent shipyards that existed on the southeastern shore of the Kiel Fjord early in the twentieth century. The shipyard originated as the SCHWEFFEL & HOWALDT MASCHINEN FABRIK UND EISENGIESSEREI (Machine Works and Iron Foundry) in 1838, and by 1850, it was beginning to build iron ships. In 1889, the Georg Howaldt shipyard merged with the Gebruder Howaldt (Brothers Howaldt) Machinery Works, Foundry, and Boiler Factory to form HOWALDTSWERKE. By 1895, Howaldtswerke had produced over 300 ships, and at the turn of the century, it was heavily engaged in warship production. Before the outbreak of the First World War, the yard built one light cruiser in 1903 and the battleship *Helgoland* in 1911. Wartime production included the battleships *Kaiserin* in 1913 and *Bayern* in 1916, as well as the light cruiser *Rostock* in 1913, and ten torpedo-boats in 1917-18.

Howaldtswerke Kiel was not heavily engaged in warship production after the war, and in 1939, the company headquarters was moved to Hamburg. The Kiel shipyard was sold to the German government at that time, and from 1940 to 1943, it produced thirty-one Type VII-C submarines for the German Navy. Howaldtswerke purchased the shipyard back in 1943, and it planned to continue U-boat production, but orders for twenty-nine more Type VII-C U-boats were cancelled as the end of the war approached. In 1945, Howaldtswerke Kiel absorbed the Deutsche Werke shipyard directly to its south. In 1968, Howaldtswerke merged with Deutsche Werft Hamburg to form HOWALDTSWERKE DEUTSCHE WERFT AG (HDW).

Howaldtswerke Kiel built two attack submarines in 1968-9 and six more in 1973-4. In 1984, Alfried Krupp wrote off the Krupp Germania shipyard further to the south, and it was subsequently acquired by Howaldtswerke, giving it the entire shipbuilding capacity at the southeastern end of the Kiel Fjord. Howaldtswerke Kiel has since built two guided missile frigates for the German Navy, with the last one completed in 1995.

## FLENSBURG

Flensburg is located at the southwestern end of the Flensburger Fjord, an inlet of the Ostsee about 50 miles northwest of Kiel. The FLENSBURGER SCHIFFBAU AG (Flensburg Shipbuilding, Inc.) began building ships at the beginning of the twentieth century, and its most notable achievement was the construction of the cargo submarine *Deutschland* in 1916. The *Deutschland* had a surface displacement of 1600 tons and could carry about 1000 tons of cargo. On her maiden voyage to Baltimore in the summer of 1916, she carried 3000 cases of dyestuffs for the American textile industry, and she returned to Germany with critically needed supplies of nickel, tin, and crude rubber.

During the Second World War, the Flensburger Schiffbau AG built twenty-eight Type VII-C submarines for the German Navy, but orders for an additional twenty boats had to be cancelled toward the end of the war. Flensburg remains an important port city and shipbuilding centre in Schleswig-Holstein.

The Baltic.

## Baltic

### Lübeck and Rostock

FLENDER WERFT was located at Lübeck, a town at the southwestern corner of the Lübecker Bay, which is an arm of the Ostsee at the western end of the Baltic Sea. Flender Werft built a total of twenty-one submarines for the German Navy prior to and during the Second World War, including two Type II coastal U-boats in 1935-6, five Type VII-B U-boats in 1939-41, and sixteen VII-C Type U-boats in 1941-2. Orders for seventy more U-boats were cancelled at the end of the war. The NEPTUNWERFT (Neptune Shipyard) was located at Rostock, a town on the Mecklenburger Bay off the Ostsee about 60 miles east of Lübeck. During the First World War, the Neptunwerft received orders for ten submarines for the German Navy, but they were cancelled at the end of the war.

### VULKAN STETTIN

VULKAN STETTIN was established around the middle of the nineteenth century at the mouth of the Oder River near the town of Stettin, about 50 miles northeast of Berlin. The shipyard began building warships for the Imperial German Navy soon after the formation of the new German Empire in 1871. Vulkan Stettin built four ironclad frigates and four ironclad corvettes in 1876-86. Vulkan Stettin began building torpedo-boats in 1884, completing ten of these vessels by the end of the nineteenth century. The shipyard built the battleships *Brandenburg* in 1893 and the *Weissenburg* in 1894, and this was followed by the protected cruisers *Herta*, *Hansa*, and *Vineta*, all in 1898. The *Weissenburg* was later sold to Turkey in 1910, and it became the *Torgut Reis* in the Turkish Navy.

In addition to warships, Vulkan Stettin was also known for the merchant ships that it produced, including the passenger liners *Friedrich der Grosse* in 1896 and the *Königin Louise* in 1897. After the turn of the century, Vulkan Stettin built one protected cruiser for Russia in 1902. The shipyard continued warship production with the battleships *Mecklenburg* in 1903, *Preussen* in 1905, and *Pommern* in 1907, and in the period 1904-09, Vulcan Stettin also produced four light cruisers. Vulcan Stettin then built the Dreadnought battleship *Rheinland* for the Imperial German Navy in 1910 and began the battleship *Salamis* for Greece in 1913, but she was never completed. Torpedo-boat construction continued with the building of seventy-six additional vessels of this type from 1900 to 1918.

Merchant vessels produced prior to the First World War included the passenger liners *Prinzessin Alice* (1900), *Prinzessin Irene* (also 1900), *Kronprinz Wilhelm* (1901), *Kaiser Wilhelm II* (1903), *Kronprinzessin Cecile* (1907), and *George Washington* (1909). After the war, Vulcan Stettin built the passenger liners *München* in 1923 and *Stuttgart* in 1924. Like other shipyards in Germany and throughout the world, Vulcan Stettin saw a gradual drop in workload, and it was severely depressed in the late 1920s and during the 1930s.

Vulcan Stettin did not play a major role in the construction of warships for the German Navy during the Second World War, completing only one Type VII-C submarine and having an order for one additional boat cancelled at the end of the war. Stettin was overrun by Soviet forces toward the end of the war, and it was later ceded to Poland under the peace treaty with Germany. Stettin was renamed Szczecin, and it continues to serve as an important port for Poland.

## SCHICHAU ELBING

In 1837, Friedrich Schichau established a shipyard at Elbing, a town on the eastern Baltic coast about 70 miles southwest of Königsberg, the ancient capital of the Kingdom of Prussia (later referred to as East Prussia). In 1884, SCHICHAU ELBING began producing torpedo-boats, and it completed 110 such vessels for the Imperial German Navy before the end of the nineteenth century. The shipyard continued to build torpedo-boats in the twentieth century, completing ninety more such vessels before the First World War, and an additional fifty boats during the war.

In addition to being the greatest producer of torpedo-boats for the Imperial German Navy, Schichau Elbing also built numerous torpedo-boats for foreign nations, including fourteen for Austria-Hungary, six for Brazil, four for Turkey, and two for China. Schichau Elbing also built five destroyers for Austria-Hungary during the First World War, but it was not involved in any significant naval construction between the two world wars. During the Second World War, the shipyard built thirty torpedo-boats for the German Navy, and another twelve torpedo-boats were left incomplete at the end of the war. In 1945, Soviet forces captured Elbing, and under the terms of the peace treaty, that area was later ceded to Poland. Elbing is now known as the Polish town of Elblag.

## SCHICHAU DANZIG

At the end of the nineteenth century, Friedrich Schichau built another shipyard at Danzig to handle the construction of larger ships. SCHICHAU DANZIG built the battleships *Odin* in 1896, *Kaiser Barbarossa* in 1901, *Wettin* in

1902, *Elsass* in 1904, and *Lothringen* in 1906. It then built the Dreadnought-type battleships *Oldenburg* (1912) and *König Albert* (1913), the battlecruiser *Lützow* (1915), and the battleship *Baden* (1916). One additional battlecruiser, the *Graf Spee*, was launched in 1917, but could not be completed before the end of the war. Schichau Danzig also built fifteen destroyers for the Russian Navy before the outbreak of the First World War.

Prior to the First World War, Schichau Danzig built the passenger liners *Bremen* in 1897 and *Grosser Kurfürst* in 1900. After the war, it resumed the production of passenger liners with the *Homeric* in 1920 and the *Columbus* in 1923. The *Columbus* was scuttled by her crew in December 1939 when she was intercepted by a British warship while attempting to return to Germany from New York after the outbreak of the Second World War. During the war, Schichau Danzig built fifty-four Type VII-C submarines for the Germany Navy, and orders for an additional forty-two submarines of the same type were cancelled at the end of the war. After the end of the war, Danzig again became part of Poland, and is now known as the Polish city of Gdansk.

# 7 Italy

Italy was not a nation as such until the unification of its various states into a confederacy, and Victor Emmanuel II of Sardinia was declared King of Italy in 1861. After the fall of the Roman Empire, there was no central control over the various states that now comprise Italy. Even under the Holy Roman Empire established by Charlemagne in AD 600, the more powerful states had a considerable degree of autonomy. These included the Papal States, which were located in the vicinity of Rome and were controlled directly by the Vatican, and the independent states of Venice and Genoa. From a naval point of view, Venice was by far the most important of those states.

Attempts to unify the Italian states had begun in the late fifteenth century with the formation of a league by certain states, but feuds among these states and incursions by the French, Spanish, and Austrians over the next three centuries precluded the establishment of a united nation. In 1800, Italy was invaded by Napoleon, and it subsequently became part of the French Empire. In 1813, the Austrians invaded, but the Armistice of Scharino Rizzino in 1814 recognised the 'Kingdom of Italy'. In 1861, most of the Italian states were unified into one nation as a result of the combined efforts of Giuseppe Garibaldi and Count Camillo Cavour.

The act of unification heralded the birth of the Italian Navy in 1861. The new nation of Italy inherited the warships of the Neapolitan, Sardinian, and Tuscan navies, as well as their naval bases and shipyards. It then became a matter of integrating those assets into a single naval establishment. The new Italian navy was soon tested in a war with Austria, but it was defeated in the Battle of Lissa in the Adriatic Sea in 1866. Italy started to lay up most of its older warships in the 1870s, and in the next decade, it began a naval construction programme with a trend toward building faster ships but with lighter armour protection than those of other European powers.

In the late nineteenth century, Italy began to establish colonies in East Africa. Italians settled along the Red Sea coast of Africa in 1880, and in 1889, Italian sovereignty over that territory was recognised by the Treaty of Uccialli.

The colony of Eritrea was officially proclaimed in the following year. About the same time, Italians were establishing trading posts in the Somali coastal region bordering on the Indian Ocean. In 1919, Great Britain ceded some of their territory in the region to Italy, and in the 1920s, the colony of Italian Somaliland was established. Great Britain and France had holdings along the Gulf of Aden known as British Somaliland and French Somaliland, respectively.

In 1911, Italy had territorial designs on Tripolitania and Cyrenaica, Turkish possessions directly across the Mediterranean Sea from Italy in North Africa. After declaring war on Turkey and invading those territories, Italy was ceded that area by the peace treaty of Ouchy in 1912. A naval base was established by the Italians at Tripoli. The territories of Tripolitania and Cyrenaica were subsequently combined in the 1930s and given the name of 'Libya'.

After its unification in 1861, Italy was actually ruled by a succession of prime ministers with the king exercising very little influence. Italy joined the other European powers in the naval armaments race that took place at the beginning of the twentieth century, and by the time that the First World War broke out, it possessed twelve battleships, four of those being of the advanced Dreadnought-type, and there were two more Dreadnoughts under construction. In 1914, Italy was still an ally of Germany, but when Austria invaded Serbia at the beginning of the First World War, Italy declared its neutrality.

In 1915, after being promised territorial gains by the Allies if it entered the war on their side, Italy renounced its previous treaty with the Central Powers and declared war against Austria. In reward for its participation in the war, Italy was ceded part of the Austrian Tyrol, the port city of Trieste, and the Istrian peninsula including the port of Pola. With Trieste, Italy acquired the most important naval shipyard of the Austro-Hungarian Empire, and it had continued to be a significant Italian shipyard up to the present time. Pola became a naval base for the Italian Navy, but after the Second World War, the Istrian Peninsula was ceded to Yugoslavia.

In 1922, the Fascist Party in Italy gained control of the government, and three years later, Benito Mussolini became the dictatorial ruler of Italy. Italy befriended the Nazi dictatorship under Adolf Hitler in Germany, and it then became one of the three 'Axis' nations that included Japan. In 1935, Italy sought further territorial expansion by invading Ethiopia, using its colonies of Eritrea and Italian Somaliland as jumping-off bases for a two-pronged assault. Ethiopia capitulated in the following year after being overwhelmed by superior Italian forces armed with modern weapons.

Italy entered the Second World War on the side of Germany by invading France in 1940. Italy's colony of Libya in North Africa was the scene of much fighting back-and-forth in 1940-2 before finally being taken by British forces early in 1943. British forces liberated Ethiopia and captured the Italian colonies of Eritrea and Somaliland in 1941. In 1943, after the invasion of Italy, its government sued for peace and then turned around and declared war on Germany. Mussolini initially escaped prison, but in April 1945, he was captured and executed by Italian partisans. As a result of its initial involvement

Italy in 1939.

in the war on the Axis side, Italy lost the Istrian Peninsula to Yugoslavia, but was able to retain the port of Trieste.

## NAVAL SHIPYARDS

*Venice*
Venice (Venezia) is one of many islands formed by silt deposits that accumulated in the Gulf of Venice in the northwestern corner of the Adriatic Sea. Venice is now connected by a causeway over two miles long to the mainland at Mestre. Venice was first settled in the middle of the sixth century, and it subsequently became an independent community. By 800, Venice had come to dominate the northern Adriatic region, and it became very wealthy as a result of its trade with the eastern Mediterranean markets of the Levant. In 1000, Venice built a fleet of warships to defend her merchantmen from pirates based in Dalmatia across the Adriatic Sea. After destroying the pirate bases in Dalmatia, Venice became the predominant naval power in the Adriatic region.

During the Fourth Crusade in the late twelfth century, Venetian shipbuilders built most of the vessels needed to transport the Christian warriors and their horses and equipment to the Holy Land. As a result of the fall of Constantinople in 1204, Venice acquired much of Dalmatia and the Ionian Islands off Greece. Venice then controlled the entire Adriatic region as well as the area of the Ionian Sea. Venice later purchased the island of Crete, extending her domain even closer to Asia Minor. Venice was challenged by Genoa for the control of trade between Europe and the Levant, and this led to almost continuous warfare between the two states in the thirteenth and fourteenth century.

Although its conflict with Genoa seesawed back and forth during that period, Venice eventually achieved final victory when it trapped and destroyed the Genoese fleet at Chioggia in 1380. Venice thereby became the dominant power in the Mediterranean with near absolute control over the eastern Mediterranean Levant trade. At the beginning of the fourteenth century, Venice established a maritime arsenal at the eastern end of the island state. Venice began to decline in the fifteenth century after the route around the Cape of Good Hope was discovered by the Portuguese navigator, Bartholomeu Dias de Novaes (Bartholomew Diaz) in 1486. That discovery opened up a direct sea route to India without the need for transporting goods overland between India and the Levant.

The state of Venice was at war with Turkey almost continuously in the sixteenth and seventeenth centuries. Venice joined in an alliance with Spain, Genoa, Malta, and the Papal States in one of its wars against Turkey, and this resulted in the complete destruction of the Turkish fleet during the famous Battle of Lepanto in 1571. Venice provided the heavily-armed galleasses that decimated the Turkish vessels before they could close with the Allied fleet and engage in hand-to hand combat.

L'ARSENALE DE VENEZIA (Venice Naval Arsenal) was the most important of the naval bases and shipyards inherited from the Italian states upon their unification into the new nation of Italy in 1861. Venice had been an important naval shipbuilding centre since the twelfth century, and it produced a variety

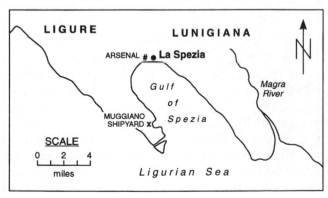

La Spezia.

of warships during its long history. Venice had built many of the wooden sailing warships and some newer steam-powered warships that became part of the Italian Navy at the time of the unification, and then continued, production including two screw-propelled frigates in 1862, the cruiser *Stromboli* in 1886, and several ironclad frigates constructed during the latter half of the nineteenth century.

Venice built the battleships *Sardegna* in 1894 and *Ammiraglio di St. Bon* in 1900, the armoured cruisers *Francesco Ferruccio* in 1905 and *San Marco* in 1908, and one light cruiser in 1911. Venice also produced three submarines for the Italian Navy in 1914. After the First World War, Venice was not an important naval shipbuilding facility, and it operated primarily as a naval base and ship repair and maintenance facility.

## La Spezia

The importance of the Gulf of Spezia as the site for a naval base was recognised in 1805 by Napoleon, but no specific action to build such a base was undertaken at the time. Finally in 1857, the construction of a naval arsenal on the Gulf of Spezia was approved by Victor Emmanuel II, who was then still

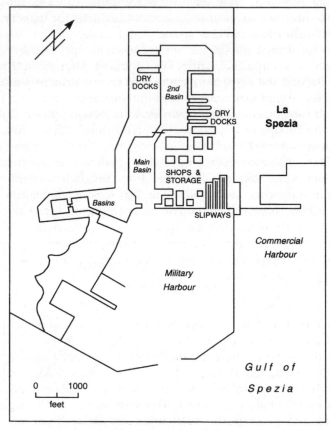

La Spezia Arsenal in 1945.

only King of Sardinia before becoming King of Italy in 1861. In 1859, plans for a naval arsenal just west of the town of Spezia were drawn up by the military engineer, Domenico Chiodo, and 85 acres of land were acquired at the site for that purpose. Construction began in the following year, and L'ARSENALE DI LA SPEZIA (La Spezia Naval Arsenal) was dedicated in 1869.

The La Spezia Naval Arsenal was designed to have one open basin, 1380 × 655ft in size, and one enclosed basin, 1280 × 655ft in size. In addition, four dry docks, two of 430ft and two of 360ft in length, and nine slipways, three of 390ft and six of 330ft in length, were contemplated. Although all of its facilities were not as yet completed, the shipyard soon began by producing steam-powered warships, such as the cruiser *Palestro* in 1871 and two gunboats in 1874. In 1875, the arsenal ordered a 160-ton hydraulic crane from W. G. Armstrong of Newcastle-upon-Tyne for use in lifting heavy guns during the fitting-out of warships at the arsenal. At that time, there were 1650 workers employed at the arsenal.

La Spezia built the pre-Dreadnought battleships *Dandolo* in 1878, *Andrea Doria* in 1887, *Re Umberto* in 1893, *Regina Margharita* in 1904, *Regina Elena* in 1907, and *Roma* in 1908, four light cruisers in 1888-94 and the armoured cruiser *Carlo Alberto* in 1898. The shipyard was electrified in 1890-1, and this soon led to the use of electric cranes to facilitate the handling of heavy machinery and ordnance items at the yard. During the First World War, La Spezia produced the battleships *Conte di Cavour* in 1915 and the *Andrea Doria* in 1916. as well as eight submarines from 1913-19. After the war, shipbuilding was discontinued at La Spezia, and the yard served primarily as a naval base and a ship repair and maintenance facility thereafter.

Although temporarily closed down after the Second World War, La Spezia was allowed to reopen in 1946, and the period from 1947-50 was devoted to the reconstruction of the yard from its extensive wartime damage. In the post-war era, La Spezia modernised three light cruisers for the Italian Navy in 1952-60. ARSENALE MILITARE MARITTIMO LA SPEZIA is currently performing ship maintenance work and providing logistic support for Italian naval vessels in the Upper Tyrrhenian Region. The shipyard currently has 35 acres of land with seven acres under cover. La Spezia has six permanent dry docks, two floating dry docks and 8500 linear feet of quay space. The yard has a total strength of 2600 people, comprising 2000 workers, 300 military personnel, 200 administrative staff, and 100 technical staff.

### Taranto

L'ARSENALE DI TARANTO (Taranto Naval Arsenal) was established in 1882 on the southeastern coast of Italy, nestled under the arch of the 'boot' that represents the shape of the country. Taranto is protected on the west by the islands of Chéradi, San Pietro, and San Páolo and breakwaters connecting these islands to the mainland. The outer harbour of Taranto, Mare Grande, affords an excellent fleet anchorage. The arsenal was under construction for seven years, and in 1889, the 390ft brick dry dock, 'Benedetto Brin', was completed. In 1901, the capacity of the arsenal was increased by the addition

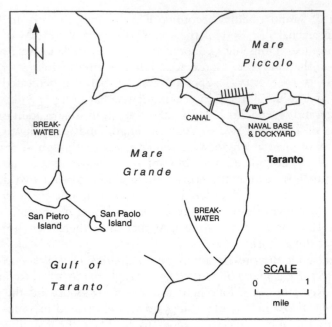

Taranto in 1945.

of a 255ft floating dry dock, and in 1916, the larger 800ft brick dry dock, 'Edgardo Ferrati', was constructed at the arsenal.

Another floating dry dock, 230ft long, was added to Taranto's facilities in 1940. When Italy entered the Second World War on the side of Germany in June of 1940, Taranto became the primary base for the Italian navy due to its sheltered harbour. On the evening of 11 November 1940, British Swordfish torpedo planes operating from the aircraft carrier HMS *Illustrious* successfully attacked the Italian warships anchored in the outer harbour of Taranto. The battleship *Conte di Cavour* was sunk, and the *Caio Duilio* was heavily damaged. In addition, the newer battleship *Littorio* was also damaged in the attack, as were two cruisers and a destroyer.

Taranto was used primarily a naval base and ship repair and maintenance facility rather than for the construction of warships. Naval shipbuilding at the arsenal was limited to the production of three frigates for the Italian Navy in 1969. Two more floating dry docks were emplaced at the arsenal in the 1970s, a 325ft dock in 1971 and a 460ft dock in 1975. In 1991, the ship repair and maintenance capacity of the Taranto arsenal was further increased by the addition of a 500ft floating dry dock at the yard.

Today, L'ARSENALE MILITARE MARITTIMO DI TARANTO remains an important ship repair and maintenance facility for the Italian Navy, and it is the most important Italian naval station in the Mediterranean. Specifically, the base is responsible for providing logistic support to Italian naval vessels in the Ionian Sea and Lower Adriatic coastal regions. The base is currently on 220 acres of land, and it has a workforce of 3000, comprising 2800 civilian and 200 military personnel.

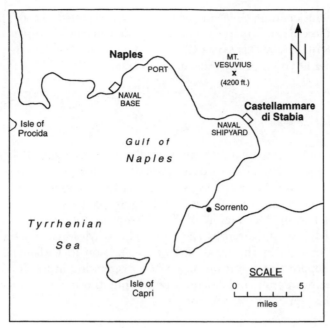

Naples.

*Castellammare di Stabia*

Another important naval shipyard was the CASTELLAMMARE DI STABIA NAVAL
ARSENAL on the Bay of Naples about 20 miles southeast of the city. The
shipyard was established late in the nineteenth century, and it soon produced
a number of ironclad warships for the Italian navy. Castellammare then built
the pre-Dreadnought battleships *Emanuele Filiberto* in 1902, *Beneditto Brin* in
1905, *Napoli* in 1908, and *Vittorio Emmanuele* in 1908. The shipyard built the
first Italian Dreadnought-type battleship, the *Dante Alighieri*, which was
completed in 1913. She displaced nearly 20,000 tons and carried twelve 12in
guns in four triple turrets, the first use of triple turrets for main naval
armament in the world.

During the period before the First World War, Castellammare also built the
armoured cruisers *Marco Polo* (1891), *Vetto Pisani* (1899), and *San Giorgio* (1908)
as well as four light cruisers in 1890-1912. In 1915, Castellammare completed
the Dreadnought-type battleship *Caio Duilio*, which also served during the
Second World War. Another battleship, the *Carraciolo*, had been launched in
1920, but work was then cancelled, and the ship was never completed.

After the First World War, Castellammare built the light cruiser *Giovanni
Della Bande Nere* in 1930. Naval construction during the Second World War
consisted primarily of the light cruiser *Giulio Germanico*, which was completed
in 1942. After the war, the shipyard was turned over to private ownership, and
it became NAVALMECCANIA CASTELLAMMARE. The yard then fell under the
Italcantieri Group and became ITALCANTIERI CASTELLAMMARE. Castellammare continued to produce warships for the Italian Navy, including the

helicopter cruisers *Caio Duilio* in 1964 and *Vittorio Veneto* in 1969. The shipyard also built three frigates in 1962 and one guided missile destroyer in 1972. In 1984, CANTIERI CASTELLAMMARE DI STABIA came under the Merchant Shipbuilding Division of the Fincantieri Group.


## NAVAL BASES

In addition to La Spezia, Taranto, and Castellammare di Stabia, Italy established a string of smaller naval bases around the coast. At the present time, La Spezia provides ship maintenance and logistic support for Italian naval units in Upper Tyrrhenian, while the naval base at Napoli (Naples) covers the Lower Tyrrhenian region. The region of Sicily and the 'toe' of the Italian geographical 'boot' is supported by the naval base at Messina, and the region of Sardinia is covered by the naval base of Cagliari on that island. The Taranto naval base supports that portion of the Navy operating in the Ionian Sea and Lower Adriatic region, and Ancona rounds out the major support bases by covering the Upper Adriatic region.


## PRIVATE SHIPYARDS

In addition to the government-operated naval arsenals mentioned above, there were several private shipyards that built warships for the Italian navy under contract with the Italian government. These shipyards extended along the Italian coastline from Genoa down along the west coast, up along the east coast, and over to Trieste. After the Second World War, there began a trend to consolidate Italian shipbuilding under central management.

In 1966, the shipyards at Riva Trigoso, Ancona, and Palermo, as well as the Genoa Repair Works, came under Cantieri Navali del Tirreno Riuniti (CNTR). In 1971, Cantieri Navali e Riuniti (CNR) took over the Odero-Terni-Orlando shipyards at Muggiano and Livorno and the Breda shipyard at Venice-Marghera. In 1975, Ansaldo Sestri Ponente absorbed the former Castellammare di Stabia naval shipyard and the Cantieri Navali Riuniti shipyard at Monfalcone under the new corporate name of Italcantieri.

Since 1984, all major private shipyards came under the Societa Finanziaria Cantieri Navali (Fincantieri Group) with its headquarters at Trieste. Its Merchant Shipbuilding Division manages the shipyards at Trieste, Monfalcone, Venice-Marghera, Ancona, Palermo, Castellammare de Stabia, and Livorno (Leghorn). Its Naval Shipbuilding Division operates the shipyards at Muggiano (La Spezia) and at Riva Trigoso, about 30 miles east of Genoa. Although Muggiano and Riva Trigoso specialise in the construction of naval vessels, other Fincantieri shipyards associated with the Merchant Shipbuilding Division also build warships.

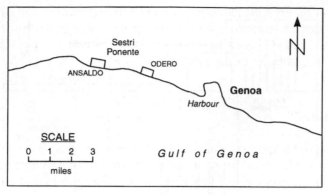

Genoa.

## Genoa

One of the first shipyards in the Genoa (Genova) area to produce warships for the new Italian Navy was the FOCE SHIPYARD located at Foce, a southeast suburb of Genoa. That yard produced three ironclad frigates in 1865-73. Another early producer of warships in the Genoa area was the ODERO SESTRI SHIPYARD, located at Sestri Ponente, a western suburb of Genoa. The Odero family acquired the shipyard from Agostino Briasco during the mid-nineteenth century, and it built several warships for the Italian Navy, including the armoured cruiser *Amalfi* in 1909 and the battleship *Leonardo da Vinci* in 1914. The yard also produced twenty-five destroyers and torpedo-boats up until the First World War. Odero Sestri was later consolidated with the Ansaldo Group.

The most prolific of the Italian private shipyards engaged in naval construction was the Ansaldo Shipyard of Sestri Ponente near Genoa. The GIO. ANSALDO & C. WORKS was established in 1853 by Cavour, the first Italian prime minister, and named for its chief engineer, Giovanni Ansaldo. The Ansaldo Works was originally involved in the production of steam loco-motives, but it soon expanded its work to include the manufacture of heavy ordnance and steam turbine engines, as well as the building of ships. In 1904, the company was incorporated as Societa Anonima Italiana GIO. ANSALDO & C., and it later acquired control over the Odera Sestri shipyard to supplement its own production capacity.

Ansaldo began building major warships for the Italian Navy early in the twentieth century. The firm produced the armoured cruiser *Giuseppe Garibaldi* in 1902 and the light cruisers *Liguria* in 1893 and *Libia* in 1914, as well as twenty-seven torpedo-boats and destroyers up to 1916. Ansaldo built the battleship *Guilio Cesare* in 1914. The shipyard laid down the battleship *Cristoforo Colombo* in 1915, but work on the ship was cancelled before it was even launched. During the inter-war years, Ansaldo built the heavy cruiser *Bolzano* in 1932 and the light cruisers *Alberto di Giussano* in 1931, *Alberico da Barbiano* in 1932, *Raimondo Montecuccoli* in 1934 and *Eugenio di Savoia* in 1935 The yard also produced ten destroyers in the 1920s and nine torpedo-boats in 1938.

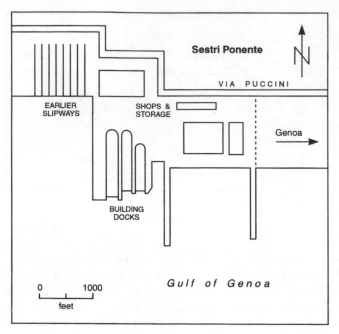

Ansaldo Genoa in 1945.

During the Second World War, Ansaldo built the 35,000-ton battleship *Littorio* (later renamed the *Italia*) in 1940. The firm also produced the light cruisers *Paolo Emilia* and *Ottaviano Augusto*, both in 1942. In 1939, Ansaldo began work on the battleship *Impero*, a sister-ship of the *Littorio*, but the programme was cancelled during the war before the ship could be completed. During its earlier years, Ansaldo also produced many liners for the Italian steamship lines, including the *Duilio* (1923), *Roma* (1926) and *Augustus* (1927), and the famous liner *Rex* (1932) which won the transatlantic Blue Riband in 1933.

After the war, the shipyard resumed the construction of passenger liners, including the *Andrea Doria* in 1953, the *Cristoforo Colombo* in 1954, and *Gripsholm* for Sweden in 1956. The *Andrea Doria* sank after a collision with the Swedish liner *Stockholm* off the coast of North America in 1956. Returning to warship production, Ansaldo built one frigate in 1957 and two destroyers, one in 1958 and the other in 1963. The yard also produced the liner *Leonardo da Vinci* in 1960.

In 1984, Ansaldo and other public shipbuilders came under the Merchant Shipbuilding Division of the Fincantieri Group. Since 1993, the Ansaldo shipyard became known as CANTIERI NAVALI ITALIANI SpA, an independent subsidiary company of Fincantieri. Cantieri Navali Italiani S.p.A. now specialises in the construction of gas carriers, marine systems, and off-shore drilling rigs. The Sestri shipyard has two dry docks, one 835ft and the other 935ft in length. These dry docks can accommodate ships of up to 80,000 tons and 140,000 tons, respectively

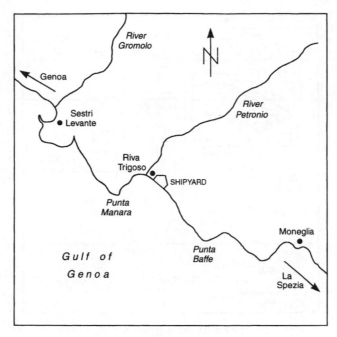

Riva Trigoso area.

*Riva Trigoso*

In 1890, Erasmo Piaggio, chairman of the board of Navigazione Generale Italiana (Italian General Navigation Company) proposed the establishment of the Società Esercizio Bacini to operate five dry docks and two workshops for repairing ships of the port of Genoa. In 1897, the Società Esercizio Bacini founded a large foundry and modern naval shipyard at Riva Trigoso on the coast of the Ligurian Sea, about 30 miles east of Genoa. At first, the shipyard produced only small fishing vessels, but it gradually came to build vessels of increasing size. The first large ship built by Riva Trigoso was a freighter in 1900.

During the First World War, the Riva Trigoso yard built eight naval tankers and several other auxiliary naval vessels for the Italian Navy. In 1925, the company was renamed Cantieri del Tirreno. The shipyard built one destroyer for the Italian Navy in 1934, and it produced two additional destroyers in 1938. During the Second World War, it produced the light cruisers *Vipsanio Agrippa* and *Claudio Druso*, both in 1942. The shipyard was severely damaged during the war, but it soon recovered and began building cargo ships again in 1946. In 1950, Cantieri del Tirreno became Cantieri Navali Riuniti-Riva Trigoso.

CNR Riva Trigoso built the helicopter cruiser *Andrea Doria* in 1964, and in 1966, the shipyard came under the Cantieri Navali del Tirreno e Reuniti (CNTR). CNTR Riva Trigoso built two guided missile frigates in 1968, two destroyers in 1969, and one guided missile destroyer in 1972. The yard also built the luxury cruise ships *Southwind* and *Spirit of London* in 1971-2. In the

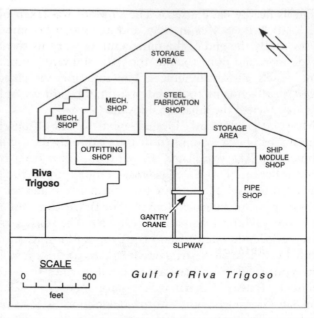

Riva Trigosa shipyard in 1990.

late 1970s, Riva Trigoso became the lead yard for the production of *Lupo* class guided missile frigates, and it produced ten of these vessels for the Italian Navy from 1977 to 1985, as well as a number for foreign navies. During this period, the yard also built another destroyer in 1979.

In 1984, the shipyard became CANTIERI RIVA TRIGOSO under the Naval Shipbuilding Division of the Fincantieri Group, which consolidated all private Italian shipyards. Cantieri Riva Trigoso built eight guided missile frigates of the *Maestrale* class from 1988 to 1998 and three guided missile destroyers in 1989-91. Since Riva Trigoso did not have a fitting-out basin, completed ships were brought to its sister shipyard, Muggiana at La Spezia, for final fitting-out.

The Riva Trigoso shipyard is situated on 42 acres of land, nearly half of which is under cover, and it has two adjacent slipways, 575ft long and with a combined width of 200ft. The slipways are served by a single travelling gantry crane that spans the entire width of the two slipways. The slipways are also served by three individual travelling cranes that move along the outside of the combined slipway, two on one side and one on the other. The Ship Module Shop with a covered area of 70,000ft$^2$ can accommodate two frigate hulls at the same time, producing one complete ship module every three weeks. Completed ship modules are moved out of the shop, picked up by the travelling gantry crane, and then positioned on the ship being assembled on the slipway.

## Muggiano

In 1883, GEORGE HENFRY & CO. established a shipyard by on the southwestern shore of the Gulf of Spezia, about four miles south of the town of La Spezia and its nearby naval arsenal. The shipyard was taken over by the CONTINENTAL LEAD & IRON CO. in 1887, and in 1899, it became CANTIERI NAVALE MUGGIANO. By the end of the nineteenth century, its workforce had increased to 1500 men, and from 1900 to 1905, the shipyard produced thirty-three merchant vessels, mostly freighters. The shipyard was taken over by CANTIERI RIUNITI of Genoa in 1906, and in 1913, the yard was sold to Fiat-San Giorgio, which owned the adjacent shipyard.

The FIAT-MUGGIANO shipyard, located next to the Cantieri Navale Muggiano shipyard, had been established in 1905 expressly for the purpose of producing submarines. Two years later, the yard was taken oven by the San Giorgio Co. and it became FIAT-SAN GIORGIO. From 1907 to 1918, Fiat-San Giorgio produced thirty submarines for the Italian Navy and an additional twelve for foreign governments, including five for Brazil, three for Spain, two for Portugal, and one each for Denmark and Sweden. The yards also fitted out five submarines produced by the Orlando Bros. shipyard in Livorno and three submarines built by Odero of Sestri Ponente (Genoa). In 1917, Fiat issued licenses for the construction of Fiat-designed submarines to Great Britain (Scotts of Greenock), Russia (Nikolaiev), and Japan (Kawasaki Kobe).

In 1913, Fiat-San Giorgio bought out the neighbouring Cantieri Reuniti shipyard, and the facilities were consolidated under the Fiat-San Giorgio name. At the end of the First World War, the consolidated Fiat-San Georgio shipyard was taken over by Ansaldo of Genoa, and it became ANSALDO SAN GIORGIO. In 1927, the Ansaldo San Giorgio shipyard was taken over by ODERO-TERNI, and it produced four submarines for the Italian Navy from then until 1929. In 1930, Odero-Terni entered into a partnership with the Orlando Bros. of Livorno, and the shipyard became known as ODERO-TERNI-ORLANDO (LA SPEZIA). Ship production was slow during the 1920s, but it began to pick up in the early 1930s.

OTO La Spezia built an additional twenty-five submarines for the Italian Navy between 1930 and 1939. During that period, the Muggiano yard also produced the heavy cruiser *Zara* in 1931 and the light cruisers *Armando Diaz* in 1933 and *Luigi di Savoia Duca degli Abruzzi* in 1937. In the 1930s, the shipyard had 64 acres of land, a force of 4000 workers, and six landing stages for ships up to 400ft in length and 14,000 tons displacement. During the Second World War, OTO La Spezia continued building submarines, completing eleven for the Italian Navy until 1943, but orders for five additional submarines were cancelled when Italy withdrew from the war in 1943. The OTO-La Spezia shipyard was left in ruins as a result of the German occupation of Italy, and in 1949, it was acquired by Ansaldo of Genoa.

The Muggiano shipyard built five small warships for South Korea in 1968-9, and in 1971, it became CANTIERI MUGGIANO SpA. Ten years later in 1981, the shipyard was turned over to Cantieri Navali Riuniti (CNR) of Genoa. The CNR-MUGGIANO shipyard built two frigates for the Italian Navy as well as ten corvettes for foreign customers through 1984. In 1984, the shipyard came under the Fincantieri Merchant Shipbuilding Division as the CANTIERI MUGGIANO. The yard has since produced six frigates of the *Maestrale* class, two guided missile destroyers, and eight corvettes for the Italian Navy as well as several small naval vessels for other governments. A recent decision by Fincantieri to transfer submarine production from Monfalcone to Muggiano will establish the latter shipyard as a submarine production centre. The yard has already received an order for two attack submarines to be delivered in 2005-6.

Cantieri Muggiano is now consolidated on 40 acres of ground, 13 acres of which is covered. The yard has a fitting-out basin with nearly 4000 linear feet of mooring space, which is served by six travelling cranes of various lifting capacities. This basin is also used for fitting out ships from other shipyards, including Cantieri Riva Trigoso, which has no fitting-out basin of its own. A 850ft floating dry dock has a lifting capacity of ships displacing up to 40,000 tons. The Muggiano shipyard has two slipways, one of which is nearly 600ft long and the other only 200ft long. Cantieri Muggiano also specialises in the construction of smaller naval craft ranging from 3200-ton frigates and corvettes down to fast patrol craft and 60-ton hydrofoils.

### Livorno

Shipbuilding at Livorno (Leghorn) on the Ligurian Sea, about 100 miles southeast of Genoa, began in the fifteenth century. It was not until 1866, however, when Luigi Orlando acquired the 37-acre San Rocco shipyard, that shipbuilding became a major industry in the area. Luigi Orlando operated the shipyard with the assistance of his brothers, Salvatore, Giuseppe, and Paolo, under the name of CANTIERE NAVALE FRATELLI ORLANDO (Orlando Bros. Naval Shipyard). Orlando produced its first warship, the 3900-ton armoured frigate *Conte Verde*, in 1871. By 1887, the workforce at the shipyard had increased from 500 to 1140.

Orlando began producing torpedo-boats in 1885, and it completed thirteen of those craft over the next ten years. In 1887, Orlando built the 13,900-ton battleship *Lepanto*, which carried four 17in guns. The yard produced one light cruiser in 1894, the protected cruiser *Adamastor* in 1897, and the armoured cruiser *Varese* in 1901. In addition, Orlando also built two armoured cruisers for Argentina in 1897-8 and a protected cruiser for Portugal in 1903. In 1904, the shipyard was renamed CANTIERE NAVALE FRATELLI ORLANDO E C. In 1909, Orlando built the 9800-ton armoured cruiser *Pisa* with four 10in guns, and that ship was followed by an armoured cruiser for Greece in 1911.

In 1911, an additional dry dock capable of accommodating ships up to 4500 tons displacement was built at the Orlando yard to supplement three earlier dry docks with a capacity of only 3200 tons. By 1912, the yard had expanded to 61 acres, 15 acres of which were covered, and employment had gradually increased over the years to 2000 workers. In 1914, a 600ft concrete-base slipway was built at the yard to accommodate larger ships. In 1912, Orlando began building submarines, and it completed eight such craft through 1917. The yard also produced four destroyers in 1913-14 and seven torpedo-boats in 1916-19. In 1915, the yard laid the keel for the 31,400-ton superdreadnought *Francesco Morosini*, but the programme was cancelled before the ship was even launched.

In the inter-war years, Orlando produced eight more destroyers from 1920-4. In 1925, the shipyard was taken over by the Società Anonime Livorno, and its name was changed to CANTIERI NAVALI ORLANDO. Orlando continued naval construction with the 10,500-ton heavy cruiser *Trento* mounting eight 8in guns, which was completed in 1929. In 1930, the company merged with the firm of Odero Terni, and the shipyard became CANTIERE NAVALE ODERO-TERNI-ORLANDO LIVORNO, or 'OTO Livorno' for short. In 1931, OTO Livorno completed a small 6800-ton heavy cruiser mounting six 7.5in guns for Argentina. The shipyard then produced the heavy cruisers *Gorizia* and *Pola* for the Italian Navy in 1931 and 1932, respectively.

In 1936, OTO Livorno built the light cruiser *Emanuele Filiberto Duca d'Aosta*, and the yard produced ten destroyers in 1937-9. Production during the Second World War included the 'Capitani Romani' class light cruisers *Attilio Regolo* in 1942 and the *Scipione Africano* in 1943, as well as three additional destroyers in 1942-3. A third cruiser of the same class, the *Caio Mario*, was begun during the war, but could not be completed before Italy's capitulation in September 1943. On 28 May 1943, Livorno was the target of American heavy bombers, and the Orlando shipyard received over 200 hits, killing 200 workers and injuring 2000 more. The Germans evacuated Livorno in early July 1944, but not before destroying cranes and other facilities and equipment at the Orlando shipyard.

After the Second World War, OTO Livorno's production was limited to commercial vessels of various types. In 1949, the shipyard was taken over by Ansaldo of Genoa, and it was renamed again as STABILIMENTO LUIGI ORLANDO LIVORNO. Warship production at the Orlando shipyard eventually resumed with five destroyers for Venezuela in 1956-7, two destroyers for Indonesia in 1956-8, and two destroyers for the Italian Navy in 1958. In 1964, the shipyard was renamed CANTIERE NAVALE LUIGI ORLANDO S.P.A. LIVORNO, and its subsequent production consisted primarily of roll-on/roll-off (RO/RO) cargo ships, large ferries, and gas carriers.

In 1975, the repair capability of the yard was greatly enhanced by the completion of a huge dry dock, 1150ft long and 184ft wide. The new dry dock, capable of taking ships up to 300,000 tons displacement, is supported by one 90-ton and three 20-ton travelling cranes. In 1984, the Orlando shipyard was taken over by the Fincantieri Group, which now manages all Italian shipyards. The yard became known as FINCANTIERI CANTIERI NAVALI ITALIANI S.P.A. (STABILIMENTO DI LIVORNO), and it continued in the production of commercial vessels. In 1996, the name of the shipyard was changed back to CANTIERE NAVALE FRATELLI ORLANDO, and it now operates as an independent shipyard under the overall corporate control of the Fincantieri Group.

## Naples

Naples (Napoli) was the home of the Officine e Cantieri Napoletani, better known as C. E T.T. PATTISON. Pattison was noted for its construction of destroyers and torpedo-boats, and from 1910 until the end of the First World War, it completed ten destroyers and twenty-four torpedo-boats for the Italian

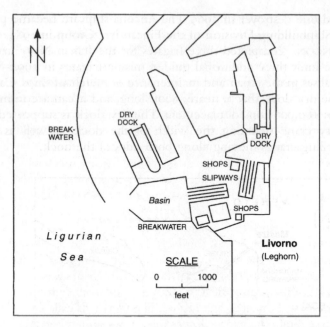

Orlando in 1990.

Navy. Patterson built six more destroyers in the 1920s, but after that, orders for warship construction diminished, and by the time that the Second World War erupted, Patterson was no longer a factor in naval construction for the Italian Navy.

Just to the south of Naples is the private shipyard of CANTIERI CASTELLAMMARE DI STABIA, which has since 1984 has been one of the shipyards under the Merchant Shipbuilding Division of the Fincantieri Group. Not currently involved in naval construction, the shipyard has one 780ft-long slipway that can support the construction of vessels up to 60,000 tons displacement.

### Taranto
Taranto is not only the site of the Taranto Naval Arsenal, but it was also home of CANTIERI NAVALE FRANCO TOSI, renown builder of submarines for the Italian Navy in the 1920s and 1930s. Tosi built five Cavallini-type submarines in 1926-8, three Bernardi-type boats in 1929-30, and four additional Cavallini-type boats in 1930-5. The yard produced seven submarines of its own design in 1930-3, and an additional ten boats in 1936-9.

### Ancona
Ancona is located high on the Adriatic coast of Italy, about 125 miles northeast of Rome and 150 miles southeast of Venice. RIUNITI ANCONA built seven destroyers for the Italian Navy between the First and Second World Wars. In 1966, Ancona came under Cantieri Navali del Tirreno e Riuniti (CNTR),

and it produced one destroyer in 1969. The Ancona shipyard became part of the Merchant Shipbuilding Division of the Fincantieri Group in 1984.

CANTIERI ANCONA completed three frigates for the Italian Navy in 1985, and it has since built three additional guided missile frigates in 1994-6. The yard now specialises in the repair and maintenance of merchant ships. Cantieri Ancona has one dry dock that is nearly 800ft long, and it can accommodate ships as large as 100,000 tons displacement. The dry dock is supported by a travelling gantry crane spanning the width of the dock, as well as three individual travelling cranes moving along both sides of the dock.

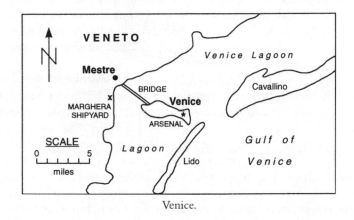

Venice.

## Venice

After the Second World War, Breda Meccanica Bresciana SpA established a modern shipyard near Venice at Marghera on the mainland just to the south of Mestre. CANTIERI NAVALE BREDA built a number of guided missile gunboats, corvettes, and minesweepers for the Italian Navy, but it specialised in the construction of tankers, bulk cargo carriers, liquid gas carriers, and container ships. In 1971, Breda came under Cantieri Navali Reuniti (CNR), and in 1984, the yard was absorbed by the Fincantieri Group.

Now known as VENEZIA-MARGHERA, the facility is one of the shipyards of the Merchant Shipbuilding Division of Fincantieri. The yard now specialises in construction of cruise ships and the repair and maintenance of merchant ships up to 250,000 tons displacement. The Marghera shipyard built the two Disney cruise ships, *Disney Magic* and the *Disney Wonder*, as well as the fastest cruise ship in the world, the Dutch cruise liner *Rotterdam*, all in 1997. The primary asset of the shipyard is a large 1150ft dry dock that can accommodate vessels up to 250,000 tons displacement. The dry dock is supported by four individual travelling cranes, two on either side of the dock.

## Monfalcone

Monfalcone, a town about 20 miles northwest of Trieste, had been part of the Austro-Hungarian Empire until the end of the First World War when the Trieste region was ceded to Italy. The CANTIERI NAVALE TRIESTINO (Naval Shipyard of Trieste) was subsequently established at Monfalcone, and it soon began producing passenger liners, including the *Saturnia* in 1927 and the *Vulcania* in 1928. In 1929, the CANTIERI RIUNITI DELL'ADRIATICO (CRDA) (United Shipbuilders of the Adriatic) was established, and it acquired the shipyards at Trieste and Monfalcone. CRDA MONFALCONE then built the passenger liners *Neptunia* in 1932 and *Oceani* in 1933. The yard also built two liners for Poland, the *Pilsudski* in 1935 and the *Batory* in 1936.

After the Second World War, CRDA Monfalcone built the passenger liners *Guilio Cesare* in 1951 and the *Raffaelo* in 1965. The shipyard also produced the *Oceanic* in 1965 for the Home Lines. In 1969, CDRA produced four submarines for the Italian Navy, and this was followed by two more boats in 1979. Around 1980, CRDA Monfalcone became ITALCANTIERI MONFALCONE, part of Italcantieri Group of Italian shipbuilders. The yard completed four attack submarines in 1980-2 and the 10,000-ton helicopter carrier *Giuseppe Garibaldi* in 1985.

The shipyard became CANTIERI MONFALCONE under the Fincantieri Group which consolidated all private major Italian shipyards in 1984. Cantieri Monfalcone produced two submarines in 1989, and from 1988 to 1995, it built four additional attack submarines for the Italian Navy. The yard also built the largest cruise ship in the world, the *Grand Princess*, for the P&O Princess Lines in 1997. Cantieri Monfalcone has one dry dock that is 1210ft long and can accommodate ships of up to 40,000 tons displacement. The yard also possesses a 1070ft slipway that can support the construction of vessels up to 140,000 tons displacement.

*Trieste*

Stabilimento Tecnico Triestino (STT) (Technical Establishment of Trieste) was the most important shipyard of the Austro-Hungarian Empire. STT produced nearly all of its capital ships and other major naval vessels since the middle of the nineteenth century. Italy acquired STT at the end of the First World War when that region was ceded to Italy by Austria-Hungary. STT had two shipyards in the Trieste area, one, the San Marco Shipyard, in the western coastal area of Trieste and the other, San Rocco Shipyard, at Muggia, a town just to the south of Trieste. Since being in Italian hands, STT San Marco built the heavy cruiser *Trieste* in 1926 and the passenger liner *Conte Grande* in 1928.

In 1929, STT merged with Cantieri Navale Triestino of Monfalcone to form Cantieri Riuniti dell' Adriatico (CRDA) (United Shipbuilders of the Adriatic). CRDA TRIESTE (San Marco) built the heavy cruiser *Fiume* in 1931, the light cruisers *Luigi Cadorna* (1931), *Muzio Attendola* (1935), and the *Giuseppe Garibaldi* (1937). The yard also produced a total of twenty-seven submarines for the Italian Navy during the period from 1931 to 1940. Prior to the Second World War, CRDA Trieste built the passenger liner *Conte di Savoia* in 1932. Wartime production included the 35,000-ton battleship *Vittorio Veneto* in 1940 and her sister ship, the *Roma*, in 1942. The *Roma* was subsequently sunk by German aircraft in 1943 after Italy had surrendered to the Allied Powers.

Trieste.

After the war, CRDA Trieste built the guided missile cruiser *Giuseppe Garibaldi* in 1962, one frigate in 1969, one submarine in 1969, and one corvette in 1979. During that period, it also produced the passenger liners *Donizetti*, *Rossini*, and *Verdi*, all in 1951, the *Augustus* in 1952, and the *Michelangelo* in 1965. Since 1984, CRDA Trieste came under the Fincantieri Group of Italian Shipbuilders, but it is no longer an important ship construction or repair facility. CANTIERI TRIESTE has three dry docks of 475, 680, and 970ft in length, and with a capacity of ships up to 25,000, 50,000, and 170,000 tons displacement respectively.

*Fiume*
CANTIERI NAVALE QUARNARO (Quarnaro Naval Shipyard) was located at Fiume, a town about 40 miles southeast of Trieste. This territory was ceded to Italy by Austria-Hungary after the First World War. It began building warships for the Italian Navy with two destroyers in 1925 and two more in 1928-9. Quarnaro built one submarine in 1933, and this was followed by two torpedo-boats in 1935-6 and four destroyers in 1937-8. The territory was ceded to Yugoslavia after the end of the Second World War, and Fiume is now known as Rijeka.

*Palermo*
Cantieri Palermo was established during the first half of the twentieth century. Palermo is located on the northwestern coast of the island of Sicily off the southern tip of Italy. Actually not heavily involved in naval construction,

Palermo produced only the light cruiser *Ulpio Traiano* in 1942. In 1966, the shipyard came under CANTIERI NAVALI DEL TIRRENO E RIUNITI (CNTR). Since 1984, the shipyard has been part of the Fincantieri Group of private Italian shipbuilders, and it now specialises in the construction and repair of ships. CANTIERI PALERMO has two dry docks, one 835ft and the other 935ft in length, and these dry docks can accommodate ships up to 80,000 tons and 140,000 tons displacement, respectively. The shipyard also has a 1030ft slipway for vessels up to 160,000 tons displacement.

# 8 Russia

Russia became a major naval power in the late nineteenth and early twentieth century, and it again achieved naval significance during the Cold War. Russia was faced with naval concerns in four widely separated areas, the Baltic Sea, the Black Sea, the Pacific Coast, and more recently the Arctic, which complicated her naval programme. Her long-time enemy in the Baltic was Sweden, and in the Black Sea, Turkey was the primary naval power to contend with. Although Russia competed with British and French interests in the Far East, her greatest antagonist in that area at the beginning of the twentieth century was the fledgling naval power of Japan.

The first serious attempt to establish a navy for Russia was undertaken at the beginning of the eighteenth century by Tsar Peter I (the Great). In 1704, he established the Admiralty Yard at St Petersburg to build warships for the Imperial Russian Navy. By building naval vessels at government facilities, Russia could avoid the need to acquire warships from private or foreign yards. He also established a naval base for the Russian Baltic Fleet on nearby Kotlin Island, which was later named Kronstadt (Kronshtadt). An additional naval shipyard, the New Admiralty Yard, was established adjacent to the original Admiralty Yard in St. Petersburg in 1800 by Tsar Paul I. Later in the nineteenth century, further Admiralty yards were established at Nikolayev and Sevastopol on the Black Sea.

Although naval shipbuilding had begun in Russia as early as the beginning of the eighteenth century, the warships produced were wooden sailing vessels. It was not until the middle of the nineteenth century that naval shipbuilding became a major industry and the construction of ironclad, steam-powered warships was undertaken. Private shipyards, such as the great Baltic Works of St Petersburg, and a number of smaller shipyards scattered throughout Russian coastal regions, began to supplement the in-house production of warships for the Imperial Russian Navy.

Russia acquired several iron and steel warships from foreign countries to learn new technologies in naval construction, as well as to expedite the build-up of the fleet. These included one ironclad frigate from Thames Iron Works, London in 1864 and one unprotected cruiser from Le Havre, France in 1881. Russia later acquired the battleship *Retvisan* (1901) and the protected cruiser *Varyag* (1900) from William Cramp, Philadelphia, the armoured cruiser *Askold* from Krupp Germania, Kiel in 1901, the protected cruiser *Bogatyr* from Vulkan Stettin in 1902, and the battleship *Tsessarevitch* and the armoured cruiser *Bayan I*, both from La Seyne, Toulon, in 1903.

In the Far East, Russia established naval bases at Vladivostok in 1872 and at Port Arthur in 1898 in territory acquired from China. Already concerned by the establishment of the base at Vladivostock, the Japanese considered the acquisition of Port Arthur as a serious threat to their own interests in that region. In 1904, the Japanese laid siege to Port Arthur, and the Russians capitulated early in the following year. The Russian Baltic Fleet, sent by Tsar Nicholas II to lift the siege, arrived too late and therefore headed on to Vladivostock.

In May 1905, the Baltic Fleet, en route to Vladivostok, sailed through the Tsushima Strait between Honshu, the main island of Japan, and Tsushima Island when it ran into the Japanese fleet under the command of Admiral Togo. In a battle that extended over two days, the Russian fleet was decimated, and it finally had to surrender to the Japanese. Russian naval losses during the Russo-Japanese War were staggering. Four battleships, the *Imperator Aleksandr III*, *Borodino*, *Kniaz Suvorov*, and *Imperatritsa Ekaterina II*, were sunk during the Battle of Tsushima. The first-line Russian battleships *Orel* (1904) and *Nikolai I* (1893), as well as the smaller coastal defence battleships *General Admiral Apraxin* (1898) and *Admiral Senyavin* (1895), were captured and subsequently incorporated into the Japanese fleet as war prizes.

In addition to the above mentioned losses, the battleships *Retvizan* (1902), *Pobieda* (1902), *Peresviet* (1901), and *Poltava* (1898), all sunk during the siege of Port Arthur, were salvaged and commissioned into the Imperial Japanese Navy. The Russian protected cruisers *Pallada* (1902), *Novik* (1901), and *Varyag* (1900) were likewise salvaged from Port Arthur and other shallow waters to become units of the Imperial Japanese Navy. After the Russo-Japanese War, Russia undertook a major naval construction programme to replace her wartime losses.

After the advent of the all-big-gun battleship with HMS *Dreadnought* in 1906, Russia began to build her own Dreadnought-type battleships. Four *Gangut* class battleships, *Gangut*, *Petropavlovsk*, *Sevastopol*, and *Poltava*, were laid down in St. Petersburg in 1909 and completed in 1914-15. These ships displaced 24,000 tons and mounted twelve 12in guns in four triple turrets, one forward, one aft, and two amidships. Three similar battleships were laid down at Nikolayev in 1911, of which the *Imperatritsa Mariya* and the *Imperatritsa Ekaterina II* were both completed in 1915 and the *Imperator Aleksandr II* in 1917. A fourth battleship, the *Imperator Nikolai I*, was laid down at Nikolayev in 1914, and although launched in 1916, it was never completed.

In addition to the warships produced by her own shipyards, Russia also acquired several warships from foreign sources, including the armoured cruiser

*Admiral Markarov* from La Seyne, Toulon and the armoured cruiser *Rurik* from Vickers Maxim, Barrow-in-Furness, both in 1908. Russia had also ordered two light cruisers from Schichau at Danzig, but they could not be delivered before the outbreak of the First World War. Those ships were subsequently seized by the German government, and they were incorporated into the Imperial German Navy upon their completion.

Recognising that some of its older shipyards could no longer produce the larger and more modern warships of the Dreadnought era, Russia planned to replace those yards with new, modern shipyards to be constructed with the technical and financial assistance of foreign shipbuilding firms. In 1911, the new Putilov Shipyard in St Petersburg was built with the assistance of the German shipbuilding firm of Blohm & Voss. In the Black Sea region, the British shipbuilding firms of John Brown Clydebank and Vickers Barrow each engineered one of the two new shipyards in Nikolayev. The New Admiralty shipyard in St Petersburg was closed down in 1910, and the Admiralty yard in Nikolayev was gradually phased out after 1912. The original Admiralty Shipyard on Galerny Island continued shipbuilding operations until they were brought to a stop by the Revolution in 1917.

Russia had laid down four additional battleships at St Petersburg in 1912, and these were somewhat larger and more heavily armed than the earlier *Gangut* class. The new *Borodino* class battleships were to displace 32,500 tons and carry twelve 14in guns in the same arrangement as with the *Gangut* class. Those battleships were actually launched in 1915-16, but they were never completed. There was little emphasis on naval shipbuilding immediately after the Revolution, and the existing warships, including the four *Gangut* class and three *Imperatritsa Mariya* class battleships that had been completed, were merely incorporated into the Soviet Navy with changed names.

The two battleships built by the Admiralty Yard (Galerny Island), the *Gangut* and the *Poltava*, were renamed the *Oktyabrskaya Revolutsia* (October Revolution) and *Mikhail Frunze*, respectively. The *Mikhail Frunze* was lost by fire in the early 1920s. The two Russian battleships that were completed by the Baltic Works, the *Sevastopol* and *Petropavlovsk*, became the *Parizhskaya Kommuna* (Paris Commune) and *Marat*, respectively. Of the Nikolayev-built ships, the *Imperatritsa Ekaterina II* was renamed the *Svobodnaya Rossia*. Although obsolete for all practical purposes, the three surviving ships all participated in the Second World War.

It was not until the 1930s that the Soviet government took a renewed interest in developing the navy. The Soviet leader, Josef Stalin, ordered the construction of two new naval shipyards each capable of building two battleships at a time as well as a number of smaller vessels. Both of those shipyards were built in 1932, and they were located where they would have free access to the sea and thereby establish the Soviet Union as a world naval power. One shipyard was built at Severodvinsk near Arkhangelsk (Archangel) on the White Sea above the Arctic Circle, about 450 miles northeast of St Petersburg. The other yard was constructed at Komsomolsk on the Amur River, about 300 miles from the mouth of the river and 600 miles northeast of Vladivostok.

The construction of three new 35,000-ton battleships of the *Sovietski Soyuz* class was begun in the late 1930s, but the outbreak of the Second World War prevented their completion. The ship being built at Nikolayev was only half finished when the city fell to the invading Germans in 1941, and it was destroyed when the Germans were later driven back from the area. Work on the two battleships laid down at Severodvinsk was suspended due to the shortage of steel and other materials needed elsewhere to support the war effort.

The Soviet Union emerged from the war as a much stronger power than she had been before it. As a result of the Allied victory, she was able to retake control of the Baltic nations of Estonia, Latvia, and Lithuania, which Russia lost as a result of the Versailles Treaty after the end of the First World War. The Soviet Union also acquired part of East Prussia from Germany and other territories in eastern Europe, as well as recovering the territory in Manchuria that Russia lost to the Japanese after the Russo-Japanese War. The continued occupation of Poland and other eastern European nations, and the eventual establishment of puppet Communist governments in those countries, enabled the Soviet Union to maintain effective control over all of eastern Europe.

Shortly after the end of the war, the Soviet Union undertook a naval construction programme intended to neutralise the overwhelming naval power of the Western World. The USSR began the construction of a massive fleet of submarines of all types, first conventional, then nuclear-powered, and finally missile-carrying submarines. The Soviet Union also built up its surface fleet, beginning with a dozen light cruisers in the 1950s and some thirty guided missile cruisers from 1960 to 1990. The nation constructed four 22,000-ton missile-carrying battlecruisers in the 1980s, and it built two helicopter carriers in the late 1960s, four 36,000-ton aircraft carriers in the 1970s and 1980s, and one 46,000-ton aircraft carrier in the early 1990s.

With the break-up of the Soviet Union in December 1991, Russia lost some of her naval facilities. The Baltic states of Estonia, Latvia, and Lithuania took over the former Soviet naval bases and shipyards in those areas when those states regained their freedom. Some of the Black Sea naval bases and shipyards are now within the independent nation of the Ukraine. The former Soviet Black Sea Fleet has been divided between the states of Russia and the Ukraine, and between 1995 and 1997, certain units of the fleet were transferred to the Ukraine. Polish independence has likewise deprived Russia of direct control over the naval bases and shipyards in that country.

### The Baltic Sea

#### St Petersburg

Tsar Peter I (the Great) founded St Petersburg in 1703, and he immediately captured the nearby strategically important island of Kotlin from the Swedes. Kotlin lies at the eastern end of the Gulf of Finland, about 25 miles northwest of St Petersburg, and guards the entrance to the city. Peter I established the

The Gulf of Finland.

Admiralty Shipyard at St Petersburg in 1704, and he soon began fortifying the city and Kotlin Island. St Petersburg became the capital of Russia in 1712, and by the middle of the eighteenth century, it had became an important point of entry into Russia for foreign trade. The Neva River at St Petersburg provided excellent features for shipbuilding, and by the latter half of the nineteenth century, three major shipyards were established there.

The three major shipyards at St Petersburg at the beginning of the twentieth century were the Admiralty Yard located on Galerny island, the adjacent New Admiralty Yard, and the Baltic Works across the Neva River from the two Admiralty shipyards. All of these yards produced capital ships for the Tsar's Navy prior to and during the early part of the First World War. Several of those ships were taken over by the Japanese as war prizes after their defeat of the Russian fleet in the Tsushima Straits in 1905. With the advent of the First World War, St Petersburg was given the more Russian-sounding name of Petrograd in 1914, but after the Russian Revolution, the city was renamed as Leningrad after the founder of the Russian Communist movement.

### ADMIRALTY

The ADMIRALTY SHIPYARD was established by Peter I (the Great) in 1704 on the banks of the southern branch of the Neva River on Galerny Island, about two miles southwest of the centre of St. Petersburg. After the establishment of the adjacent New Admiralty Shipyard in 1800, the Admiralty Shipyard became known as the GALERNY ISLAND WORKS to distinguish it from its sister yard. From 1884 to 1891, the shipyard became the FRANCO-RUSSIAN WORKS in view of its joint ownership by a Franco-Russian concern. During the latter half of the nineteenth century, the Galerny Island Works produced five ironclad frigates in 1865-96.

The Galerny Island Works built the protected cruisers *Vitiaz* (1886), *Rynda* (1887), *Pallada* (1902), and *Diana* (1902). The yard also began building battleships in that period, including the *Sevastopol* and *Petropavlovsk* in 1899. After the turn of the century, the Galerny Island Works built the battleships *Orel* (1904), *Andre Pervozvanny* (1910), *Poltava* (1914), and *Gangut* (1915). The

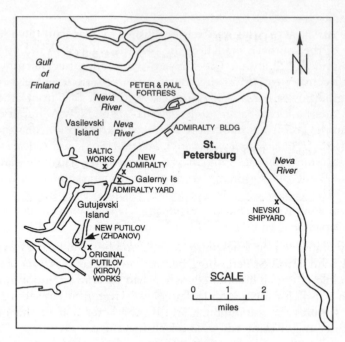

St Petersburg.

*Orel* was captured by the Japanese during the Battle of Tsushima in 1905 and was incorporated into the Imperial Japanese Navy as the *Iwami*.

The Galerny Island Works was one of two shipyards chosen to build the latest Dreadnought battleships for the Imperial Russian Navy. The keels for the *Borodino* and *Ismail* were laid down in 1912, and they were launched in 1915 but were never completed. The ships would have displaced 30,000 tons and carried twelve 14in guns, but shortages of construction material prevented their completion before the Russian Revolution. After the Revolution, the *Poltava* and *Gangut*, which displaced 23,400 tons and carried twelve 12in guns, were renamed *Mikhail Frunze* and *Oktyabrskaya Revolusia* respectively.

The original Admiralty Shipyard (Galerny Island Works) was administratively merged with the New Admiralty Shipyard in 1908 to form the UNITED ADMIRALTY SHIPYARD, but in 1914, the name reverted back to just the ADMIRALTY SHIPYARD. While the New Admiralty Shipyard was gradually phased out at that time, the original Admiralty Shipyard remained in operation after the Revolution. The yard, however, was not involved in any major naval construction between the wars, or even during the Second World War, and it was not until after the war that it resumed the construction of warships. The Admiralty Shipyard built the light cruisers *Aleksandr Nevski*, *Ordzhonikidze*, both in 1951, and the *Aleksandr Suvarov* in 1952.

Soon after the Second World War, a new facility, the SUDOMEKH SHIPYARD, was established adjacent to the Admiralty Shipyard for the construction of submarines. From 1952 to 1961, Sudomekh produced over fifty conventional submarines for the Soviet Navy.

## NEW ADMIRALTY

The NEW ADMIRALTY SHIPYARD was established by Tsar Paul I in 1800 on the east bank of the southern branch of the Neva River, just to the north of the original Admiralty Shipyard. The shipyard was modernised during the mid-nineteenth century to permit the construction of iron and steel vessels with steam engine power. The New Admiralty yard built one ironclad frigate in 1864, and later built two battery ships in 1891-4. The New Admiralty Shipyard then began the construction of more advanced battleships, such as the *Admiral Senyavin* (1895), *Admiral Ushakov* (1895), *Poltava* (1898), and *Oslyabia* (1901).

The battleship *Admiral Senyavin* was captured by Japanese naval forces during the Battle of Tsushima in 1905 and renamed *Mishima* as it became a war prize. The *Poltava* was salvaged by the Japanese after being sunk during the siege of Port Arthur, and it was renamed *Tango* when it also joined the Imperial Japanese Navy. The New Admiralty Shipyard also produced a number of cruisers at the turn of the century, including the armoured cruisers *Dmitri Donskoi* (1885), *Bayan II* (1911), and *Pallada* (also in 1911) and the protected cruisers *Aurora* (1903) and *Oleg* (1904). The *Aurora* had the distinction of firing the shot that signalled the start of the Bolshevik Revolution in October 1917, and it is now maintained in St Petersburg as a museum and memorial to the Revolution.

In 1908, the New Admiralty Shipyard was administratively merged with the original Admiralty Shipyard to form the UNITED ADMIRALTY SHIPYARD, but the combined yards were later renamed just the ADMIRALTY SHIPYARD. The facilities of the New Admiralty Shipyard were not adequate to build the larger, more modern warships contemplated for the Imperial Russian Navy, so it was gradually phased out prior to the Russian Revolution in favour of continuing work at the original Admiralty Shipyard on Galerny Island.

## BALTIC WORKS

The BALTIC WORKS (Baltiyski) was established as a private shipyard at the southern tip of Vasilevski Island near the mouth of the Neva River in 1856, and 10 years later in 1866, it built the ironclad frigate *Kreml* for the Tsarist navy. In 1877, the company officially became the BALTIC CO., but it remained known as the Baltic Works. The shipyard soon began building a number of armoured cruisers for the Imperial Russian Navy, including the *Gerzog Edinburghski* (1877), *Minin* (1878), *Vladimir Monomakh* (1885), *Admiral Nakhimov* (1888), and *Pamiat Azova* (1890). In 1894, control of the shipyard was taken over by the Tsarist government, but it was still managed by a private concern. Baltic Works continued to build armoured cruisers for the Imperial Russian Navy, including the *Rurik* (1895), *Rossia* (1897, and *Gromoboi* (1900).

At the end of the nineteenth century, the Baltic Works began building a series of battleships for the Imperial Russian Navy, including the pre-Dreadnought battleships *General Apraxin* (1898), *Peresviet* (1901), *Pobieda* (1902), *Slava* (1903), *Imperator Aleksandr III* (1903), and *Kniaz Suvarov* (1904). Of these ships, the *Slava* was the only survivor of the Russo-Japanese War. Both the *Imperator Aleksandr III* and the *Kniaz Suvarov* were sunk during the

Battle of Tsushima in 1905. The *General Apraxin*, *Peresviet*, and *Pobieda* were all sunk during the Japanese siege of Port Arthur, but they were subsequently salvaged and incorporated into the Japanese Navy as war prizes.

In 1910, the Baltic Works completed the battleship *Imperator Pavel I*, but having been laid down in 1903 and launched in 1907, it still represented the pre-Dreadnought design concept. During the early part of the First World War, the Baltic Works produced the Dreadnought-type battleships *Sevastopol* (1914) and *Petropavlovsk* (1915), which displaced 23,400 tons and carried twelve 12in guns in four triple turrets along the centreline of the ships. The yard also began work on two additional battleships, the *Navarin* and *Kinburn*, both begun in 1912 and launched in 1915-16. These ships would have displaced 30,000 tons and carried twelve 14in guns, but work had to be stopped on them just before the Russian Revolution due to the shortage of materials.

After the Revolution, the battleship *Sevastopol* was renamed the *Parishaya Kommune* in honour of the Paris Commune, the communist insurrection in Paris in 1871. Likewise, the *Petropavlovsk* was renamed *Marat* after the French revolutionary leader of the eighteenth century, Jean Paul Marat. The Baltic Works was not used extensively for naval construction between the two world wars and in the Second World War, it came under fire from German artillery and air attacks during the siege of Leningrad.

After the war, the newly designated BALTIC YARD 189 built seven of the new light cruisers being produced for the rejuvenated Soviet Navy. These light cruisers included the *Sverdlov* (1950), *Admiral Lazarev* (1951), *Varyag* (1951), *Zhdanov* (1951), *Admiral Ushakov* (1952), *Dmitri Pozharski* (1953), and *Admiral Senjavin* (1954). The Baltic Yard became active again in the 1980's, producing all four of the new 22,000-ton guided missile battlecruisers authorised, the *Kirov* (1980), *Frunze* (1983), *Kalinin* (later *Admiral Nakhimov*) (1988), and *Yuri Andropov* (later *Pyotr Velkiv*) (1992).

## PUTILOV

The Putilov family established the PUTILOV WORKS, a major armaments factory located in the southwestern suburbs of St Petersburg, in 1801. The Putilov Works continued to expand throughout the nineteenth century, to include the establishment of the marine steam engine plant and the construction of a small shipbuilding activity in the harbour area around 1880. To keep up with the increasing demand for larger and more modern warships, a new PUTILOV SHIPYARD was constructed in 1911 with the technical and financial assistance of the German shipbuilding firm of Blohm & Voss. The shipyard was built on landfill at the southern tip of Gutujevski Island, across the canal from the original Putilov Works. When the First World War broke out, several Blohm & Voss engineers were trapped in Russia and had a harrowing time escaping back to Germany.

The Putilov Shipyard completed the light cruisers *Admiral Butakov* and *Admiral Spiridov* in 1916 and two destroyers before the Russian Revolution brought a halt to shipbuilding activity. In 1918, the Putilov Shipyard was renamed the SEVERNY SHIPYARD (Northern Shipyard), and the Putilov armaments plant was renamed the Kirov Works. There was little shipbuilding activity during the 1920s, but early in the 1930s, the Severny Shipyard began to produce pre-fabricated submarine components for assembly at other shipyards. In 1935, the shipyard was again renamed as the ZHDANOV SHIPYARD after a Communist official, and the yard retained that name during the remainder of the twentieth century.

The Zhdanov Shipyard completed the heavy cruisers *Kirov* in 1938 and the *Maksim Gorki* in 1940. These ships displaced nearly 9000 tons and carried nine 7in guns in three triple turrets, two forward and one aft. At the beginning of the Second World War, the Zhdanov Shipyard completed four destroyers for the Soviet Navy before the German invasion and siege of Leningrad interrupted warship production at the yard. After the Second World War, the Zhdanov Shipyard was modernised, and it became one of the most important shipyards for producing warships for the Soviet Navy.

The Zhdanov Shipyard built several destroyers in the 1950s before producing a long line of guided missile cruisers, including the *Admiral Fokin* (1962), *Admiral Golovka* (1963), *Grozny* (1964), *Varyag* (1965), *Admiral Zozulya* (1967), *Vladivostok* (1968), *Vitse-Admiral Drozd* (1968), *Sevastopol* (1968), and *Kronshtadt* (1969). During the 1970s, the shipyard continued building guided missile cruisers, such as the *Admiral Isakov* (1970), *Admiral Nakhimov* (1971), *Admiral Marakov* (1972), *Marshal Voroshilov* (1973), *Admiral Oktyabrsky* (1973), *Admiral Isachenkov* (1974), *Marshal Timoshenko* (1975), *Vasily Chapayev* (1976), and *Admiral Yumaschev* (1977). In the 1980s, the shipyard reverted to the production of guided missile destroyers, completing some twenty such vessels in that decade.

## Nevski

The NEVSKI SHIPYARD was founded during the middle of the nineteenth century on the west bank of the Neva River, about 5 miles southeast of St Petersburg. Being some distance upstream from the mouth of the Neva River at St Petersburg, the Nevski shipyard was limited to the production of relatively small ships. In 1875, it built the armoured cruiser *General Admiral*, and it later produced the protected cruisers *Uzumrud* and *Jemtchug*, both in 1904. From the turn of the century to the time of the Russian Revolution in 1917, the Nevski Shipyard produced over twenty-five destroyers and a number of submarines and auxiliary vessels for the Imperial Russian Navy. In view of its limited capability, the Nevski shipyard was not used extensively for naval construction by the Soviet Navy, completing only one destroyer in 1928.

## Kronstadt

Russia's major naval base in the Baltic Sea was at Kronstadt (Kronshtadt) on the island of Kotlin at the eastern end of the Gulf of Finland near St Petersburg. Commanding the approaches to St Petersburg, Kotlin Island was captured from the Swedes and transformed into a fortress by Peter the Great at the beginning of the eighteenth century. In 1823, a naval base was established at Kronstadt at the eastern end of Kotlin Island, and it became the primary naval base for the Russian Baltic Fleet. Kronstadt was also involved in the construction of minor warships for the Imperial Russian Navy in the latter half of the nineteenth century, but it served mainly as a ship repair and refit facility for the Baltic Fleet.

### Reval

The RUSSO-BALTIC SHIPBUILDING CO. at Reval (now Tallinn) in Estonia built the light cruisers *Svetlana* and *Admiral Grieg* in 1916, as well as several destroyers and submarines during the early part of the First World War. The light cruiser *Krasni Krim* was laid down at Revel in 1913, but it was not completed until 1924, after Estonia had become an independent nation. Russia had earlier used Reval as a naval base and anchorage for the Baltic Fleet, and it was from here that the fleet began its fatal voyage to the Far East to meet its doom at the hands of the Japanese in the Battle of Tsushima in 1905.

### Kaliningrad

After the Second World War, the Soviets established a shipyard near the city of Kaliningrad (Königsberg), the former capital of the old Kingdom of Prussia. The YANTAR SHIPYARD (Kaliningrad 820) built four frigates from 1969 to 1981, and those ships were followed by seven guided missile destroyers in 1985-95 and two guided missile frigates in 1993-8.

### Other Baltic Sea Bases

In the Baltic Sea region, Russia also had naval bases at Helsinki (Helsingfors) and Liepaja (Libau) before Finland and Latvia became independent nations after the First World War. The Soviet Union again used Reval and Libau as naval bases after the Second World War while Estonia and Latvia were occupied by Soviet forces. The bases reverted back to Estonian and Latvian ownership in 1990 when those nations again achieved their independence.

## The Black Sea

### Sevastopol

During the latter half of the eighteenth century and under the leadership of Catherine II (the Great), Russia acquired the Crimean Peninsula and the northern coastline of the Black Sea. Recognising the strategic value of the Crimean Peninsular, the Russians selected Sevastopol on the south-western tip of the peninsular as their primary naval base in the Black Sea area. The site was fortified during the early part of the nineteenth century, and by the end of the century, Sevastopol had become exclusively a naval arsenal (Admiralty shipyard).

The ROPIT SHIPYARD at Sevastopol produced the battleships *Chesma* (1889), *Sinope* (1890), and *Georgi Pobiedonosets* (1896). In 1905, the SEVASTOPOL SHIPYARD built the protected cruiser *Kagul*, later renamed the *Ochakov*. The last and largest major warship built at Sevastopol was the 12,800-ton battleship

The Black Sea.

*Ioann Zlatoust*, which was completed in 1910. By then, naval shipbuilding in the Black Sea region was being concentrated at Nikolayev, leaving Sevastopol to serve primarily as a naval base for the Russian Black Sea Fleet.

### Nikolayev

The port of Nikolayev was established in the eighteenth century at the confluence of the Ingul and Bug rivers about twenty-five miles north of the mouth of the Bug River and about 75 miles northeast of Odessa on the Black Sea. At the beginning of the nineteenth century, an Admiralty shipyard was established at Nikolayev, and the NIKOLAYEV SHIPYARD soon became a major naval shipbuilding facility. In 1889, the shipyard built the battleship *Imperatritsa Ekaterina II*, which was later sunk by a Japanese naval force during the Battle of Tsushima in 1905. The Nikolayev Admiralty Shipyard also produced the battleships *Tri Sviatitelia* (1895), *Rostislav* (1899), and *Kniaz Potemkin* (1904) (later renamed *Panteleimon*).

The *Kniaz Potemkin* was involved in a Communist-inspired mutiny in 1905, and it was later immortalised in the classic Soviet film 'Battleship Potemkin' directed by Sergei Eisenstein. The Nikolayev Shipyard produced the protected cruiser *Pamiat Murkuria* in 1905 and the battleship *Sviatitoi Evstafi* in 1910 before it was closed down in that latter year. Since the facilities were limited and not suited to the production of larger and more sophisticated warships, the Nikolayev Shipyard was replaced by a pair of shipyards in the same area. The Nikolayev (North) and Nikolayev (South) Shipyards were both established with the help of foreign capital and engineering, mostly from British firms.

### NIKOLAYEV (NORTH)

The NIKOLAYEV (NORTH) SHIPYARD was established in 1911 by the Russian Shipbuilding Co. (Russud) with the aid of foreign capital and engineering, especially from John Brown, the famed Scottish shipbuilding company. Often referred to as the RUSSUD SHIPYARD, it produced the battleships *Imperatritsa Mariya* (1915) and *Imperator Aleksandr III* (1917), just before the Russian

Revolution caused a suspension of naval shipbuilding activity. In 1914, the yard laid the keel for the battleship *Nikolai I*, and although the hull was launched in 1916, the could not be completed before the Revolution. Also left incomplete on the building ways was one light cruiser that had been laid down in 1914.

In 1917, after the Russian Revolution, both the Nikolayev North and Nikolayev South yards were renamed Marti North and Marti South, respectively, after a noted communist revolutionary leader. Under the Soviet regime, the MARTI (NORTH) SHIPYARD produced the light cruiser *Admiral Nakhimov* in 1927. Naval shipbuilding at Marti (North) was brought to a halt during the Second World War when the Germans occupied the area after their invasion of Russia in 1941. Nikolayev (North) resumed the production of warships for the Soviet Navy in the 1970s, when it built the 8200-ton guided missile cruisers *Nikolayev* (1971), *Ochakov* (1973), *Kerch* (1974), *Azov* (1975), *Petropavlovsk* (1976), *Tashkent* (1977), and *Tallinn* (1978).

Nikolayev (North) later became known as NIKOLAYEV SHIPYARD 445 (61 Kommuna). The yard produced the 9800-ton guided missile cruisers *Slava* (later renamed *Moskva*) in 1982, *Marshal Ustinov* in 1986, *Chervona Ukraina* (subsequently renamed *Varyag*) in 1990, and the *Admiral Lobov* (1993).

NIKOLAYEV (SOUTH)
The NIKOLAYEV (SOUTH) SHIPYARD was established at the end of the nineteenth century with the aide of foreign capital and engineering. The English firm of Vickers-Barrow was the primary contributor to the technical skills required to build the shipyard. Like Nikolayev (North), the Nikolayev (South) is located south of Nikolayev at the junction of the Ingul and Bug Rivers about 40 miles from the mouth of the Bug River. The Nikolayev (South) Shipyard began building warships at the turn of the century, and in 1907, the yard became known as the NIKOLAYEV NAVY YARD. The yard was soon enlarged to enable it to increase its warship production prior to the breakout of the First World War.

During the war, Nikolayev (South) produced the battleship *Imperatritsa Ekaterina II* in 1915, but it could not complete one light cruiser that had been laid down in 1914. After the Revolution, the Nikolayev Navy Yard became known as the MARTI (SOUTH) SHIPYARD. There was little naval shipbuilding activity in the 1920s, but in the 1930s, there was renewed interest in naval construction by the Soviet regime. In 1932, the Marti (South) Shipyard built the light cruiser *Admiral Lazarev*, which was later renamed *Krasni Kavkaz*. Just at the beginning of the Second World War, the yard produced the heavy cruisers *Molotov* and *Voroshilov*, both completed in 1940. As with the Marti (North) Shipyard, naval construction ceased at Marti (South) during the German occupation of the area during the war.

With its excellent facilities for the construction of large ships, the Nikolayev (South) Shipyard became a major naval construction facility for the Soviet Navy after the Second World War. The shipyard produced the 16,000-ton light cruisers *Dzerzhinski* in 1950 and the *Mikhail Kutusov* in 1953, and it began

building aircraft carriers after that. Nikolayev (South) later became known as
NIKOLAYEV SHIPYARD 444 (Nosenko). The yard built the small helicopter carriers *Moskva* in 1967 and the *Leningrad* in 1968, and these were followed by
the 37,000-ton aircraft carriers *Kiev* in 1975, *Minsk* in 1978, *Novorossiysk* in
1982, and *Admiral Gorshkov* (ex-*Baku*) in 1987. In 1991, the Nikolayev (South)
Shipyard built the 46,000-ton aircraft carrier *Admiral Kuznetsov*, the largest
warship completed by the Soviet Union.

## Kerch

A small shipyard was established at Kerch, a town at the eastern tip of the
Crimean Peninsula, at some time after the Second World War. From 1969 to
1990, the shipyard produced a total of eleven frigates of the 'Krivak I, II, and
III' classes.

## Inland Shipyards

### Gorki

The SORVOMO SHIPYARD began building small warships for the Tsar during
the middle of the nineteenth century. It is located at the confluence of the
Oka and Volga Rivers near the town of Gorki (Niznij Novgorod) about 200
miles east of Moscow. Since the Second World War, Sorvomo has been
involved in the construction of submarines for the Soviet Navy, including the
pre-fabrication of submarine sections that are transported to other shipyards
for final assembly.

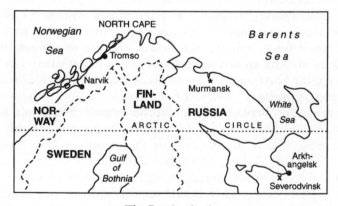

The Russian Arctic.

## Arctic

### Severodvinsk

The SEVERODVINSK Shipyard was established in northern Russia by the Soviet
regime in the 1930s to allow its warships free access to the oceans via the
Barents Sea. Passage of Soviet ships from their Baltic shipyards to the North
Sea was severely constrained by the narrow waters between the Scandinavian

countries. Likewise, Soviet naval units in the Black Sea must pass through the bottlenecks created by the confining Turkish and Greek waters of the Bosporus and Dardanelles, as well as the Straits of Gibraltar, before reaching the Atlantic Ocean. The Severodvinsk Shipyard is located on the Dvina Gulf about 30 miles southwest across the delta of the Dvina River from the port city of Arkhangelsk (Archangel).

In the late 1930s construction was begun on two 35,000-ton battleships of the *Sovietski Soyuz* class, but work had to be deferred during the Second World War due to the shortage of critically needed materials. With the utility of battleships diminished as a result of wartime experience, no further effort was undertaken to complete these ships, and they were broken up on the ways. After the war, Severodvinsk built the light cruisers *Oktvabrskaya Revolutsiya* (1952) and the *Murmansk* (1953), which displaced nearly 16,000 tons and carried twelve 6in guns in four triple turrets.

Since the 1950s, the SEVERODVINSK SHIPYARD 402 has been a major producer of submarines for the Soviet Navy, including nuclear and missile-carrying types. From 1950 until 1963, Severodvinsk produced over one hundred conventional submarines, and it subsequently built over fifty nuclear attack submarines. In 1969, the yard began constructing nuclear-powered ballistic missile submarines, including ten 'Delta I' class in 1969-74, nine 'Delta III' class in 1976-82, seven 'Delta IV' class in 1981-9, and six Type 941 in 1981-9. Severodvinsk continues producing submarines for the Russian Navy with the launching of another nuclear-powered ballistic missile submarine in 1996.

### Archangel and Murmansk
Although Arkhangelsk (Archangel) and Murmansk were not considered as permanent naval bases for Russia or the Soviet Union, they became temporary bases for Allied warships during the Second World War. These warships were involved in the protection of convoys delivering food and war materials to those ports which were the only European entry points into the Soviet Union at that time. There continues to be a naval presence in those areas to provide a measure of security for the Arctic coastline of Russia.

## The East

### Vladivostok
In 1858, under Tsar Alexander II, Russia acquired the eastern coastal region of Manchuria from China as part of the Treaty of Aigun which ended the war between China and her adversaries, England and France. Within two years, the Russians began settling the area and founded the town of Vladivostok. In 1872, they established a naval base there, and by 1917, the Trans-Siberian Railroad had been extended to Vladivostok. In the 1930s, the naval shipyard at Vladivostok built a number of destroyers and submarines for the Soviet Far East Fleet. With the establishment of a shipyard at Komsomolsk in that time frame, Vladivostok was no longer needed for shipbuilding, and it could serve primarily as a naval base for the Soviet Far East Fleet.

## Port Arthur

Russia acquired the Chinese naval base at Lushun (Port Arthur) in Liao-Tung Province, Manchuria in 1898 as a result of a 25-year pact with China. The harbour, which is ice-free throughout the year, provided an excellent anchorage for the Russian Far East Squadron, which was normally based at Vladivostok. In 1904, the Japanese attacked Port Arthur and blockaded the Russian Far East Fleet, consisting of several battleships and cruisers and a sizeable number of destroyers. Nicholas II ordered the Russian Baltic Fleet to the Far East to lift the Japanese siege of Port Arthur, but the base had already capitulated to the Japanese at the beginning of 1905 before the arrival of the Russian Baltic Fleet.

Several Russian warships, including four battleships, were sunk during the siege of Port Arthur, but they were salvaged by the Japanese and incorporated into their own navy. As a result of the Treaty of Portsmouth (New Hampshire) in 1905, Russia ceded her rights to Port Arthur, and Japan retained that base until the end of the Second World War. Soviet forces seized Port Arthur in August 1945, and it held joint control over Port Arthur with China until 1955, when the port reverted to Chinese control exclusively.

## Komsomolsk

The KOMSOMOLSK SHIPYARD was established in the 1930s to provide the Soviet Union with a second major naval shipbuilding activity where their naval units would have free access to the oceans of the world. The Komsomolsk Shipyard is located on the Amur River nearly 300 miles upstream from its mouth and about 600 miles north of Vladivostok. The shipyard began with the construction of destroyers in the late 1930s, and then it built the heavy cruisers *Kaganovich* and *Kalinin* during the Second World War. After the war, the Komsomolsk Shipyard continued to build surface vessels for the Soviet Navy, mostly destroyers and frigates, but it soon began to specialise in the construction of submarines.

Now known as KOMSOMOLSK SHIPYARD 199, the yard built over fifty conventional submarines from 1955 to 1965. From 1958, Komsomolsk began producing nuclear-powered attack submarines, completing over ten such vessels to date. In addition, the yard produced four nuclear-powered cruise missile submarines in 1961-2 and eight 'Delta I' class nuclear ballistic missile submarines in 1969-74. Being located upstream on a river, Komsomolsk is restricted as to the size of warships that can built at that facility.

# 9 The Netherlands

O nce part of the Holy Roman Empire and later occupied by Spanish forces under Philip II, the seven northern provinces of the Netherlands declared their independence and were confederated under the Union of Utrecht in 1579. The Dutch undertook their first voyage to the East Indies in 1595-8, and in 1602, the Dutch East India Company was formed. Turning toward the New World, the Dutch under Henrik Hudson discovered the mouth of the Hudson River in 1609, and in 1623, the permanent settlement of New Amsterdam was founded in that region. During the first half of the seventeenth century, the Netherlands was involved in a number of conflicts with Spain.

The Dutch captured a fleet of vessels transporting silver from Mexico in 1628, and in 1639, Admiral Tromp defeated a Spanish fleet in the Downs. Dutch independence from Spain was finally recognised by the Treaty of Münster and the Peace of Westphalia in 1648. The Netherlands gradually built a new navy under the direction of John de Witt during the latter half of the seventeenth century to defend its colonial empire. During that time frame, a naval shipyard was established at Amsterdam. A series of wars broke out between the Netherlands and England, beginning with the first Anglo-Dutch War in 1652-4, which involved a number of indecisive naval clashes.

In 1664, the British attacked the Dutch colony at New Amsterdam, and after its surrender, the British promptly renamed it New York after the Duke of York. Toward the end of the second Anglo-Dutch War (1665-7), a Dutch squadron under Admiral De Ruyter raided the Royal Dockyards at Sheerness and Chatham on the River Medway, burning English warships and shore facilities. During the third Anglo-Dutch War (1672-4), the British attacked the Dutch merchant fleet in the Channel, causing considerable

The Netherlands.

damage. After peace was restored, the Dutch continued to build up their navy.

By the end of the seventeenth century, the Dutch had a fleet of fourteen ships-of-the-line, mostly two-decked ships with 80-90 guns, but also a few three-decker, First Rate ships with one hundred or more guns. The Dutch also had a number of frigates and smaller naval vessels, including ships of a unique Dutch design known as the fluit (fluyt or flute). The fluit was a long vessel, about the size of a sloop, with a rounded bow and stern. The ship displaced only 100-125 tons, and it carried an average of twenty guns on a single gun deck. The fluit was designed as a merchant vessel with a large cargo-carrying capacity, but it could be adapted as an armed escort vessel or as a coastal defence ship.

In 1701, the Dutch completed their first dry dock at their shipyard in Vlissingen (Flushing). After the War of the Spanish Succession (1701-14), the Netherlands navy declined rapidly, and it was not until the middle of the nineteenth century that interest in the navy was renewed. In 1850, the Koninklijk Instituut voor de Marine (Royal Naval Institute) was established at Breda, but just four years later, it was moved to its present site at Willemsoord near Den Helder. The Dutch naval shipyards at Amsterdam and Flushing converted from sail and wood to steam power and iron along with the rest of the world naval powers. The Flushing yard produced an ironclad frigate in 1853, and then the Amsterdam and Flushing yards shared production for ten wooden, screw-propelled frigates and corvettes in the 1860s.

The Netherlands acquired several turret ships and monitors from various British and French shipyards to learn the new technologies incorporated into these naval vessels, but after that, they produced their own warships. Dutch yards built eleven monitors, six light cruisers, and two turret ships from 1870 to 1890. In the 1890s, the Dutch built ten coastal defence ships ranging in size from 3500 tons to 6500 tons displacement. These coastal defence ships, alternately considered to be protected cruisers or small battleships, were followed by six additional ships of that type during the first decade of the twentieth century.

When the self-propelled torpedo became an important instrument of war, the Netherlands procured a number of torpedo-boats from the Yarrow shipyard at Scotoun on the River Clyde in Scotland. The Dutch then built a total of forty-one torpedo-boats in their own yards. The Netherlands was neutral during the First World War, and its fleet was used primarily to protect its colonies. After the war, the Dutch fleet gradually declined with age. New construction failed to keep pace with those losses, and by the time the Netherlands became involved in the Second World War, the Dutch Navy had only three light cruisers, eight destroyers, thirteen submarines, and a number of smaller warships that were completed by 1940.

The Netherlands lost two light cruisers and several destroyers and smaller ships during the Second World War, but after the end of the war, the Dutch completed one light cruiser left incomplete during the German occupation. To build up its fleet in the post-war period, the Netherlands acquired a number of surplus warships from Great Britain and the United States. Those ships included the British aircraft carrier HMS *Venerable*, procured in 1948 and renamed *Karel Doorman*, four destroyers from Great Britain, six destroyer escorts from the United States and two submarines each from Great Britain and the United States.

In the 1950s, the Dutch built two light cruisers, twelve destroyer escorts, four submarines, and a number of smaller vessels in its own shipyards. The Dutch navy now consists of four attack submarines and twenty guided missile frigates, all produced in Dutch yards.


ROYAL SHIPYARDS AND NAVAL BASES

The KONINKLICHE WERF AMSTERDAM (Amsterdam Royal Shipyard) was established around 1660, and by the end of the seventeenth century, it had produced over ten ships-of-the-line as well as a number of frigates and smaller ships. Amsterdam continued to produce wooden sailing vessels for the Dutch Navy until the middle of the nineteenth century, when it began to convert to steam power and iron construction. The shipyard built one wooden screw-propelled frigate in 1867, seven wooden screw-propelled corvettes from 1860-72, four sloops from 1864-82, one turret ram in 1870, and six monitors from 1869-78.

Amsterdam then built six light cruisers in 1876–86. Those light cruisers were followed by the protected cruiser *Sumatra* in 1890 and the coastal defence battleships *Koningin Wilhelmina der Nederlanden* (1892), *Piet Hein* (1894), *Holland* (1896), *Utrecht* (1898), *Koningin Regentes* (1900), *Hertog Henrik* (1902), *Marten Tromp* (1904), *Jacob van Heemskerck* (1906), and *De Zeven Provincien* (1909). Amsterdam also built some ten torpedo-boats for the Dutch Navy before the First World War. The Amsterdam Naval Shipyard was turned over to private ownership before the war, and it became the Nederlandsche Dok en Scheepsbouwe Maatschappij (Netherlands Dock and Shipbuilding Co.).

A KONINKLICHE WERF (Royal Shipyard) was established at Vlissingen (Flushing) before the end of the seventeenth century, and in 1701, a dry dock was built at that installation to facilitate the repair and maintenance of their warships. The town of Flushing is located on the southern coast of the island of Walcheren where it commands the mouth of the Schelde River leading to the important Belgian port city of Antwerp. During the eighteenth and early nineteenth centuries, the shipyard assisted the Amsterdam shipyard in the construction, repair, and maintenance of the wooden sailing warships for the Dutch Navy. In the middle of the nineteenth century, Flushing converted to the construction of steam-powered and ironclad warships. In 1853, Flushing completed the ironclad 74-gun ship-of-the-line *De Ruyter*, and in 1861, it built the wooden screw-propelled frigate *Adolf Hertog van Nassau*.

Den Helder is located on the northwestern point of the mainland of the province of North Holland near the North Sea coast. Den Helder consists of a naval complex encompassing Willemsoord and Nienwediep. The WILLEMSOORD RIJKSWERF (National Shipyard), in addition to its primary mission of ship repair and maintenance, built five patrol boats for the Dutch Navy in 1954–5. An important naval base for the Dutch Navy, Willemsoord is also the site of the KONINKLIK INSTITUUT VOOR DE MARINE (Royal Institute for the Navy), the Dutch naval academy. HELLEVOETSLUIS was a relatively minor facility capable only of ship repair and maintenance. Hellevoetsluis is located in the Voorne District on the Haring Waterway between Voorne and Overflaakkee in the province of Holland, about thirteen miles southwest of Rotterdam.

In addition to its main naval base at Den Helder, the Netherlands had several small naval stations near Amsterdam and Rotterdam and along its seacoast to support its coastal defence and patrol operations. Overseas, the Dutch had naval bases at Batavia (now Jakarta) and Surabaya on the island of Java and at Sabang on Sumatra in the Dutch East Indies (now Indonesia). These naval bases were intended primarily for refuelling and resupply purposes, and they could perform only limited repair and maintenance on Dutch warships operating in that region.

## PRIVATE SHIPYARDS

The major private shipyards that have been engaged in naval shipbuilding for the Netherlands are all concentrated in the area of Rotterdam, its most important port and shipbuilding centre. Those shipyards included the Royal Schelde Co. at Flushing, the Fijenoord Dock and Shipyard Co. at Schiedam, the Rotterdam Dry Dock Co., the Burgerhouts Shipyard, and the P. Smit Jr. Machine Works and Shipyard.

ROYAL SCHELDE

The KONINKLICHE MAATSCHAPPIJ DE SCHELDE (Royal Company of the Schelde) was founded in 1875, and four years later, it built its first torpedo-boat for the Royal Netherlands Navy. The ROYAL SCHELDE CO., as the shipyard became to be known, produced an additional five torpedo-boats in 1881-8, and these were followed by three light cruisers in 1896-1900. The yard then produced eight torpedo-boats from 1902 to 1907 and six destroyers in 1911-13. Royal Schelde began the production of submarines for the Royal Netherlands Navy in 1906, and it completed three of those craft before the outbreak of the First World War. Wartime production included four torpedo-boats and four submarines.

In the inter-war years, the Royal Schelde Co. produced five submarines in 1920-3. The light cruiser *Java* was built at the yard in 1925, and it was followed by one submarine in 1926 and one destroyer in 1928. The shipyard then produced three submarines for the Royal Netherlands Navy in 1931-6 and one submarine for Poland in 1939. During this period, the yard also built three passenger liners in 1928-31 for the Rotterdamse Lloyd Line. Royal Schelde completed two destroyers before Holland was invaded by Germany in 1940. During the German occupation, the yard built six minesweepers for the German Navy in 1944, and it began work on four destroyers, but they could not be completed before the end of the war.

After the war, the Royal Schelde Co. completed the passenger liner *Willem Ruys* for the Rotterdamse Lloyd Line in 1947. The ship had been laid down in 1938, but it could not be competed before the German invasion. The shipyard concentrated on the production of merchant ships, completing forty-three cargo vessels and eleven tankers from 1949 to 1975. During that period, Royal Schelde built the passenger liner *Kungsholm* for Sweden in 1953. The yard resumed the production of warships with the completion of four anti-submarine warfare destroyers in 1955-7. In 1963, Royal Schelde merged with Rotterdam Dry Dock to form Rhine Schelde Shipyards (RS), but it continued to operate under its own name.

Royal Schelde built two frigates in 1967 before the next series of corporate changes. In 1970, Rhine Schelde merged with Wilton-Fijenoord, and in the following year, that combination merged with Verolme United Shipyards of Rotterdam to form RHINE SCHELDE VEROLME SHIPYARDS (RSV). Verolme United Shipyards was the ship repair facility that in 1960 completed the British aircraft carrier *Vengeance*, which had been launched by Swan Hunter in 1944, after the ship had been sold to Brazil and renamed the *Minas Gerais*. Rhine Schelde Verolme built ten *Kortenaer* class frigates in 1978-83, but in 1983, Rhine Schelde Verolme went bankrupt. Royal Schelde thereupon became an independent corporation again as the Koninklijke Schelde Groep B.V. (Royal Schelde Group, Inc.)

The SCHELDE SHIPBUILDING Division of the Royal Schelde Group is now responsible for the design, engineering, construction, and conversion of naval surface vessels, including frigates, auxiliary oil replenishment ships (AOR), and amphibious troopships. Two other operating divisions of the group are the Scheldepoort Repair yard, which is responsible for ship repairs, and Schelde Gears, which produces reduction gear boxes for turbine engines. Schelde Shipbuilding produced two *Jacob van Heemskerck* class frigates in 1985-6, and eight *Karel Doorman* class frigates in 1990-5. Royal Schelde laid down two guided missile destroyers in 1998, which are scheduled for delivery in 2002-5.

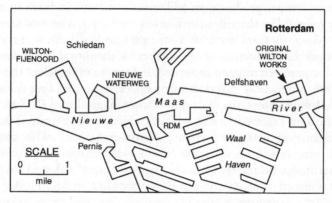

Rotterdam.

## WILTON-FIJENOORD

In 1823, Gerhard M. Roentgen, a former Dutch naval officer, founded the Nederlandsche Stoomboot Maatschappij (Netherland's Steamboat Co.) at Rotterdam. Two years later in 1825, Roentgen became involved in shipbuilding, and the ETABLISSEMENT FIJENOORD was created. Fijenoord initially concentrated on the production of steamships for use by its steamboat company, but it later get involved in the production of warships. The shipyard built two monitors in 1871 and two more in 1876-8. Fijenoord then built the small coastal defence battleships *Evertsen* in 1894, *Friesland* in 1896, *Geldenland* in 1898, and *De Ruyter* in 1901.

From 1879 to 1916, Fijenoord produced a total of twenty-six torpedo-boats for the Royal Dutch Navy, and during the First World War, the yard built two destroyers. Fijenoord produced nine submarines from 1916 to 1923, three 'K' class submarines in 1924, one 'O' class submarine in 1925, two sloops in 1925, and two destroyers in 1928. From 1927-30, the shipyard also produced three submarines for foreign customers. In 1929, Etablissement Fijenoord merged with Wilton's Machinenfabrik en Scheepswerf N.V. to form Dok en Werf-Maatschappij Wilton-Fijenoord N.V. (Wilton-Fijenoord Dock and Shipyard Co. Inc.).

Bartel Wilton had established the WILTON'S MACHINENFABRIK EN SCHEEPSWERF N.V. (Wilton's Machinery Shop and Shipyard Co.) in 1854, using the municipal dry dock at Rotterdam to do repair work on ships out of the water. In 1907, Wilton built its first dry dock at the shipyard, and the yard continued repairing ships and engines prior to and during the First World War. In 1918, Wilton procured a tract of land at Schiedam, a western suburb of Rotterdam, as the possible site of a future shipyard.

In 1920, Wilton acquired a 40,000-ton floating dry dock from the German firm of Blohm & Voss. Originally intended for the Austro-Hungarian shipyard at Pola, the dry dock was delivered to Wilton before it could be seized by the Allies for war reparations under the Versailles Treaty. After a harrowing voyage under tow in the North Sea, the dock was delivered to the Nieuwe Waterweg where it was manoeuvred into its prescribed berth. Wilton's Machinenfabrik en Scheepswerf N.V. merged with Etablissement Fijenoord to become DOK EN WERF MAATSCHAPPIJ WILTON-FIJENOORD B.V. (Wilton-Fijenoord Dock and Shipyard Co., Inc.) in 1929. Wilton-Fijenoord settled on the land previously acquired by Wilton at Schiedam, and it constructed a new shipyard on the north bank of the Nieuwe Maas River

In 1936, Wilton-Fijenoord built the 6500-ton light cruiser *De Ruyter*, which was later sunk in the Battle of the Java Sea in February 1942. The yard then completed the liner *Zaandam* for the Holland-America Line in 1939. Wilton-Fijenoord produced three submarines in 1939-40, but one fell into German hands when the country was invaded in May 1940. After the war, Wilton-Fijenoord resumed its production of passenger liners for the Holland-America Line with the 12,000-ton *Westerdam* in 1946 and the twin 15,000-ton liners *Ryndam* in 1951 and *Maasdam* in 1952, respectively. The yard also built the 15,000-ton Polish liner *Stephen Batory* in 1952.

In 1953, Wilton-Fijenoord completed the 9700-ton light cruiser *De Ruyter*, which had been laid down in 1939. Wilton-Fijenoord then built two 'O' class submarines in 1954, one destroyer in 1957, two destroyer escorts in 1955-7, and three minesweepers in that same period. The yard also produced the liner *Statendam* for the Holland-America Line in 1957. In addition, Wilton-Fijenoord built one frigate for Nigeria in the 1950s. Wilton-Fijenoord built two further submarines for the Royal Dutch Navy in 1965-6 and two more submarines for foreign nations in 1965.

In 1970, Wilton-Fijenoord merged with Rhine Schelde Shipyards (RS), but it continued to operate under its own name. This was followed a short time later by another merger with Verolme United Shipyards to form Rhine Schelde Verolme Shipyards (RSV) in 1971. Wilton-Fijenoord produced three corvettes for Indonesia in the late 1970s, and it built two *Kortenaer* class guided missile frigates for the Royal Dutch Navy in 1981-2. The yard then produced two submarines for foreign customers in 1982-3.

Rhine Schelde Verolme Shipyards went bankrupt in 1983, and the Dok en Werf Maatschappij Wilton-Fijenoord B.V. again became an independent company. Shipbuilding continued with the production of two submarines for Taiwan in 1988. In 1998, RDM Technology Holding Co. acquired the shares of Wilton-Fijenoord, but the shipyard continues to operate independently as a subsidiary of RDM Technology Holding Co., as does RDM Submarines.

*Rotterdam Dry Dock*

In 1856, a shipyard was established near Rotterdam by the Scottish engineer, Duncan Christie, and his sons, David and George. The CHRISTIE & SONS shipyard was located in the village of Delfshaven on the north shore of the Merwe River (later called Nieuw Maas River) just to the southwest of the city of Rotterdam. The shipyard produced a small number of merchant vessels before the Christies took on Arnoldus Nolet as a partner in 1865, and the yard became CHRISTIE & NOLET. The addition of another partner, Franciscus de Kuijper (Kuyper), caused another name change to CHRISTIE, NOLET & DE KUIJPER in 1870. During this period, the shipyard produced a number of steamships, small warships, and dredgers.

In 1879, Christie, Nolet & De Kuyper went bankrupt, and the company was taken over by the SOCIETÉ ANONYME DES FONDERIES ET CONSTRUCTIONS NAVELES DE LA MEUSE (Society of Foundries and Naval Construction of the Meuse, Inc.), a Paris-based concern. In 1880, a new company, MAATSCHAPPIJ 'DE MAAS', was formed to take over the holdings of Christie, Nolet & De Kuyper. Although the name of the new company was changed in 1881 to Maatschappij Schoonerloo, the name of a local town, it reverted back to Maatschappij 'de Maas' two years later in 1883. In 1899, the company acquired an 11-acre plot of land at Heyplaat on the southern bank of the Nieuw Maas River, and the facilities of the shipyard were then transferred to the new location.

In 1902, the ROTTERDAMSCHE DROOGDOK MAATSCHAPPIJ N.V. (RDM) (Rotterdam Dry Dock Co. Inc.) was founded as the successor to Maatschappij 'de Maas'. In the following year, RDM procured two floating dry docks from the Scottish firm of William Hamilton of Port Glasgow. Those docks, referred to as Prins Hendrik Docks Nos. 1 and 2, could accommodate ships of up to 3000 tons and 7500 tons, respectively, and they were inaugurated into service in 1904. By 1909, RDM had three slipways of up to 360ft in length and nearly 40,000ft² of covered shop space. In 1911, the shipyard was extended westward by the acquisition of nearly four additional acres of land at the fishing village of Pernis, and a new slipway was added to the shipyard at that time.

Rotterdam Dry Dock was electrified in 1911, and in 1913, two electric cranes were installed at the yard. By the beginning of the First World War, its workforce was up to 2600 employees. RDM built twenty-two cargo ships up to 1914, and an additional twenty-one cargo ships during the war. As construction materials became scarce toward the end of the war, shipbuilding was reduced in favour of other products, but after the war, shipbuilding was resumed. In 1920, the yard completed the 20,000-ton passenger liner *Scythia*, which was launched by Vickers Barrow, but could not be completed by that firm due to a labour strike in Great Britain. Rotterdam Dry Dock built the twin 17,400-ton liners *Leerdam* and *Spaarndam* for the Holland-America Line in 1921-2.

In 1922, the 19,000-ton Prins Hendrik Dry Dock No.3 was built at the shipyard for the company's own use, and in 1924, the yard was further expanded with additional slipways, travelling cranes, and office space. During this period, shipbuilding demands dropped off, and Rotterdam Dry Dock had to cut its workforce in half down to 1300 workers. In 1925, RDM took over 'De Nieuwe Waterweg' Shipbuilding Co., a ship repair facility at Schiedam in the western suburbs of Rotterdam, that had been established in 1914. 'De Nieuwe Waterweg' produced a number of merchant ships during and immediately after the war, and its acquisition increased the production capability of RDM significantly.

In 1929, RDM received a contract to build three submarines for the Royal Netherlands Navy, its first effort in naval shipbuilding. In 1930, the yard had over 3000 workers, but in the following year, its workforce had dropped to under 2000 men. The capacity of the shipyard was increased in 1933 by the Prins Hendrik Dock No. 4, a floating dry dock that was built at its Nieuwe Waterweg facility. Rotterdam Dry Dock received a big boost in 1938, when it built the 36,700-ton passenger liner *Nieuw Amsterdam* for the Holland–America Line. In 1939, Rotterdam Dry Dock received an order to build the 9700-ton light cruiser *De Zeven Proviciën* (The Seven Provinces), one of two ships of the *De Ruyter* class authorised at that time. The keel of the ship was laid in 1939, but work was suspended upon the German invasion of Holland in 1940.

Rotterdam Dry Dock completed one submarine for Poland in 1939, and this was followed by two 'O' class submarines built for the Dutch Navy in 1940. Two additional 'O' class submarines were still under construction at the time of the German invasion of Holland in 1940, and these were subsequently completed for the German Navy in 1941. One destroyer was completed by the yard in 1940, but it was sunk and later salvaged by the Germans. Another destroyer was completed for the German Navy in 1942. During the Second World War, the shipyard was forced to produce four torpedo-boats and eight minesweepers for the Kriegsmarine. Work had begun in 1942 on two destroyers for the German Navy, but these ships were never completed before the end of the war.

The Rotterdam Dry Dock shipyard suffered some damage during the war, but restoration was immediately begun after the end of the war. The yard was enlarged at the time, and its workforce had soon reached over 6000 workers as ship construction work boomed. In 1948, RDM procured its eighth floating dry dock, the 32,000-ton capacity Prins Bernhard Dock, from Greenock, Scotland, and it was put into service one year later in 1949. Rotterdam Dry Dock Co. built four passenger liners under 20,000 tons displacement, seven tankers, and three cargo ships from 1945 to 1955. The yard completed the light cruiser *De Zeven Provincien* in 1953, and it then produced two destroyers in 1954-8.

In 1959, Rotterdam Dry Dock built the 37,800-ton passenger liner *Rotterdam*, the fifth ship to bear that name. Resuming its production of submarines, the yard built two such craft in 1960-1. Rotterdam Dry Dock Co. merged with the Royal Schelde in 1963 to form RHINE SCHELDE SHIPYARDS (RS), but it still continued to operate under its own name. Further mergers took place in 1970 when RS combined with Wilton-Fijenoord in 1970 and with Verolme United Shipyards in 1971 to form RHINE SCHELDE VEROLME

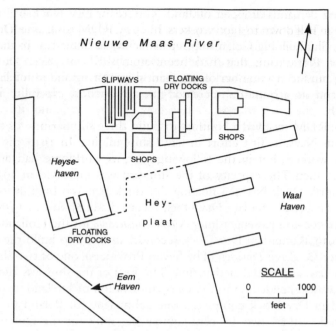

RDM Shipyard in 1990.

SHIPYARDS (RSV). RSV built the 17,500-ton liner *Cunard Adventurer* in 1971, and in 1972, the yard produced two additional submarines. Rhine Schelde Verolme went bankrupt in 1983, and shipbuilding at RDM was severely curtailed.

Rotterdam Dry Dock Co. completed four attack submarines for the Netherlands Navy in 1992-4. In 1996, the holdings of RDM were taken over by RDM Technology Holding Co. B.V., and RDM SUBMARINES was established as its operating marine branch. RDM Technology Holding Co. acquired the shares of Wilton-Fijenoord in 1998, taking over control of shipbuilding in the Rotterdam area.

### Other Private Dutch Shipyards

The NEDERLANDSCHE DOK EN SCHEEPSBOUWE MAATSCHAPPIJ (Netherlands Dock and Shipbuilding Co.) was established to take over the Amsterdam Royal Dockyard, which had been privatised prior to the First World War. During the war, the yard did not produce any major naval vessels for the Royal Dutch Navy. Between the wars, Amsterdam built one 'O' class submarine in 1925 and the light cruiser *Tromp* in 1937. The shipyard began construction on the light cruiser *Jacob van Heemskerck* in 1939, but it could not be completed before the German invasion in 1940. The ship was finally completed after the war. The Amsterdam yard built four destroyers 1956-8 and three frigates in 1967 for the Royal Dutch Navy.

The BURGERHOUTS SHIPYARD played only a minor role in naval shipbuilding for the Royal Dutch Navy. It produced three destroyers in 1926-7 and another two in 1929-30. The MACHINEFABRIK EN SCHEEPSWERF VAN P. SMIT, JR. (P. Smit Jr. Machine Works and Shipyard) was also of little significance in warship production for the Netherlands Navy. After completing the passenger liner *Noordam* in 1938, P Smit began construction of a 'K' class frigate in 1939. The ship was launched in 1941 and completed in 1942 while the Netherlands was under German occupation. After serving in the German Navy, the frigate was returned to the Netherlands at the end of the war, and it was finally commissioned in the Dutch Navy in 1946.

# 10 Scandinavia

The Scandinavian tribes became a major naval influence in Europe at the end of the ninth century when hordes of Norsemen from the Scandinavian peninsula and the Kingdom of Denmark began raiding the British Isles and the European mainland. These so-called 'Vikings' pillaged and plundered many cities, towns, and villages along their route of destruction, but they also established settlements in fertile areas of the British Isles and in central Europe that were in sharp contrast to their own rugged environment.

The Norsemen from the western half of the Scandinavian Peninsula (now Norway) were perhaps the earliest Vikings to begin raiding expeditions against other European nations. They first occupied the islands off Northern Scotland in the late eighth century and then drove down the western coast of Scotland to Ireland, which they invaded and eventually occupied during the ninth century. The Norwegian Vikings continued their raiding expeditions southward along the Atlantic coast of France and the Iberian Peninsula, into the Mediterranean, and then along the coast all the way to the southern coast of France. They also sailed westward to establish settlements in Iceland, Greenland, and Labrador, eventually reaching Newfoundland in their explorations.

The Norsemen from the eastern half of the Scandinavian peninsula (now Sweden) drove eastward to the Baltic and south to the Caspian and Black Seas. They established settlements in Russia, including one at Kiev, and went as far south as Constantinople. The Danes concentrated their efforts along the coastlines of Friesland, France, and England and pillaged cities and towns along European rivers as far as Hamburg on the Elbe, Paris on the Seine, and Nantes on the Loire during the ninth century. They also established settlements in Normandie and East Anglia during the same period, and they finally conquered England in 1013. A great Anglo-Scandinavian kingdom, including Norway and parts of Sweden, was then established under the Danish king Knut I (Canute).

The Vikings made their forays in unique, oar-propelled 'longships'. These were long, narrow, relatively light craft having a shallow draught, but with excellent sea-keeping qualities. They were usually 80-100ft long, pointed at both ends and often had the head of a dragon or other fierce creature mounted above its bow to frighten its foes. The ships were manned by 40-60 oarsmen. The long boat had one large square sail to assist in its voyages across the seas, but the ship was manoeuvred by its oarsmen during battle and when coming to land.

The political histories of the Scandinavian nations continued to be interwoven after the Viking era. Norway and Sweden subsequently became separate kingdoms, but were they united in 1319. They then joined the Kingdom of Denmark in a Scandinavian union as a result of the Treaty of Kalmar in 1397. Ruled by Danish kings for the next 125 years, Sweden finally broke from Denmark in 1523, but it was not until 1814 that Norway separated from Denmark. Then followed an uneasy union between Norway and Sweden for another 90 years before Norway became totally independent in 1905.

## NORWAY

After the Viking era, the naval power of Norway gradually diminished into insignificance at the time in came under the influence of Sweden and then Denmark. Norway became part of Sweden in 1319 and part of the Scandinavian confederation from 1397 to 1523. Although united with Sweden by a common king from 1523 until 1905, Norway exercised some degree of political independence after becoming separated from Denmark and establishing its own constitution in 1814. Norway began to build a navy to protect her sizeable merchant marine and established naval bases to support her fledgling navy. A naval shipyard was established at Horten on the west side of the Oslo Fjord about 40 miles south of Oslo, and Norway had several excellent private shipyards that could also provide warships for her navy.

During the mid-nineteenth century, Norway undertook a programme to build a modern fleet by procuring steam-powered warships from foreign sources. Norway purchased the coastal defence battleships *Harald Haarfagre*, *Tordenskjold*, *Norge*, and *Eidsvold* from Armstrong Elswick in 1896-1900. Other foreign acquisitions included several destroyers and torpedo-boats from Schichau Elbing around the turn of the century and three submarines from Krupp Germania in 1913. Other warships in the Norwegian Navy were built by Norwegian shipyards before and after the First World War.

Norway had been neutral during the First World War and she tried to maintain her neutrality at the outbreak of the Second World War. She was, however, caught in a power play between Great Britain and Germany, and this led to the German invasion of Norway in April 1940 and its subsequent occupation by German forces until the end of the war. Once her sovereignty had been restored, Norway began to build up its navy from surplus British and

Scandanavia.

Canadian vessels, including five destroyers, twelve frigates, and five submarines. In addition, Norway was awarded three former German U-boats at the end of the war. Norway later purchased six submarines in 1964-6 and six more in 1989-92, all from the German Nordseewerke Emden.

### Naval Shipyards and Naval Bases

The HORTEN NAVAL SHIPYARD was the only naval shipyard established by Norway. The shipyard began as a naval base at the town of Karl-Johansvaen, which was then fortified and expanded into a naval shipyard, early in the nineteenth century. The naval base and shipyard now takes its name from the larger nearby town of Horten, located on the west bank of the Oslo Fjord about 40 miles south of the capital city. Horten began building wooden warships for the Norwegian Navy in the middle of the nineteenth century, including two wooden screw-propelled frigates in 1856-60 and three wooden screw-propelled corvettes in 1855-62. From 1863 to 1903, Horten produced two monitors and seven gunboats, and it built the small protected cruisers *Viking* in 1891 and *Frithjof* in 1896.

Prior to the outbreak of the First World War, Horten completed three destroyers for the Norwegian Navy. After the war, Horten built six submarines from 1923-9 and four frigates in 1936-8. One destroyer, begun in 1939, was severely damaged during the German occupation and was not completed until 1948. After the war, Horten built five guided missile frigates in 1966-8. These ships, together with the twelve submarines purchased from German yards in the post-war era, constitute the major part of the current Norwegian Navy.

The main naval bases for the Norwegian Navy are located at Horten, Kristiansand, Bergen, Trondheim, and Narvik, all strategically strung along the coastline of the country. Starting with Horten on the Oslo Fjord, these bases run westward around the southern tip of Norway and then northward along the Norwegian Sea. Smaller naval stations are located at other strategic points and extend as far north as the Arctic region.

### Private Shipyards

Norway has several private shipyards that are capable of producing warships, but the most important is the FREDRIKSTAD MEKANISKA VERKSTED (mechanical works). Fredrikstad is located at the mouth of the Glama (Glommen) River on the eastern shore of the Oslo Fjord about 60 miles south of Oslo. With nearly all naval construction orders going to Horten Naval Shipyard, Fredrikstad actually produced only one frigate for the Norwegian Navy in 1939. While Norway was still under Swedish influence, the Swedish shipyard at NORRKÖPING, about 40 miles south of Stockholm, produced a monitor for the Norwegian Navy in 1868.

### SWEDEN

Sweden was the more dominant power on the Scandinavian peninsula, having acquired Norway in 1319 and then maintaining dominance over that kingdom until 1814. Even after 1814, the Swedish king also had the Norwegian crown until 1905, when Norway achieved its total independence. Sweden herself was ruled by the King of Denmark from 1397 until 1523. The union with Denmark had been unpopular with the citizenry of Sweden, and considerable animosity had arisen between the two populations. In 1523, the Swedes broke away from Danish rule and elected Gustavus I Vasa as their king, thereby establishing the so-called 'New Sweden'. Sweden began to build up a navy and established a number of naval bases along its coastline.

Early in the sixteenth century, Sweden established a naval shipyard at Stockholm. During the mid-sixteenth century, there were a series of wars between Sweden and Denmark in which Sweden achieved a number of naval victories. By the end of that century, the Swedish navy held the balance of power among the fleets of the Baltic nations, and it continued to grow in strength in the seventeenth century. In 1634, King Gustav I founded the Swedish Royal Navy College at Näsby and continued to build up the Swedish fleet. During the seventeenth century, Swedish shipyards turned out twenty frigates with 40-50 guns, fourteen ships-of-the-line with 60-72 guns, one 88-gun ship, and the great First Rate *Stora Kronan* mounting over 120 guns.

One of the ships built in this period was the proud 64-gun *Vasa*, completed at Stockholm in 1628. On her maiden voyage she foundered just outside the harbour when a sudden gust of wind caused her to heel over, water rushing in through her open lower gun ports and capsizing her. The ship was rediscovered in 1956 and subsequently raised to be restored in a Stockholm museum as one of the now more famous ships in history.

In the eighteenth century, Sweden continued to be the dominant naval power in the Baltic. Around 1790, Sweden was involved in a war with Russia that resulted in several inconclusive naval battles. By the end of the eighteenth century, Sweden had achieved control of the Baltic Sea south of the Bay of Finland. In the nineteenth century, Sweden's navy began to decline, and by the middle of the century, it was down to two small 2600 to 2800-ton steam-powered, screw-driven battleships, the *Karl XIV Johan* and *Stockholm*, and a number of smaller vessels. Those other warships included two screw driven corvettes, seven wooden sailing ships-of-the-line, two wooden sailing frigates, and seven sloops.

With the threat of Russian naval expansion in the Baltic at the latter half of the nineteenth century, Sweden began the construction of several small coastal defence battleships, cruisers, monitors, and other smaller vessels at various naval and private shipyards. Sweden, like the other Scandinavian countries, maintained its neutrality during the First World War. After the war, Sweden began to modernise its fleet with a number of warships from various native shipyards. These ships included two coastal defence battleships, one light cruiser, and a number of destroyers, submarines, and frigates. Sweden again remained neutral in the Second World War, and warship production during the war consisted of several destroyers, submarines, frigates, and smaller vessels. In the post-war era, Sweden produced a number of additional destroyers, submarines, and corvettes to supplement its existing fleet.

### Naval Shipyards and Naval Bases

Sweden had naval shipyards at Stockholm, Karlskrona, and Gothenburg, but only the first two were equipped for building ships while Gothenburg remained a ship repair and maintenance facility. STOCKHOLM NAVAL SHIPYARD was the first Swedish naval shipyard, and it produced many of the wooden sailing ships-of-the-line, frigates, and smaller warships since the sixteenth century. Stockholm produced three gunboats in 1877-9 and nine First Class torpedo-boats in 1882-1903. The shipyard also built three submarines in the period prior to the First World War.

### KARLSKRONA NAVAL SHIPYARD

In 1679, Admiral Hans Wachtmeister, Chief of the Swedish Navy, recommended the establishment of a naval shipyard near the naval base of Blekinge on the southeast coast of Sweden. Upon the approval of the proposal by King Karl XI, land was procured on the island of Trossö and nearby

Lindholmen on the mainland. From 1680-4, three ships-of-the-line were built at the Blekinge naval base, but before operations were shifted to Trossö upon completion of the shipyard facilities at that location, which included three slipways. At about that time, the shipyard was named KARLSKRONA NAVY YARD after the name of a nearby village.

From 1684 to 1709, Karlskrona produced twenty ships-of-the-line, including the 108-gun *Konung Karl* in 1694 and thirteen frigates. Early in the eighteenth century, the shipyard employed about 500 workers. In 1724, Karlskrona built the 230 × 50ft 'Christoffer Polhem Dock', the first dry dock built in Sweden, and in 1729, it acquired a 25-ton capacity mast crane from the N. J. Swahn Co. From 1710 to 1782, the workload at the yard slowed down, and only thirteen Second and Third Rate ships-of-the-line and ten frigates were produced during that period.

In 1756, work was begun on a planned complex of ten dry docks radiating outward from a common basin. By 1780, half of the complex with five dry docks had been completed, and plans for the additional five docks were dropped. In addition to the expansion at Karlskrona, new slipways were added at Lindholmen in 1763, and one of those slipways was covered by the large barn-shaped 'Vasa Shed'. This would allow ships to be built indoors and protected from the elements. In 1782, Fredrik Henrik af Chapman became manager of the Karlskrona shipyard, and he introduced the technique of building large vessels in sections. Using this technique, the yard produced ten 62-gun ships-of-the-line and ten 40-gun frigates in three short years, from 1782-5.

After this short burst of production, work at Karlskrona again began to decline, and for the next 36 years from 1786-1822, the yard produced only two 74-gun ships-of-the-line, in 1799 and 1819. During that period, the shipyard produced one 40-gun frigate in 1803, but it was kept busy producing nearly fifty smaller naval vessels. Karlskrona began using dry docks for the construction of naval vessels early in the nineteenth century. In 1822, Karlskrona built its first steam-powered vessels, two postal paddle steamers. The yard built its first steam-powered warship, a corvette, in 1841, and in 1847, it built its first screw propeller-driven ship, another corvette.

Karlskrona built one screw-driven frigate in 1862 and a screw-driven corvette in 1870. In 1874, Karlskrona acquired a 50-ton capacity crane from James Taylor & Co., Britannia Engine Works, Birkenhead, England for lifting heavy objects on to ships under construction. During that same year, a large workshop building with two slipways was constructed at the shipyard to allow ships to be completely built and assembled in one building. Karlskrona built three gunboats in 1877, and nine torpedo-boats in 1891-1902. In 1903, the 'Oscarsdoken' (Oscar's Dry Dock) was completed at the yard. Continuing with warship production, Karlskrona produced six additional torpedo-boats in 1907-10 and four submarines in 1914-16.

Before 1919, the workers at Karlskrona were hired by the Swedish Navy and had no representation on the naval management staff, but during that year, they became members of a trade union that afforded them some protection. The workload decreased after the end of the First World War, and by 1923, the

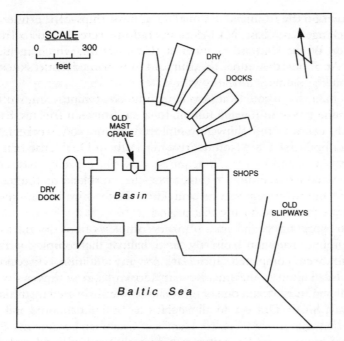

Karlskrona in 1900.

yard was down to 1600 workers. Karlskrona produced two additional submarines in 1921 and another four such boats from 1926-30. Turning back to surface vessels, the shipyard built three destroyers in 1932-19. Wartime production included four coastal type submarines in 1942-4

The workforce at Karlskrona had grown from 1600 workers in 1939 to over 2100 workers in 1945, not including an administrative staff of nearly 150 employees. In 1945, the MARINVERKSTÄDERNA (MVK) (Marine Workshops), with a civilian Work Manager, was established over the industrial segment of the shipyard. This placed the shipbuilding effort outside of the naval structure, but still within the overall command of the Swedish Navy. The shipyard was now permitted to take orders from private customers, which greatly stabilised its workload during slack periods of naval construction.

In the post-war period, further improvements and modernisation of the yard was begun, and in 1948, a Works Council was established to provide greater representation of the workers in the management process. Karlskrona built four submarines from 1956-61, and during this period, a new 100-ton capacity travelling crane was acquired for the yard in 1959. In 1961, the Marine Workshops at the yard was privatised, and shipyard then became KARLSKRONAVARVET A.B. (Karlskrona Shipyard Co.), which is addressed below.

### Private Shipyards

#### Malmö
Since the mid-nineteenth century, Sweden has relied heavily on the shipbuilding capacity of its private shipyards to supplement the warship

production of its naval shipyards. One of the most important private shipyards in Sweden is KOCKUMS MEKANISKA VERKSTADS AKTIEBOLAG (Kockums Mechanical Works Co.), located at Malmö on the southern tip of Sweden. The Kockums Works was founded in 1840 by Frans Henrik Kockum on a plot of land he owned on the town's waterfront. In 1842, the facility at the time was basically a boiler factory with fifty-two employees, but Kockums soon decided to get into shipbuilding. In 1851, Kockums received municipal approval to build a dry dock at the site, and that dock was completed seven years later in 1858. Next came two slipways and a small shipbuilding workshop.

Kockums completed its first ship, a 700-ton steam-driven cargo vessel in 1873, and it produced the first torpedo-boat for the Swedish Navy two years later in 1875. Kockums built one gunboat in 1877, and then it undertook an expansion programme adding six new slipways and several additional workshops. The armoured cruisers (coastal defence battleships) *Tapperheten* and *Manligheten*, were completed at the yard in 1903 and 1904 respectively. These ships displaced about 3700 tons and carried two 8.3in guns and six 6in guns. The yard produced three destroyers in 1908-12. In 1913, the shipyard was moved to a location closer to the port after a fire destroyed much of the original shipyard.

From 1875 to 1914, Kockums had built a total of 114 ships with an aggregate displacement of 64,000 tons. By 1914, the shipyard had a total of 1200 employees. Turning to submarine production, Kockums built two submarines of Italian design in 1914, and these were followed by three more of the same type during the First World War. The coastal defence battleship *Gustav V den Femta*, which had been laid down before the outbreak of war, was finally completed in 1922. After the war, Kockums became one of the pioneers in the use of electric welding in shipbuilding. The yard was further expanded in 1923, and it built one frigate in 1927 and one destroyer in 1932.

Returning to submarine production, Kockums built nine submarines in 1938-41 and an additional twelve boats during the Second World War. By 1939, Kockums had a workforce of 2400 workers, and in 1940, the yard built the first fully-welded ocean-going cargo ship in the world, the M/T *Braconda*, for Norway. In 1941, Kockums built four torpedo-boats for the Swedish Navy, and it completed fourteen submarines from 1940-3 at the rate of one per quarter. After the war, Kockums built one frigate in 1948, and in that year, the yard began another expansion programme with the addition of two 25,000-ton capacity slipways and another large dry dock. By 1951, Kockums had become one of the most productive shipyards in the world.

A naval drawing office was built at Kockums in 1954 to permit the design, engineering, and technical support for the ships that it produces. During that same year, a new 65,000-ton capacity shipbuilding berth (No. 8) was also constructed at the shipyard. Kockums built one destroyer in 1957, but the yard was then beginning to specialise in submarine construction. Kockums resumed submarine production with two conventional submarines in 1956-7. In 1961, shipbuilding berth No. 7 was expanded to accommodate ships of up

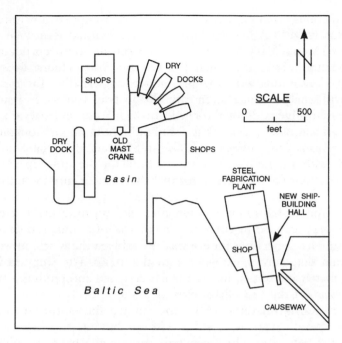

Karlskrona in 1990.

to 130,000 tons displacement. One year later, the shipyard delivered a 81,000-ton tanker, the largest vessel produced at the yard to date.

In 1967, Kockums designed a submarine for prolonged submersion, and the yard then built two submarines in 1968-9. A large crane and workshop No. 8 were added to the shipyard in 1974. In the early and mid-1970s, Kockums was delivering super tankers of over 350,000-ton displacement, LNG carriers, and other large vessels at a production rate of nearly ten ships a year. By 1978, however, workload was beginning to decline, and the shipyard had to lay off its workers by the hundreds. This downward trend continued until 1982, when the shipbuilding business began to pick up again. After completing the advanced cruise liners *Celebration* and *Jubilee* in 1986, Kockums decided to discontinue the production of commercial vessels. This caused another personnel reduction of 900 workers.

The year 1987 turned out to be a banner year for Kockums. The yard had just been selected to build six Kockums Type 471 submarines for the Australian Navy after a stiff international competition. This immediately led to the establishment in 1987 of the Australian Submarine Corporation (ASC) as a subsidiary of Kockums Naval Systems, Celsius Group to build that type of submarine in Australia. In addition to Kockums Malmö and ASC, Karlskronavervat is now also part of Kockums Naval Systems, Celsius Group. By 1990, KOCKUMS MALMÖ had built over 600 vessels, including more than one hundred warships. The shipyard continues to produce submarines for the Swedish Navy, completing three attack submarines in 1996-7.

*Karlskrona*

KARLSKRONAVARVET AB evolved from the privatisation of the Marine Works of the Karlskrona Navy Yard in 1961. Under the new corporate set-up, union representatives were included on the management board of the company. Continuing with the production of warships for the Swedish Navy, Karlskrona produced seven torpedo-boats in 1965-6, two submarines in 1968, and twelve additional torpedo-boats in 1972-6. In 1970, control of the shipyard was taken over by the Swedish State Holding Company, and in 1977, Karlskrona came under the Swedish Shipyards Association. In 1977, a new plant with a central workshop was built for the ship repair section of the yard. Karlskrona built eight patrol boats for various foreign navies in 1978-81.

In 1980, the workforce was down from the wartime high of over 2100 people in 1945 to 1000 in 1980 and 700 in 1983. In 1978, Karlskrona began building submarine sections for eventual assembly at the Kockums shipyard in Malmö, and this activity extended into the 1990s. The shipyard built two coastal corvettes in 1984-5, and in 1989, it designed and produced the coastal corvette *Göteborg*, the first of that class of vessel.

In 1990, Karlskronavarvet AB came under the corporate control of Kockums Naval Systems, Celsius Group, but it still operates as an independent activity. The shipyard produced three further coastal corvettes of the *Göteborg* class in 1990-1. In addition to shipbuilding, Karlskrona is in the lead for naval development work. The firm is a pioneer in the construction of ships with fibre-reinforced plastic hulls and the development of unmanned, remote-controlled magnetic and acoustic minesweepers for Sweden and the United States. Karlskronavarvet currently has four corvettes under construction with scheduled delivery dates of 2001-3.

*Göteborg*

LINDHOLMENS MEKANSKA VERKSTAD OCH VARF (Lindholmen Mechanical Works and Shipyard) is located at Göteborg (Gothenburg) on the southwestern coast of Sweden. The yard produced the coastal defence battle-ships *Svea* (1886), *Göta* (1891), *Niord* (1899), *Dristigheten* (1900), *Aran* (1902), and the *Oscar II den Andra* (1907). Lindholmens also built one torpedo-gunboat in 1896, one First Class torpedo-boat in 1904, and two destroyers in 1917.

GÖTAVERKEN (Göta Works), also at Göteborg, built one destroyer in 1911, and this was followed by the coastal defence battleships *Sverige* in 1917 and *Drottning Viktoria* in 1922. The shipyard then produced one frigate in 1927, the light cruiser *Gotland* in 1934, two destroyers in 1936-41, and two frigates in 1942. After the Second World War, Götaverken produced the light cruiser *Tre Kronor* in 1947 and three destroyers in 1955-9.

Another Göteborg shipyard, ERIKSBERG MEKANSISKA VERKSTAD, built two destroyers in 1939-41 and one frigate in 1942. Post-war production included the light cruiser *Göta Lejon* in 1947 and two destroyers in 1956-9.

*Stockholm*

BERGSUNDS MEKANISKA VERKSTAD OCH VARF (Bergsund Mechanical Works and Shipyard) at Stockholm built the coastal defence battleships *Thule* in 1893, *Oden* in 1897, *Thor* in 1899, and *Vasa* in 1902. Other naval shipbuilding around the turn of the century included the armoured cruiser *Fylgia* in 1905, three torpedo-gunboats in 1898-9, and five First Class torpedo-boats in 1887-1903. Bergsund also built two submarines in 1911-15 and a number of small naval vessels for the Swedish Navy prior to the First World War. The NÖRRKÖPING shipyard, about 40 miles south of Stockholm, built four monitors in 1865-71 and five gunboats in 1872-5. Other private shipyards engaged in naval construction included ORESUNDSVARVET, which produced one frigate and a number of smaller vessels during the Second World War.

## DENMARK

Of the Scandinavian countries, Denmark was perhaps the most advanced politically and militarily. It had a formal kingdom prior to the ninth century while various Norse tribes occupied the Scandinavian Peninsula. Denmark's Viking forces invaded England and France and established settlements in East Anglia and Normandie during the ninth century. In 1013, Sweyn I conquered England, and in the following year, a great Anglo-Scandinavian kingdom was established under Knut I (Canute). In 1375, the Danes persuaded Sweden, which was already united with Norway, to join in a Scandinavian Union under the Danish king. This union lasted until 1523 when Sweden broke away from Denmark and re-established its own monarchy.

During the fifteenth century, a naval base and naval shipyard was established at Copenhagen, which earlier in that century had become the seat of the king of Denmark. Denmark controlled the narrow sound between the Danish island of Sjaelland (Zealand) and Sweden, and it began to exact tolls on trade between western Europe and the Baltic region which had to pass through the sound. This led to a series of conflicts in the fifteenth and sixteenth centuries with the Hanseatic League, which had interests on both sides of the bottleneck. After peace had been restored, Denmark prospered as foreign trade grew rapidly in the sixteenth and seventeenth centuries.

During the seventeenth and eighteenth centuries, Denmark was constantly at war with Sweden, over which it tried to regain control but without success. In this time frame, Denmark had a sizeable fleet consisting of many ships-of-the-line of various rates, including a number of first rate ships mounting one hundred or more guns. At the beginning of the nineteenth century, Denmark allied herself with other European powers against Great Britain to thwart Britain's claim of the right to search ships at sea. This led Britain to attack the Danish Navy in the Battle of Copenhagen in 1801, and again in 1807, destroying or capturing much of the Danish fleet. Denmark was never able to fully recover from that loss, and it remained a second-rate sea power thereafter.

### Naval Shipyards and Naval Bases

In recent times, Denmark had only one naval shipyard, COPENHAGEN ROYAL
SHIPYARD, which had produced many of the Danish wooden sailing ships-of-
the-line, frigates, and smaller naval vessels of the past. In the nineteenth and
twentieth centuries, nearly all Danish warships were built by Copenhagen or
were procured from foreign shipyards. Copenhagen built two ironclad frigates
in 1863-4, and it then produced the coastal defence battleships *Lindormen*
(1868), *Gorm* (1870), *Odin* (1872), *Helgoland* (1878), *Iver Hvitfeldt* (1886), *Skjold*
(1896), *Herluf Trolle* (1899), and *Olfert Fischer* (1903).

Copenhagen also produced two screw-driven frigates in 1860-2, one sloop
in 1861, and one screw-driven corvette in 1871. The shipyard then built one
light cruiser in 1882, the protected cruisers *Valkyrien* (1888), *Hekla* (1890), and
*Heimdal* (1894), and three First Class torpedo-boats in 1896-8. After the First
World War, Copenhagen began the construction of submarines for the Danish
Navy, completing seven of these craft from 1930 to 1939. Copenhagen laid
down two destroyers early in the Second World War, but they were not
completed until 1947. After the war, it produced six torpedo-boats in 1946,
four submarines in 1954-64 and two attack submarines in 1970.

### Private Shipyards

While most Danish naval construction was performed by the Copenhagen
Royal Shipyard, a few warships were contracted from private shipyards, both
foreign and domestic. BURMEISTER & WAIN of Stockholm built the protected
cruiser *Gejser* in 1892. AALBORG VAERFT on Lim Fjord in the northern end of
the Jylland (Jutland) Peninsula produced two frigates in 1963, one frigate in
1976, and this was followed by three guided missile frigates in 1980-2.
SVENDBORG VAERFT, located on the southeastern shore of the island of Fyn,
built one frigate in 1963 and four frigates in 1991-2. Several additional frigates
were produced by private yards, including one by AARHUS FLYDEDOK in 1962
and two by HELSINGÖRS J. & M. in 1966-7.

# 11 Other European Nations

## SPAIN

Prior to the fifteenth century, Spain consisted of a number of kingdoms and small states often competing with one another for power. These states included Asturias (later León), Navarre, Aragon, Castile, Catalonia, and Valencia. Sancho III the Great of Navarre added Aragon to his kingdom at the beginning of the eleventh century, but it was not until the marriage of Queen Isabella of Castile to Ferdinand II of Aragon in 1479 that much of what is now Spain was united into one nation. In 1492, unification of Spain was completed with the conquest of the Moorish kingdom of Granada at the southeastern section of the Iberian Peninsula.

During the reign of Alfonso X the Wise of Castile in the latter half of the thirteenth century, the first significant step was taken to build a navy in Spain by the establishment of an Admiralty. A naval shipyard was established at Cádiz on the southern Atlantic coast after its capture by Alfonso X in 1262. A shipbuilding industry had already been in existence by that time, and the shipyards were turning out galleys and then galleons, mostly for trade. With Spanish overseas explorations sponsored by Queen Isabella, and the subsequent discovery of the New World at the end of fifteenth century, Spain was soon thrust into becoming a major sea power.

Spain and Portugal.

When English pirates began plundering Spanish galleons bringing back gold and other treasures from the New World, Spain was forced to arm her ships and often provide warships as armed escorts. Antagonism between Spain and England heightened in 1587 with the destructive English raid on Cádiz, which at that time was the main port of Spanish treasure ships returning from the New World. A naval squadron under the command of Sir Francis Drake entered the harbour and burned the ships in port as a pre-emptive strike against an armada being formed to invade England.

Philip II vowed to put an end to English sea power, and in 1588, he reconstituted his fleet of ships for the invasion of England. While sailing up the English Channel, the Spanish Armada was outmanoeuvred by the British fleet, and the Spanish were forced to abort their invasion attempt. The Armada headed north into the North Sea, and there it encountered severe storms which resulted in the loss of many ships. During its return to Spain around the northern coast of Scotland, the Armada was further devastated by additional storms in the North Atlantic. Despite this setback, Spain remained a significant naval power until the nineteenth century.

In 1805, a combined French and Spanish fleet was defeated by a British fleet under the command of Lord Nelson at Trafalgar. In 1808, Spain was occupied by Napoleon, and for the next six years, the nation was involved in a struggle for independence, which it finally achieved in 1814. With its declining naval power, many of Spain's American colonies were achieving their independence, further eroding Spain's influence in the world. The final blow came in 1898 with the Spanish-American War. American naval victories in Manila Bay and off Santiago, Cuba decimated what was left of the Spanish fleet. As a result of the war, Spain lost the Philippines and Puerto Rico to the United States, as well as Cuba, which won its independence.

In addition to its primary naval shipyard at Cádiz (also known as Carraca), Spain constructed naval shipyards at Ferrol at the northwestern tip of the country and at Cartegena on the Mediterranean coast. Warships were also built by a private shipyard at Bilbao on the Bay of Biscay in the northern part of the country. In addition to warships built in Spanish yards, Spain acquired a number of warships from private yards in other countries.

### Naval Shipyards

The CÁDIZ NAVAL SHIPYARD, Spain's oldest, is located on the southern Atlantic coast of Spain, about 60 miles north of the southern tip of Spain. Cádiz began building galleons and eventually frigates and ships–of–the–line since before the fifteenth century. Cádiz converted from wooden sailing vessels to iron and steel ships driven by steam power in the nineteenth century. The shipyard built four light cruisers in 1881-7, the protected cruiser *Marques de la Ensenada* in 1890, the armoured cruisers *Emperador Carlos V* in 1895 and *Princesa de Asturias* in 1896, and the protected cruiser *Estramadura* in 1900. Naval construction by Cádiz during the twentieth century was limited to one frigate in 1936 and two minesweepers in 1955.

The FERROL NAVAL SHIPYARD is located on the northern Atlantic coast of Spain, about 30 miles south of the northwest tip of Spain. Ferrol also began building wooden sailing vessels, but then it became the leading Spanish producer of iron and steel, steam-driven warships. The yard built one wooden screw-propelled frigate in 1864 and two ironclads in 1863-9. Ferrol produced four light cruisers in 1881-7, and it then completed the protected cruiser *Alfonso XIII* in 1891, the armoured cruiser *Cardenal Cisneros* in 1897, and the protected cruiser *Reina Regenta* in 1906.

In the early part of the twentieth century, Ferrol built the battleships *España* (1914), *Alfonso XIII* (1915), and *Jaime I* (1921). The shipyard then produced the anti-aircraft cruiser *Mendez Nuñez* in 1925 and the light cruisers *Almirante Cervera* and *Galicia*, both in 1927, and the *Miguel de Cervantes* in 1930. In 1936, Ferrol completed the 10,700-ton heavy cruisers *Canarias* and *Baleares*, the largest warships ever built in Spanish yards. From 1937 to 1943, the yard produced six frigate minelayers, and after the war, Ferrol produced eight frigates in 1946-51, nine anti-submarine frigates in 1953-6, and three fast frigates in 1959-60.

The CARTEGENA NAVAL SHIPYARD, like the other Spanish naval shipyards, also began with wooden sailing ships and then converted to iron and steam in the nineteenth century. Cartegena produced one wooden screw-propelled frigate in 1864, one ironclad frigate in 1867, and four light cruisers in 1879-88. Further construction included the protected cruiser *Lepanto* in 1892 and the armoured cruiser *Cataluna* in 1900. Cartegena built one frigate in 1923, and this was followed by fourteen destroyers from 1924 to 1936. After the Second World War, Cartegena built three submarines in 1947-54, two destroyers in 1950-1, five minesweepers in 1953-4, and six corvettes in 1954-9.

### Private Shipyards

Spain's only private shipyard that was involved in the construction of major warships for the Spanish Navy until the late twentieth century was the BILBAO SHIPYARD. Bilbao is located on the Bay of Biscay along the northern coast of Spain, about 70 miles west of the French border. Bilbao produced the armoured cruisers *Infanta Maria Teresa* in 1890 and the *Vizcaya* and *Almirante Oquendo*, both in 1891.

Since 1950, most naval shipbuilding in Spain has been carried out by EMPRESA NACIONAL BAZÁN at their yards in Ferrol, Cartagena, and Cádiz. BAZÁN FERROL built one destroyer in 1959, thirteen guided missile frigates from 1973-94, and the 17,200-ton helicopter carrier *Principe de Asturias* in 1988. Four more guided missile frigates have been ordered from Bazán Ferrol for delivery in 2002-6. BAZÁN CARTAGENA produced eight frigates from 1950-79, eight attack submarines from 1973-86, and four guided missile frigates in 1978-80. Bazán Cartagena also provided seven frigates for the Portuguese Navy in 1970-5. The least productive yard, BAZÁN CÁDIZ, built two frigates for the Spanish Navy in 1959-60.

### Foreign Acquisitions

With only a limited shipbuilding capability, Spain was required to obtain part of her naval strength from outside sources. Several ironclads were purchased from British and French shipyards. Blackwall (London) provided one ironclad frigate in 1864 and two light cruisers in 1881. Armstrong Elswick built two protected cruisers for Spain in 1886, and in 1890, the French yard of La Seyne built the battleship *Pelayo* for Spain.

With the advent of the torpedo-boat at the end of the nineteenth century, Spain purchased a number of these vessels from foreign sources. Those ships included a total of twelve torpedo-boats from the British yards of John Brown Clydebank, Thornycroft and Yarrow, three from German yards, and one each from La Seyne and Normand in France. Spain later acquired three submarines, two from Italy in 1938 and one from Germany in 1942. After the Second World War, the United States turned over two *Fletcher* class destroyers to Spain in 1957.

## PORTUGAL

Even thought it was known for its navigators and colonisation in the far reaches of the world, Portugal never became a significant naval power. Portugal shared the Iberian Peninsula with Spain, and its history closely paralleled that of its neighbour. There were often close royal family ties through marriage, but there was also frequent conflict between the two countries. Once associated with the Spanish states of Castile and León,

Portugal became an independent state in the twelfth century when it broke away from León. In 1317, Diniz (Denis), son of Alfonso X of Castile, began to build a navy for Portugal with the assistance of a Genoese admiral.

In 1340, Portugal assisted Spain in driving out the Moslems from the southern part of the Iberian Peninsula, but then engaged in warfare with Spain throughout the remainder of the fourteenth century. During the fifteenth century, Portugal began to explore the west coast of Africa, and by 1446, it reached Sierra Leone. Portuguese explorers also visited the islands off the African coast, including the Madeiras, Canaries, and Azores. In 1458-71, Portugal sent military expeditions into Morocco and captured Tangier and Arzila. Continuing down the west coast of Africa, the Portuguese discovered Angola in 1482, and they soon began colonising that territory. Portugal established its sovereignty over Angola in 1617, and later it established a naval base at Luanda, earlier known as S. Paulo de Loanda.

In 1488, the Portuguese rounded the Cape of Good Hope and reached the east coast of Africa, which opened the gateway to India. Portugal sent its first expedition to India, headed by Vasco da Gama, in 1497. By that time, Columbus had discovered the New World, and Spain claimed all lands discovered on the far side of the Atlantic Ocean. This claim was later limited by the Treaty of Tordesillas in 1494 to lands over 1100 miles west of the Cape Verde Islands. This limitation left the eastern tip of South America open to others, and Portugal was quick to seize the opportunity. In 1500, Portuguese explorers discovered Brazil and claimed it for their country.

Vasco da Gama founded the town of Mozambique on the east cost of Africa in 1498, and the Portuguese began to settle that area in 1506. As the settlement expanded, it eventually became the colony of Portuguese East Africa with its capital at Mozambique. Portugal also established colonies at Diu and Goa on the west coast of India in the early part of the sixteenth century, and Goa was subsequently declared to be the capital of 'Portugal-East'. The Portuguese then sent expeditions to the Moluccas (Spice Islands) in the Malay archipelago. Continuing eastward around the southern coast of China, the Portuguese established a colony at Macao near the British Crown Colony of Hong Kong. The Portuguese fortified their holdings along the trade routes, and they were able to drive off incursions by the Dutch and other nations attempting to seize those possessions for their own use.

Portugal was occupied by Spain under Philip II from 1580 until 1640, when the Duke of Braganza drove out the Spanish and became John IV of Portugal. Strife continued between Spain and Portugal, but in 1668, Spain finally recognised the sovereignty of Portugal. Although at first neutral, Portugal in 1703 joined the Grand Alliance with England, Holland, Denmark, Austria, and some German states in their war against France during the War of the Spanish Succession. In retaliation, France sacked Rio de Janeiro in the Portuguese colony of Brazil in 1711. Peace was restored in 1715, and Portugal prospered during the remainder of the eighteenth century.

Portugal was attacked by Napoleon on several occasions in 1807-10 after he had occupied Spain, but peace was restored with Napoleon's defeat in 1814.

Portugal established Brazil as a kingdom under its empire in 1815, but this did not last long with Brazil becoming an independent nation in 1825. Portugal had become a republic in 1910, and in 1914, it joined the Allies against the Central Powers. In the Second World War, however, Portugal maintained its neutrality.

Portugal had a naval shipyard at Lisbon and a naval base at Luanda in Angola on the west coast of Africa. Lisbon produced most of the wooden sailing ships used by Portugal over the years, and in 1862-4, the shipyard produced two sloops-of-war. These were followed by six gunboats, the protected cruiser *Rainha Dona Amelia*, and one destroyer from 1869 to 1903. In addition to the output of warships from Lisbon, Portugal ordered several warships from foreign shipyards late in the nineteenth century, including the coastal defence battleship *Vasco de Gama*, obtained from Thames Iron Works (London) in 1876. Portugal also acquired several protected cruisers from outside sources, including one from Orlando Livorno in 1896, two from Le Havre in 1898, and one from Armstrong Elswick, also in 1898.

In 1933-4, Portugal acquired four sloops from Hawthorn Leslie at Newcastle-upon-Tyne and two destroyers from Yarrow Scotstoun. The Lisbon naval shipyard then produced two sloops and three destroyers in 1935-6, based on the design of the ships they had just received from Britain. After the Second World War, Portugal procured three submarines from Great Britain in 1948, and those ships were followed by two 'River' class frigates from Britain in 1949. Portugal then acquired from the United States four minesweepers in 1955 and two frigates (destroyer escorts) in 1957. Also in 1957, Portugal ordered one fast anti-submarine frigate from Castellammare di Stabia in Italy. More recent naval acquisitions included three submarines from Dubigeon-Normandie Nantes and four frigates from Ateliers et Chantiers de Nantes, all in 1967-9. Portugal also procured seven frigates from Empresa Nacional Bazán Cartagena in 1970-5 and three frigates from Blohm + Voss Hamburg in 1970. In 1991, Portugal acquired two guided missile frigates from Howaldtswerke Kiel and another one from Blohm + Voss.


## AUSTRIA-HUNGARY

Austria, once part of the Holy Roman Empire, became an empire in itself in 1804, just two years before the Holy Roman Empire was dissolved by Napoleon Bonaparte. At that time, the Empire of Austria included the Kingdom of Hungary, and it extended to the Adriatic Sea. As a result of the Treaty of Paris following Napoleon's defeat in 1814, Austria reacquired the Illyrian provinces which had been earlier lost to Napoleon. This territory included Trieste and a strip of land along the Dalmatian coastline south to the border of Albania. In 1867, Austria and Hungary formed the joint Austro-Hungarian Empire under the Hapsburg Emperor Franz Joseph.

Austria-Hungary established a navy and undertook a naval construction programme around the middle of the nineteenth century. To begin with,

Austria–Hungary in 1914.

Austria acquired several warships from foreign shipyards, including two steam frigates and a corvette from the Venice Arsenal. A major naval shipyard was established at Pola, and naval bases were set up at Zara, Sebenico, Gravosa and Cattaro along the Dalmatian coast. Several commercial shipyards were also engaged to produce warships for the Austro-Hungarian fleet, the most noted of which was the Stabilimento Tecnico Triestino at Trieste. Other private shipyards that produced warships for Austria–Hungary included the Cantiere Navale Trestino at Monfalcone near Trieste and Danubius Shipyard at Fiume.

Austria–Hungary quickly recognised the value of the new Whitehead self-propelled torpedo, and in 1875-9, it acquired three torpedo-boats from British yards. After gaining the technical knowledge of their construction, the Pola Naval Shipyard began producing torpedo-boats of their own design. Austria–Hungary continued the procurement of new torpedo-boats and destroyers from foreign sources, such as the German shipyard of Schichau at Elbing and the British firm of Yarrow, while also producing newer models at Pola and other domestic yards. By 1913, Austria–Hungary had a fleet of some seventy torpedo-boats and twenty-five destroyers, of which more than two thirds were produced by domestic shipyards.

As the international situation began to deteriorate during the early part of the twentieth century, Austria–Hungary kept up with the armaments race and accelerated its own naval construction programme. The rate of battleship production was increased to an average of two per year from 1910 to 1914. With the outbreak of the First World War, the naval construction programme for even newer and more powerful battleships was cancelled in favour of higher priority land warfare armaments. After the war, the Austro-Hungarian Empire was required to turn over all of its navy to the Allies under the 1919 Treaty of St. Germain-en-Laye. The empire was then broken apart into the smaller independent republics of Austria and Hungary, and all of its territory along the Adriatic coast was lost to either Italy or Yugoslavia.

The POLA NAVAL SHIPYARD was established in the 1860s, and it completed one corvette and one sloop in 1869. The shipyard then produced two ironclad ships in 1873-8 and the barbette ship *Kronprinz Erzherzog Rudolf* in 1889. Pola built the protected cruisers *Kaiserin Elisabeth* in 1892, *Zenta* in 1899, *Aspern* in 1900, and *Szigetvan* in 1901, and it completed the battleship *Monarch* in 1898. After the turn of the century, Pola built the armoured cruiser *Sankt Georg* in 1905 and the protected cruiser *Admiral Spaun* in 1910, but then the yard was used mainly for warship refitting and repair work. Pola was lost to Italy as a result of the Allied victory in the First World War.

The STABILIMENTO TECNICO TRIESTINO (STT) at Trieste was by far the greatest producer of major warships for the Austro-Hungarian fleet, and it was often regarded as a naval shipyard. The shipyard was established at the middle of the nineteenth century, and it began producing wooden, steam-powered, screw-propelled frigates for the navy in 1857. STT built seven broadside-battery ironclad frigates from 1862 to 1865, seven central-battery ironclad frigates from 1871 to 1881, and the barbette ship *Kronprinzessin Erzherzogin Stefanie* in 1889. The shipyard produced one light cruiser in 1888, the protected cruiser *Kaiser Franz Joseph I* in 1890, and the armoured cruisers *Kaiserin und Königin Maria Theresa* in 1894 and *Kaiser Karl IV* in 1898. In 1898, STT also built the battleships *Wien* and *Budapest*.

After the turn of the century, STT built a succession of battleships that made Austria-Hungary the strongest naval power in the Mediterranean area. The shipyard produced the battleships *Hapsburg* (1902), *Arpad* (1903), *Babenburg* (1904), *Erzherzog Karl* (1906), and *Erzherzog Friedrich* and *Erzherzog Ferdinand Max* (both in 1907). STT then built the Dreadnought battleships *Erzherzog Franz Ferdinand* (1910), *Zrinyi*, *Radetsky*, and *Viribus Unitis* (all in 1911), and the *Tegetthoff* and *Prinz Eugen* (both in 1912). Trieste was lost to Italy after the end of the First World War, but STT remained in business producing warships for the Italian Navy.

The DANUBIUS SHIPYARD at Fiume was established early in the twentieth century to increase Austria-Hungary's capacity for warship construction during the armaments race prior to the First World War. By the outbreak of war, the yard had produced three major warships, including the protected cruisers *Helgoland* and *Novara* and the battleship *Szent Istvan*, the last capital ship produced for the Austro-Hungarian Navy, all in 1914, but naval construction ceased thereafter. A Whitehead torpedo factory was also established at Fiume to provide torpedoes for the Austro-Hungarian fleet of torpedo-boats. Fiume was included in the portion of the territory that was ceded by Austria-Hungary to Italy at the end of the war.

## GREECE

Greece was a major naval power in the eastern end of the Mediterranean Sea as early as the twelfth century BC. At that time, Greece joined the other 'Peoples of the Sea' (Phrygians, Philistines, Achaeans, Danaans, and Libyans) in a military campaign against the Egyptians. The attack, however, was turned back by Ramses III. During the first millennium BC, the Greeks improved upon the design of the standard galley used in that region by adding another bank of oars at a different height and staggered to avoid interference. This 'bireme' was later followed by the 'trireme', sporting three banks of oars to further increase the propulsion of the vessel without extending its length. In 480 BC, the Greeks defeated the Persian fleet at Salamis, primarily with the use of triremes.

Greece remained a significant naval power in the eastern Mediterranean until 1453 when the Turks invaded Europe, capturing Constantinople and occupying Greece. The Greeks revolted in 1821, but their freedom was not assured until an Allied fleet consisting of British, French, and Russian warships defeated the Turks in the Battle of Navarino Bay in 1827. The Greeks never regained their former naval strength, and in modern times, the nation acquired most of its major naval vessels from foreign sources. Greece eventually established a naval shipyard at Salamis on a small island, about ten miles west of Athens, primarily as a ship repair and maintenance facility. The Greek Navy also uses the excellent harbour facilities of the port of Salonika as a naval base.

In 1867-9, Greece acquired two ironclad frigates, one from Thames Iron Works and the other from Stabilimento Tecnico Triestino in Austria-Hungary. This was followed by one protected cruiser from La Seyne in 1879, two armoured cruisers from Granville in 1889-90, and one armoured cruiser from St Nazaire in 1889, all French shipyards. Greece then procured one armoured cruiser from Orlando Livorno in 1911 and one protected cruiser from New York Shipbuilding, Camden in 1913. During this period, the Greeks also obtained a total of fourteen destroyers from various foreign shipyards.

After the First World War, Greece acquired the former American battleships USS *Mississippi* (BB-23) and USS *Idaho* (BB-24), which were renamed *Lemnos* and *Kilkis*, respectively. In 1926-7, Greece purchased six submarines from French shipyards, including four from Ateliers et Chantiers de la Loire at Nantes, one from Chantiers de la Gironde at Bordeaux, and one from the Granville Shipyard. Greece was occupied by Italian and German forces during the Second World War, but the country was liberated with the German defeat in May 1945. From 1942 to 1945, Britain turned over ten destroyers and six submarines to Greek seaman in exile to allow them to continue the war in concert with the Royal Navy.

Greece began to build up its fleet after the war by the acquisition of warships from outside sources. In 1950, Greece received the former Italian light cruiser *Eugenia di Savoia* as part of Italy's war reparations. The United States transferred two destroyers and four destroyer escorts to the Hellenic Navy in 1951. Greece later received eight 'Hunt' class frigates from the Royal

Greece and Turkey.

Navy and two *Gato* class submarines from the US Navy, all in 1957. The US Navy then transferred six *Fletcher* class destroyers to Greece in 1959-62, one *Balao* class submarine in 1965, six additional destroyers in 1971-7, and two *Guppy* class submarines in 1972-3. Greece also purchased four attack submarines from Howaldtswerke Kiel in 1971-2.

Greece subsequently obtained four additional attack submarines from Howaldtswerke Kiel in 1979-80, as well as six guided missile frigates from the Royal Schelde Shipyard at Vlissingen (Flushing) in The Netherlands in 1978-82. In 1992, the US Navy transferred four *Adams* class guided missile destroyers and three guided missile frigates to the Hellenic Navy. The German Blohm + Voss Shipyard built two guided missile frigates for Greece in 1992-6, and these are being followed by two additional guided missile frigates under construction by the Hellenic Shipyard Skaramanga.

## TURKEY

Turkey rose to become a first-class sea power in the eastern Mediterranean Sea during the sixteenth century, but it fell to near insignificance in later centuries. The Ottoman Empire was established in 1290 by the Ottoman Turks with other Asiatic Turkish tribes. Turkey then controlled the southern shore of the Black Sea and the Sea of Marmara, and it bordered on the Bosporus and Dardanelles waterways between the Byzantine and Ottoman Empires. During much of the fourteenth century, the Ottoman Empire was at war with the Greeks, and in 1356, the Turks invaded Europe, capturing Adrianople in the Byzantine Empire in 1365.

The Ottoman Empire soon became a threat to Venice, the predominant naval power in the Mediterranean, and in 1416, the Venetians destroyed the

Turkish fleet off Gallipoli. after that defeat, Sultan Murad II began building a strong Turkish navy during the second quarter of the fifteenth century. In 1453, the Turks captured Constantinople and began to move further westward into Europe, conquering Serbia, Bosnia, Albania, Styria, and the Crimea. In 1499, the Turks defeated Venice in the first naval Battle of Lepanto at the beginning of the second war between Venice and the Ottoman Empire.

Turkey became a first class sea power during the reign of Sultan Suleiman I the Magnificent in the first half of the sixteenth century. In 1538, a Turkish fleet under the command of Admiral Khair ud-Din Barbarossa defeated a Venetian fleet under Admiral Andrea Doria. Concerned about the increasing strength of the Turks in eastern Europe, Venice secured an alliance with Spain and the Papal States to put an end to further Turkish encroachments to the west. In 1571, a combined fleet assembled by the Allies and commanded by Don Juan of Austria met and defeated the Turkish fleet at Lepanto. The Turks used mostly galleys while the Venetians supplemented their fleet with cannon-armed galleasses with devastating effect.

The defeat at Lepanto, as well as the later naval defeats at Tchesme (1770), Navarino (1827), and Sinope (1850), destroyed forever Turkey's desire to become the greatest sea power in the Mediterranean. In modern times, Turkey acquired most of their major naval vessels from foreign sources. A naval shipyard was established at Constantinople, and it produced a number of wooden frigates, a few ironclad vessels, and a cruiser during the nineteenth century, but all subsequent major warships were built by foreign yards. Another naval shipyard was established at Ismit, and its production was also limited to a few wooden frigates. In 1891, Ismit laid down two cruisers, but work on those ships were cancelled before they were even launched.

Ships acquired from foreign sources include seven ironclads and three battleships built by British firms of Napier, Thames Iron Works, Samuda Bros., and Armstrong Elswick. Five ironclads were built by the French shipyards of La Seyne and Bordeaux, and one was built at the Austro-Hungarian yard at Trieste. In 1903, one protected cruiser was produced by William Cramp & Sons of Philadelphia and another by Armstrong.

Turkey purchased two old battleships from Germany in 1910, and then acquired the more modern German battlecruiser *Goeben*, renamed *Yavuz Sultan Selim*, shortly after the outbreak of the First World War. On the outbreak of war, Britain had seized two battleships building for Turkey in British yards, and these were subsequently completed for the Royal Navy. In 1931, four destroyers were acquired from Italian yards.

Turkey remained neutral during the Second World War, and soon after the end of the war, it procured four surplus destroyers from Great Britain and another four from the United States, as well as seven *Balao* class submarines in 1948-54. A further seventeen destroyers were acquired from the United States from 1967-83. Turning to other European sources, Turkey procured three attack submarines in 1976-8 and one Meko 200 type guided missile frigate in 1988 from Howaldtswerke Kiel and three more Meko 200 frigates from

Blohm + Voss Hamburg in 1987–96. Eleven *Oliver Hazard Perry* class frigates were then acquired from the United States in 1996–7.

The CONSTANTINOPLE NAVAL SHIPYARD was established early in the nineteenth century, and it produced a number of wooden frigates for the Turkish Navy. Later, the yard built two ironclads in 1873–1885. In 1892, the Constantinople Naval Shipyard completed one cruiser and began work on another cruiser and a battleship. Neither of the latter ships were completed.

Some time after the Second World War, Turkey began to develop a domestic naval shipbuilding capability, and in 1972–5, the GÖLCÜK NAVAL SHIPYARD completed two frigates of the *Berk* class. GÖLCÜK ISMET built three attack submarines in 1981–90 and completed two Meko 200 type guided missile frigates in 1988–9, and two additional Meko 200 frigates are presently under construction there. In 1994–9, the GÖLCÜK KACAELI shipyard produced four attack submarines.

Poland – Stettin.

## POLAND

Before the First World War, Poland was part of the Russian Empire and it therefore had no a maritime industry of its own. As a result of the Treaty of Versailles, the former Kingdom of Poland was recreated from a large section of Russia and with a strip of land carved out of Germany that extended to the Baltic Sea. At the Baltic end of the so-called 'Polish Corridor', the port of Gdynia served as the base for Polish shipping, but there were no shipbuilding

Poland – Danzig.

facilities within that area. There was an excellent shipyard, the former German Schichau Shipyard, at nearby Danzig, but that port was declared a 'Free City' by the Treaty of Versailles.

During the Second World War, the Polish Navy operated several destroyers and submarines acquired from other nations, including Great Britain, France, and The Netherlands. Its merchant shipping was also obtained from foreign shipyards, including two large liners, the *Batory* and *Pilsudski,* produced by Cantieri Reuniti dell' Adriatico at Monfalcone near Trieste, Italy in 1935 and 1936. After the Second World War, Poland was ceded additional territory from Germany, which extended to the Oder River and included the Pomeranian seaport of Stettin (renamed Sczcecin by the Poles). In addition to the Vulkan Shipyard at Stettin, Poland also acquired the former Schichau Shipyard at Danzig (Gdansk), which was also incorporated into the new Polish Republic.

While the acquisition of former German shipyards greatly enhanced her shipbuilding capability, Poland received most of her naval strength from the Soviet Union since the war. The Soviets supplied these vessels to their partners in the Soviet bloc of Warsaw Pact nations to ensure standardisation of equipment for operational and logistics reasons. In recent years, the ships provided by the Soviet Union included three submarines, one guided missile destroyer, and four patrol corvettes. Since 1987, Poland has built eight frigates and three corvettes for its own navy at the Northern Shipyard at Gdansk. Poland now has naval bases at Swinouyscie (Sweinemünde) and Kolobrzeg (Kolberg) on the Baltic Sea coast in addition to one at Gdansk.

# 12 The Rest of the World

## CANADA

In 1910, the Dominion of Canada established the Royal Canadian Navy and took over the HALIFAX DOCKYARD from the Royal Navy. In that year, Canada also established the Royal Naval College of Canada at Halifax. In 1917, Halifax was rocked by the explosion of a French munitions ship after it collided with another vessel in the harbour. Over 6000 people were killed or injured, and extensive damage was done to the city and dockyard. While the damage was gradually repaired and the dockyard restored to order, the authorities decided to transfer the Royal Naval College to Esquimault on the Pacific coast of Canada in 1918.

The Halifax Dockyard was closed in 1922 for financial reasons, but it was reopened six years later in 1928. In 1938, the dockyard built four mine-sweepers for the Canadian Navy. During the Second World War, Halifax served as the main western terminal for convoys between Canada and the British Isles, and the naval base supported the Royal Navy's ships on convoy duty in the North Atlantic. Having no dry dock of its own, the Halifax Dockyard had to rely on the 600ft dry dock established by the Halifax Graving Dock Co. Ltd. at the suburb of Richmond in 1889.

Like the Halifax Dockyard, the ESQUIMAULT DOCKYARD was taken over by the newly formed Royal Canadian Navy in 1910. With most of the naval

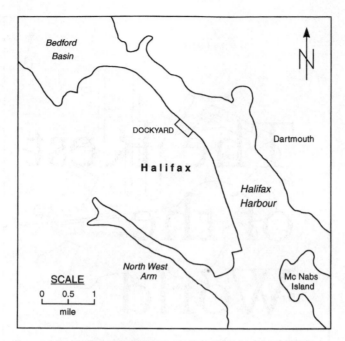

Halifax, Nova Scotia.

Lower Vancouver Island.

activity being in the Atlantic region during the First World War, Esquimault was not able to contribute to the Allied war effort to any great degree. Esquimault did, however, actively supported Royal Canadian Navy operations in the Pacific during the Second World War and the Korean War. The yard continues to be involved primarily with the repair and maintenance of Canadian warships based on the West Coast. The Esquimault Dockyard now also serves as the headquarters for the Canadian Maritime Forces Pacific (MARPAC), which is responsible for the protection of Canadian interests in the Pacific Region.

The Canadian West Coast Fleet consists of mostly patrol frigates, a couple of destroyers, and a number of auxiliary vessels. The nearby Naden Annex was

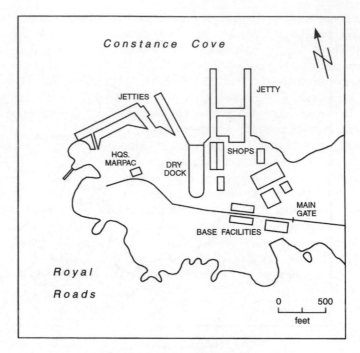

Esquimault Dockyard in 1990.

established in 1922, and it features a large dry dock capable of accommodating the largest warships and ocean liners of the time. The annex also houses the Canadian Forces Fleet School Esquimault (CFFSE) which trains enlisted seamen. Junior naval offices are trained at the Venture Naval Officers Training Centre (NOTC) located at Work Point, another annex located near the entrance to Victoria Harbour.

When the ROYAL NAVAL COLLEGE OF CANADA was transferred from Halifax to Esquimault in 1918, it was housed in buildings at the dockyard converted for that purpose. The Royal Naval College of Canada was disestablished in 1922, mostly for financial reasons, but in 1940 it was re-established as part of the Royal Roads Military College of Canada at Hatley Park across Royal Roads from Esquimault. The Royal Military College of Canada was operated until 1995, when it was closed for financial reasons. The government of British Columbia then took over the facility, and it is now a business school known as the Royal Roads University.

Many warships of the Royal Canadian Navy were acquired from Great Britain over the years, including the light cruisers *Ontario* (ex-HMS *Minotaur*) and *Quebec* (ex-HMS *Uganda*) and seven destroyers, all transferred from the Royal Navy in 1943-5. After the war, the Royal Canadian Navy also acquired the light fleet aircraft carrier *Bonaventure* (ex-HMS *Powerful*) from the Royal Navy on a loan basis. Canada obtained two British-built destroyers in 1951, and in 1965-8, it acquired three *Oberon* class attack submarines built by the Chatham Royal Dockyard.

Private shipyards in Canada, however, have also been constructing naval vessels for the Royal Canadian Navy since the beginning of the twentieth century. The CANADIAN VICKERS CO. of Montreal produced ten 'H' class submarines toward the end of the First World War. Canadian Vickers later built two frigates in 1956-63. HALIFAX SHIPYARDS LTD. in Halifax produced four 'Tribal' class destroyers and a number of smaller ships for the Canadian Navy during the Second World War. After the war, Halifax Shipyards produced four frigates in 1956-64 and one destroyer in 1964.

MARINE INDUSTRIES, Ltd. of Sorel, located on the St Lawrence River about 80 miles northeast of Montreal, built five frigates in 1956-64, one destroyer in 1964, and two guided missile destroyers in 1972. DAVIE SHIPBUILDING AND REPAIRING CO. of Lauzon (Lévis-Lauzon), located on the St Lawrence River directly across from city of Quebec, built two frigates in 1958-63 and two guided missile destroyers in 1972-73. From 1956 to 1963, frigates were also produced by the BURRAND DRY DOCK & SHIPBUILDING CO., the VICTORIA MACHINERY DEPOT CO., and the YARROW LTD. shipyard at Lang's Cove near the Esquimault Dockyard in British Columbia.

## AUSTRALIA

Australia became a self-governing Dominion of the British Commonwealth of Nations in 1901, and in 1911, the Royal Australian Navy was officially established. The Royal Australian Navy continued to acquire its warships from Great Britain, including the protected cruisers *Melbourne* and *Sydney*, both in 1911, the light cruiser *Encounter* in 1911, and the battlecruiser *Australia* in 1912. Later acquisitions from Great Britain included the heavy cruisers *Australia* and *Canberra*, both in 1928. The *Canberra* was lost during the Battle of Savo Island while covering the landing of American troops at Guadalcanal in August 1942, and it was subsequently replaced by the heavy cruiser *Shropshire* in 1943.

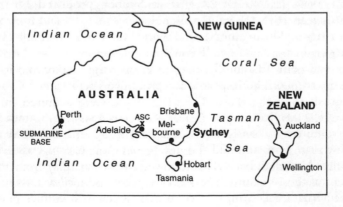

Australia and New Zealand.

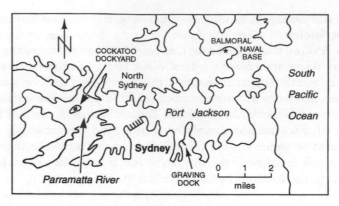

Sydney.

Three light cruisers were later transferred from the Royal Navy to the Royal Australian Navy in 1938, namely, the *Sydney* (ex-HMS *Phaeton*), *Hobart* (ex-HMS *Apollo*), and the *Perth* (ex-HMS *Amphion*). Both the *Sydney* and the *Perth* were casualties of the Second World War. HMAS *Sydney* disappeared with all hands after it was hit and set on fire by the German auxiliary cruiser *Kormoran* in the Pacific in November 1941. The *Kormoran* also sank as a result of the damage sustained in its fight with the *Sydney*. HMAS *Perth* was lost with the American heavy cruiser USS *Houston* during an engagement with superior Japanese naval forces in Sunda Strait after the Battle of the Java Sea in February 1942.

After the war, Australia acquired the aircraft carriers *Sydney* (ex-HMS *Terrible*) in 1948 and *Melbourne* (ex-HMS *Majestic*) in 1955 and four destroyers in 1950, all from the Royal Navy. In addition, three attack submarines were obtained from Scotts in Greenock, Scotland in 1969 and 1978. Australia also procured three guided missile destroyers in 1965-7 and four *Oliver Hazard Perry* class guided missile frigates in 1981-4 from American shipyards.

Australia had established a shipbuilding capability by the beginning of the twentieth century, and it now produces nearly all of its naval requirements. The COCKADOO ISLAND DOCKYARD at Sydney produced the protected cruiser *Brisbane* in 1912, the light cruiser *Adelaide* in 1922, and four *Swan* class frigates in 1936-40. During the Second World War, Cockatoo built two 'Tribal' class destroyers in 1942 and two 'River' class frigates in 1944-5. After the war, Cockatoo built one 'Battle' class destroyer in 1951 and two *Voyager* class destroyers in 1957-9. The shipyard also produced six frigates in 1961-4 and another one in 1971.

The AUSTRALIAN SUBMARINE CORPORATION (ASC) was founded in 1987 as a joint venture between Kockums Submarine Systems AB of Sweden and several Australian firms to build the new generation *Collins* class submarines for the Royal Australian Navy. This followed the acceptance by the Australian government of the Kockums Type 471 design for the *Collins* class submarines after an international competition. While Kockums would provide the technical expertise, the Australian firms would contribute the financial, industrial, and management aspects of the venture, in which Australia has the controlling interest.

In 1989, ASC established a submarine construction facility on the west bank of the Port River at Osborne, several miles to the northwest of the city of Adelaide in South Australia. In 1990, the keels were laid for six 3000-ton *Collins* class diesel-electric submarines. HMAS *Collins*, the first of that class of submarines, was launched in 1993 and entered service in 1996. The second submarine of that class was completed in 1997, and the remaining four ships are scheduled to enter service during the remainder of the decade. These submarines will be based at the site of the Royal Australian Navy Submarine School just to the south of Perth in Western Australia.

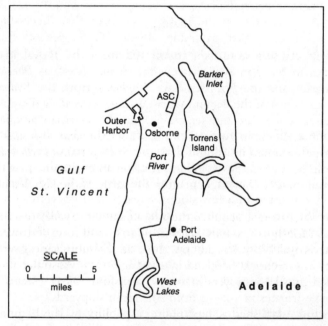

Adelaide in 1998.

Another Australian yard, the WILLIAMSTOWN DOCKYARD AT Melbourne, built one frigate in 1945, one *Voyager* class destroyer in 1958, three *Yarra* class frigates in 1961–70, and two *Adelaide* class (*Oliver Hazard Perry* class) guided missile frigates in 1992–3. Williamstown has begun producing Meko 200 type frigates (the *Anzac* class) and expects to complete eight of them by the year 2004.

## NEW ZEALAND

After New Zealand became a self-governing Dominion in 1907, it established its own navy. New Zealand then took over the dockyard that had been constructed by the British at Devonport, just to the north of Auckland, to service ships of the Royal Navy operating in that region. The dockyard now continues to operate as a ship repair and maintenance facility under contract with BABCOCK NEW ZEALAND LTD., a subsidiary of the Babcock International Group. New Zealand does not have a major naval shipbuilding capability, and it must rely on outside shipyards to provide its warships.

Ships of the Royal New Zealand Navy have been generally provided by Great Britain, with the Dominion paying for their annual maintenance and upkeep. Under this arrangement, New Zealand continued to acquire warships from Great Britain, including the two *Dido* class light antiaircraft cruisers *Black Prince* and *Royalist*, at the end of the Second World War. The Royal New Zealand Navy also operates several British-built anti-submarine frigates. Ships of the Royal New Zealand Navy often operated with the Royal Navy, especially during wartime. During the Second World War, HMNZS *Achilles* was one of the three cruisers in the British task force that successfully hunted down the German pocket battleship *Admiral Graf Spee* off the coast of Uruguay in South America in December 1939.

## INDIA

India became a self-governing dominion under the British Commonwealth of Nations in 1947. The Royal Indian Navy had operated under the guidance of the Royal Navy, and it relied heavily on the provision of its warships from Great Britain. Up until the Second World War, the Royal Indian Navy consisted of a few sloops, frigates, and corvettes for patrolling its coastline. At the end of the war, India obtained one British 'River' class frigate in 1945. After its independence, India acquired several warships from Great Britain, including the aircraft carriers *Vikrant* (ex-HMS *Hercules*) in 1957 and *Viraat* (ex-HMS *Hermes*) in 1988. India also obtained the light cruisers *Delhi* (ex-HMNZS *Achilles*) in 1948 and *Mysore* (ex-HMS *Nigeria*) in 1957.

India acquired ten additional frigates from Great Britain from 1953 to 1960, but after that, it turned to other nations to supply its smaller warships. In 1969, India obtained ten frigates from the Soviet Union, and this was followed by orders for four additional frigates and six submarines from Soviet yards in 1970-4. India then obtained five guided missile destroyers from the Soviet Union in 1980-8. In 1986, India purchased one attack submarine from the German Howaldtswerke in Kiel in 1986 and eight attack submarines from the Soviet Sudomekh shipyard in St Petersburg in 1986-91.

India gradually developed a limited naval shipbuilding capability of its own over the years. The MAZAGON DOCKS LTD. of Bombay produced eight guided missile frigates from 1974 to 1985, four attack submarines in 1992-4, and one guided missile destroyer in 1997. An additional two guided missile destroyers are presently under construction at the yards. Another shipyard, the GARDEN REACH SHIPYARD at Calcutta, built two corvettes in 1991, and it currently has programmes to build three guided missile frigates and four corvettes up to

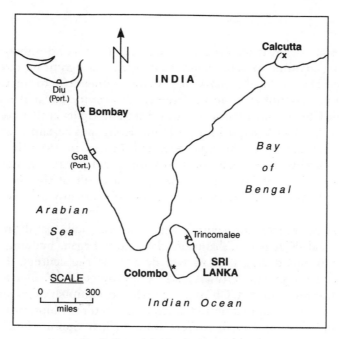

India and Sri Lanka in 1998.

2003. The GOA SHIPYARD, a small shipyard on the west coast of India, built three corvettes in 1993–7

## PAKISTAN

Pakistan was partitioned from India in 1947, and each of those nations achieved dominion status under the British Commonwealth of Nations at that same time. Pakistan soon established its own navy, and like India, it had to rely on outside shipyards to produce its naval vessels. In 1951, Pakistan approached the German firm of H.C. Stülcken Sohn to build ships for its navy, but Germany was still prohibited at that time from building such ships by the Allied Control Council established after the Second World War. Stülckenwerft suggested the construction of a shipyard in Pakistan to produce the ships desired, and this soon resulted in the establishment of the Karachi Shipyard & Engineering Works Ltd, with the assistance of Stülcken engineers.

Pakistan acquired the light anti-aircraft cruiser *Babur* (ex-HMS *Diadem*) in 1957, as well as eight destroyers and four frigates from the Royal Navy in 1954–8. The PAKISTAN DOCKYARD was established at Karachi on the Arabian Sea, primarily for the repair and maintenance of Pakistani warships. Karachi is also the site of the Pakistan Naval Academy and seamen training schools. Pakistan established a naval base at Chittagong on the Bay of Bengal in East Pakistan, but in 1971, East Pakistan seceded from Pakistan to become the independent nation of Bangladesh.

## CHINA

China, despite its great civilisation dating back the second millennium BC, and its long coastline to defend, never emerged as a significant naval power. The lack of a formidable navy left China vulnerable to incursions by European powers and Japan in the nineteenth century. Great Britain waged war against China from 1839 to 1844 over trading rights in that country, and this led to the British acquisition of Hong Kong and certain trading rights in other Chinese ports. Portugal acquired Macao in 1887. In 1894, the upstart naval power of Japan attacked China, and Japan was subsequently awarded the island of Formosa (Taiwan). As a result of the Sino-Japanese War, Korea became a free nation, and it was subsequently annexed to Japan in 1910.

Late in the nineteenth century, the Chinese built naval shipyards at Foochow and Kiangnan (Shanghai). Foochow began building gunboats around 1870, and during the last two decades of the century, it built one armoured cruiser, six light cruisers, and six destroyers. The Kiangnan Shipyard built two frigates in 1872-3. China also purchased a number of major warships from foreign sources in that period, including two turret ships, two armoured cruisers, and four protected cruisers from Vulkan Stettin, four protected cruisers from Armstrong Elswick, two protected cruisers from Mitchell; and two protected cruisers from Howaldtswerke Kiel. In addition, Schichau Elbing provided six destroyers, and Yarrow Scotstoun built another two destroyers for China.

At the end of the nineteenth century, the European powers made further choice acquisitions in China, but most of these were subsequently legalised by long-term leases. In 1897, Germany took Tsingtao, and a year later, the Russians occupied Port Arthur and Dairen. In a countermove, Great Britain immediately established a naval base at Wei-Hai-Wei across the bay from Port Arthur, which the Russians began to fortify. Also in 1898, the French signed a 99-year lease for Kuang-chou Wan in Kwantung province. The unsuccessful Boxer Rebellion against foreigners in 1900 brought further recriminations against the Chinese, but European imperialism began to decline as the major powers turned their attention to one another in the First World War.

After the end of the war, the major powers recognised China as a sovereign nation under the Treaty of Washington (1921-2). China began to build a navy with the construction of three gunboats by the Kiangnan Dock Co. in Shanghai, as well as the acquisition of several warships from foreign sources. In 1931, the Japanese invaded Manchuria and established a puppet regime in what became the independent state of Manchoukuo. Over the next few years, Japan made further inroads into Chinese territory until 1937, when a major conflict erupted. The Sino-Japanese War extended into the Second World War, and it did not end until the defeat of Japan by the Allied Powers in 1945.

After the end of the Second World War, China began to rebuild its navy, primarily with former Japanese warships turned over to them. The Chinese also acquired several warships from other foreign sources, including the light cruiser *Aurora* from Great Britain and two destroyers from the United States. In 1949, the Communists overthrew the Nationalist government of China, which fled to the island of Formosa (Taiwan). The Nationalist regime was able to save most of its warships, but a few, including the former British light cruiser *Aurora*, fell into Communist hands.

The naval needs of Communist China were satisfied mostly by warships provided by the Soviet Union, but in recent years, smaller warships were produced by shipyards mostly in the Shanghai area. The HUTANG SHANGHAI shipyard built four frigates in 1958-9, and an additional four were produced by various Chinese yards in 1967-9. During this period, yards including the JIANGNAN and WUHAN shipyards, both of Shanghai, were also producing submarines based on the Soviet 'Romeo' and 'Whiskey' types. Jiangnan Shanghai also produced a number of guided missile frigates of the 'Jianghu I' and 'Jianghu II' types from 1975-96, and two modern guided missile destroyers in 1994-6. Further 'Jianghu' and 'Jiangwei' type guided missile frigates were built at the Shanghai shipyards of Hudong and Huangpu.

The United States turned over three destroyers to the Nationalist regime on Taiwan in 1954-5, and it continues to protect Taiwan against Chinese threats to reunite that island with the mainland of China.

## SOUTH AMERICA

The large 'ABC' countries of Argentina, Brazil, and Chile, with long coastlines to defend, were the primary naval powers in South America. None of the South American nations have a significant shipbuilding capability, and therefore all of their major warships have to be obtained from outside sources, primarily the United States, Great Britain, France, Canada, Italy, and Spain. In recent years, Colombia, Peru, and Venezuela have each established a navy consisting of several destroyers and frigates, with Peru also maintaining a small fleet of submarines. The other South American nations, as well as those of Central America and the Caribbean, have only a small number of frigates, gunboats, and small patrol craft that constitute their navies.

In addition to the independent republics of South America, naval stations were established along the northern coast of the continent by the colonial powers of Britain, The Netherlands, and France. Their respective colonies in the Guiana area were known as British Guiana, Dutch Guiana, and French Guiana, beginning with British Guiana on the border with Venezuela to the west and extending eastward to French Guiana on the border with Brazil to the east. Those colonies lacked the features for a good naval base, and the naval stations located there were of relatively minor importance. British Guiana later became the independent nation of Guyana, and Dutch Guiana became the independent country of Surinam.

South America.

## Argentina

Argentina revolted against Spain in 1810 and proclaimed its independence in 1816. A stabilised regime, however, was not established until the constitutional assembly of 1852 and the consolidation of the nation in 1860. Argentina soon began to build a navy, ordering the battleship *Almirante Brown* from Great Britain in 1880. Argentina later procured two additional battleships from Britain, the *Indepencia* in 1892 and the *Libertad* in 1893. Around that time frame, Argentina also purchased an old coastal defence battleship built by Samuda Bros. Poplar (London) and four armoured cruisers from Italian sources, two from Ansaldo Genoa and two from Orlando Liverno.

By the turn of the century, Argentina had established naval arsenals (shipyards) at Buenos Aires, Bahia Blanca (Puerto Belgrano), and Rio Santiago to maintain its warships. Before the First World War, Argentina purchased four destroyers from German shipyards, two from Schichau Elbing and two from Krupp Germania Kiel. In 1914-5, Argentina acquired two battleships from American shipyards, the *Rivadavia* from Fore River and the *Moreno* from New York Shipbuilding Camden. In 1931, Argentina purchased two heavy cruisers from Italian shipyards, the *Almirante Brown* from Odero Sestri Ponente (Genoa) and the *25 de Mayo* from Orlando Liverno (Leghorn). Argentina also acquired the light cruiser *La Argentina* from Vickers-Armstrong Barrow in 1939.

The RIO SANTIAGO NAVAL SHIPYARD built a number of small warships, including eight minesweepers in 1936-8, two frigates in 1946, and two frigates in 1956-7. The Rio Santiago yard also built one British Type 42 guided missile destroyer in 1978 and four Meko 140 guided missile frigates in 1985-90. Two more Meko 140s ordered by the Argentine Navy have already been launched and are scheduled for completion in 2002-2.

After the Second World War, the Argentine Navy was modernised by the acquisition of two American 10,000-ton light cruisers mounting fifteen 6in guns in 1951. The ex-USS *Phoenix* (CL-46) was renamed the *General Belgrano*, while the ex-USS *Boise* (CL-47) became the *9 de Julio*. The *General Belgrano* was sunk by a British submarine on 3 May 1982 during the Falklands War with a loss of over 350 lives out of a crew of nearly 1050 men. In addition to the two light cruisers, Argentina also purchased four frigates from the United States after the Second World War. Argentina continued to procure warships from foreign sources, including five destroyers from the United States in 1961 and the British aircraft carrier *Venerable*, renamed *25 de Mayo*, in 1968. A further three destroyers were acquired from the United States in 1972-3, a attack submarine from Howaldtswerke Kiel in 1974, one guided missile destroyer from Vickers Barrow in 1977, and three guided missile frigates from Lorient Dockyard in 1978-81. In 1984-5, Thyssen Nordseewerke Emden supplied another attack submarine for the Argentine Navy.

## Brazil

The native population of Brazil revolted against Portuguese rule in 1789, but it was not until 1822 that Brazil was declared to be an independent nation with Dom Pedro as its emperor. The empire collapsed in 1889, and two years later, Brazil became a constitutional republic. Faced with a rivalry against its sister republics of Argentina and Chile, Brazil also began to develop a naval establishment which soon became the most powerful naval force in South America. Brazil had naval shipyards at Rio de Janeiro and Para (Belem), as well as a number of private shipyards. The shipyard of Ilha das Cobras at Rio de Janeiro was capable of building warships as large as destroyers, and Ilha Vieana, also at Rio de Janeiro, built a number of small naval vessels.

In 1899, Brazil acquired the pre-Dreadnought battleships *Marshal Floriano* and *Marshal Deodora* from the French shipyard of La Seyne near Toulon, and in 1910, Brazil procured the Dreadnought battleships *Minas Gerais* and *Sao Paulo* from Vickers Barrow. Brazil subsequently ordered another battleship, the 27,000-ton *Rio de Janeiro*, from Armstrong Elswick, but the country ran out of funds, and the incomplete ship had to be sold to Turkey in 1913. Renamed the *Sultan Osman I*, the ship was confiscated by the British at the outbreak of the First World War, and she joined the Royal Navy as HMS *Agincourt*.

In 1937, three destroyers of American design were laid down at the ILHA DAS COBRAS shipyard in Rio de Janeiro, and these were completed in 1943 for the Brazilian Navy. In 1940-1, six destroyers of British design were laid down at that yard, but due to the absence of parts from Great Britain during the war, the ships could not be completed until 1949-51. Warships obtained from foreign sources included three submarines delivered by Odero-Terni-Orlando of Spezia, Italy in 1938 and eight US destroyer escorts, which were transferred to Brazil in 1944.

In 1951, Brazil purchased two American 10,000-ton light cruisers that carried fifteen 6in guns in five triple turrets. The ex-USS *Philadelphia* (CL-41) became the Brazilian cruiser *Barroso*, while the ex-USS *St Louis* (CL-49) was renamed the *Tamandare*. Brazil then ordered ten corvettes from The Netherlands, and these were delivered in 1954-5. In 1956, Brazil acquired the former British 13,200-ton aircraft carrier HMS *Vengeance,* which was renamed the *Minas Gerais*. Further naval acquisitions by Brazil included eleven destroyers and seven submarines from the United States in 1972-3. From Great Britain, Brazil received three submarines in 1973-7, and four destroyers and four guided missile frigates in 1976-8. Subsequently, one submarine was acquired from Howaldtswerke Kiel in 1989, four guided missile frigates from American shipyards also in 1989, and four guided missile frigates from Yarrow Scotstoun in 1995-7.

In the 1970s, Brazil made a determined effort to establish a domestic naval shipbuilding capability. The ARSENAL DE MARINHA in Rio de Janiero built two destroyers in 1978, two guided missile frigates in 1979-80, and two corvettes in 1989-91. The Arsenal de Marinha is currently also building submarines, having completed three boats based on a Howaldtswerke design in 1994-9.

*Chile*

The Chilean population rose up against Spain in 1817, and the country immediately began to build a navy to clear the coastline of Spanish ships. After rebel victories at Chacabuco in 1817 and Maipo in 1818, freedom was assured, and Chile became an independent nation under the dictatorship of Bernardo O'Higgins. In 1831, a republic was established, and with a stabilised political structure, the country began to flourish. Rivalry with Argentina and Brazil caused Chile to begin building a strong navy at the beginning of the 20th century. A naval shipyard was established at Talcehuano, about 300 miles south of the capital city of Santiago.

Two 28,500-ton Dreadnought battleships designed to carry ten 14in guns were ordered from Armstrong Elswick. The *Almirante Latorre* was laid down on 1911, and it was followed by its sister-ship, the *Almirante Cochrane*, 2 years later. Work was suspended on both ships at the outbreak of the First World War, but construction was soon resumed on the *Almirante Latorre* after it had been acquired by the British government. The ship was completed, and it served in the Royal Navy during the war as HMS *Canada*. After the war, the ship was returned to Chile. The hull of the *Almirante Cochrane* was retained by the Britain, and the ship was eventually completed as the aircraft carrier HMS *Eagle*.

In 1928-9, Chile received six destroyers ordered from Thornycroft Southampton, as well as three submarines ordered from Vickers-Armstrong

Barrow. After the end of the Second World War, Chile purchased six frigates from Canada in 1946 and two 10,000-ton light cruisers from the United States in 1951. Of the former American cruisers, the ex-USS *Brooklyn* (CL-43) was renamed *O'Higgins* after the Chilean liberator, Bernardo O'Higgins, and the ex-USS *Nashville* (CL-40) was renamed *Prat*. In 1955, Chile ordered two destroyers from Vickers-Armstrong Barrow, and these were commissioned in 1960.

Chile subsequently acquired one *Balao* class submarine, four destroyers and three frigates from the United States in 1961-5. In 1971, the Swedish light cruiser *Göta Lejon* was purchased and renamed *Almirante Latorre*. Acquisitions from Great Britain included two *Leander* class frigates in 1973-4, an *Oberon* class submarine in 1976, and four 'County' class guided missile destroyers in 1982-7. Chile also acquired two submarines from Howaldtswerke Kiel in 1984, and in 1998, two more submarines were ordered from DCN Cherbourg for delivery in 2004-5.

# Glossary

**A-frame.** Two poles connected together at the top, but spread apart at the bottom, to form a structure like the sides of the letter 'A'. A-frames were usually used for the installation or replacement of masts on a sailing vessel. Two A-frames were often used together, one across from the other on opposite sides of a slipway, to allow heavy objects to be transported laterally over a ship under construction. Also called 'sheer-legs'.

**Atelier.** French term for a shipyard involved primarily in the repair of ships.

**Armament.** The guns of various calibres carried on a warship for offensive or defensive purposes. In the pre-missile age, the main armament constitutes the primary weapon system of the ship with the larger calibre guns, whereas the secondary armament refers to all other guns of a smaller calibre.

**Armour.** Iron or steel plating applied to a warship to protect its vital components from enemy fire. As the penetrating power of projectiles increased as a result of technology advancements, the thickness, composition, and treating of armour plating also improved over time.

**Armoured cruiser.** An all-steel cruiser that was protected by a thick armoured belt along both sides of the ship to protect its magazines and power plant. Also called a 'belted cruiser'.

**Arsenal.** French term for naval shipyard.

**Arsenale.** Italian term for naval shipyard.

**Barbette.** 1. Originally, an armoured turntable mounting one or two large-calibre guns that could be traversed to fire forward and to the sides of a ship. 2. A cylindrical heavily armoured structure that protected the ammunition while being hoisted from the magazine of the ship to the turret.

**Barbette ship.** A nineteenth-century armoured steel vessel carrying one or two barbettes (one forward and one aft).

**Basin.** A large body of water within a shipyard facility, usually square or rectangular-shaped, used for fitting out ships after they have been launched. The sides of the basin are usually constructed of concrete to support cranes and other facilities used in the outfitting of ships. Tidal basins are open to the surrounding water while enclosed basins have a gate or lock to keep the water within the basin at a constant level unaffected by tides.

**Battleship.** A term derived from the line-of-battle ship of the sailing era. A capital warship usually of the largest displacement, heaviest armament, and greatest armour protection possible within the current state of the art.

**Battlecruiser.** A capital warship with battleship-calibre armament but higher speed, often achieved by compromising armour protection. Battlecruisers normally had a greater length to beam ratio than battleships for greater speed, and they were often referred to as 'fast battleships' by some navies.

**Belted cruiser.** *See* Armoured cruiser.

**Berth.** The space allocated for a ship, usually at a dock or pier. The term is also used for a building way.

**Boom.** A spar extending from the lower portion of a mast of a sailing vessel to support the bottom of a fore-and-aft sail.

**Bore.** The centre hollow part of a gun barrel through which the ball or projectile travels from the breech to the muzzle end of the gun.

**Bowsprit.** A large spar extending forward from the bow of a sailing vessel to support the lower ends of the head sails.

**Breakwater.** A cape, reef or man-made structure that protects a harbour or anchorage from the open sea. Breakwaters can be created by dumping rocks or other material and by using concrete barriers partially around the harbour or anchorage.

**Breech.** The rear end of a gun from which the propellant charge is ignited to fire the gun. On a muzzleloader, the breech constitutes the repository for the propellant charge and ball or projectile before the gun is fired. The breech must absorb the greatest pressure created when the propellant charge is ignited, and it therefore is the thickest part of the gun tube.

**Breech-loader.** The type of gun in which the projectile and propellant charge is loaded from the breech end of the gun.

**Breech mechanism.** The mechanical parts of the breech of a breech-loading gun which allows the breech end of the gun to be opened for loading the projectile and propellant charge and to be closed after the loading the projectile

and propellant charge to prevent the leakage of propellant gases after firing.

**Building dock.** A dry dock used for the construction of a ship in lieu of a building way. Upon completion of the ship under construction, the dock is merely flooded, allowing the ship to be floated out and towed to the outfitting basin.

**Building way.** A slipway on dry land on which a ship is built and then launched by sliding down the rails of the way into a body of water.

**Calibre.** The size of the bore of a gun measured across its diameter in linear dimensions. Calibre also refers to the effective length of a gun tube measured by the number of times it can be divided by its bore size. For example, a 16in gun with a 67ft long gun tube is considered to be a 50 calibre gun (67 × 12/16= 50).

**Cantiere.** Italian term for a shipyard.

**Cantiere Navale.** Italian term for a naval shipyard.

**Capital ship.** A major warship, traditionally a battleship or battlecruiser, that represents one of the most powerful naval vessels of a nation. Formerly referred to as 'ship-of-the-line', a capital ship is capable of direct combat engagement against the most powerful ships of an enemy fleet. In the modern era, the term has been applied to aircraft carriers and nuclear submarines.

**Carronade.** A large calibre muzzle-loading naval gun with a relatively short barrel used at close range.

**Casemate.** A fixed armoured enclosure around the breech end of a naval gun positioned between decks along the side of a steel warship to protect the crew from enemy fire while loading and firing the gun.

**Chantier.** French term for a shipyard.

**Chronometer.** A highly accurate timepiece that is used in locating the position of a ship at sea based on sextant readings and astronomical tables.

**Compass.** A device that is attracted to the magnetic poles of the earth and is therefore used for navigational purposes. (See also Gyrocompass.)

**Composite ship.** A ship with a wrought iron keel, stem and stern posts, and frames, but with wooden side planking. This type of construction process evolved during the period of transition from all wood to all iron or steel.

**Compound engine.** A steam engine that uses two pistons, one small high-pressure steam piston and a larger low-pressure steam piston arranged to allow steam to expand in that sequence for grater efficiency over a simple one-piston steam engine. Also called a 'double expansion' steam engine.

**Compression-ignition (CI) engine.** An internal combustion engine in which the fuel-air mixture is ignited by its compression in the cylinder. Also known as a diesel engine.

**Corvette.** 1. A sailing warship smaller than a frigate and mounting 20 to 30 guns, used primarily for patrol purposes in the eighteenth and early nineteenth century. 2. A steel, steam-powered warship, smaller than a frigate, used in European navies primarily for patrolling and imperial policing. 3. A modern warship, smaller than a frigate, used by navies throughout the world for patrolling and coastal defence purposes.

**Crane.** A device for lifting heavy objects used in connection with the construction and repair of ships. *See also* cantilever crane, floating crane, gantry crane, hammerhead crane, jib crane, and spar crane.

**Cruiser.** Originally, a term applied to any warship on detached, patrolling duties. The term was later applied to medium-sized surface warships, usually with a displacement of 5000 to 15,000 tons. *See also* unprotected cruiser, protected cruiser, armoured cruiser, light cruiser, heavy cruiser, anti-aircraft cruiser, helicopter cruiser, and guided missile cruiser.

**Diesel engine.** An internal combustion engine, invented by Rudolf Diesel of Germany, in which ignition of the fuel-air mixture is achieved by its compression by the piston in each cylinder. It is also known as a com-pression-ignition (CI) engine. The Diesel engine has been the primary power plant for non-nuclear powered submarines, and it has been used in other marine applications, including Germany's pocket battle-ships.

**Dock.** A structure on a shoreline that permits the loading and unloading of ships.

**Dockyard.** The British term for a naval shipyard.

**Dreadnought.** The name of the first battleship, HMS *Dreadnought*, to encompass the 'all-big-gun' concept of having its entire main armament consist of the largest guns of a single calibre instead of a mixture of guns of various calibres. The term was later applied to any battleship of any nation that was built under this concept.

**Dry dock.** A structure that allows a ship to be repaired fitted out, or otherwise worked on when completely out of the water. It has closed sides that allows the ship to enter through a gate that can be closed to seal it from the outside water. The structure can then be emptied of water, allowing the ship to settle on wooden blocks positioned on the floor of the dock to fit the configuration of the ship's hull. Dry docks may also be used for the construction of ships which are then launched by merely flooding the dry dock.

**Engineering company.** In British terminology, a company that has the capability to design and manufacture engines and other machinery for the propulsion of ships.

**Engineering and shipbuilding company.** In British terminology, a company that had the capability to build both ships and their propulsion machinery.

**Engine works.** A facility that specialises in the design and manufacture of engines and other propulsion machinery for ships.

**Fire control equipment.** The optical and electronic equipment used to assist in the proper laying of the main and secondary gun systems or missiles aboard a warship.

**Fitting out.** The process of completing a ship after it has been launched, usually at a fitting-out basin or quay, by adding its superstructure and armament.

**Floating crane.** A heavy-lift crane mounted on a barge that can be positioned beside a ship and used for the installation and removal of heavy objects from the ship. Floating cranes have the flexibility of being moved from place to place and avoiding the cost of individual heavy-lift cranes at each site.

**Floating [dry] dock.** A floating structure that serves the purpose of a dry dock. The dock is lowered into the water by flooding until a ship can be moved into it. Once the ship is properly positioned in the structure, the floating dry dock is raised again by pumping the water out of its ballast tanks, allowing the ship to settle on wooden blocks set onto the floor, and eventually come out of the water.

**Fore-and-aft sail.** A sail rigged in line with the centreline of a sailing vessel, often supported at the top by a gaff and at the bottom by a boom, but also refers to jibs and staysails which have no yards at all.

**Fore deck.** The forward part of the main deck of a ship.

**Foremast.** The forward mast of a sailing vessel with two or more masts (unless it is a ketch or a yawl, which have no foremast).

**Forge.** In general, the facility at a shipyard that specialises in the forging of metals to impart shape and toughness to rough castings. Also, a French term for the iron works specifically associated with the construction of iron and steel ships.

**Foundry.** A facility that specialises in the casting of metal components that are subject to further machining operations to provide components for a warship.

**Frigate.** 1. A fast sailing warship of moderate size, mounting 28 to 44 guns, and usually operating alone on any of a variety of naval missions during the eighteenth and early nineteenth century. 2. A steam-powered warship, smaller than a destroyer, used primarily for anti-submarine warfare by European navies early in the twentieth century. 3. A destroyer-leader in the US Navy during the mid-twentieth century. Many such ships equipped with guided missiles were later reclassified as guided missile cruisers. 4. In the US Navy, a warship that evolved from the destroyer escort of the Second World War and are now equipped with guided missiles. 5. A small modern warship equipped with sophisticated offensive and defensive weapons systems and used by most navies of the world. Some of the later types are equipped with gas turbine engines for greater speed.

**Gaff.** A spar extending diagonally upward from the mast of a sailing vessel to support a fore-and-aft sail. Also a sprit.

**Galleon.** A large sailing ship of the fifteenth and sixteenth centuries used primarily for trade, but also for naval warfare. The galleon was derived from the carrack, and it usually had four masts, of which the foremast and main mast were square-rigged with three sails apiece and the two mizzenmasts were rigged with lateen sails. Galleons were usually also equipped with bowsprit sails.

**Galliot.** A ship similar to a galley, but somewhat smaller and built especially for speed.

**Galley.** A wooden ship propelled primarily by oars but equipped with one or more sails to assist propulsion on the open sea.

**Gantry crane.** A crane that straddles a slipway or building dock and can move heavy objects both longitudinally and laterally over a ship under construction. The fixed gantry crane has a steel framework over the entire slipway to support the movement of a crane travelling along its longitudinal axis. The elevated gantry crane travels on raised supports on either side of the slipway extending for its entire length. The newer travelling gantry crane is a high structure that straddles over an open slipway or building dock and moves on rails at ground level along its longitudinal axis. In any event, lateral movement is by a carriage travelling crosswise along the crane itself.

**Gas turbine engine.** A turbine engine that uses hot gases generated from the combustion of fuel to impart rotary motion to the drive shaft. Similar to jet engines, gas turbine engines are currently used to provide high-speed performance to warships generally up to frigate size, although some larger ships have been fitted with them (*eg* the British *Invincible* class aircraft carriers).

**Graving dock.** British term for dry dock.

**Guided missile cruiser.** A cruiser built during the latter half of the twentieth century that has guided missiles as its primary armament system instead of guns.

**Gun.** For the purpose of this work, a naval cannon of either muzzle-loading or breech-loading type and of any size or calibre above that of small arms.

**Gunboat.** An small, heavily-armed, shallow-draft vessel intended for patrolling or the bombardment of enemy shore installations.

**Gun shield.** An armoured hood over the breech end of an open-mounted naval gun to protect the crew from enemy fire while loading and firing the weapon.

**Gyrocompass.** An electro-mechanical device with a moveable element free to rotate around its vertical axis and equipped with a gyroscope that causes the element to turn to the geographic north pole due to the influence of the earth's rotation on the gyroscope. A gyrocompass is usually placed in a central location on the ship, and the bearing of the ship is electrically transmitted to repeater compasses located on the bridge and other locations. On naval vessels, the gyrocompass is used for gunfire control purposes as well as for navigational needs.

**Hammerhead crane.** A large crane with a fixed counterbalancing jib designed to lift heavy objects that is used primarily for the outfitting of ships at naval shipyards. These cranes are capable of lifting gun turrets and other heavy components of warships.

**Helicopter cruiser.** In some navies, a cruiser built during the latter half of the twentieth century that is equipped with a large platform on its quarter (after) deck for carrying, launching, and retrieving helicopters.

**Internal combustion engine.** An engine that derives its power from the combustion of a fuel-air mixture inside of its cylinders to force down the pistons and impart rotary motion to the drive shaft by means of a cranking action. Internal combustion engines can be either the compression-ignition (Diesel) type or the spark-ignition type generally used in private automotive applications.

**Iron works.** A facility that specialises in the design and manufacture of products made primarily out of iron and steel, including ships.

**Jib boom.** A spar extending forward from the bowsprit of a sailing vessel to support the lower ends of the most forward jib sails.

**Jib crane.** A shipyard crane consisting of a vertical support structure with a jib-like member that is hinged partway up the vertical structure and can be swung out and rotated to lift and position heavy objects between the ship and the ground.

**Jib sail.** A triangular sail rigged from the foremast of a sailing ship to the bowsprit or jib boom.

**Lateen sail.** A triangular sail set fore and aft from the mast of a sailing vessel. This type of sail originated in the Mediter-ranean area as a single sail, but it was later also used on two and three-masted caravels and the mizzenmasts of carracks and galleons.

**Launching way.** *See* slipway.

**Lock.** A basin with a swinging gate, usually of two sections that come together at the centre, that can be closed after the entry of a ship so that the dry dock can be pumped free of water or the basin can be kept at a certain level without being influenced by tides.

**Machinery.** The engines (including steam reciprocating engines, steam turbine engines, diesel engines, and gas turbine engines), steam boilers, reduction gear assemblies; and any other mechanical equipment needed to provide propulsion for the hull and structure of a ship.

**Machine shop.** A facility that specialises in the machining of metal components to reduce them to their final shape and size and with required features by the use of highly precise machine tools, such as lathes, shapers, drill presses, punches, automatic screw machines, etc.

**Main armament.** The primary gun system of a warship consisting of the largest-calibre guns carried on the ship and their protective turrets. It also includes the elevating mechanism to elevate the guns to the proper angle at which the projectiles fired from the guns will reach the target, the traversing mechanism to rotate the turrets to the correct azimuth in line with the target and the ammunition supply system.

**Main deck.** The upper deck of a ship that extends the entire length of a ship except possibly for a lowered fantail.

**Main mast.** The tallest and heaviest mast of a sailing vessel, usually at the centre of the ship especially in the case of three-masted vessels.

**Marine Railway.** A railway-like structure consisting of cross-ties with two rails that gradually slopes from the shore into a body of water and is used to haul small vessels onto land by means of a carriage riding on those rails.

**Mast.** A tall, heavy, wooden installed upright on a sailing ship to primarily support its rigging and sails. Later on engine-powered steel vessels, a tubular steel post installed upright to support its wireless rigging, signal flags, warning lights, radar antennas, and other equipment.

**Mast pond.** A small body of water at a shipyard where mast timbers were seasoned and stored.

**Mizzen mast.** The most rearward mast of a sailing vessel with three masts, or the after mast of a ketch or yawl.

**Monitor.** 1. Originally, a small steam-powered, screw-propelled ship with a low freeboard, constructed of iron plates, and armed with two large calibre guns in a rotating turret located at the centre of the deck. Later monitors had two turrets, one forward and one aft, and they were the precursor to the turret ship. 2. In more modern times, a small ship with large-calibre guns intended for the bombardment of shore positions.

**Muzzle-loader.** A naval gun that is loaded from its forward end by having the propellant charge and then the ball or projectile rammed down its tube into the breech end of the gun.

**Naval base.** A government-owned and operated naval facility that supports the operations of a naval unit or activity. A naval base includes storage facilities for fuel, ammunition, provisions, supplies, and other needs, but usually with very limited ship repair capability.

**Naval shipyard.** A government-owned and operated naval facility established for the construction, refit, and repair of naval vessels. Some naval shipyards are used only for the refit or repair of warships and have no shipbuilding or launching capabilities.

**Naval station.** A naval base with limited support capability to include refuelling and resupply of warships on operational missions, such as patrolling and convoy protection.

**Navy yard.** A term synonymous with naval shipyard. In the United States, naval shipyards were called navy yards until 1945, near the end of the Second World War.

**Ordnance works.** A facility that specialises in the design and manufacture of armaments and their ammunition.

**Paddle wheeler.** A steam-powered ship that uses a paddle wheel, or pair of paddle wheels, to propel the ship. Double paddle wheels consist of a pair of paddle wheels that are mounted externally on either side of the ship (side-wheeler). Stern-wheelers have a single paddle-wheel aft.

**Panzerschiff.** German for 'armoured ship'. Specifically, the term was applied to each of three capital ships built by Germany in the inter-war years with a standard displacement of only 10,000 tons and mounting six 11in guns in two triple turrets to meet the limitations imposed by the Versailles Treaty. It was given the nickname of 'pocket battleship' by other nations.

**Pedestal mount.** Usually a conical-shaped structural pedestal on which a light or medium-calibre single naval gun is mounted with manually-operated traversing and elevation controls.

**Pocket battleship.** See 'Panzerschiff'.

**Pounder.** The size of a muzzle-loading cannon based on the weight in pounds of a solid round shot that could be fired from the gun.

**Pre-Dreadnought.** The term applied to any battleship built prior to HMS *Dreadnought* or whose main armament still consisted of guns of various calibres instead of following the 'all-big-gun' concept adopted for the *Dreadnought*.

**Private shipyard.** A shipyard owned and operated by a private firm, which may be contracted to build warships, especially when the capacity of domestic naval shipyards is inadequate

to meet the needs of national naval construction.

**Protected cruiser.** An early all-steel cruiser with a moderate degree of armour protection over its vital components, usually by mostly horizontal deck armour.

**Quadrant.** A simple device used to measure the vertical inclination of a star from the horizon to determine the location of a ship at sea by means of astronomical tables. The forerunner to the more sophisticated sextant.

**Reciprocating engine.** An engine that uses one or more pistons to impart rotary motion to a crankshaft by means of connecting rods and crank arms attached to the crankshaft. Early steam engines and later internal combustion engines are of this type.

**Reduction gearing.** A gear train assembly used to reduce the high speed of a turbine engine to the much slower speed of a propeller shaft for ship propulsion.

**Refit.** The process of modifying or modernising a ship at a shipyard in accordance with prescribed procedures to bring the ship up to more current standards of performance.

**Repair.** The process of restoring a ship to its prior state by the replacement of worn or damaged components and other maintenance operations.

**Ropery.** A long building at a shipyard used for the manufacture of rope, especially during the sailing era. Also called a rope-walk.

**Rudder.** A broad flat movable structure at the stern of the ship that is used by means of a tiller or other device to steer the ship. Early sailing vessels had steering oars attached to the side of the ship near its stern for the same purpose.

**Rudderpost.** The stern post of a ship on which the rudder is mounted and which provides the pivot for turning the rudder.

**Rudder stock.** The forward part of a ship's rudder that is attached to the rudderpost or sternpost of a ship to provide the hinge on which the rudder is turned.

**Schooner.** A small fore and aft-rigged sailing vessel with two or more masts. Schooners built as warships were usually under 200 tons, less than 100ft long, and carried 12 guns or less.

**Secondary armament.** All guns on a warship other than its main armament, including all anti-aircraft guns.

**Sextant.** A device used for measuring the vertical inclination of a star from the horizon to determine the location of a ship at sea by means of a chronometer and astronomical tables.

**Ship.** Generally, any sea-going vessel. Occasionally the term was used to designate a particular type of ship, depending on the method used for rigging its sails, such as a three-masted sailing vessel with at least three square sails attached to each mast and with a bowsprit sail.

**Ship-of-the-line.** The largest sailing warship of the eighteenth and early nineteenth centuries intended to form a line with similar ships and slug it out with an enemy fleet sailing on a parallel course. Ships of the line were rated as to their firepower, with First Rates having one hundred or more guns on three decks, Second Rates having 90-98 guns on three decks, and Third Rates having 60-80 guns on two decks. The term 'ship-of-the-line' gradually evolved into 'line-of-battle' ship and finally just 'battleship'.

**Shipbuilding company.** A company that specialises in the construction of ships.

**Shipbuilding and engineering company.** A company that not only builds ships, but also has the capability to design and produce their propulsion machinery.

**Shipyard.** A facility, usually located along a protected body of water, where ships can be built, launched, outfitted, and/or repaired.

**Side-wheeler.** A steam-powered vessel that is propelled by two large paddle wheels centrally mounted on either side of the ship.

**Slipway.** A structure of primarily large timber rails extending into a protected body of water on which a ship is built and launched. The ship is supported in an upright position by cradles that slide over the wooden rails which have been heavily greased to reduce friction during launching. As the ship enters the water, its own buoyancy lifts it up from the supporting cradles as it floats as it is brought under control and moved to a fitting out facility.

**Sloop.** 1. A fore and aft-rigged single-masted sailing vessel. A sloop armed with 10-20 guns and used primarily for patrol purposes (sloop-of-war). 2. A small warship used primarily for convoy defence and patrol purposes in the British Royal Navy and other navies.

**Spanker.** A fore-and-aft sail usually hoisted on a gaff on the mizzen (after) mast of a square-rigged ship.

**Spar.** Any pole such as a mast, yard, boom, or gaff used to support or extend a sail of a sailing vessel.

**Spar crane.** A shipyard crane that consists of a vertical support structure with a spar attached to a rotating base that can be used to move heavy objects between a ship and the shore.

**Spar deck.** The upper deck of a sailing vessel that extends the full length of the ship.

**Sprit.** A spar extending diagonally upward from a mast of a sailing vessel to support a fore-and-aft sail.

**Sprit sail.** A fore-and-aft sail supported by a sprit or gaff on a sailing vessel. Also a square sail carried on the bowsprit.

**Square-rigged.** A sailing vessel rigged with primarily square sails for propulsion.

**Square sail.** A square, rectangular, or trapezoidal-shaped sail held by a 'yard' across the mast of a sailing vessel.

**Steamer.** A ship powered by a steam engine.

**Steam turbine engine.** A turbine engine driven by high-pressure steam acting on a series of blades mounted radially from the drive shaft to impart rotary motion to the shaft.

**Sternpost.** A vertical structural member at the stern of a ship that supports the rudder of the ship. Also referred to as a rudderpost.

**Sternwheeler.** A steam-powered vessel that is propelled by a single broad paddle wheel attached to its stern.

**Triple-expansion engine.** A steam engine in which the steam is passed progressively into three cylinders of increasing size for greater overall efficiency.

**Turbine engine.** An engine powered by steam or hot gases acting on sets of blades to impart rotary motion to the output shaft. Due to the high speed achieved by turbine engines, a reduction gear assembly must be used to reduce the speed of the drive shaft for propulsion purposes.

**Unarmoured cruiser.** The same as an unprotected cruiser.

**Unprotected cruiser.** An all-steel light cruiser that evolved directly from the wooden, sailing frigate without significant armour protection for any part of the ship.

**Varvet.** Swedish term for shipyard.

**Verksted.** Norwegian name for shipyard (workshop)

**Way.** *See* slipway.

**Werf.** Dutch term for shipyard.

**Werft.** The German term for a shipyard.

**Werke.** The German term for 'works', including a shipyard.

**Works.** A facility that specialises in the design and manufacture of a specific category of product, such as ships, engines, ordnance equipment, items made of metal, etc.

**Yard.** On a sailing vessel, a slender spar tapered toward each end attached at or near its centre crosswise to the mast of a sailing vessel to support a square sail.

**Yardarm.** The end section of a 'yard' of a sailing vessel, sometimes used for the hanging of crewmen charged with a capital offence.

# Bibliography

Ahern, Joseph-James, *Philadelphia Naval Shipyard* (Philadelphia 1997).

Auphan, Paul, and Mordal, Jacques, *The French Navy in World War II* (Annapolis 1959).

Banbury, Philip, *Shipbuilders of the Thames and Medway* (Newton Abbot 1971).

Bath Iron Works, *A Legacy of Pride; A Future of Promise* (Bath, Maine 1984).

Bathe, Basil W, *Seven Centuries of Sea Travel – from the Crusades to the Cruises* (New York 1973).

Bekker, Cajus, *Deutsche Schlachtschiffe und Kreuzer 1925-1945* (Oldenburg/Hamburg 1966).

——, *Das Grosse Bildbuch der deutschen Kriegsmarine* (Oldenburg/Hamburg 1973).

——, *Hitler's Naval War* (Oldenburg/Hamburg 1971).

Bess, H H, *Die Marine der Bundesrepublik Deutschland – The Federal German Navy* (Herford 1971).

Bethlehem Shipbuilding Corporation, *Bethlehem Ship Repair Facilities* (Bethlehem, Pennsylvania 1924).

Bonnici, Joseph, and Cassar, Michael, *The Malta Grand Harbor and Its Dockyard* (Valetta 1995).

Boyd, David F, *U.S. Navy Yard Portsmouth* (Portsmouth, New Hampshire 1931).

Bradatin, Marc' Antonio, *The Italian Navy in World War II* (Annapolis 1957).

Brett, Bernard, *Modern Sea Power* (London 1980).

Breyer, Siegfried, *Soviet Warship Development* (London 1992).

——, and Koop, Gerhard, *The German Navy at War 1939-1945, Volume 1 – The Battleships* (West Chester, Pennsylvania 1989).

——, *The German Navy at War 1939-1945, Volume 2 – The U-Boat,* (West Chester, Pennsylvania 1989).

——, *Von der 'Emden' zur 'Tirpitz'* (Koblenz/Bonn 1981).

Brown, D K, *A Century of Naval Construction* (London 1983).

Burns, K V, *The Devonport Dockyard Story* (Liskeard 1984).

Chappell, Howard I, *The History of American Sailing Ships* (New York 1935).

——, *The History of the American Sailing Navy* (New York 1949).

Charleston Navy Yard, *The Industrial History of the Charleston Navy Yard 1939-1945* (Charleston, South Carolina 1945).

*Conway's All the World's Fighting Ships, 1860-1905* (London 1979).

*Conway's All the World's Fighting Ships, 1906-1921* (London 1985).

*Conway's All the World's Fighting Ships, 1922-1946* (London 1980).

*Conway's All the World's Fighting Ships, 1947-1995* (London 1995).

Edwards, Bernard, *Salvo – Classic Naval Gun Actions* (London 1995).

Evans, David C (ed), *The Japanese Navy in World War II* (Annapolis 1969).

Fahey, James C, *The Ships and Aircraft of the U.S. Fleet* (First through Seventh Editions, Ships and Aircraft, New York/Falls Church, 1941–1958).

——, *The Ships and Aircraft of the U.S. Fleet* (Eighth and Subsequent Editions, Annapolis, 1965–present).

Farr, Gail E, and Bostwick, Brett F, *Shipbuilding at Cramp & Sons* (Philadelphia 1992)

Galuppini, Gino, *L'Arsenale di La Spezia nel centenario della sua inaugurazione* (La Spezia 1969).

——, *Warships of the World – An Illustrated Encyclopedia* (Milan 1983 and New York 1986).

Gardiner, Robert (ed), *Conway's History of the Ship – Cogs, Caravels, and Galleons – The Sailing Ship 1000-1650* (London 1994).

——, *Conway's History of the Ship – Eclipse of the Big Gun, The Warship 1906-1945* (London 1992).

Garzke, William H, Jr, and Dulin, Robert O, Jr, *Battleships, Allied Battleships in World War II* (Annapolis 1980).

——, *Battleships, Axis and Neutral Battleships in World War II* (Annapolis 1985).

——, *Battleships, United States Battleships, 1935-1992* (Annapolis 1976).

George, James I, *History of Warships* (Annapolis 1998).

Gillett, Ross, *Australia's Navy: Past, Present, and Future* (Brookvale, New South Wales 1986).

Hailey, Foster, and Lancelot, Milton, *Clear for Action – The Photographic Story of Modern Naval Combat 1898-1964* (New York 1964).

Hamlin, Paul W, *History of the Boston Naval Shipyard, 1800-1937* (Boston 1948).

Hansen, Hans Jürgen, *The Ships of the German Fleets 1848-1945* (Annapolis 1988).

Harris, Brayton, *The Age of the Battleship, 1890-1922* (New York 1965).

Hastings, D J , *The Royal Indian Navy, 1612-1950* (Jefferson, North Carolina 1988).

Hewison, W S, *Scapa Flow in War and Peace* (Kirkwall 1995).

Holland, A J , *Ships of British Oak – The Rise and Decline of Wooden Shipbuilding in Hampshire* (Newton Abbot 1971).

Hood, John, *The History of Clydebank* (Clydebank).

Horton, Edward, *The Illustrated History of the Submarine* (New York 1974).

Hough, Richard, *Dreadnought – A History of the Modern Battleship* (New York 1964).

Hughes, Terry, and Costello, John, *The Battle of the North Atlantic* (New York 1977).

*Jane's Fighting Ships* (all editions)(London).

Jenkins, John, *A Short History of the Portsmouth Royal Dockyard* (Portsmouth 1984).

Jensen, Oliver, *Carrier War* (New York 1945).

Jentschura, Hansgeorg, Jung, Dieter, and Mickel, Peter, *Warships of the Imperial Japanese Navy, 1869-1945* (Annapolis 1977).

Jordan, John, *Soviet Warships 1945 to the Present* (London 1992).

Kemp, P K (ed), *History of the Royal Navy* (New York 1969).

Kirk, John, and Klein, Aaron, *Ships of the U.S. Navy* (New York 1988).

Koburger, Charles W, *Naval Strategy East of Suez, The Role of Djibouti* (New York 1992).

Kuckuk, Peter, *Die A.G. 'Weser'* (Bremen 1987).

——, *Grosswerften im Dritten Reich* (Bremen 1993).

——, *Werften und Schiffbau in Bremen und die Unterweserregion in 20. Jahrhundert* (Steintor 1983).

Le Fleming, H M, *Warships of World War I* (London 1962).

Lenton, H T, and Colledge, J J, *Warships of World War II* (London 1962).

Lobley, Douglas, *Ships Through the Ages* (London 1972).

Lott, Arnold S, *A Long Line of Ships: Mare Island's Century of Naval Activities in California* (Annapolis 1954).

Lyon, Hugh, *The Encyclopedia of the World's Warships* (London 1978).

MacDougall, Philip, *Royal Dockyards* (London 1982).

Macintire, Donald, and Bathe, Basil W, *Man-of-War – A History of the Combat Vessel* (New York 1968).

Mallmann Schowell, Jak P, *The German Navy in World War II – A Reference Guide to the Kriegsmarine, 1935-1945* (London 1979).

Mansfield, George O Q , *Historical Review: Boston Naval Shipyard* (Boston 1957).

Mare Island Naval Shipyard, *Mare Island Navy Yard Centennial 1854-1954* (Vallejo, California 1954).

Middlemiss, Norman L, *British Shipbuilding Yards* 3 vols (Newcastle-upon-Tyne 1995).

Miller, Nathan, *The United States Navy – An Illustrated History* (Annapolis 1977).

Mitchell, C Bradford, *Every Kind of Shipwork – A History of Todd Shipyards* (New York 1981).

Morison, Samuel Eliot, *History of United States Naval Operations in World War II, Vols I-XIV* (Boston, 1947-1960)

——, *The Two-Ocean War – A Short History of the United States Navy in the Second World War* (Boston 1963).

Myllenberg, Arne, *300 Years and 400 Vessels – A Book of Karlskronavarvet* (Karlskrona 1981).

New York Shipbuilding Corporation, *50 Year* (Camden 1949).

Newport News Shipbuilding and Dry Dock Company, *Three Generations of Shipbuilding (1886-1961)* (Newport News 1961).

Norberg, Erik (ed), *Karlskronavarvets Historia* (Karlskrona 1993).

Palmers Shipbuilding and Iron Co. Ltd, *From Colliers to Battleships, Palmers of Jarrow 1852-1933* (Jarrow 1950).

Parks, Oscar, *British Battleships 'Warrior' 1860 to 'Vanguard' 1950: A History of the Design, Construction, and Armament* (London 1966).

Pawlowski, Gareth L, *Flat-tops and Fledglings – A History of American Aircraft Carriers* (New York 1971).

Peebles, Hugh P, *Warshipbuilding on the Clyde* (Edinburgh 1987).

Polmar, Norman, *Guide to the Soviet Navy* (Annapolis 1970).

Portsmouth Naval Shipyard, *From Sails to Atoms* (Portsmouth, New Hampshire 1963).

——, *Cradle of American Shipbuilding* (Portsmouth, New Hampshire 1978).

Potter, E B, *Illustrated History of the United States Navy*, (New York 1971).

Prager, Hans Georg, *Blohm+Voss, Ships and Machinery for the World* (Herford 1977).

Preston, Anthony, *Aircraft Carriers, Battleships, Cruisers, Destroyers,* and *Submarines* (separate volumes) (Greenwich 1982).

——, *Battleships of World War I* (London 1972).

——(ed), *Warships in Profile, Volume 3* (Windsor 1973).

Raven, Allen, and Roberts, John, *British Battleships in World War Two* (London 1976).

Reh, Louise M, *Fifty Dollars an Acre: A History of the Puget Sound Naval Shipyard* (Washington 1983).

Ritter, A R , *A Brief History of the Philadelphia Navy from its Inception to December 31, 1920* (Philadelphia 1921).

Rohwer, Jürgen, *War at Sea 1939-1945* (London 1996).

Ropp, Theodore, *The Development of a Modern Navy: French Naval Policy* (Annapolis 1987).

Roscoe, Theodore, and Freeman, Fred, *Picture History of the U.S. Navy* (New York 1956).

Roskill, S W, *White Ensign – The British Navy at War, 1939-1945* (London 1960).

Rössler, Eberhard, *The U-boat, The History of German U-boat Construction* (Annapolis 1975).

Ruge, Friedrich, *Der Seekrieg – The German Navy's Story, 1939-1945* (Annapolis 1957).

Sarcone, Anthony F, and Rines, Lawrence F, *A History of Shipbuilding at Fore River* (Quincy, Massachusetts 1975).

Schofield, William G, *Destroyers – 60 Years* (New York 1962).

Sears, Stephen W, *Carrier War in the Pacific* (New York 1966).

Showell, Jak P Mallmann, *The German Navy in World War II, A Reference Guide to the Kriegsmarine 1935-1945* (Annapolis 1979).

Silverstone, Paul H, *US Warships of World War II* (New York 1965).

Skiera, Joseph A (ed), *Aircraft Carriers in Peace and War* (New York 1965).

Slade, K A, *The Historic Dockyard, Chatham* (Chatham 1993).

Smith, Marilyn Gurney, *The King's Yard: An Illustrated History of the Halifax Dockyard* (Halifax, Nova Scotia 1985).

Stephen, Martin, *Sea Battles in Close up: World War 2* (Annapolis 1988).

Stern, Robert Cecil, *Kriegsmarine – A Pictorial History of the German Navy 1935-1945* (Carrollton, Texas 1979).

Swann, Leonard Alexander, *John Roach – Maritime Entrepreneur* (Annapolis 1965).

Terzibaschitsch, Stefan, *Battleships of the U.S. Navy in World War II* (New York 1977).

——, *Cruisers of the U.S. Navy 1922-1962* (Annapolis 1984).

United States Strategic Bombing Survey, Naval Analysis Division, *The Campaigns of the Pacific War* (Washington 1946).

Von der Porten, Edward P, *The German Navy in World War II* (New York 1969).

Walker, Fred M, *Song of the Clyde – A History of Clyde Shipbuilding* (New York 1984).

Walser, Ray, *France's Search for a Battle Fleet: Naval Policy and Naval Power* (New York 1992).

Warner, Oliver, *The British Navy: A Concise History* (London 1975).

——, *Great Battle Fleets* (London 1973).

——, *Great Sea Battles* (London 1968).

Whitley, M J, *Cruisers of World War Two – An International Encyclopedia* (Annapolis 1995).

Willmott, H P, *Warships – Sea Power Since the Ironclad* (London 1975).

Wingate, John (ed), *Warships in Profile Volume 1* (Windsor 1971).

——, *Warships in Profile, Volume 2* (Windsor 1973).

Witthöft, Hans Jürgen, *Lexikon zur deutschen Marinegeschichte* (Herford 1977).

Yarrow Shipbuilding Ltd, *Yarrow 1865-1990* (Scotstoun 1992).

# Index

This Index lists major naval vessels having the same name by date, but it does not necessarily include all warships that have ever borne that name. The name of each ship listed in this Index represents the full name of the ship, including first name and/or title, but not with the article 'the'.

**Abbreviations**

Arg = Argentina; Aus = Australia; A-H = Austria-Hungary; Br = Great Britain; Bzl = Brazil; Can = Canada; Carib = Caribbean; CSS = Confederate States Ship; Den = Denmark; Eng = England; Fr = France; Ger = Germany; Grk = Greece; HMAS = His (Her) Majesty's Australian Ship; HMCS = His (Her) Majesty's Canadian Ship; HMIS = His (Her) Majesty's Indian Ship; HMNZS = His (Her) Majesty's New Zealand Ship; HMS = His (Her) Majesty's Ship; It = Italy; Jpn = Japan; Neth = Netherlands; NZ = New Zealand; Nor = Norway; Pak = Pakistan; Pol = Poland; Port = Portugal; Rus = Russia/USSR; Scot = Scotland; Sp = Spain; Swe = Sweden; Trk = Turkey; US = United States of America; USS = United States Ship